This memorial wall in the "Valley of the Communities" at Yad Vashem in Jerusalem bears the names of the 29 of the 50 communities about which this book was written.

Protecting Our Litvak Heritage

A History of 50 Jewish Communities in Lithuania

By Josef Rosin

Introduction by Professor Dov Levin
The Hebrew University in Jerusalem

Edited by Susan Levy and Joel Alpert

Published by The Friends of the Yurburg Jewish Cemetery, Inc.
Coral Gables, Florida

Protecting Our Litvak Heritiage

A History of 50 Jewish Communities in Lithuania

By Josef Rosin

Copyright © by Josef Rosin and Joel Alpert 2009

First Printing: February 2009, Shevat 5769

Editors: Susan Levy and Joel Alpert
Layout: Joel Alpert
Cover Design: Adina Alpert

The Friends of the Yurburg Jewish Cemetery, Inc.
628 Navarre Avenue
Coral Gables, Florida, 33134

Printed in the United States of America by Lightning Source, Inc.

Library of Congress Control Number (LCCN): 2008944297
ISBN-13: 978-0-9822282-0-3
ISBN-10: 0-9822282-0-1
(hard cover: 480 pages, alk. paper)

Cover photograph: the Hebrew Gymnasium in Shavl *(Siauliai)*.

This book is dedicated to the

memory of

my father Yehudah-Leib Rosin,

my mother Hayah nee Leibovitz

and

my little sister Tekhiyah

who were murdered by the Nazis and their

Lithuanian helpers

Pikeliai
Laizuva
Latvia
Zidikai
Ylakiai
Akmene
Vieksniai
Pasvitinys
Seda
Suvainiskis Onuskis
Plateliai
Tryskiai
Pumpenai Vabalninkas
Kursenai
Zarenai
Kamajai
Luoke
Rietavas
Seduva
Svedasai
Vaiguva
Laukuva
Kraziai Tytuvenai
Grinkiskis Krekenava
Troskunai
Kaltinenai
Nemaksciai Siluva
Ramygala
Vainutas
Raseiniai
Surviliskis
Vidukle
Girkalna
Moletai
Erzvilkas
Cekiske
Seredzius
Gelvonai
Velsuona
Zapiskys
Russia
Griskabudis
Kaunas
(East Prussia)
Garliava
Vilnius

Baltic Sea

Z E M A I T I J A

A U K S T A I T I J A

Belarus

Liudvinavas

Miroslavas

Poland

Leipalingis

Map of Lithuania with the 50 Towns

TABLE OF CONTENTS

PREFACE

The book I am presenting here contains articles on the history of fifty Jewish communities, about half of them in the *Zemaitija* region (Akmene, Kursenai, Vidukle etc.) and half in the *Aukstaitija* region (Krekenava, Moletai, Miroslavas etc.)(see map). Most of the towns had a small Jewish population that during the years became smaller and smaller because many of it emigrated to South Africa, America and *Eretz-Yisrael*.

I wrote these articles in English and half of them were edited by Sarah and Mordehai Kopfstein, Haifa, Israel, by Fania Hilelson-Jivotovsky, Montreal, Canada, by Sue Levy of Perth, Australia and by Joel Alpert, Boston, USA.

The pictures included in the articles come from various sources: the names of the people who allowed me to use their pictures are printed beneath the pictures. Other sources are the four volumes of <u>*Yahaduth Lita*</u> published by "The Association of Lithuanian Jews in Israel", Tel-Aviv, and the Archives of the Association and <u>*Yahaduth Lita*</u> by way of *"Mossad HaRav Kook"*, Jerusalem. Pictures of the massacre sites and the monuments erected on them were taken mostly from <u>The Book of Sorrow</u>, Vilnius 1997.

Josef Rosin

ACKNOWLEDGEMENTS

Many thanks to my relative and friend Joel Alpert for initiating, compiling, editing and publishing this book. In large part, this book, on the subject of commemoration of the Lithuanian Jewish communities would not have been written if it wasn't for the encouragement and advice of my good friend, Professor Dov Levin. Thanks and much appreciation go to my friends Sarah and Mordehai Kopfstein who edited my poor English in half of the articles and to my cousin Fania Hilelson-Jivotovsky for editing the English in the other half of my articles; their work greatly improved the readability of the text. Thanks go to Sue Levy for her final editing and proof reading the entire manuscript. I want to thank my beloved wife Peninah, for her wise and sensitive remarks. And lastly, I want to thank the "Friends of the Yurburg Jewish Cemetery, Inc." for their willingness to publish this book.

J. R.

EDITOR'S NOTE

Josef Rosin has documented the history of a total of 52 Litvak towns in his two volumes of Preserving Our Litvak Heritage, Volumes I and II. Because these two books were so well received, he has decided to continue his documentation of the history of another 50 Litvak towns in this current volume, Protecting Our Litvak Heritage. The editor urges the reader to first read the **INTRODUCTION** in order to fully appreciate and understand the context of the history of each town. The Introduction was written by the eminent scholar of Lithuanian Jewish History, Professor Dov Levin, retired chair of the Department of Oral History at the Hebrew University, Jerusalem.

Both Dr. Dov Levin and the author, Josef Rosin, are natives of Lithuania, raised in that Jewish community and therefore entitled to be called "Litvaks," a title they both proudly wear. Levin grew up in Kovno and Rosin in Kibart, each living in their hometowns until the start of World War II. They met in the Kovno Ghetto where they were active in the anti-Nazi underground and later in the forests of Lithuania as partisan fighters against the German and Lithuanian Nazis. Both men, now retired, have devoted many years to collecting and assembling information on Litvak history.

In 1996 Yad VaShem published their work, *Pinkas Hakehilot Lita* in Hebrew (Encyclopedia of the Jewish Communities in Lithuania); it is a monumental work of more than 750 pages detailing the specific history of over 500 Litvak towns. Professor Levin was the editor and Josef Rosin, who wrote about 80% of the entries, was the assistant editor. Unfortunately this significant work is not accessible to the English reading public because it is written in Hebrew. This current book by Josef Rosin provides an account of 50 of those Litvak communities, in even more detail than was presented in *Pinkas Hakehilot Lita* , as the author is now able to elaborate and offer details that could not be included due to space limitations. In addition, Rosin has mined the memories and photograph albums of many former residents of these towns now living in Israel and elsewhere, to compile an even more comprehensive picture of these communities. It is truly fortuitous that he accomplished this task in good time, because today, in 2009, those survivors who were young adults in 1941 are now well past their 80th birthday. As we discovered, the younger generations are finally starting to search for their history that existed in their Litvak past, and so we are all extremely fortunate to be able to benefit from the thorough research on which this book is based.

It is my distinct honor and pleasure to have been able to work with Josef Rosin and Professor Dov Levin and thus bring this book to the English reading public.

Joel Alpert, Editor

By Professor Dov Levin, The Hebrew University, Jerusalem

On the eve of the Shoah the Jewish population of Lithuania, including the Vilna region and the refugees from Poland, numbered approximately a quarter of a million souls. Although this represented only around 0.9% of world Jewry during the twenty years of independent Lithuania, it was long recognized as a specific religious-cultural unit as compared to the neighboring Jewish centers of Poland, Belarus and Ukraine. Lithuanian Jews were distinguished by their intellectual and rational attitudes. For good reason the Lithuanian Jews were not only nicknamed *Litvak*, but also *Tseilem Kop* ("Cross Head"), suggesting that the Lithuanian Jew would be ready to strike out vertically and horizontally (in the form of a cross, G-d forbid) in order to achieve his goal, or alternatively to cross-check his findings in order to reach absolute truth.

These attributes and others not only had implications in daily life, but also resulted in various phenomena, currents and systems in the socio-cultural strata, for example the reservation of the majority of Lithuanian Jews to the concepts of "False Messiahs" and their opposition to *Hasiduth* (Chassidism). Their diligence was exemplary in studying the Torah in the Synagogues (*Batei Midrash*), the *Yeshivoth Ketanoth* (Junior Yeshivoth) and especially in the Great *Yeshivoth*. Jewish Lithuania was famous for the great *Yeshivoth* of Slabodka (Vilijampole), Telzh (Telsiai), Ponivezh (Panevezys) and Kelm (Kelme) where hundreds of foreign students also studied. The Salant community was also well known, because it was from here that the *Musar* (Ethics) movement began and spread through Rabbi Yisrael Salanter. The *Musar* principles were based on the use of intellectual activity and knowledge to correct and improve the behavior of the individual. Lithuanian Jewry was also known for fostering the *Hibath Zion* movement and later for practically adopting the Zionist idea, while exhibiting an almost simultaneous openness to the challenge of the *Haskalah* (the Enlightenment Movement), whether it be in Yiddish, Hebrew, Russian or German.

The city of Vilna (often referred to as the "Jerusalem of Lithuania") not only became a worldwide center of Jewish religion but was also the abode of such famous persons as Rabbi Eliyahu (the Vilna *Gaon*), Rabbi Hayim-Ozer Grodzensky and many others; moreover it was the cradle of the religious Zionist movement (*Mizrahi*) on the one hand and of the socialist workers movement (*Bund*) on the other. In due course the Institution of Yiddish Culture (YIVO), now established in New York, was born in this city.

Historically it seems that these impressive attributes and achievements, as well as the special character of Lithuanian Jewry within the Jewish world, developed alongside prolonged struggles for their economic and civil rights among their ethnic Lithuanian neighbors, and this in spite of frequent changes of rulers.

INTRODUCTION

The first settlement of Jews in the Great Lithuanian Duchy, also named *Magnus Ducatus Lithuaniae*, began in the fourteenth century by invitation of the Grand Dukes Gediminas and Vytautas (Witold). In 1388, one year after the Christian-Catholic religion was introduced throughout Lithuania, the Jews were also granted a preferred civil status and incomparable bills of rights in many different spheres, such as protecting their bodies and property; freedom to maintain their religious rituals; significant alleviation in the field of commerce and money lending, in relation to Christians. There was also a particular regulation protecting Jews against blood libels. But in 1495, only three years after the expulsion of Spanish Jewry, Grand Duke Alexander expelled all Jews, then numbering more than 6,000, from Lithuania and confiscated their property. Eight years later, when he was elected King of Poland according to the joint rule of these two countries, he allowed Lithuanian Jews to return to their homes and gave them back some of their property. Most of the privileges granted by Vytautas were left intact: for a long period after this event these privileges were of some importance in preserving the legal, civil and economic status of the Jews.

This situation often caused envy among the Christian townspeople, mostly Germans, who were organized in merchant and artisan unions (*cechy*) and who for a long time had enjoyed the Magdeburg Rights according to the precedent granted to merchants in the town of Magdeburg in Germany; they now perceived the Jews as competitors who had to be fought. For example, they managed to have an edict proclaimed (*De non tolerandis Judaeis*) forbidding Jews to settle in Vilna, the capital of the duchy, and to trade there. In time this interdict lost its significance. However, insults to Jews by urban Christians, including students at theological seminars in this town and others, continued for centuries.

This was not the same problem that confronted the Jewish population in the north-western region of the Lithuanian Duchy known as Zemaitija or Samogitia (the Jews called it Zamut). In contrast to the eastern region, Aukstaitija, and the south-eastern parts of the duchy, most of this region was settled by ethnic Lithuanian tribes who, in contrast to most of their brethren, had accepted the Christian-Catholic religion relatively late (1413) and, because of their religious background, had not yet been stricken with Judophobia.

The first Jewish settlers in Zamut earned their living by customs and tax collection. A further wave of Jews settled in this region following the expulsion of Jews from Vilna (1527) and Memel (1567). At this time there were already Jewish settlements in Zamut − in Alsiad (Alsedziai), Utyan (Utena), Birzh (Birzai), Zhager (Zagare), Yurburg (Yurbarkas), Palongen

(Palanga), Plungyan (Plunge), Pokroy (Pakruojis), Keidan (Kedainiai), Kelm (Kelme), Shadeve (Seduva)*[1] and other towns.

A considerable improvement in the condition of the Jewish population and in the relationship between Jews and the entire population occurred during the period of the unification of the Great Lithuanian Dukedom with Poland within the framework of the Polish Republic *Rzeczpospolita* (1569-1795).

Then and for many decades after, feudalism reigned in Lithuania. Most of the population continued to make their living from agriculture as before and from breeding cattle and poultry, from fishing in the rivers and lakes and from harvesting trees. A few, mainly Jews, were peddlers, while even fewer Jews dealt with the import and export of agricultural products. Very few Jews, generally those close to the establishment, were granted the privilege of leasing the collection of levies. With the improvement of roads and sailing routes on the rivers, most of which flowed into the Baltic Sea, there was a gradual increase in commercial activity, especially the export of timber, flax, grains, poultry, cattle and dairy products. As a result taverns and storehouses were established near the crossroads and at river ports. These small settlements developed into villages and towns where many Jewish artisans and merchants settled. Until the eighteenth century in the area of ethnic Lithuania, recognition as a town was granted to 83 settlements and rights to commercial trade to 87 settlements. In fact there was no significant difference in rights between a small (shtetl) and a big town.

An additional factor for Jews becoming firmly established in the economic sphere was the significant growth in the number of Jews employed by nobles and estate owners to manage their estates, and also in the leasing of barrooms and taverns in rural areas. As a result, the Jewish bartender or manager was exposed to the hostility of the rural population, which regarded him as an agent of the noblemen who wished to exploit them.

Although most ethnic Lithuanians were already Christians, the belief in devils and ghosts had not yet disappeared and now the Jew replaced these evil symbols. It was not difficult for the Lithuanians to believe in the veracity of the blood libels, a phenomenon that continued to exist until recently.

Despite this, Western Lithuania, and in particular the Zamut region, became a relatively safe haven for thousands of Jewish refugees who survived the Period of Tribulation (1648-1667) that started with the mutiny of the Cossacks headed by Bogdan Khmielnitsky, and ended with the occupation of Vilna by the Russian army. At the same time, the Black Plague ravaged the population of the region.

The *Va'ad Medinath Lita* (The Lithuanian Jewish Council) played an important role in maintaining good relations between the general population and the Jews, as well as among the Jews themselves. This *Va'ad* was a quasi-

---

[1] * indicates that this town is one of the 50 towns covered in this book.

autonomic authority of the union of Jewish communities in the Polish Republic *Rzeczpospolita*. During the 138 years from 1623 to 1761, this authority effectively and honorably represented the day-to-day interests of about 160,000 Jews in the Lithuanian Dukedom vis-a-vis the rulers and also managed to protect their physical safety and dignity against hostile elements in the Christian population. After the *Va'ad* was organized, the communities of the Ethnic Lithuania region were included in an administrative unit called *Galil* Zamut. Later this was renamed *Medinath* Zamut which included several sub-units in Birzh, (Birzai), Vizhun (Vyzuonos), Plungyan (Plunge) and elsewhere.

Far-reaching changes in the legal and civil status of the Jews occurred during the third division of Poland in 1795; then, most of Lithuania was annexed to Russia and became known as The North-Western Zone, thereby becoming an integral part of the Russian empire. In addition to the Provinces (*guberniae*), Vilna in the northeast and Grodno in the south, the provinces of Kovno in the northwest and Suwalk in the southwest were also added. These two included most of the 50 towns presented in this book. This arrangement continued more or less until World War I. (see map taken from *The Litvaks*).

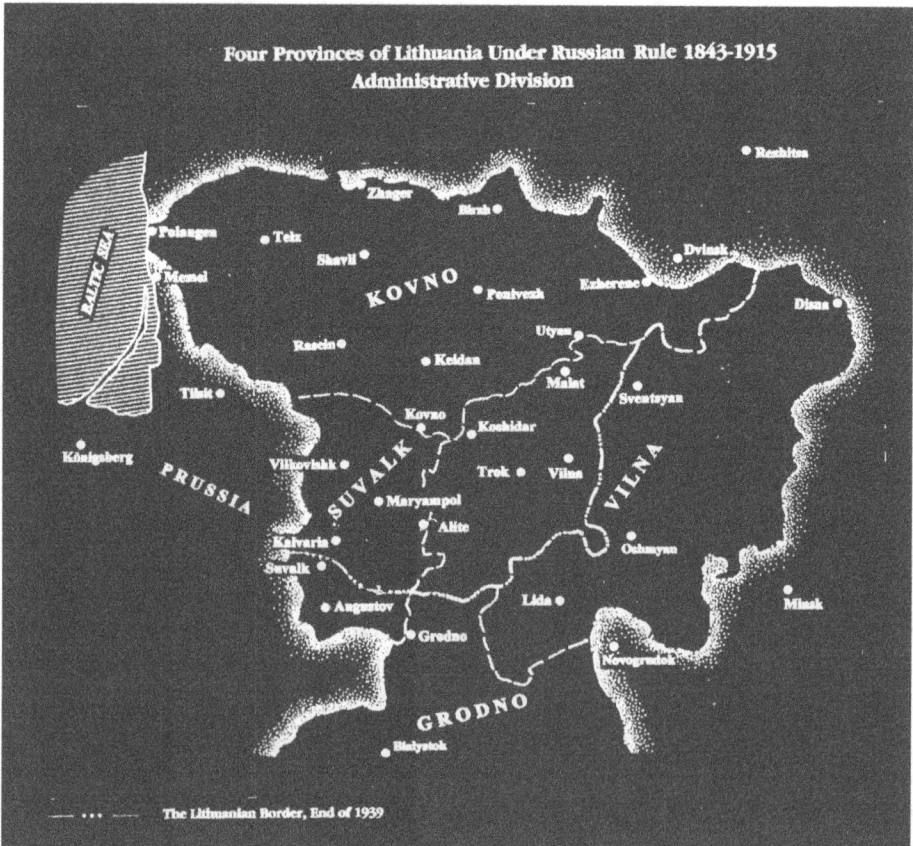

Four Provinces of Lithuania Under Russian Rule 1843-1915
Administrative Division

At the end of the eighteenth century there were several areas in this region where half of the population was Jewish, while in a few the Jews enjoyed a decisive majority. In urban settlements, Jews usually tended to concentrate in a defined area, a Jewish quarter, sometimes called "The Jews' Street." Jews who were scattered or lived outside this area were strongly linked to and remained in close contact with those living within the Jewish quarter.

As in other areas in western Russia at this time, this region was also proclaimed as belonging to the *Tehum HaMoshav HaYehudi* (The Jewish Pale of Settlement), where many restrictive edicts and harsh limitations were imposed on the Jewish population, resulting in great hardship and which continued almost until World War I.

At the same time the government was troubled by the isolation of the Jews and tried to deal with this problem in different, sometimes contradictory ways. Thus in 1804 Jews were forbidden to live in the villages and to sell alcohol to peasants, but they were allowed to live as peasants on land allocated to them by the government. Schools were opened for Jews, and in Vilna, a *Beth Midrash* (Seminary) for Rabbis was permitted. In fact these institutions served as centers for the development of a stratum of learned men who spoke Russian, which gave them entry into the lower echelons of the social and academic establishments. Most Jews, whose main living was based on contact with peasants and the poor and who lived in the villages and in small towns, managed to survive with a minimal knowledge of the Polish and Lithuanian languages. However, among the narrow layer of Lithuanian intelligentsia, still loyal to a great extent to Polish culture and statehood, there were accusations that these Jews were, in fact, causing the spread of Russian culture on behalf of the ruling class. As a result the Jews found themselves "between the hammer and the anvil" in times of war, as during the invasion of Lithuania by Napoleon in 1812. Some of them, favorably impressed by their contacts with French officers, supported the provisional authority established by the French army and even helped to provide information. But the majority remained patriotic to mother Russia. The Jews were thrown into even more critical situations during the Polish uprisings against Russian rule in 1831 and in 1863: on the one hand they were suspected of sympathy with the rulers and some of them were murdered, whereas on the other hand the Cossacks, who had been sent by the rulers against the Poles, abused the Jews after expelling the rebels.

During the 1905 Russian revolution, progressive circles among Lithuanian Jews expressed their support for the Lithuanians, requesting national autonomy in ethnic Lithuanian regions; i.e. in most of the areas of the Vilna and Kovno *Guberniae* and, in particular, in the Neman (Nemunas) and Vilija (Neris) river basins.

In view of the elections to the all-Russian parliament (*Duma*) which took place in the years 1906-1917, preliminary agreements were arranged for collaboration between Jews and Lithuanians: as a result three Jewish delegates were elected from the Kovno and Vilna *Guberniae*. At approximately the same time the local branch of the social democratic party in Lithuania published a proclamation in Lithuanian denouncing pogroms against Jews in these Provinces.

From the start of World War I the Russian army organized attacks on Jews in several towns in Lithuania, including Kuziai, on the pretext that they supplied information to the German army. Despite this libel being strongly refuted by a committee on behalf of the Duma, the military authorities did not retract their accusation. Furthermore, in the summer of 1915, before their retreat from the Kovno *Gubernia* when under pressure by the German army, they exiled 120,000 Jewish citizens into remote Russia.

The German military administration (*Oberost*) imposed strict adherence to orders on Jews as well as on other residents, but their relationship to Jews was correct and they even made allowances for Jewish cultural requirements.

This attitude was prompted by the presence of several Jewish officers in the German army. Also the identity cards issued to Jews were printed in German and Yiddish. For political reasons the Germans did not allow the establishment of an autonomous framework for Jews, despite the intercession of noted German Jews. A deputation of prominent local Jews, including the chairman of the Vilna community, Dr. Ya'akov Vigodsky, Rabbi Yisrael-Nisan Kark from Kovno and others, represented Jewish interests. Some of them advocated collaboration with Lithuanian delegates regarding the establishment of an independent Lithuania.

Considerably closer relations between Lithuanian Jewry and Lithuanians at the political level could be seen at the end of World War I when Lithuania was proclaimed an independent state. Being interested in acquiring the support of world Jewry, the Lithuanian government granted a broad cultural autonomy to the Jewish minority. Despite the massive participation of Jews in the independence war of Lithuania and their empathy in the struggle against the seizure of the Vilna region by the Polish army, many Jews were nevertheless wounded in pogroms by Lithuanian soldiers in Ponevezh (Panevezys), Vilkomir (Ukmerge), Kovarsk (Kavarskas) and other places. Frequent organized offensives against Jews, such as smearing tar on signs written in Yiddish on shops and on the premises of liberal professionals, were carried out in the temporary capital of Kovno (Kaunas) and in other towns.

In the short period 1920-1925, which can be called the Golden Era of Lithuanian Jewry and the peak of its autonomous status, public Jewish issues were managed by local community committees: these were supported and guided in their daily functions by such central institutions in Kovno as the Jewish National Council, the highest institution of the autonomy, and the Ministry for Jewish Affairs.

Map of Lithuania 1918-1940
The Jewish Communities

The territory of Lithuania in mid-1939

The Vilna region conquered by Poland in 1920 and annexed to Lithuania in October 1939

The Klaipėda (Memel) district annexed by Germany in March 1939

Annexed to Lithuania from Soviet Belorussia in 1940

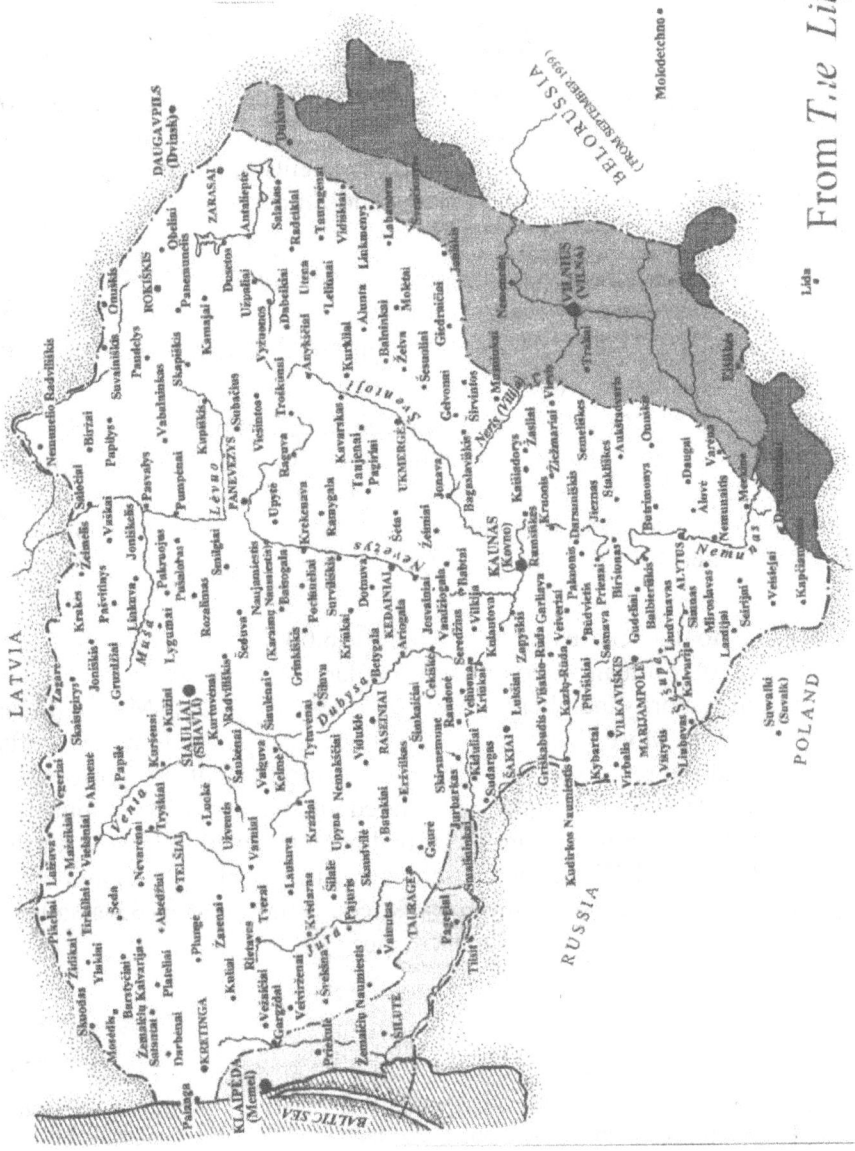

From T.ıe Litvaks

BELORUSSIA (FROM SEPTEMBER 1939)

Molodetchna

Lida

DAUGAVPILS (Dvinsk)

ZARASAI

ROKIŠKIS

PANEVEŽYS

UKMERGĖ

KĖDAINIAI

RASEINIAI

ŠIAULIAI (SHAVLI)

TELŠIAI

KRETINGA

KLAIPĖDA (Memel)

ŠILUTĖ

TAURAGĖ

ŠAKIAI

VILKAVIŠKIS

MARIJAMPOLE

ALYTUS

VILNIUS (VILNA)

KAUNAS (KOVNO)

LATVIA

POLAND

RUSSIA

BALTIC SEA

Left: Stamp of the Minister for Jewish affairs.
Right: Stamp of the National Council of Lithuania's Jews.

The education system in Hebrew and Yiddish, serving about 90% of the Jewish children[2] and the network of popular banks (*Folksbank*) in 85 settlements, were some of the many achievements of the autonomy period. In most towns, branches of Zionist parties and Zionist youth organizations were active.

Between the two world wars a considerable number of Jews emigrated to *Eretz-Yisrael*. Hayim-Nakhman Bialik, when visiting Lithuania and hearing Hebrew spoken in the streets, was so impressed that he called Lithuania the *Eretz-Yisrael* of the Diaspora.

In contrast to the Zionists, the radical religious camp (*Agudath Yisrael*) and the Yiddishist camp (Folkists, Bundists and Communists) were numerically smaller. Although Hebrew was spoken in educational institutions, in youth organizations and also in a number of houses, the daily language was Yiddish, which was also the language of the six daily newspapers and other publications.

According to the census of 1923, the 156,000 Jews (7.6% of the entire population of Lithuania) comprised the largest minority in the state. The Lithuanian majority numbered 1,701,000 persons (84%). Most Lithuanians were peasants. More than half of the Jews dealt in commerce, crafts and industry and the remainder worked in transportation, liberal professions and agriculture. Two-thirds of the Jews lived in the temporary capital city of Kovno (Vilna and a region around it had been annexed to Poland during this period after World War I) and in cities such as Ponevezh, Shavli (Siauliai) and Vilkomir Ukmerge), while the rest could be found in 33 smaller cities and in 246 smaller towns and rural villages.

---

[2] In 1938 and 39 there were 78 primary schools of the Hebrew *Tarbuth* chain, and many fewer of the Hebrew religious *Yavneh* chain and a few run by Yiddishists in Lithuania.

The central committee of the *Tarbuth* organization

Front row from left: Zalman Traub, Dov Aloni

Second row from left: Josef Margolin, Aizik Brudni, --, Dr. Y.L. Barukh, Shoshanah Alperin, Dr. M. Shvabe, Dr. Josef Berger, Efraim-Nahum Prakhyahu (Prokhovnik)

Back row from left: Avraham Kisin, A. Zabarsky, L. Shapira, Mosheh Cohen, Dr. Aharon Berman, Nathan Goren (Grinblat), Y. Lobman- Haviv, Shepshelevitz.

The central committee of the Jewish Popular Bank (*Folksbank*)

From left: Agr. Kelzon (speaking), Dr. Grigori Volf, Leib Garfinkel, Gedalyahu Halperin, Adv. H. Landoi, Fain, --, Katz.

INTRODUCTION

In spite of the high degree of loyalty, which Jews showed to Lithuania and their willingness to fulfil their civil obligations to the state, by the end of the 1930s a considerable sector of the Lithuanian public and authorities decided to restrict the economic livelihood of the Jews. A prominent role in a defamation and incitement campaign on this subject was carried out in cities and towns by members of the association of Lithuanian merchants and artisans, *Verslininkai*. In their journal *Verslas* they even advocated the prohibition of the employment of Lithuanian women by Jews.

At the same time the number of blood libel incidents, the so-called use of blood of Christian children for baking matzoth, increased. Assaults on Jews increased, on students in Kovno University, and also on people in the streets. Given that specific malicious incidents, such as shattering windows in synagogues and setting fire to wooden Jewish houses, were carried out in several villages simultaneously, one can only conclude that they were organized countrywide. It eventually became clear that some nationalist circles, which favored these actions, had close contacts with various groups in neighboring Nazi Germany, in spite of the fact that at about the same time (March 1939) Germany annexed the Lithuanian port of Klaipeda (Memel), through which numerous Jewish residents narrowly escaped.

This situation, as well as economic depression during this period, which affected the Jewish sector in particular, strengthened left wing political circles among the Jews. Due to international tension and the prospect of war, emigration to America, South Africa and *Eretz-Yisrael* was restricted.

With the return of the Vilna region to Lithuania at the beginning of World War II (October 10th, 1939), the Jewish population, including war refugees from Poland, increased to 250,000. Despite the difficult situation, Lithuanian Jews came to the assistance of the Polish refugees and warmly welcomed the return of Vilna Jews, with whom contact was renewed after 19 years of separation. This stopped to a great extent on June 15th, 1940 when all Lithuania fell to the Red Army and Soviet-Communist rule was implemented, with all that this implied. Despite the misgivings of many Jews, mainly business owners and those from the Zionist sector, the new regime was accepted positively, particularly when the alternative was that Nazi Germany could have taken over instead.

Despite Soviet rule in Lithuania lasting for only one year, from June 1940 until June 1941, the Jews experienced severe changes to their social and economic status. With Sovietization they were adversely affected by the nationalization of the commercial (83%) and industrial (57%) sectors; by the elimination of the Hebrew education system and the religious institutions, the pride of Lithuanian Jewry; by reduction of the Yiddish press and the closing of all public and political organizations except those connected to the Communist party. A section of Jewish youth, particularly former members of Zionist youth organizations and Hebrew educational institutions, organized secret underground circles, where they maintained intellectual and social activities in Hebrew in a national spirit.

During that year the Soviet government imprisoned several Jewish leaders, local Zionist activists and merchants. All were exiled to Siberia and to other remote areas in the Soviet Union. Others who were destined for the same fate, but had meanwhile been overlooked for some reason, changed their addresses. During this period about 7,000 Jews, including refugees from central Europe and Poland (among them Menahem Begin, the future Prime Minister of Israel) were detained and exiled.

Even though Soviet rule caused obvious suffering to the Jewish population, the Lithuanians blamed the Jews for the loss of their independence, calling for revenge. Meanwhile the Lithuanian national underground (L.A.F. – the Lithuanian Activist Front) which had been established in Berlin on November 17th, 1940, strengthened its secret contacts with Nazi Germany and incited Jews, preparing for an uprising against Soviet rule in expectation of an invasion by the German army.

And indeed, during the first days of war between Germany and the Soviet Union in June 1941, many Jews were cruelly murdered by inhumane Lithuanians. Only a small number managed to escape to the Soviet Union, where some fought against the Nazi German army in the Lithuanian 16th Division of the Red Army.

Since the German army managed to overrun Lithuania in a few days, the majority of Lithuanian Jews remained under Nazi occupation, while the hostile Lithuanian population stepped up their bloody pogroms, raping and robbing their Jewish neighbors.

Very often these terrible events occurred long before the soldiers of the German army arrived at the settlements where Jews had lived for generations. Thousands of Jews all over Lithuania were imprisoned in jails and in other locations which would later serve as mass murder sites, following a precise German plan which was executed with great enthusiasm by the Lithuanian military, the police force and local volunteers. The "Organized Murder Units" would appear in villages where Jews lived, usually after the first pogroms. The scared and hapless Jews were brutally concentrated into synagogues (which became, in fact, torture sites), in market places, on isolated farms or in other buildings. From there they were led, first the men, then the women and children, to the mass murder sites. Here they were forced, while being tortured, to hand over jewellery and other valuables they had carried with them, to undress and to descend into previously prepared pits where they were shot by gun and machine-gun fire. The wounded and those still alive were buried together with the dead in mass graves; their clothes and property were plundered by the murderers and local residents.

INTRODUCTION

About 40,000 Jews who survived the mass murders in the summer and autumn of 1941 and who were destined to serve as a temporary labor force for the German war effort, were imprisoned in ghettos in Vilna, Kovno, Shavli, Shventsian (Svencionys) and in several labor camps in eastern Lithuania. The despairing Jews were subject to inhumanly organized murders, euphemistically called "Actions", and many were deported to countries outside Lithuania. With the Soviet-German front drawing nearer at the end of 1943 and in the first half of 1944, the ghettos and labor camps were liquidated and their remnants transferred to concentration camps in Estonia and Germany. When the Red Army returned to Lithuania in the second half of 1944, there were then about 2,000 Jews in Soviet partisan units and the same number in hiding places, where they had not been discovered. Others had found shelter with non-Jews, mostly in villages far from the central towns of Lithuania. If one adds the number of Lithuanian Jewish survivors to those who escaped or were exiled to Russia, and to those who survived the concentration camps in Germany, Estonia and elsewhere, it would seem that 94% of the 220,000 Jewish residents fell victim to the Nazi occupation, the greatest percentage in all Europe. It is not surprising that most of the remnants of the *Shoah* left Lithuania's blood-soaked earth: a considerable number of these survivors emigrated to *Eretz-Yisrael*.

One of those privileged to arrive in *Eretz-Yisrael* before the State of Israel was established, was the engineer Josef Rosin, the author of this book, having alone survived when his entire family was murdered in 1941 together with all the Jews in Kibart (Kybartai), in western Lithuania.[3]

As in other places in Lithuania the massacre of this community was carried out by Germans along with Lithuanians, who availed themselves to the Germans in the cruel liquidation of their Jewish neighbors, and since then this community no longer exists.

Nearly fifty years after the complete destruction of his community, Josef Rosin decided to commemorate the loss of his family and community by producing the Yizkor Book *Kibart*, which was published in Haifa in 1988 by the Association of Former Kibart Citizens in Israel. In October 2003 a second extended and updated edition of this book was published, including more impressive photographs of Kibart community members, their institutions, their houses and important documents of community life.

---

[3] English readers interested in additional material on this subject are referred to:
1) **Dov Levin, THE LITVAKS, A Short History of the Jews in Lithuania**, Yad Vashem, **Jerusalem.** Contains: Maps, Bibliography, List of Jewish Communities, Index of names, Statistical tables.
2) **Dov Levin**, LITHUANIA, The YIVO Encyclopedia of Jews in Eastern Europe, Yale Vol. 1. pp 1068-1076.

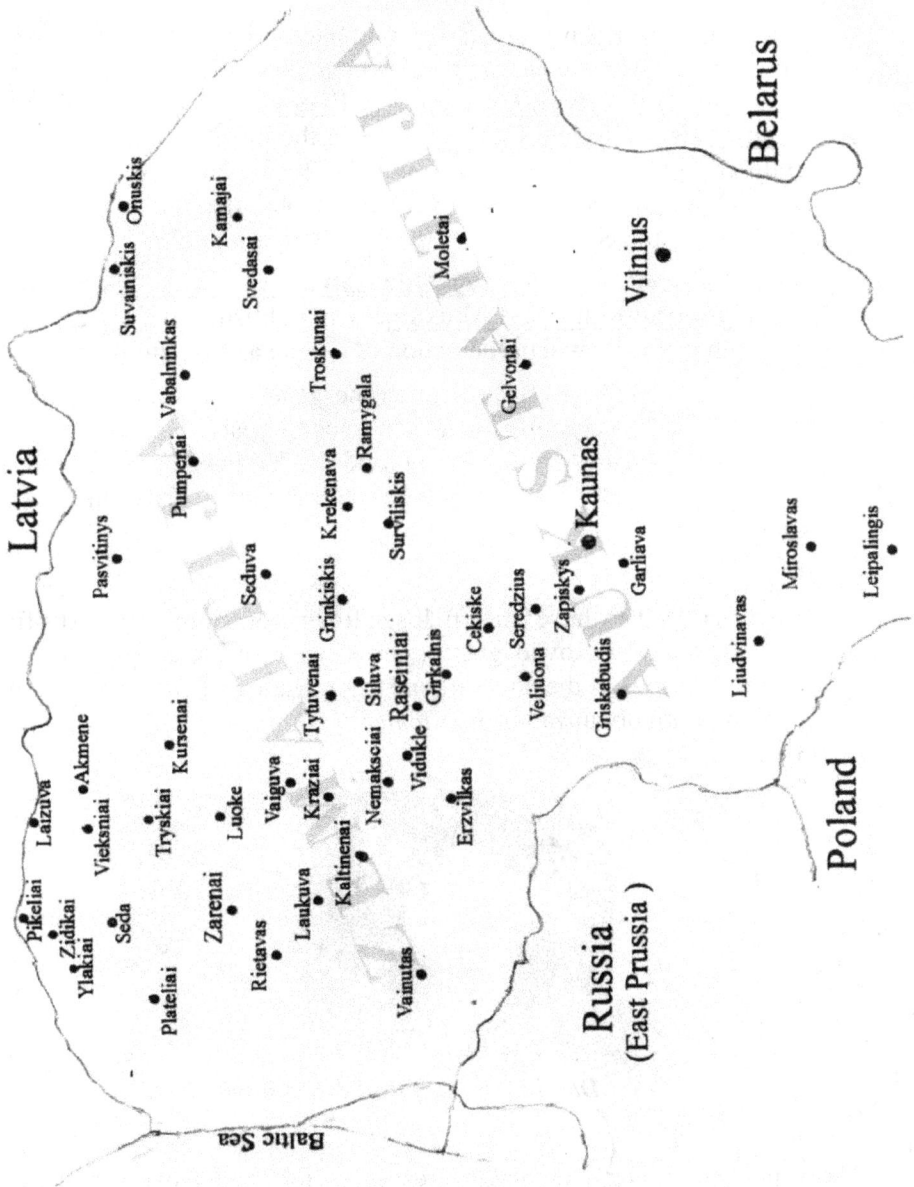

Map of Lithuania with the 50 towns contained in this book.

Since then Josef Rosin's documentation has expanded to 102 articles on other Lithuanian Jewish communities, which are included in three books: **Preserving Our Litvak Heritage - A History of 31 Jewish Communities in Lithuania,** edited by Joel Alpert, with the introduction by Professor Dov Levin, and published by JewishGen, Inc. 2003. This first book includes the *Yizkor* Book of Kybartai and 30 articles on other communities, some of which were situated relatively close to Kybartai.

The second book, **Preserving Our Litvak Heritage - A History of 21 Jewish Communities in Lithuania**, was published by JewishGen, Inc. in 2007 with the dedicated participation of people and institutions as above.

Now we are privileged to present to the general public and in particular to "Litvaks" (and surely to the historians, sociologists and genealogists) a third book, now published by the Friends of the Yurburg Jewish Cemetery, Inc. This book includes 50 articles on communities from all over Jewish Lithuania.

*

I am privileged to have known Josef Rosin for more than sixty-five years, since 1943 in the Kovno ghetto: there, we became partners in social and cultural activities in the underground organization of survivors of the Zionist-Socialist youth organization *HaShomer HaTsair*.

Dov Levin (left) and Josef Rosin today

By that time Josef was already respected for his outstanding knowledge of many subjects and his moderate and balanced point of view. In particular, he gave us immeasurable pleasure in the depressing atmosphere of the ghetto - he would play his wonderful music on his *Garmoshka* (Mouth organ). Later his melodies soothed us in the heavily forested partisan woods of eastern Lithuania, where we were privileged to be partners in the fight against the German Nazis and their local allies. This pleasant tradition continued, when in October 1945 we were together on an Italian fishing vessel, which transported 171 illegal *Shoah* (Holocaust) survivors to *Eretz-Yisrael*. During those seven very difficult and trying days on board ship, he was given the job of allocating the scarce drinking water to the passengers. (It is doubtful that he then foresaw that, within about six years, he would hold the position of a department head of TAHAL - The Water Planning Authority for Israel!).

We arrived safely in *Eretz-Yisrael*, having evaded capture by the British police as illegal immigrants. Both of us joined Kibbutz Beth-Zera in the Jordan valley and there we worked for some time in the banana plantations. Even after Josef went to study at the Technion in Haifa and I at the Hebrew University in Jerusalem, we would meet at least annually with other friends who had shared our ideals and life in the Kovno ghetto. And, of course, we and our families would again enjoy the music from his ever-present mouth organ.

In due course we came to cooperate even more positively at this scientific-literary level. This happened at the beginning of the 1990s, when I was elected by the directorate of Yad Vashem to serve as chief editor of the book *Pinkas Kehilot Lita*. [4]

Knowing well his involvement and expertise concerning Jewish life in Lithuania and also his accuracy when writing, it was natural to approach Josef Rosin to accept the assignment of assistant editor. I am glad to state that from that time until the publication of the first edition of the *Pinkas Kehilot Lita* in 1996, we were blessed with productive and beneficial working relations, which, if indirectly, gave rise to the two books mentioned above and in the course of the issue I will refer to the content, significance and particularity of this third book.

The author also deserves appreciation for his care in including with awesome reverence most of the names of his hometown Jews. In view of the terrible tragedy that the Jewish people experienced, it is essential, in my opinion, to repeatedly mention the Jewish names of villages and even more so the names of Jews, particularly those who did not leave relatives or descendants. We hope that, in this way, their names, at least, will not be lost.

The author should be commended for using the old Jewish names of the towns, as a reminder to some of the Litvaks in Western Europe and America who may not know them or prefer to use the official Lithuanian names as enforced by the government for nationalistic-political reasons.

The results of this destructive and draconian policy can be seen in most of the names of the towns presented in this book; so much so that it is sometimes difficult to identify a town by the Hebrew or Yiddish or other name it has had for

---

[4] Pinkas Kehilot Lita, Encyclopeadia of Jewish Communities in Lithuania from their foundation till after the Holocaust. Editor: Dov Levin. Assistant Editor: Josef Rosin. Yad Vashem, Jerusalem 1996.

hundreds of years, according to Jewish historiography and literature. In the 1930s the local Yiddish press was forced to use the official Lithuanian names. [5]

Some of the 50 towns in this book have names that are quite different from their Yiddish names (shown in parentheses): examples include Seredzius (Srednik), Luoke (Luknik), Svedasai (Sviadushch), Moletai (Maliat), Leipalingis (Leipun), Plateliai (Plotel), Ylakiai (Yelok), Tytuvenai (Tsitovyan) and Garliava (Gudleve).

As in the previous volumes, which received positive reviews, the author presents his material in this book in a similar manner to that of the Hebrew book "*Pinkas Kehilot Lita*" mentioned above.

On page xv above a map shows the reader the geographical location of each of the 50 towns that are included in the book. [6]

No less important in this volume is the way in which the history of every community is divided into the three main periods of its growth and development since it first came into existence. These periods were:

1) From the settlement of the first Jews (often during the fourteenth century) during or even before the period of the *Va'ad Medinath Lita* (1623-1761) until World War I in 1914. [7]

2) The period of independent Lithuania between the two world wars, 1918 to 1940.

3) The duration of World War II (1940-1945) and in particular the fate of the Jewish communities at the hands of the Nazis and their Lithuanian neighbors, with losses of about 94% of the Jewish population. Also described in this period is the fate of the few known survivors to date.

In order to complete the knowledge of the Jews who lived in the 50 towns during past centuries two tables of authentic information (based on official censi) on the numbers of Jews in each town are presented. [8]

---

[5] The first indications of the organized oppression and terror against the public use of the Yiddish language were evident at the beginning of the young Lithuanian state, when Jewish volunteers still fought in its war for independence. In one night of February 1923, in an organized action in tens of towns, Jewish and Hebrew signs on shops were smeared with tar. See also **The Litvaks**, p. 125

[6] It could be of interest to the reader to know that about half (24) of the 50 towns were included in 4 districts: 8 in Mazheik District, 7 in Rasein, 5 in Kovno, 4 in Ponevezh and 3 in Shavl District. The other towns were scattered in 12 Districts as follows: Alite, Birzh, Keidan, Kretingen, Mariampol, Rakishok, Shaki, Utyan, Seiny, Tavrig, Telzh, Vilkomir, (altogether there were 23 Districts in Lithuania).

[7] Communities that were already established in the seventeenth century include: Gelvan*, Grinkishok*, Vekshne*, Pumpyan*, Kruzh*, Rasein*, and in the eighteenth century were Akmyan*, Grishkabud*, Zhidik*, Maliat*, Siad*.

[8] People interested in checking the names and the regular spelling of the communities in Yiddish and in Lithuanian in specific periods can find the information in Dov Levin's book, **The Litvaks**, pp.268-282.

Table 1. Jewish population according to censi of 1847, 1855-1857, 1897

Town (in Yiddish)	1847	%	1855-57	%	1897	%	Remarks
Akmyan	667				543	36	
Anishok					80-90 families		about 400 persons
Erzhvilik					144	20	
Gudleve					469	49	
Gelvan			90 *				1914 families *
Girtegole					530	82	
Grinkishok					---		
Grishkabud					30 families		about 150 persons
Kaltinan					---		
Kamai	453				944	85	
Krakinove	594				1,505	69	
Krozh			236*		906	51	1816*
Kurshan					1,542	48	
Laizheve					434	46	
Loikeve					418	55	
Ludvinove			1,055	69	369	34	
Leipun					134	10	
Luknik	949				798	49	
Miroslav					60 families		about 300 persons
Maliat	1,006		725*	60	1,948	81	1866*
Nemoksht	255				954	81	
Pashvitin					435	57	
Pikeln					1,206	68	
Plotel					171	28	
Pumpyan	694	69			1,017	69	
Remigole	190				650	49	
Rasein			5,000	59	3,484	47	
Riteve					1,397	80	
Sapizishok					---		
Siad	1,729				1,384	69	
Shadeve	1,211				2,513	56	
Srednik	1,090				1,174	71	
Shidleve	245				506	42	
Survilishok	250*						1873*
Suvainishok					684	80	
Svadushch					528		

Trashkun					779	64	
Trishik					681	34	
Tsaikishok					432	65	
Tsitevyan					---		
Vabolnik	508		545	46	1,828	78	
Vaigeve					193	36	
Vainute					---		
Velon					573	70	
Vidukle					---		
Vekshne	1,120				1,646	56	
Yelok					775	57	
Yezne			170*	31			1866*
Zharan					---		
Zhidik					914	73	
Total	**10,961**				**35,458**		

Table 1 includes data of the Jewish population and its percentage of the total population gleaned from the three census surveys of 1847, 1855/57 and 1897 carried out in Lithuania under Czarist Russian rule. In addition to the overall growth in the number of Jews in almost all of the 50 towns, they were the absolute majority in 22 of these centers by the end of the century. It is proper to note that during the nineteenth century the Jewish population in the 50 towns in this book grew by 25,000 despite the great emigration of Lithuanian Jews to overseas countries during this period.

In the 17 communities for which we have census figures for Jewish residents in both 1847 and 1897, 12 of them showed an increase: Kamai*, Krakinove*, Kruzh*, Maliat*, Nemoksht*, Srednik*, Pumpyan*, Remigole*, Shadeve*, Shidleve*, Vabolnik*, Vekshne* while in 5 others, Akmyan*, Ludvinove*, Luknik*, Siad* and the district center Rasein*, a decrease was recorded.

In the following towns the Jews constituted an absolute majority of the total population:
Kamai (85%), Girtigole (82%), Maliat (81%), Nemoksht (81%), Suveinishok (80%), Riteve (80%), Bolnik (78%), Zhidik (73%), Srednik (71%), Velon (70%), Siad (69%), Krakinove-69%, Pumpyan-69%, Pikeln-68%, Tsaikishok-65%, Trashkun (64%), Yelok (57%), Pashvitin (57%), Vekshne (56%), Shadeve (56%), Loikeve (55%), Kruzh (51%).

Table 2. Jewish population of all 50 towns during the period of Independent Lithuania, according to the census of 1923.

Town (in Yiddish)	Jewish Population in 1923	% 0f Total Population	1945	After 1945
Akmyan	360	25		
Anishok	60-70 families	About 400 persons	0	
Erzhvilik	222	46	0	
Gudleve	311	33	0	
Gelvan	473		0	
Girtegole	213		0	
Grinkishok	235	24	0	
Grishkabud	92	12	0	
Kaltinan	130	20	0	
Kamai	336	54	0	
Krakinove	527	50	0	
Krozh	470		0	
Kurshan	841		0	
Laizheve	127	15	0	
Loikeve	305	42	0	
Ludvinove	85	14	0	
Leipun	160	21	0	
Luknik	513	40	0	
Miroslav	124	32	0	
Maliat	1,343	76		In 1959 - 1
Nemoksht	704	69	0	
Pashvitin	274	33	0	
Pikeln	286	34	0	
Plotel	150	23	0	
Pumpyan	372	33	0	
Remigole	480	38	0	
Rasein	2,035	39	6	In 1989 - 2
Riteve	868	50		In 1959 - 1
Sapizishok	293	50	0	
Siad	815	44	0	
Shadeve	916	29		In 1959 - 4
Srednik	449	48	0	
Shidleve	365	37	1	woman
Survilishok	104	24	0	
Suvainishok	250*			1921*
Svadushch	245		0	
Trashkun	424	48	0	

Trishik	335	26	0	
Tsaikishok	324	56	0	
Tsitevyan	221	19		In 1959 - 1
Vabolnik	441	32	0	
Vaigeve	118	30	0	
Vainute	348	27	0	
Velon	335	71	0	
Vidukle	221	32	0	
Vekshne	300*		0	1921*
Yelok	409	41	0	
Yezne	286	29	0	
Zharan	174	45	0	
Zhidik	799	89	0	
Total	**20,508**			**10**

Over 50% of the population: 9 towns

Table 2 gives data of the Jewish population in the 50 towns during the period of independent Lithuania revealed by the census of 1923. It would seem that their numbers had decreased to a noticeable degree in 41 of the towns (altogether about 15,000 persons). Despite administrative manipulations by the authorities, the Jews retained their majority in nine towns (Kamai*, Krakinove*, Maliat*, Nemoksht*, Riteve*, Sapizishok*, Tsaikishok*, Velon* and Zhidik*).

Population statistics presented in the two tables show the early growth of Jewish communities in the 50 towns by the end of the first period (1897), their reduction during the second (1923-1940), and finally their absolute destruction in the third (1941-1945).

There is no doubt that the diminishing numbers of Lithuanian Jews was a result of the increasingly hostile attitude to Jews in the Lithuanian provinces. This foreshadowed the impendion of the slaughter of Jews in Lithuanian towns in the summer of 1941 long before the first German soldier appeared.

The multitude of zeroes in the penultimate column (1945) in Table 2 serves as a grim reminder that 100% of the Jews were exterminated in those places between 1941 and 1945.

After World War II and the shocking events of the Shoah the handful of Jews who returned to live in a few places of the state decreased from year to year from natural causes and also because of continued murders by local gangs who could not tolerate Jewish existence on Lithuanian soil. Also the number of Russian Jews who migrated to Lithuania after the war decreased greatly. In fact the Lithuanian government that once supported the local murderers of Jews and failed to order restitution of Jewish property to its owners, is now making an effort to reconstruct a few Jewish institutions such as cemeteries in order to encourage Jewish tourists to visit the graves of their relatives, many of whom were murdered by their own neighbors.

On a final note, the reader will understand the considerable differences in religious and cultural life between relatively large communities of more than a thousand Jews in the period of independent Lithuania (e.g. Rasein*, Maliat*) and smaller communities which numbered only several hundreds (e.g. Kurshan*, Shadeve*, Zhidik*, Siad*) and very small communities which numbered only a few dozen (Ludvinove*, Grishkabud*, Vaigeve*).

Despite this difference and others, the Jewish Popular Bank (Folksbank) had branches in almost all the communities described in this book.

The basic way of life of the communities featured in this book shows community life directed first of all to fulfilling religious commandments, e.g. *Hevroth Kadisha* (burial societies), cemeteries, synagogues and different *Minyanim*. In bigger communities there were prayer houses for groups of worshipers of the same profession, such as artisans, merchants, shop owners, and synagogue beadles. Special institutions for studying the Torah were established: *Batei Midrash* for adults, *Hadarim* for children and *Yeshivoth Ketanoth* (small *Yeshivas*) for youngsters. In most of the communities various groups of volunteers, acting under different names, worked in welfare organizations, including *Bikur Holim* for medical aid and hospitalization; *Linath Hatsedek* to support the poor and sick and to supply free medicines; *Gemiluth Hesed* providing small interest free loans to the needy; *Zokhrei Petirath Neshamah,* for commemoration of the deceased, and more.

Several communities established Volunteer Fire Brigades. These brigades, on more than one occasion, fulfilled an effective role in protecting Jewish communities in times of pogroms and riots. Here it must be noted that almost every town in Lithuania was ravaged by fire. Since most houses and synagogues were constructed of wood, most of the Jewish population was at some time rendered homeless. In such cases, the community Rabbis would publicize the disaster by mail, messengers and in later years also in the Jewish press in Hebrew and Yiddish, pleading for aid from near and far communities. On the whole help arrived as requested, and similar methods were adopted when other disasters struck, such as a virulent cholera epidemic.

INTRODUCTION

Table 3: Jewish population according to census of 1897 and numbers of donors for the victims of the Persian famine and for the settlement of *Eretz-Yisrael*

Town (in Yiddish)	1897	%	Comment	Donors for the victims of the Persian famine 1871*	Donors for the Settlement of *Eretz-Yisrael* 1873-1904**
Akmyan	543	36		---	---
Anishok	80-90 families		about 400 persons	---	---
Erzhvilik	144	20		---	---
Gudleve	469	49		---	---
Gelvan			families 1914*	---	---
Girtegole	530	82		---	---
Grinkishok	---			67	33
Grishkabud	30 families		About 150 persons	---	---
Kaltinan	---			---	11
Kamai	944	85		---	---
Krakinove	1,505	69		---	190
Krozh	906	51	1816*	24	17
Kurshan	1,542	48		75	---
Laizheve	434	46		---	---
Loikeve	418	55		---	---
Ludvinove	369	34		---	2
Leipun	134	10		---	---
Luknik	798	49		---	29
Miroslav	60 families		About 300 persons	---	---
Maliat	1,948	81	1866*	---	---
Nemoksht	954	81		---	96
Pashvitin	435	57		24	several
Pikeln	1,206	68		130	12
Plotel	171	28		---	---
Pumpyan	1,017	69		---	---
Remigole	650	49		---	91
Rasein	3,484	47		74	234
Riteve	1,397	80		---	89
Sapizishok	---			---	---
Siad	1,384	69		---	53
Shadeve	2,513	56		128	57
Srednik	1,174	71		---	several

Shidleve	506	42	---	---
Survilishok			1873*	---	---
Suvainishok	684	80	---	---
Svadushch	528		---	---
Trashkun	779	64	---	---
Trishik	681	34	62	14
Tsaikishok	432	65	101	---
Tsitevyan	---		---	1
Vabolnik	1,828	78	41	20
Vaigeve	193	36	---	---
Vainute	---		57	---
Velon	573	70	25	---
Vidukle	---		---	61
Vekshne	1,646	56	118	58
Yelok	775	57	---	19
Yezne			1866*	---	---
Zharan	---		---	---
Zhidik	914	73	43	---
Total	**35,458**		**14 Towns of 50 (28%)**	**20 Towns of 50 (40%)**

* Compiled by Jeffrey Maynard from *HaMagid*
** Compiled by Jeffrey Maynard from *HaMelitz*

In **Table 3** one can see the Jewish solidarity in the communities of Girtigole*, Rasein*, Pikeln*, Kamai*, Shadeve*, Nemoksht*, Tsaikishok*, Vainute*, Vekshne* and others, that expressed itself in donations of money to Jewish communities outside Lithuania, as far away as Persia (Iran) and certainly *Eretz-Yisrael*.

To illustrate this phenomenon, hundreds of donors' names are listed in this book. They were published in the pages of *HaMagid* from 1871 and *Hamelitz* from 1873 to 1904. This may be valuable for descendants seeking reference to their ancestors from genealogical viewpoint or whose tombstones in the cemeteries of Lithuania have been ruined by weathering or vandalism.

*

A few days before signing this Introduction the author and myself lost our long standing and devoted friend Hayim Galin who was with us for more than fifty years, beginning in the period of organizing resistance in the Kovno ghetto, our fighting in the partisan woods and finally in Israel.

INTRODUCTION

Finally, it is appropriate to mark with gratitude and appreciation the professional work of the outstanding American-born Litvak, our mutual friend Joel Alpert, who invested much energy in preparing this book with all its components and appendices which also have great historical value and human importance. This is an act of true kindness (*Hesed shel Emeth*) for the hundreds of people of the fifty Jewish communities that were destroyed, never to rise again.

Professor Dov Levin, Hebrew University of Jerusalem

Yerushalayim, May 20, 2008

The Author, Josef Rosin, About Himself

I am a native of Kybartai (Lithuania). I was born on January 24, 1922 to Hayah (nee Leibovitz) from Marijampole and Yehudah Leib Rosin from Sudargas (Lithuania). They were the owners of a paper and stationary shop in Kibart (the Yiddish name of the town).

I received my elementary and high school education in Kibart, Virbalis and Marijampole. During the years 1939 to 1941 I was a student at the Civil Engineering Faculty of the Kovno (Kaunas) University.

I left my home for the last time on Friday, June 20, 1941, just two days before the German invasion into the USSR began. My parents and my sister stayed in Kibart and were murdered together with all the Jews of the town in July of the same year. I was in the Kovno Ghetto for more than two and a half years until the beginning of February 1944 when I escaped into the woods (first into the Rudniki forests and later into the Naliboki forests in Belarus). I remained there until the liberation by the Red Army. In August 1944 I returned to Kovno. At the end of March 1945, I joined a group of young Lithuanian Jews who determined that we should leave Europe and make our way to *Eretz Yisrael*; we became part of the movement that became known as the *"Brikhah" (Flight)* movement. I left Lithuania and after the tribulations of the illegal travel through Poland, Slovakia, Rumania, Hungary, Austria and Italy, I arrived in *Eretz Yisrael* on October 24, 1945 on a ship of *"Ma'apilim" (Illegal Immigrants)*. During the stay in Rumania I married Peninah (nee Cypkewitz) from Wloclawek, who had made a similarly difficult journey from Poland.

We lived in Kibbutz Beth-Zera in the Jordan Valley for nine months. In the autumn of 1946 we left the Kibbutz and moved to Haifa, with the aim of continuing my studies at the Civil Engineering Faculty of the Technion. I was accepted in the second course (as a second year student) and after a further year delay because of the War of Independence; I completed my studies in 1950 with the degree of Engineer. In 1958 I received my M.Sc. in Agricultural Engineering from the Technion.

During the War of Independence I served in the Air Force in the Aerial Photography Unit and was discharged with the rank of Staff Sergeant. I served in the Army Reserves until the age of 54.

During the years 1950-1952 I worked at the Water Department of the Ministry of Agriculture and with the establishment of "Water Planning for Israel" (Tahal), I joined this firm, where I worked until my retirement on the first of April 1987. For more than twenty years I held the position of Head of the Drainage and Development Department of that firm.

In 1989, I published my "Memoirs" in Hebrew and in 1994 in English.

During the years 1987 through 1994 I wrote many entries for the Hebrew book _Encyclopedia of the Jewish Communities in Lithuania_ (_Pinkas Hakehilot-Lita_) and participated in publishing this book as the Assistant

Editor. This book was published by Yad Vashem in 1996, edited by Dov Levin.

In 2001 and 2002 I acted as the assistant editor for the publication of the Memorial Book of the Jewish Community of Yurburg, Lithuania-Translation and Update.

Most recently I wrote two books on the history of 52 Lithuanian Jewish communities, Preserving Our Litvak Heritage, Volumes I and II, published by JewishGen in 2005 and 2007, respectively.

I have a married son and a married daughter and four grandchildren.

****

Common sources used in most of the articles were:

Yad-Vashem Archives, Jerusalem.

Central Zionist Archives, Jerusalem: 55/1788; 55/1701; 13/15/131; Z-4/2548.

YIVO, NY-Lithuanian Jewish Communities Collection.

Kamzon Y.D. *Yahaduth Lita*, (Hebrew) Mossad HaRav Kook, Jerusalem 1959.

Yahaduth Lita, (Hebrew) Tel-Aviv, 1960-1984, Volumes 1-4.

Cohen Berl, *Shtetl, Shtetlach un Dorfishe Yishuvim in Lite biz 1918* (Towns, Small Towns and Rural Settlements in Lithuania till 1918) (Yiddish) New York 1992.

Pinkas haKehiloth Lita (Encyclopedia of Jewish Communities in Lithuania) (Hebrew), Editor: Dov Levin, Assistant editor: Josef Rosin, Yad Vashem. Jerusalem 1996.

Masines Zudynes Lietuvoje (Mass Murder in Lithuania) vol. 1-2, Vilnius 1941-1944 (Lithuanian).

The Book of Sorrow (Hebrew, Yiddish, English, Lithuanian), Vilnius 1997.

The Lithuanians Encyclopedia, Boston, 1953-1965, (Lithuanian).

The Small Lithuanian Encyclopedia, Vilnius, 1966-1971, (Lithuanian).

From Beginning to End (The History of *HaShomer HaTsair* Movement in Lithuania) (Hebrew).

HaMeilitz (St. Petersburg) (Hebrew).

Dos Vort, Kovno (Yiddish).

Folksblat, Kovno (Yiddish).

Di Yiddishe Shtime, Kovno (Yiddish).

Specific references of each town appear at the end of each article.

Notes to the Reader:

All the Yiddish and Hebrew names were transliterated anew according to the rules issued by YIVO for this purpose.

Dates in the book are written according to the European standard, as day-month-year, so that, for example, Dec. 15, 1955 would be abbreviated as 15.12.55.

Because of technical difficulties the Lithuanian names of the towns and places (except of the captions of the articles) are printed without the particular Lithuanian letters and symbols.

Agadah - Homiletic passages in Rabbinic literature
Agudath-Yisrael - Orthodox anti-Zionist organization
Aliyah (Ascent) - Immigration to Israel
Aron Kodesh - The Holy Ark in the Synagogue
Ashkenazi - Jew from Central or Eastern Europe
Benei-Akiva - Religious Zionist youth organization
Berith-Milah - Circumcision
Beth Midrash - A Synagogue for praying and studying the Torah
Bikur-Holim - Welfare society for helping the Ill
Beitar (Brith Yosef Trumpeldor) - The Revisionist youth organization
Bimah - Platform, mostly in the middle of the Synagogue, for reading the Torah
Brith HaKanaim - the youth organization of the Grosmanists
Bund - Jewish anti-Zionist workers organization
Ein Ya'akov - collection of legends and homilies from the Talmud
Eretz-Yisrael - The Land of Israel
Ezrah (Help) - welfare society who took over the functions of the
Community Committees after their liquidation in many communities
Gabai, (pl. Gabaim) - Manager of a Synagogue
Gemara - Talmud
Gemiluth Khesed - Small loans without interest to the poor
Gordonia - Zionist Socialist youth organization
Grosmanists - Jewish State Party led by Meir Grosman
Gubernia (Russian) - Province
Gubernator – Head of Gubernia
Hakhnasath Kalah - Welfare society for helping poor brides to get married
Hakhnasath Orkhim - Welfare society for accommodate passers-by
Halakhah - Legal part of Jewish traditional literature
Hamelitz - a Hebrew weekly newspaper founded in 1860 in Odessa, later a
daily newspaper in St.Petersburg, was closed in 1903
HaMagid - a Hebrew weekly newspaper, founded in 1856, was printed in
Prussia near the border with Russia, was closed in 1890
HaNoar HaZioni - The youth organization of the General Zionist party
HaPoel - the sport organization of the Z.S. party
HaShomer-HaTsair - Leftist Zionist youth organization. In Lithuania its
official name was: "The Young Guard Organization of Hebrew Scouts"
HaShomer-Hatsair-Netsakh - a splitting of the main organization
HeKhalutz (Pioneer) - Organization with the goal to enable its members to
move to Eretz-Yisrael after first undergoing a serious course of training
particularly in agriculture
Ivrith uThekhiyah - Hebrew and Revival
Khalutz or **Halutz, (pl. Halutsim, Halutsoth) -** Pioneer
Hitakhduth - Federation of several Zionist Socialist parties
Hovev Zion (pl. Hovevei) – lover of Zion

Humash - First Five Books of the Bible (Pentateuch)
Joint – Joint Distribution Committee
Kadish - Liturgical doxology said by the mourner
Kahal - Assembly
Kantonist – a Jewish boy removed from his family to serve in the Russian army
Karaite - member of Jewish sect originating in the 8th century, which rejects the Oral Law
Khalah, Halah - Loaf of bread made of white flour, prepared specially for Shabath
Khevrah-Kadisha (Hevrah) - Burial Society
Kheder (pl. Hadarim) - Religious Elementary School
Kheder Metukan - Improved Kheder in which secular subjects were also taught
Khupah - Marriage ceremony
Keren Kayemeth Le'Yisrael (KKL) - The Jewish National Fund. Its goals were buying land, planting groves and other reclamation works in Eretz-Yisrael
Keren Tel-Hai - The fund of the Revisionists after they split from the Zionist Organization
Keren Ha'Yesod - Jewish Foundation Fund
Khibath Zion (Love of Zion) - a 19th century movement to build up the Land of Yisrael before the establishment of the Zionist organization
Khovevei Zion - Members of the above-mentioned movement
Khasidim - a sect in Judaism founded by Rabbi Yisrael Ba'al Shem Tov
Khevrah - Society
Kibutz Hakhsharah - Training Kibutz for the Halutsim before their Aliyah to Eretz Yisrael
Klois - a small prayer room
Kultur Lige - Culture League, association of Yiddishists
Lekhem Aniyim - Welfare society for supplying bread to the poor
Linath HaTsedek - Welfare society for helping the ill
Magdeburg Rights - the Constitution of Magdeburg was an example of almost full autonomy for many towns in Eastern Europe
Magen David (The Shield of David) - The national emblem of the Jewish people
Maoth - Money
Maoth Khitim - Charity Fund for the poor for buying flour for Matsoth
Matsah (pl. Matsoth) - Unleavened bread for Passover
Matsah Shemurah - Guarded Matsah of wheat kept dry from the time of reaping
Melamed (pl. Melamdim) - Teacher in a Kheder
Meshulakh - Emissary for collecting money for different institutions in Eretz-Yisrael

GLOSSARY

Midrash - Homiletic interpretation of the Scriptures

Mikveh - Ritual bath

Minyan (pl. Minyanim) - Ten adult male Jews, the minimum for congregational prayer

Mishnah - Collection of Oral Laws compiled by Rabbi Yehudah haNasi, which forms the basis of the Talmud

Mithnagdim - Opponents to Hasidim

Mizrahi - Religious Zionist party

Mohel - Circumciser

Moshav Zekeinim - Home for the Aged

Oleh (pl. Olim) (Ascending) - Immigrant to Israel

Olim LaTorah - called up to the weekly bible portion

Orakh Hayim - The first column of the Shulhan Arukh of Rabbi Josef Caro

ORT Chain - International organization for spreading vocational education among the Jews

OZE (Initials of the Russian name) - International organization for improving the public and personal hygiene of the Jewish population, in particular of the school children

Pinkas - Notebook, Register

Pesakh - Passover

Poalei Zion (Workers of Zion) - Socialist workers party

Poale Zion-Smol (Workers of Zion-left) - Radical leftist party, was forbidden by the Lithuanian government

Rosh Yeshivah - Head of a Yeshivah

Sepharadi - Jew of Spanish stock

Shabbat – The Sabbath (Friday night / Saturday)

Shamash - Synagogue beadle

Shas (Abbreviation of Shisha Sidrei Mishnah) - The six books of the Mishnah

Shekhitah - Ritual slaughtering

Shekel (pl. Shekalim) - the membership card of the Zionist organization that granted the privilege to vote at the Zionist Congresses

Shokhet (pl. Shokhtim) - Ritual slaughterer(s)

Shtibl (pl. Shtiblakh) - Small prayer room for people of the same profession

Shul - Synagogue

Shulhoif-The backyard of the Synagogue

Shulkhan Arukh (The prepared table) - authoritative code of Jewish laws, written by Yoseph Caro (1488-1575)

Sidur - Prayer book

Simhath Torah - Rejoicing of the Law (Festival)

Somekh Noflim - Loans without interest for people who have lost their business or property

Tallith (pl. Tallithoth) - Praying shawl

Talmud - The commentaries on the Mishnah

Talmud Torah - Religious school
Tarbuth Chain (Culture) - Zionist Hebrew chain of elementary schools
Tehilim - Psalms
Tefillin - Phylacteries
Tifereth Bakhurim - Orthodox boys' organization
Tomkhei Aniyim – Supporters of the Poor
Tomkhei Tsedakah - Charity
Tsair - Young
Tseirei Zion - Young Zionists party
Tsedakah Gedolah - Charity
Va'ad - Committee
Va'ad Kehilah - Community committee
Va'ad Medinath Lita - Autonomous organization for Jewish communities in Lithuania (1623-1764)
Verslas - Lithuanian Merchants Association
WIZO - Women International Zionist Organization
Yavneh Chain - Religious Zionist Hebrew schools
Yerushalayim - Jerusalem
Yeshivah (pl. Yeshivoth) - Talmudical college
Yeshivah Ketanah - Small Yeshivah
Yiddishist - Ideological fan of Yiddish
Z.S. - Zionist Socialist Party
Z.Z. - Tseirei Zion Party - Young Zionists

Lithuanian	Yiddish,	Russian,	Polish,	Coordinates
Akmenė	Akmyan	Okmyany	Okmiani	56° 15' 22° 45'
Čekiškė	Tsaikishok	Chekishky	Czekiszki	55° 10' 23° 31'
Eržvilkas	Erzhvilik	Erzhvilki	Erzwilki	55° 16' 22° 43'
Garliava	Gudleve	Godlevo	Godlewo	54° 49' 23° 52'
Gelvonai	Gelvan	Gelvany	Gielwany	55° 04' 24° 42'
Girkalnis	Girtegole	Girtakol	Girtokol	55° 19' 23° 13'
Grinkiškis	Grinkishok	Grinkishki	Grynkiszki	55° 34' 23° 38'
Griškabūdis	Grishkabud	Grishkabudy	Gryszkabuda	54° 51' 23° 10'
Jieznas	Yezne	Ezno	Jezno	54° 36' 24° 10'
Kaltinėnai	Kaltinan	Koltynyany	Koltyniany	55° 34' 22° 27'
Kamajai	Kamai	Komai	Komaje	55° 49' 25° 30'
Krekenava	Krakinove	Krakinovo	Krakinow	55° 33' 24° 06'
Kražiai	Kruzh	Krozhi	Kroze	55° 36' 22° 42'
Kuršėnai	Kurshan	Kurshany	Kurszany	56° 00' 22° 56'
Laižuva	Laizeve	Laizovo		56° 23' 22° 34'
Laukuva	Loikeve	Lavkovo	Lawkow	55° 37' 22° 14 '
Liudvinavas	Ludvinove	Liudvenovo	Ludwinow	54° 29 23° 21'
Leipalingis	Leipun		Lejpuny	54° 05' 23° 51'
Luokė	Luknik	Lukniki		55° 53' 22° 31'
Miroslavas	Miroslav	Miroslavo		54° 20 23° 54'
Molėtai	Maliat	Malyaty	Malaty	55° 14' 25° 25'
Nemakščiai	Nemoksht		Nemokszty	55° 26' 22° 46'
Onuškis	Anishok	Onushki	Hanuszyszki	56° 08' 25° 32'
Pašvitinys	Pashvitin		Paszwityn	56° 09' 23° 49'
Pikeliai	Pikeln	Pikeli	Pikele	56° 25' 22° 07'
Plateliai	Plotel	Ploteli	Plotele	56° 03' 21° 49'
Pumpėnai	Pumpyan	Pompyany		55° 56' 24° 21'
Ramygala	Remigole	Remigolo	Remigola	55° 31' 24° 18'
Raseiniai	Rasein	Rossieni		55° 22' 23° 07'
Rietavas	Riteve	Retovo		55° 44' 21° 56'
Seda	Siad	Siady		56° 10' 22° 06'
Šeduva	Shadeve	Shadov	Szadow	55° 46' 23° 46'
Seredžius	Srednik	Sredniki	Srednike	55° 05' 23° 25'
Šiluva	Shidleve	Shidlovo	Szydlowo	55° 32' 23° 14'
Surviliškis	Survilishok		Surwiliszki	55° 27' 24° 02'
Suvainiškis	Suveinishok		Suwejnuszky	56° 10' 25° 17'
Svedasai	Svadushch	Sviadostse	Swiadoscie	55° 41' 25° 22'
Troškūnai	Trashkun		Traszkuny	55° 36' 24° 51'
Tryškiai	Trishik	Trishki	Tryszki	56° 04' 22° 35'
Tytuvėnai	Tsitevyan	Tsytovyany	Cytowiany	55° 36' 23° 12'
Vabalninkas	Vabolnik	Vobolniky		55° 58' 24° 45'
Vaiguva	Vaigeve	Vayguva	Wajgowa	55°42' 22°45'

Vainutas	Vainute	Vainuto	Wojnuta	55°22'	21°50'
Veliuona	Velon	Velioni	Wieliona	-----	-----
Viduklė	Vidukle	Vidukli	Widukle	55°24'	22°54'
Viekšniai	Vekshne	Vyekshny	Wiekszne	56°14'	22°31'
Ylakiai	Yelok	Ilakyay	Illoki	56°17'	21°51'
Žarėnai	Zharan	Zorany		55°50	22°13'
Zapyškis	Sapizishok	Sapezhishki	Sapiezyszisky	54°55	23°40'
Židikai	Zhidik	Zhidiki	Zydyki	56°19'	22°01'

Akmenė (Akmyan)

Akmene (Akmyan in Yiddish) is in the northwestern part of Lithuania, on the Dabikine Stream, a tributary of the Venta River in the Zamut (*Zemaitija*) region. The town was built in the first half of the sixteenth century. In the seventeenth century it became a county administrative center. During the Northern War with the Swedes in 1705 it was totally destroyed. In 1792 Akmyan was granted the Magdeburg rights for self rule and received permission to hold four annual fairs.

Until 1795 Akmyan was included in the Polish-Lithuanian Kingdom. According to the third division of Poland in the same year by the three superpowers of those times, Russia, Prussia and Austria, Lithuania was divided between Russia and Prussia. As most of Lithuania, Akmyan became a part of the Russian Empire, first in the Vilna province (*Gubernia*) and from 1843 in the Kovno *Gubernia*.

By 1859 there were 62 houses in town. For some time following the Polish rebellion of 1863 the town was under the control of the rebels. As a result of the railway construction from Romni in Ukraine to Liepaja (Libau) in Kurland in 1873, the development of Akmyan was arrested. Akmyan managed to retain its status as a county administrative center during independent Lithuania (1918-1940) and during the Soviet rule (1940-1941).

Jewish settlement till World War II
Most likely Jewish settlement in Akmyan began in the middle of the eighteenth century. Jews made their living by peddling in the surrounding villages, and in crafts. A small number worked in agriculture. In the first half of the nineteenth century Jews made up about 80% of the total population. In 1847 there were 667 Jews in the town and in 1859 the total population numbered 790 people. In the village of Alkishok (Alkiskiai), not far from Akmyan, the Jewish cemetery may be found in the southwest corner of the Christian cemetery.

A Jewish peddler

In 1893 a fire caused great damage to the Jewish community. An appeal for help by the local rabbi Aharon-Eliyahu Kahana appeared in the Hebrew newspaper *HaMelitz* on behalf of the sixty Jewish families made homeless and destitute by the fire. At this time the Jews of Akmyan made up one-third of the population, as can be seen from the all Russian census of 1897: "543 Jews among the total of 1,501 (36%)," but the number was steadily decreasing due to ongoing emigration abroad before World War I. By the order of the retreating Russian army in the summer of 1915, Akmyan Jews were exiled to remote parts of Russia.

After the war following the establishment of independent Lithuania in 1918, a number of the exiled Akmyan Jews returned home. In 1921 there were 150 Jews in town and the first census performed by the new government in 1923 counted 1,453 residents in Akmyan; 360 (25%) of people in the entire county were recorded as Jews.

Following the passage of the Law of Autonomies for Minorities by the new Lithuanian government, the Minister for Jewish Affairs, Dr. Menachem (Max) Soloveitshik, ordered elections to community committees, *Va'adei Kehilah,* to be held in the summer of 1919. In Akmyan a community committee of five members was elected: three *Akhduth (Agudath Yisrael)*, one General Zionist and one representing the workers. The committee worked for several years in most fields of Jewish life.

A Jewish house in Akmyan

The exodus of Jews from Akmyan continued during this period, mainly due to the worsening economic situation.

According to the government survey of 1931, there were fourteen shops in town, eleven of them (79%) were Jewish: four textile shops, three butcher shops, one grocery, one grain merchant, one shoe store and one for sewing machine repairs. There was also a flourmill owned by a Jewish person.

In 1937 seven Jewish trades people worked in Akmyan: a baker, a carpenter, a tinsmith, a butcher, a watchmaker and two others. In 1925 a Jewish doctor, Rivkah Gurevitz, provided medical services.

Many Jewish people received loans at the Akmyan branch of the Jewish Popular Bank (*Folksbank*). In 1927 the bank had 94 members and in 1929 there were 108 members. It was one of the smallest branches. The total paid out to bank members in loans was about 45,000 Litas (about $4,500). In 1939, there were 36 telephone subscribers in Akmayan, six of them Jewish.

Despite dwindling numbers in the community, the activity of the main institutions such as the synagogue and the *Yavneh* school continued. Rabbi Nahum-Mordehai Verbovsky, who began duties in Akmyan in 1907, was the last rabbi of the community. He was murdered by Lithuanians in the summer of 1941.

Many Akmyan Jews belonged to the Zionist camp. In the elections for the first *Seimas* (Parliament) in 1922, the Zionist list received 66 votes, the religious list *Akhduth* 31 votes and the Democrats one vote.

The division of votes for two Zionist congresses is given in the table below:

Cong No.	Year	Total Shek	Total Votes	Labor Party Z"S Z"Z	Rev	Gen Zion A B	Gros	Miz
18	1933	---	40	19	3	8 ---	1	9
19	1935	---	60	39	---	2 3	---	16

Key: Cong No. = Congress Number, Tot Shek = Total Shekalim, Rev = Revisionists, Gen Zion = General Zionists, Gros = Grosmanists, Miz = Mizrahi, NB = National Block

Zionist youth organizations were represented by *HaShomer HaTsair* and *Beitar*.

During this period relations between Jews and their Lithuanian neighbors were generally amicable. But in the second half of the 1930s the situation began to deteriorate, In March 1939 Lithuanians attacked a group of Jews who resisted the attackers, forcing them to retreat.

During World War II and afterward

In 1940, Lithuania was annexed to the Soviet Union and became a Soviet Republic. During the year of the Soviet rule (1940-1941), Zionist groups were disbanded across Lithuania, and great changes affected the economy.

At the end of June 1941, a short time after the German army invaded Lithuania on June 22, Lithuanian nationalists of Akmyan rounded up all the Jewish men. In collaboration with the few Germans who arrived in Akmyan, they shot the former textile shop owner Shmit as well as Josef and Faivush Joselevitz. On August 4, 1941, all the Akmyan Jews were taken to the large barn on the shore of the Venta River near Mazheik. The men were forced to dig pits and the women were imprisoned with other Jewish women previously held in Mazheik. All were murdered together with the Jews of Mazheik and the surrounding areas on August 9, 1941 (Shabbath, 15th of Av, 5701).

A few years after the war the murder site was fenced in and a monument erected.

The mass grave and the monument in Mazheik

The monument at the entrance of the murder site (seen in the back of he above photo) with the inscription in Yiddish and Lithuanian: "At this site Hitler's murderers and their local helpers executed about 4000 Jews and people of other nationalities."

Sources:
Yad Vashem archives, Jerusalem, M-1/E-1771/1673; Koniukhovsky collection 0-71, file 21
Oshri, *Hurban Lite*, pages 260-263
Kamzon Y.D., *Yahaduth Lita*, page 73
Levin, Dov, Akmyan, *Pinkas Hakehiloth-Lita*, Yad Vashem, Jerusalem 1996
Di Yiddishe Shtime, Kovno, 29.10.1924
Der Yiddisher Kooperator, Kovno, # 11 (34), 1929, page 11
HaMelitz, St. Petersburg, 4.4.1893
Cartographic survey of Jewish cemeteries in Lithuania, 1990

Čekiškė (Tsaikishok)

Tsaikishok (in Yiddish) lies in central Lithuania, on the main Kaunas-Raseiniai road near the Dubysa River, about 36 km. northwest of Kaunas. Apparently a settlement already existed on this site in 1457, but by the beginning of the seventeenth century there was substantial evidence of Tsaikishok's existence. In 1762 the town was granted the privilege to maintain a weekly market and a yearly fair. During the period of Russian rule (1795-1915) Tsaikishok was at first included in the province (*Gubernia*) of Vilna, and thereafter from 1843 in the Kovno *Gubernia*. During the years 1915-1918 the town was under German military occupation, and during the period of Independent Lithuania (1918-1940) it was a county administrative center in the Kovno district.

Jewish settlement till after World War I
Jews probably settled in Tsaikishok at the end of the eighteenth century. It is certain that in the second half of the nineteenth century an organized Jewish community existed, headed by a Rabbi.

According to the Russian census of 1897 there were 668 residents in Cekiske, including 432 Jews (65%).

A list dated 1871, of donors who gave money for the needy in Lithuania through the Aid Committee of Memel, contains quite a few names of Tsaikishok Jews. The fund raisers were Nakhman Shlezinger and Yisrael Segal.

The Hebrew newspaper *HaMagid* (1872) published a list of donors for victims of a famine in Persia, which included the names of 101 Tsaikishok Jews (see **Appendix 1**).

In 1887 a fire destroyed all the town's houses, including the two prayer buildings and the precious holy books housed there. A young woman was burnt to death, and only three houses were left undamaged. About 160 Jewish families were left roofless and in great poverty. The local rabbi, Avraham Levental, a wealthy man, also lost all his property. Jews of the neighboring towns Vilki (Vilkija), Srednik (Seredzius), Rasein (Raseiniai), Girtigola and others, were the first people to bring carts loaded with bread and other food products to the victims of the fire, who were camping in the open. The Hebrew newspaper *HaMelitz* from July 8th, 1887 published an appeal for help, signed by Eliyahu Gurland in the name of the victims.

In 1914, before World War I, about 200 Jewish families lived in Tsaikishok. During World War I, in 1915, the retreating Russian army carried out pogroms against the Jews in many towns, with the participation of local peasants. Men were cruelly abused and women raped. Tsaikishok Jews were later relieved to receive their exile orders to Russia, which saved them from this unbearable situation.

After the war few of the exiles returned to Tsaikishok and the number of the Jews decreased from year to year, until only about 60 families remained in the town before World War II.

During the period of independent Lithuania (1918-1940)

Following the passage of the Law of Autonomies for Minorities by the new Lithuanian government, the Minister for Jewish Affairs, Dr. Menachem (Max) Soloveitshik, ordered elections for community committees (*Va'adei Kehilah*) to be held in the summer of 1919. In Tsaikishok a community committee of seven members was elected, four from *Tseirei-Zion*, two from *Mizrahi* and one from the artisans. This committee functioned until about the end of 1925 when the autonomy was annulled by a new Lithuanian government. For several years the committee was active in all aspects of Jewish life in town.

According to the first census performed by the government in 1923 there were then 577 residents, including 324 Jews (56%).

Tsaikishok Jews made their living from shopkeeping, commerce and crafts. According to the government survey on shops and industry in 1931 there were then twelve shops, all in Jewish hands: six textile shops, three restaurants, one grain shop, one pharmacy and one miscellaneous shop. Jews owned a wool combing plant, a leather-producing plant and a felt-producing factory. Later a steam-operated flourmill and a sawmill were added. Many Jews rented fruit gardens, selling the fruit in the summer.

In 1937 there were eleven Jewish artisans: three tailors, three butchers, two shoemakers, one baker, one glazier and one barber.

The Jewish Popular Bank (Folksbank) played an important role in the economic life of Tsaikishok Jews. The bank was established in 1920 and was one of the first in Lithuania, beginning with 39 members. In 1927 their number had increased to 72, but in 1933 there were 60.

Of the eight telephone owners in 1939, one was Jewish.

Jewish children studied at the Yiddish elementary school. Beside the school there was a library with about 500 books.

A number of Tsaikishok Jews had adopted the Zionist ideal by the time of the first Zionist congresses. A delegate from Tsaikishok participated in the regional conference in Vilna in 1899. During the period of Independent Lithuania, many became members of the Zionist movement with all its nuances.

Among the Zionist parties and youth organizations there were the Z"S Education Society in the name of Nakhman Sirkin, as well as *HaShomer*

HaTsair and others. Sport activities were organized at the local *Maccabi* branch, with forty members on average participating.

The results of the elections for the Zionist Congresses are given in the table below:

Cong No.	Year	Total Shek	Total Votes	Labor Party		Rev	Gen Zion		Gros	Miz
				Z"S	Z"Z		A	B		
14	1925	40	----	----	----	--	----	----	---	---
15	1927	6	6	4	2	---	----	----	---	---
16	1929	29	----	----	----	----	----	----	----	----
17	1931	30	11	3	3	----	3	---	----	2
18	1933	----	25	18		----	4	---	2	1
19	1935	----	108	102		----	4	1	---	1

Key: Cong No. = Congress Number, Total Shek = Total Shkalim, Rev = Revisionists, Gen Zion = General Zionists, Gros = Grosmanists, Miz = Mizrahi

After the great fire of 1887, a new brick synagogue was built to serve also as a place for learning Torah, because the *Beth Midrash*, which had been destroyed in this fire, was not rebuilt.

The following are the Rabbis who officiated in Tsaikishok: Avraham HaCohen Levental (from 1859 until his death in 1894); Avraham Gordon (from 1903); Ya'akov Abramovitz (in the 1920's) and the last Rabbi Shemuel-Ze'ev Melamed, who was murdered in the Holocaust.

Persons of note born in Tsaikishok include Rabbi Mordehai Eliashberg (1817-1889), an enthusiastic *"Hovev Zion"*, about whom Ahad-Ha'am wrote that his book "The Book of the Golden Path" (Warsaw, 1897) was more meaningful than a settlement in Eretz-Yisrael. Also Rabbi Mosheh Zilber (who died in 1949 in Jerusalem), the father of Aba Hilel Silver, a famous leader of American Zionists.

During World War II

With the annexation by the Soviet Union, Lithuania becoming a Soviet Republic in 1940, and some Jewish-owned shops and plants in Tsaikishok were nationalized. All Zionist parties and youth organizations were disbanded. About 60 Jewish families lived in the town at this time.

German soldiers entered Tsaikishok a week after the war between Germany and the Soviet Union began on June 22nd, 1941. However, even before a single German soldier was seen in town, Lithuanian nationalists took over. They detained Jews, mistreated them and murdered eighteen Jewish men.

According to Nazi documents (Jaeger report), on September 4th, 1941, 22 Jewish men, 64 women and 60 children were murdered.

It is known that Jews from Tsaikishok were also murdered in Eiragole (Ariogala) and Vilki (Vilkija).

A mass grave in the forest of Pakarkle, 2 km. from Veliuona, where the remains of those murdered in Tsaikishok were transported and buried.

Sources:
Yad Vashem archives, Jerusalem, O-3/1015

Central Zionist Archives: 55/1788; 55/1701; 13/15/131; Z-4/2548

YIVO, New York, Collection of Lithuanian Communities, file 1539, pages 69705-06

Dos Vort, Kovno (Yiddish), 10.9.1935; 2.1.1939

Di Yiddishe Shtime, Kovno (Yiddish),16.4.1923; 28.12.1937; 23.2.1938; 19.9.1938

Der Yiddisher Cooperator, Kovno (Yiddish), # 2-3, 1930

HaMelitz, St, Petersburg (Hebrew), 8.7.1887; 17.7.1887; 28.7.1887; 9.3.1893

Folksblat, Kovno (Yiddish), 15.8.1935; 2.1.1938

Appendix 1

A list of 101 contributors from Tsaikishok for the victims of the Persian famine in 1872. It was published in *HaMagid* #10 (1872)

(JewishGen. Org. > Databases, compiled by Jeffery Maynard)

BERNE	Moshe
BLOCH	Zalman
BOROWSKE	Binyamin
BOROWSKE	Gavriel Bentzion
BORSHTEIN	Leib
BORSHTEIN	Sender
BORSHTEIN	Shimon
CARMEL	Yosef
DOKTER	Daniel
EPSHTEIN	Kalman
FEIN	Abba
GOLD	Moshe
GRINBERG	Shmuel (from Seredzius)
HALEVI	Abba
HALEVI	Yitzchok
KA"TZ	Avraham
KARPEL	Hillel
KATZ	Nechemiah Aharon
KATZ	Shraga
KATZ	Yeshiyahu Yitzchok
KELMER	Mordechai
KILWINSKE	Shlomo
LAZBAN	Eli
LAZBAN	Nisan
MEHL	Zalkind

METZNER	Hirsh
MILNER	Avraham
MIRAGOLE	Dovid Bentzion
PEISECHOWITZ	Matat
PEISECHOWITZ	Zalman
PERIL	Avraham
PERIL	Mordehai
PERIL	Yechezkel
SEGAL	Chaim
SEGAL	Isser
SEGAL	Yisroel ben Shmuel
SEGAL	Zachariah
SENDERS	Zale
SHLEZINGER	Nachman ben Avraham
SHMID	Eliezer
SHOR	Avraham
SHTREICHMAN	Tzvi
SHTREINMAN	Aharon
TZIGELNIK	Meir
WASHKEITZ	Moshe
WEINER	Eizik
WELLER	Betzalel
YABLONSKI	Moshe
YAFE	Yisroel
YUDKOWSKE	Avraham Yosef
YUDKOWSKE	Bentzion
YUDKOWSKE	Lea
YUDKOWSKE	Moshe Yitzchok
ZILBER	Isser
ZILBER	Moshe Mordechai

ZILBER	Yisroel
	Abba ben Hillel
	Aharon ben Dov
	Aharon ben H
	Aharon Hillel
	Ari ben Yitzchok (from Vilkija)
	Avraham
Rabbi	Avraham ben Dov Ber HaCohen
	Avraham ben Yitzchok
	Avraham Yitzchok
	Binyamin ben Reuven
	Chanoch Zondil (Cantor & Shohet)
	Dov ben Helman
	Dovid ben P
	Dovid ben Y
	Ephraim ben D
	Ephraim ben Yitzchok
	Hirsh ben Eizik
	Leib ben A
	Leib ben Moshe
	Leib ben Ozer
	Mattitiyahu ben Avraham
	Menachem ben Yisroel
	Mordechai
	Mordechai ben Meir
	Moshe ben N
	Moshe ben Zev
	Nachum ben Moshe
	Nechemiah ben L
	Reuven ben Binyamin

	Shabasai Yosef
	Shalom ben A
	Shalom ben Avraham
	Shlomo ben Boruch
	Shlomo ben Tzvi
	Shmuel ben Hillel
	Tzvi ben Dovid
	Tzvi ben Yakov
	Yakov ben Moshe
	Yakov ben Peretz
	Yehuda ben Tzvi
	Yitzchok ben Ch A
	Yitzchok ben Dov
	Yitzchok ben Pesach
	Yitzhok ben M
	Zerach ben Yehuda

Appendix 2
List of 142 Tsaikishok donors to the Settlement of Eretz Yisrael
(From JewishGen.Org.>Databases>Lithuania>Hamelitz. Compiled by
Jeffrey Maynard)

Surname	Given Name	Comments	Source: Hamelitz	Year
BEINE	Yakov		#205	1903
BERELOWITZ	Chaim Pinchos		#184	1899
BERELOWITZ	Pinchos	from Widokle	#179	1900

Surname	Given Name	Comments	Source: Hamelitz	Year
BERNE	Libe		#179	1900
BERNE	Libe		#263	1900
BERNE	Yakov		#179	1900
BERNE	Yakov		#263	1900
BERNE	Yakov		#240	1902
BLUMZOHN	Shimon Yitzchok		#205	1903
BLUMZOHN	Shimon Yitzchok		#240	1902
BLUMZON	Chana		#179	1900
BLUMZON	Shimon Yitzchok		#179	1900
BLUMZON	Shimon Yitzchok		#263	1900
BORON	Rivka		#205	1903
BORON	Rivka		#240	1902
BORON	Rivka wife of Yakov Glazer		#263	1900
BORON	Yakov Hilel		#179	1900
BORON	Yakov Hillel		#184	1899
BORON	Yakov Hillel		#205	1903
BORON	Yakov Hillel		#263	1900
BORON	Yeshiahu Yitzchok		#263	1900
BORON	Yeshiyahu Yitzchok		#179	1900
BORON	Yeshiyahu Yitzchok		#205	1903
BORON	Yeshiyahu Yitzchok		#240	1902
BOROWIK	Avraham		#205	1903

Surname	Given Name	Comments	Source: Hamelitz	Year
	Shlomo			
BOROWIK	Pesha		#205	1903
BORSHTEIN	Boruch		#205	1903
BORSHTEIN	Boruch		#240	1902
DOV	Yehuda		#263	1900
FIN	Moshe		#205	1903
FIN	Moshe		#263	1900
FIN	Moshe		#240	1902
FIN	Sarah wife of Shimon Yitzchok Blumzon of Keidan	wed	#85	1899
FLOKCHIN	Leib Yitzchok	Rabbi	#240	1902
FLOKCHIN	Mashe		#240	1902
FRIDMAN	Shmuel		#205	1903
FRIDMANN	Shmuel		#240	1902
GANDEL	Leib		#179	1900
GANDZ	Leib		#205	1903
GANZ	Leib		#240	1902
GELFAND	Leib		#240	1902
GITELMAN	Shmuel		#263	1900
GITELMANN	Shmuel		#240	1902
GITLMAN	Shmuel		#179	1900
GODSON	Ari Leib		#179	1900
GOLD	Elimelech		#179	1900
GOLD	Elimelech		#205	1903
GOLD	Elimelech		#263	1900
GOLD	Elimelech		#240	1902

Surname	Given Name	Comments	Source: Hamelitz	Year
GOLD	Yitzchok		#205	1903
GOLD	Yitzchok		#263	1900
GOLD	Yitzchok		#240	1902
GOLDPOND	Leib		#263	1900
GONDIN	Avraham		#263	1900
GORDON	Avraham		#179	1900
GORDON	Avraham	Rabbi Gaon	#205	1903
GORDON	Avraham		#240	1902
GORDON	Leib		#263	1900
GORDON	Raphel Leib		#184	1899
GORDON	Raphel Leib		#77	1899
GROSMAN	Rafel		#263	1900
HELFAND	Leib		#205	1903
ITZKOWITZ	Yehuda		#205	1903
ITZKOWITZ	Yehuda		#240	1902
KERMANT	Reuven		#240	1902
KRIWANT	Aba		#263	1900
KRIWANT	Aba		#240	1902
KRIWANT	Gedalia		#205	1903
KRIWANT	Reuven		#205	1903
KRIWANT	Tzvi		#205	1903
LIPMAN	Chaim Aharon		#184	1899
LIPMAN	Chaim Aharon		#179	1900
LIPMAN	Chaim Aharon		#263	1900
LIPMAN	Libe		#179	1900
LIPMANN	Chaim		#205	1903

Surname	Given Name	Comments	Source: Hamelitz	Year
	Aharon			
LIPMANN	Chaim Aharon		#240	1902
MELER	Lipman		#263	1900
NEIMAN	Mordechai		#263	1900
NEIMANN	Yisroel		#240	1902
NEIMARK	Mordechai		#205	1903
PASAREWITZ	Matitiyahu		#179	1900
PEISACHOWITZ	Matitiahu		#263	1900
PEISACHOWITZ	Matitiahu		#240	1902
PEISACHOWITZ	Zalman		#205	1903
PEISACHOWITZ	Zalman		#263	1900
PEISACHOWITZ	Zalman		#240	1902
PEREL	Ari		#263	1900
PERL	Ari		#179	1900
PERL	Ari		#205	1903
PERL	Avraham		#205	1903
PERL	Miriam		#240	1902
PESIL	Avraham		#240	1902
PLENER	Yakov		#205	1903
PLOKCHIN	L		#60	1899
PLOKCHIN	Levi Yitzchok		#179	1900
PLOTCHIN	Levi Yitzchok		#205	1903
PLOTCHIN	Masha		#205	1903
PLOTKIN	Mashe	female	#263	1900
PLOTKIN	Yitzchok		#263	1900
PLOTZKIN	Levi Yitzchok		#231	1899
PREGER	Reuven		#240	1902

Surname	Given Name	Comments	Source: Hamelitz	Year
PREGER	Yakov		#240	1902
PRENER	Yakov		#263	1900
RAVITZ	Dovid Moshe		#179	1900
ROTKOWSKI	Shmuel		#263	1900
ROZENBERG	Tzvi Yakov		#179	1900
ROZENBERG	Tzvi Yakov		#263	1900
ROZENBERG	Yakov Tzvi		#205	1903
ROZENBERG	Yakov Tzvi		#240	1902
SHAFER	Chana Miriam		#205	1903
SHAFER	Chanah Miriam		#240	1902
SHAFER	Naftali Hertz		#263	1900
SHAFER	Naftali Hertz		#240	1902
SHAFER	Naphtali Hertz		#179	1900
SHAFER	Naphtli Hertz		#205	1903
SHITNOWITZ	Binyomin	Rabbi	#179	1900
SHTREICHMAN	Rivka		#179	1900
SHTREICHMAN	Yitzchok		#179	1900
SHTREICHMAN	Yitzchok		#263	1900
SHTROBMANN	Yitzchok		#240	1902
SHUB	Shlomo Noach		#263	1900
STREICHMANN	Aharon		#205	1903
WEBTER	Mordechai		#205	1903
WECHTER	Mordechai		#240	1902
WEINIK	Yosef		#205	1903
WEIS	Dov Ber		#240	1902

Surname	Given Name	Comments	Source: Hamelitz	Year
WEISS	Dov Ber		#205	1903
WELER	Lipman		#179	1900
WELER	Lipmann		#240	1902
WELLER	Lipmann		#205	1903
WIGDEROWITZ	Yitzchok		#205	1903
WINIK	Yosef		#240	1902
WOROBUK	Avraham Shlomo		#240	1902
YAMKOWSKI	Moshe Yitzchok		#205	1903
YASKOWSKI	Sh		#205	1903
YOTKOWITZ	Shmuel		#240	1902
YOTKOWSKI	Avraham Shimon		#179	1900
YOTKOWSKI	Moshe Yitzchok		#179	1900
YOTKOWSKI	Moshe Yitzchok		#240	1902
YUDKOWSKI	Yisroel Yitzchok		#205	1903
YUTKOWSKI	Moshe Yitzchok		#263	1900
	Roshel	Rabbi's wife	#205	1903

Eržvilkas (Erzhvilik)

Erzvilkas (Erzhvilik in Yiddish) lies in western Lithuania on the right-hand bank of the Saltuona River, 32 km. east of the district administrative center of Tavrig (Taurage). The town was mentioned in historical documents of the eighteenth century. In 1706 a church was built in the town.

Erzhvilik was included in the Polish-Lithuanian Kingdom until 1795. According to the third division of Poland in the same year by the three superpowers of those times, Russia, Prussia and Austria, Lithuania was divided between Russia and Prussia. As most of Lithuania, Erzhvilik became a part of the Russian Empire, first in the Vilna province (*Gubernia*) and from 1843 in the Kovno *Gubernia*. Erzhvilik was a county administrative center after 1745 and again during the period of independent Lithuania (1918-1940) in Tavrig district.

Jewish settlement till World War II

Jews probably first settled in Erzhvilik in the beginning of the nineteenth century. Their main living was in the small trades. According to the all-Russian census of 1897, the population of the town was 709, of whom 144 were Jewish (20%). Before World War I about 100 Jewish families lived in the town.

In 1918 the Lithuanian State was established. Following the passage of the Law of Autonomies for Minorities by the new Lithuanian government, the Minister for Jewish Affairs, Dr. Menachem (Max) Soloveitshik, ordered that elections be held for the community committees *(Va'adei Kehilah)* in the summer of 1919. In Erzhvilik a *Va'ad (*community committee) with seven members was elected: four general Zionists and three non-party men. The committee was active in all fields of Jewish life until the end of 1925.

The first government census of 1923 counted 484 residents in Erzhvilik, 222 being Jewish (46%). During this period the number of the Jews decreased as a result of emigration overseas. Before World War II only about 150 to 180 Jews (about 45 families) remained.

In the elections for the County Council in 1921, two of the twenty-two members elected were Jewish.

At that time most Erzhvilik Jews dealt in the small trades, and a few in the crafts. Almost all had land, horses and cattle and managed a rural life as did their Lithuanian neighbors, with whom they had good relations. Nevertheless many families received financial support from their relatives abroad. In general the economic situation of Erzhvilik Jews was favorable.

According to the government survey of 1931 there were five shops in the town, with one tavern and three mixed goods shops being in Jewish hands. In 1937 there were six Jewish artisans: a glazier, a carpenter, a shoemaker, a barber, a butcher and a watchmaker.

In 1939 there were 23 telephone subscribers, four of them Jewish.

The Jewish children received their elementary education at the local Hebrew School and there was a library containing Hebrew and Yiddish books.

Religious life concentrated around the *Beth Midrash*. Among the rabbis who officiated in Erzhvilik were:
Ze'ev-Volf Lerman from 1890
Nathan-Neta Dogliansky
Ze'ev Rapeiko, from 1933, who was murdered together with his community.

Erzhvilik Jews began to take an interest in Zionism through the *Hibath Zion* movement. During the period of Independent Lithuania there was Zionist activity in Erzhvilik and there were supporters for almost all Zionist parties. The table below shows how they voted at two Zionist congresses:

Cong No.	Year	Total Shek	Total Votes	Labor Party Z"S	Z"Z	Rev	Gen Zion A	B	Gros	Miz
18	1933	---	56	39		---	11	---	1	5
19	1935	---	118	50		---	---	39	3	26

Key: Cong No. = Congress Number, Tot Shek = Total Shekalim, Rev = Revisionists, Gen Zion = General Zionists, Gros = Grosmanists, Miz = Mizrahi

From 1932 branches of *HeHalutz* and *Hehalutz HaTsair* were active. Among other things they were involved in the fundraising for the National Funds *KKL* and *Keren HaYesod*.

Among the personages born in Erzhvilik were: Herman (Tsevi-Hirsh) Shapira (1840-1898), who studied in a *yeshivah* in Tavrig, became a rabbi and head of a *yeshivah*, left his position to study languages and science, dealt in business and became prosperous. In 1878 he quit his business and moved to Berlin and Heidelberg to study mathematics. In 1887 he became Professor of mathematics at Heidelberg University. Shapira was one of the founders of the *Hibath Zion* movement and supported the establishment of the *Keren Kayemeth L'Yisrael* Fund. At the first Zionist congress in Basel he proposed the creation of an institution for higher education in Jerusalem. He died in Köln.

Herman Shapira

Shimon Glazer (1877-1939), translated the *Mishne Torah* of the Rambam into English (New York, 1927) and published "The History of the Jews" in six volumes in English (New York, 1930).

During World War II and afterwards
In June 1940, Lithuania was annexed to the Soviet Union and became a Soviet Republic. All the Zionist parties were disbanded and the Hebrew school was closed. The small traders who made their living mostly in their auxiliary farms were not harmed economically under the new regime. In 1940 approximately 150 to 180 Jews lived in Erzhvilik.

On June 22, 1941 the German army invaded Lithuania and on that same evening they entered Erzhvilik. The Jews who escaped to nearby villages were forced to return home after several days because their Lithuanian acquaintances would no longer help them. They found on returning that the Lithuanians had looted their homes of all their possessions. The finer houses were seized by the Germans.

The Lithuanian police registered the names of the returning Jews and concentrated them in the *Beth Midrash*. After two days all Jews were ordered to move into seven houses in the Bath street. This area was encircled by a barbed wire fence; the Lithuanian auxiliary police guarded it, and using threats, they robbed the Jews of their money, valuables, boots. etc.

From there the Jews had to present themselves for work every morning at the market square. The labor insisted of such unpleasant tasks such as cleaning latrines by hand, burying the dead Soviet soldiers, and washing the floors at German and Lithuanian flats. The police beat and abused them.

On August 21, 1941, four Jewish youngsters who were active during Soviet rule and four Lithuanian Communists were shot. On August 28, 1941, the Lithuanians brought several Jewish men, owners of farms in the vicinity, and 31 local men, and imprisoned them in the *Beth Midrash*. At night the Lithuanians mistreated them and forced them to perform "gymnastics" for their entertainment. They also robbed them of everything that they had in their pockets and also took their garments and boots. The next morning they led them half-naked to the sand pit opposite the municipality. There 42 Lithuanian police waited ready to shoot the Jews, but the appearance of the German commander meant that the murders were delayed a few weeks.

The Lithuanians spread rumors among the Jews that they would be transferred to Batok (Batakiai) camp, about 18 km. from Erzhvilik. They also encouraged them to take anything they wanted with them.

At dawn on September 15, 1941 (23rd of Elul, 5701) all Erzhvilik Jews were loaded onto carts belonging to local peasants and were brought to the police station, where the police chief forced them to hand over all their money and valuables that they still possessed. They were then taken to the Batok camp. From the camp trucks transferred them to the Gryblaukis Forest, about 22 km. northeast of Tavrig. About 2 km. on the right side of the Tavrig-Shkudvil (Taurage-Skaudvile) road vast pits already contained the bodies of hundreds of Jewish victims. In these pits the Erzhvilik Jews were also cruelly murdered.

According to Soviet sources about 1,000 bodies were later unearthed, mainly of women and children.

The mass grave with the monument at the Gryblaukis forest

A few dozen Jews managed to hide in the homes of Lithuanians, but after a short time they were caught and murdered, including the rabbi Rapeiko with his family. Of all the Erzhvilik Jews, only 22 survived, because they had been hidden by Lithuanian peasants. After the war these survivors delivered the names of the murderers to the Soviet authorities and many were caught and punished. A few were hanged. Eight Erzhvilik Jews had managed to escape to Russia at the beginning of the war; two of them died there.

The names of a number of the Lithuanian rescuers are recorded in the archives of Yad Vashem. So are the names of the murderers.

Sources:
Yad Vashem archives, Jerusalem, M-9/15(6); M-8/45/36/291, 278
Koniukhovsky collection 0-71, files 10, 10a, 10b
Dos Vort, Kovno, 17.12.1934
Di Tsait, Kovno, 4.10.1933
Masines Zudynes Lietuvoje (Mass murder in Lithuania), Vol. 2
Sviesa (Jurbarkas) 13.4.1991

Garliava (Gudleve)

Garliava (Gudleve in Yiddish) lies about 9 km. south of Kovno, along the railway line to Prussia. At the beginning of the nineteenth century, the town began to develop on the estate owned by Gudlevsky, as a settlement of one street along the main road from Kovno (Kaunas) via Mariampol (Marijampole) to Warsaw.

Until 1795, Gudleve was included in the Polish-Lithuanian Kingdom. According to the third division of Poland in the same year by the three superpowers of those times, Russia, Prussia and Austria, Lithuania was divided between Russia and Prussia. The parts on the left bank of the River Neman (Nemunas), including Gudleve, were handed over to Prussia.

During the years 1807-1815 Gudleve belonged to the Great Dukedom of Warsaw. From 1815, after Napoleon's defeat, all of Lithuania, including Gudleve, was annexed to Russia and later it was attached to the Suwalk Province (*Gubernia*). During Russian rule and also during independent Lithuania (1918-1940), Gudleve was a county administrative center in the Kovno (Kaunas) district.

Jews probably began to settle in Gudleve as soon as it was founded. It was reputed that Gudlevsky, the estate owner, built their first prayer house. According to the Russian census of 1897 there were 962 residents, including 469 Jews (49%).

The census of 1898 for the *Parafia* (parish of the church) included 41 villages and 33 farms with 14,861 inhabitants, including 2,218 Jews.

Most Gudleve Jews made their living in small trade and crafts, and almost every family had an auxiliary farm beside the house. Near the town there were several Jewish farms (Shvartz, Segalovsky). Yits'hak Segalovsky received his farm as a gift from Gudlevsky, the estate owner, for serving as translator between him and Mosheh Montefiore, when the latter passed through the town on his way to Russia.

During World War I the town was burnt down almost completely.

According to the first census performed by the new Lithuanian government in 1923, there were then 936 residents, 311 being Jews (33%). During the period of independent Lithuania the number of Jews diminished, mainly because of economic problems. Many Gudleve Jews emigrated to America, Canada, South Africa and *Eretz-Yisrael*. Before the Shoah about 50 families remained in the town.

Following the passage of the Law of Autonomy for Minorities by the new Lithuanian government, the minister of Jewish affairs, Dr. Menachem (Max)

Soloveitshik, ordered elections for community committees *(Va'adei Kehilah)* to be held in the summer of 1919. In 1921 a Community Committee was elected in Gudleve, which was active until 1923, and dealt mainly with registration of births, marriages and deaths.

A Jewish house in Gudleve

According to the 1931 government survey, there were 16 shops in town, 14 of them in Jewish hands (87%): three pubs and restaurants, two grain trade shops, two textile shops, three for machines and tools, one grocery, one butcher's shop, one shoe shop and one haberdashery. The same survey showed 17 enterprises, of them 10 Jewish owned (59%): two brick factories, two flourmills, two workshops for cleaning the bowels of cattle, one factory producing oil, one dying plant, one leather factory and one barber shop. In 1939 Gudleve had 38 telephone subscribers, seven of them Jewish.

During the period of independent Lithuania, Jewish children received their elementary education at the Hebrew *Yavneh* School and at a Yiddish school, each school having an average of 45 pupils. The proximity of Gudleve to Kovno made it easier for the graduates of the schools to continue their studies in the big city.

Many Gudleve Jews belonged to the Zionist movement, and supporters of all Zionist parties took part in elections for Zionist Congresses.

The election results are given in the table below:

Cong No.	Year	Tot Shek	Total Votes	Labor Party		Rev	Gen Zion		Gros	Miz
				Z"S	Z"Z		A	B		
14	1925	16	----	----	----	--	----	----	----	----
15	1927	20	12	---	1	6	1	---	---	4
16	1929	52	---	---	---	---	---	----	----	---
17	1931	13	10	1	---	5	1	----	----	3
18	1933	----	11	5		3	2	---	---	1
19	1935	---	59	28		--	6	9	9	7

Key: Cong No. = Congress Number, Tot Shek = Total Shekalim, Rev = Revisionists, Gen Zion = General Zionists, Gros = Grosmanists, Miz = Mizrahi

The *Beth Midrash*

The *Shamash*

The seal of the *Beth Midrash*

Religious life in town concentrated around the *Beth Midrash*. Among the rabbis who officiated in Gudleve were: Hayim HaLevi Katz (1854-1932); Yehudah Barshtein, from 1900; Harakshansky from 1922, and from 1926 the last rabbi, Kalman Levin, who was murdered in the Shoah.

Rabbi Hayim Halevi Katz

Native born Rabbi Josef-Reuven Katz, who officiated in Vishinta and Glubok, was an activist of the *Mizrahi* party in Vilna.

In 1940 Lithuania was annexed to the Soviet Union and became a Soviet Republic. Following new rules, the factories, most of them owned by Jews, were nationalized, as were Jewish shops. All Zionist parties and youth organizations were disbanded and the Hebrew school was closed. The supply of goods decreased, and as a result, prices soared. The middle class, mostly Jewish, bore the brunt of this situation and its standard of living dropped gradually.

The war between Germany and the USSR began on June 22, 1941. By the end of the month all Lithuania had been occupied by the German army. Lithuanian nationalists immediately took control of the country and began to plot and mistreat the Jews. This also happened in Gudleve, and the murder of Jews began on August 28, 1941 (5th of Elul, 5701). A few days previously, Jewish men had been taken to the valley of the Jiesia River beside the town, where they were ordered to dig a pit 80 metres long and 2 metres wide.

When they were finished they were ordered to hand over all their money and valuables, and to take off their garments and shoes. They were then pushed into the pit and shot dead by Germans and Lithuanians. On that same day or possibly the next, the women and children were murdered and buried in a mass grave. According to a German source, 73 Jewish men, 113 women and 61 children were murdered in this place between August 28 and September 2, 1941.

The mass grave near the Jiesia River

The monument with the inscription in Yiddish and Lithuanian:
"In this place Hitler's murderers and their local helpers murdered 274 children, women and men, on August 28, 1941."

The commission for investigating German crimes in Soviet Lithuania determined in 1944, after opening the grave, that about 400 people - Jews from Gudleve, Mavruch (Mauruciai), Pakun (Pakuonis), Veiver (Veiveriai) and other small settlements in the surroundings - were buried in this pit.

Sources:
Yad Vashem archives, Jerusalem, 0-3/3217, 3259.

Central Zionist Archives: 55/1788; 55/1701; 13/15/131; Z-4/2548.

YIVO, New York, Collection of Lithuanian Jewish Communities, File #146, pages 7615-7622.

Gelvonai (Gelvan)

Gelvonai (Gelvan in Yiddish) is in central Lithuania, about 20 km. south of the district administrative center Vilkomir (*Ukmerge*). In the 1385 manuscripts of the Crusader order it was written that a small village named Gelvon belonged to the wealthy Zabas family. In 1744 King August III granted Gelvan the rights of a town. At the end of the eighteenth century the town began to grow quickly, but because of the Polish rebellions against the Czar's rule in 1831 and 1863 and the Napoleonic Wars, the town was badly damaged and its population declined. In 1863 there were only 30 houses in Gelvan. In 1895 a fire broke out and burned down the churches and other buildings. Two years later the estate owner of Gelvan, Graf Plater, erected a new church.

During World War I, from 1915 until 1918, Gelvan was under German military rule. From December 1918 until March 1919 a Soviet Bolshevik Revolutionary Council ruled the town. Because of the military activities of the Bolsheviks and later the Poles, independent Lithuanian rule was established only in the autumn of 1920 in Gelvan.

Jews first settled in Gelvan during the seventeenth century. A headstone dated 1659 has been found at the Jewish cemetery. Not far from the town headstones were scattered in a meadow; unfortunately the inscriptions can no longer be read. According to local tradition a Jewish cemetery existed before the current one was established.

Before the war Gelvan Jews dealt mainly in grain and exported poultry, fruits and milk products to Vilna. At that time Gelvan was considered an affluent town. The Jews had commercial connections with Vilna. Twice a week the Gelvan carters would travel to Vilna with agricultural products and come back laden with goods for the local merchants.

The craft professions were in Jewish hands. In 1913 Gelvan had ten shoemakers, six tailors, three carpenters, two blacksmiths, two painters, one engraver and one miller, all Jewish. The peasants from the surrounding villages were assisted only by Jewish craftsmen. More than a few Jews earned their livelihood on the estates in the vicinity. There were also Jewish middlemen who had business with the estate owners and hence also earned their livelihoods through the estates. Relations between the Jews and the non-Jews during this period were generally good.

During this time Gelvan had a solid stone church, a wooden synagogue, 75 houses, 22 shops, a pharmacy, a post office, a public library and an elementary school.

During World War I 500 Jewish families, who had been expelled from Vilkomir (Ukmerge), Yaneve (Jonava) and Kovno (Kaunas) by the Russian military, arrived in Gelvan and other nearby towns, but after a few weeks they were moved on again. The Gelvan Jews were afraid that their fate could be the same, but by intercession to the authorities, they were allowed to remain in their homes. The leaders of the community swore on their lives that no Gelvan Jews would be found spying for the Germans.

In 1918, during the preparations for the establishment of the independent Lithuanian state, two committees were established with German approval, one Lithuanian and one Polish. Gelvan Jews joined the Lithuanian committee. The Poles tried to convince the Jews to join them, and even threatened them, but the Jews were not swayed. Then the Poles tried to incite the local non-Jewish population against the Jews. Their speakers demanded expulsion of the Jews, they cut the *Eiruv* wire (the wire encircling the town according to the *Shabat* law) and called upon the non-Jews to boycott the Jewish shops, however their campaign didn't make any real impact.

During the period of Independent Lithuania (1918-1940)
After the war and the establishment of Independent Lithuania (1918-1940) the Polish army occupied Vilna and its region. After Gelvan was cut off from Vilna the economic situation of many of Gelvan Jews worsened.

In 1919 and 1920 the community received financial help from the *YeKoPo* committee (the Jewish committee for aiding the victims of the war, whose center was in Vilna) with sums ranging from 1,500 to 26,000 marks.

Following the passage of the Law of Autonomies for Minorities by the new Lithuanian government, the Minister for Jewish Affairs, Dr. Menachem (Max) Soloveitshik, ordered elections to community committees, *Va'adei Kehilah,* to be held in the summer of 1919. In Gelvan, the elected committee operated until April of 1925. In these years the committee activated social and religious institutions.

The census of 1923 recorded 473 Jews living in Gelvan.

According to the government survey of 1931 there were twelve Jewish businesses in Gelvan: four textile shops, a grain business, a flax business, a butcher shop, a heating fuel shop, a leather shop, a wool combing workshop, a bakery and a textile factory.

The Lithuanian Merchants Association (*Verslas*) ran an open propaganda campaign urging Lithuanians to boycott the Jewish shops and not to associate with the Jewish artisans. Of the many Jewish artisans who had worked there before the war, only three shoemakers, two tailors and one engraver remained. The town's economy declined and the number of the Jews decreased. A number of young people joined *Kibbutsei Hakhsharah* and emigrated to *Eretz-Yisrael*. Many emigrated overseas or moved to the bigger towns in Lithuania. Those remaining dealt in peddling and many subsisted by the help of relatives in America.

Before the war Gelvan was a predominantly Jewish town. Ninety of the one-hundred families that lived in town were Jewish; the ten non-Jewish families worked in Jewish enterprises. Then the number of Jewish families decreased to 70 while the number of Christian families increased to 90. The Lithuanians had their own shops, cooperatives and a Lithuanian bank. While Jewish numbers continued to fall, the big *Beth Midrash* that was built when the community flourished fell into disrepair, and the stone bath house that was heated only three times a year because of the cost also fell into disrepair. The Jewish community in Gelvan gradually disintegrated and the Christians' attitude towards the Jews changed.

Some Lithuanians spread rumors and libels against the Jews and also demanded that the Jews be expelled from the town. They also demanded a boycott of Jewish shops. In 1925, the 70-year-old Eideman couple were murdered in their home by robbers. The murderers were caught and sentenced to death.

In 1918 the teacher Glintershchik established a Hebrew school, but due to the influence of the Yiddishists, the school became a Yiddish one. In 1923 another reversal occurred and it was changed back into a Hebrew school of the *Tarbuth* chain.

Many of its graduates continued their studies at the Hebrew or Yiddish gymnasiums in Vilkomir. During these years the Zionists established a Hebrew library in town. A Yiddish library had already existed, but only a few people made use of its 400 books. Beside the new library, a reading room was established and lectures on cultural subjects were given there.

The Hebrew School

Many Gelvan Jews were Zionists. The Zionist Socialist (Z"S) party was the largest of the Zionist parties. The table below shows how Gelvan voted in five Zionist congresses:

Cong No.	Year	Total Shek	Total Votes	Labor Party Z"S	Z"Z	Rev	Gen Zion A	B	Gros	Miz
16	1929	17	15	13	---	---	1	---	---	1
17	1931	17	16	14	---	---	1	---	---	1
18	1933	---	25	23		---	1	---	---	1
19	1935	---	90	84		---	2	3	---	1
21	1939	29	26	4		---	4		N.B. 18	

Key: Cong No. = Congress Number, Total Shek = Total Shekalim, Rev = Revisionists, Gen Zion = General Zionists, Gros = Grosmanists, Miz = Mizrahi, N.B. = National Block

At the end of the 1920s Gelvan expatriates living in America sent $1,000 to establish a popular bank in town. In 1930, at the request of the local Jews, a branch of the Jewish Popular Bank (*Folksbank*) was established. Following the appeal by the former Gelvaners in New York, the Federation of Lithuanian Jews in America allocated 10,000 litas for the bank. However in the years of economic decline in Lithuania the bank had difficulties and the supervising authorities demanded that it close or combine with the Lithuanian bank in Gelvan. Over this time five banks operated, one of them being a private one based in the shop of H. Goldshtein.

Among the rabbis who officiated during the years in Gelvan were:
  Menahem-Mendel Lifshitz
  Yehoshua Klevan, in Gelvan till 1925, emigrated to America
  Zalman-Pinhas Kaplan (1840-1921) died in Gelvan
  Daniel Ainshtein, the last Rabbi of Gelvan, murdered in the Holocaust.
  The *Shohet* who served for many years was Zusman-Gershon Bitsik.

During World War II

In summer 1940 Lithuania was annexed to the Soviet Union and became a Soviet Republic. Following the new regulations some of the Jewish businesses were nationalized, the Zionist parties and some of the community institutions were disbanded. The Hebrew school was converted into a government Yiddish school. A number of the Zionist activists were exiled to Siberia.

On June 22, 1941 the German army invaded the USSR. Even before Germans were seen in Gelvan, local Lithuanians began to mistreat the Jews, desecrating the *Beth Midrash* and plundering many Jewish shops. After the Germans entered the town, the Lithuanian activists detained many Jews suspected of being Communists. They were transferred to the jail in Vilkomir where they were murdered.

At the beginning of July 1941 armed Lithuanians expelled the Jews from their houses, and took them to a swampy area near the town. There the men were tortured by being required to perform "gymnastics;" they were forced to run, to dance, to fall and stand up and so on. After a few hours they were brought back to the town where they found their houses had been looted. Of course this had been planned ahead of time. Many decent Lithuanians were angry about it and on the next Sunday the local priest made a vehement speech in the church against this crime. Indeed some Lithuanians returned stolen property to the Jewish owners. However the persecution against the Jews did not stop; it became worse each day.

On September 5, 1941 (13th of Elul, 5701) all the Gelvan Jews were taken out of the town and led to the Pivonija Forest near Vilkomir, where on the same day all were murdered together with Jews from nearby towns.

Only one family was saved: Hayim Goldshtein, his wife and their seven year-old twins. Hayim was born in Gelvan and owned an iron wares shop. The family hid at Lithuanian acquaintances, with whom the Goldshteins had deposited their property beforehand. The Lithuanians, who were afraid that they would have to give back the property to the Jews, handed over the family to the police and at the end of 1941 the Goldshtein family all were murdered.

The mass grave in Pivonija Forest

The entrance gate to the murder site at Pivonija Forest

The monument at Pivonija Forest

Sources:
Yad Vashem archives, Jerusalem, 0-33/879, Collection of Lithuanian Jewish
Communities 0-57-testimony of Reuven Kronik;
Koniukhovsky collection 0-71, file 97
YIVO, New York, Lithuanian Jewish Communities Collection, file1512
Julius Rafael, Gelvan, *Pinkas HaKehiloth-Lita*, Yad Vashem, Jerusalem 1996
Shohat M.; Memories, *Yiddishe Shtime*, 9.6.1922
Yiddisher Kooperator, Kovno, # 1930
Morgen Journal, New York, 18.8.1947
Folksblat, Kovno, 4.8.1935

The inscription of the tablet at the monument reads in Yiddish, Hebrew and Lithuanian: "At this site in the year 1941 Hitler's murderers and their local helpers murdered 10,239 Jews, men, women and children."

Girkalnis (Girtegole)

Girkalnis (Girtegole in Yiddish) is situated in the center of Lithuania, about 10 km. southeast from the district administrative center Rasein (*Raseiniai*) and 2 km. southwest from the main road between Kaunas and Klaipeda. Girtegole was mentioned in historical documents at the beginning of the fifteenth century. The estates of the town and county belonged to the Bishops of Zemaitija.

Until 1795 Girtegole was included in the Polish-Lithuanian Kingdom. At the time of the third division of Poland by the three superpowers of those times, Russia, Prussia and Austria, Lithuania was divided between Russia and Prussia. Similarly to most of Lithuania, Girtegole became a part of the Russian Empire, first in the Vilna province (*Gubernia*) and from 1843 in the Kovno *Gubernia*. From 1745 Girtegole was a county administrative center until the end of the period of independent Lithuania (1918-1940), after which it was included in the Rasein district.

During World War I the town was under German military rule from 1915 to 1918.

Jewish settlement till World War II
According to the Russian census of 1897, 648 people lived in Girtegole, 530 being Jewish (82%). During the period of Independent Lithuania their number decreased, so that by the start of World War II only 27 Jewish families remained in the town.

A view of Girtegole

In 1918 Lithuania became an independent state, and following the passage of the Law of Autonomies for Minorities by the new Lithuanian government, the Minister for Jewish Affairs, Dr. Menachem (Max) Soloveitshik, ordered elections for community committees (*Va'adei Kehilah*) to be held in the summer of 1919. In Girtegole the election for the committee took place in August 1919. Of 200 eligible voters, only 72 voted and a community committee of seven members was elected: three from the *Akhduth (Agudath Yisrael)* list, one from the General Zionist party, one from *Tseirei Yisrael* and one independent. In the elections of 1921 a committee of five members was elected, all non-party men. This committee functioned until the end of 1925 when the autonomy was annulled by the Lithuanian government. During those years the committee was active in all aspects of Jewish life in town.

In elections to the first Lithuanian *Seimas* (Parliament) in October 1922, Girtegole Jews voted as follows: Zionists 92, *Akhduth* six and Democrats one.

Girtegole Jews mostly made their living in trade, with some in crafts and agriculture. According to the government survey of 1931 three textile shops and one grocery were Jewish-owned. In 1937 six Jewish tradesmen worked in town: two butchers, one oven builder, one blacksmith and two others.

In 1939 there were eight telephone subscribers, only one of them Jewish.

Many of the Girtegole Jews belonged to the Zionist movement and among them were voters for the Zionist congresses as presented in the table below:

Cong No.	Year	Tot Shek	Total Votes	Labor Party Z"S	Z"Z	Rev	Gen Zion A	B	Gros	Miz
15	1927	3	3	---		1	2	---	---	---
19	1935	---	50	20		---	13	5	---	12
21	1939	29	27	3		---	20	---	4	---

Key: Cong No. = Congress Number, Tot Shek = Total Shekalim, Rev = Revisionists, Gen Zion = General Zionists, Gros = Grosmanists, Miz =Mizrahi, N.B.=National Block

The religious life of Girtegole Jews concentrated around the Beth Midrash. Among the rabbis who officiated in town were:
   Yehudah-Leib Openheim.
   Shemuel-Naftali HaLevi Epshtein.
   Meir Stolevitz (1871-1951), in Girtegole from 1903, emigrated to *Eretz-Yisrael* in 1933 and became Rabbi of the Jerusalem suburb Zikhron Mosheh. He published many books and died in Jerusalem.
   Yits'hak-Izik Broide, later a rabbi in America.
   Ya'akov-Mosheh Lesin, in Girtegole from 1922
   Hayim-Yits'hak Osovsky, the last rabbi, who was murdered by Lithuanians in 1941.

In 1902 the Hebrew newspaper *HaMelitz* #229 listed one donation from Girtegole for the settlement of *Eretz-Yisrael,* on the occasion of a wedding, as shown below:

Surname	Given Name	Comments	Town
FRIDMAN	Chaim Tzvi husband of Chaya Druzinski from Kelme	wed in Kelme 14 Elul	Girkalnis, Lith.

During World War II and afterwards
On June 15, 1940 the Red Army entered Lithuania. The state was annexed to the Soviet Union and became a Soviet Republic. Following new rules, the larger Jewish businesses were nationalized. All Zionist parties and youth organizations were disbanded.

On June 22, 1941, the first day of the war between Germany and the Soviet Union, local Lithuanians took over rule of the town. They removed the Torah scrolls from the Beth Midrash, trampled and danced on them. They took the rabbi into the street, abused him and plucked his beard out together with the skin, leaving him bleeding. Groups of Lithuanians with white stripes on their sleeves abused Girtegole Jews. They took several men and five elderly women, including Mrs. Zilberman with her two sons who would not leave her, led them all out of the town and shot them.

A few days later all the Girtegole Jews, about 120 persons, were crowded into three houses belonging to Shemuel Tatz, Shimon Goldberg and Avraham Bliakher. There they were kept without food for a week. On August 21, 1941, (28th of Av, 5701) they were dragged to a place about one kilometer from the village of Kurpiskes, where they were forced to undress and then murdered. During the murder there was a thunderstorm with heavy rain and the murderers, after finishing their job, ran to a nearby grove seeking shelter. One Jew, Yits'hak Bliakher, covered with the blood of his little son, half naked and soaked from the rain, was only lightly wounded. He managed to crawl out of the pit and ran to the local blacksmith. This righteous man helped him wash off the blood, bandaged his wounds, and supplied him with clothes and shoes, instructing him to disappear quickly. Mr. Bliakher wandered from place to place over the following years, managed to survive and was able to recall his own shocking experiences and the tragic end of the Jewish community of Girtegole. A few Jews were hidden by Lithuanian peasants in the surroundings, one of whom was detained by the authorities.

According to Soviet sources a mass grave with 1,600-1,650 bodies was found near the village of Kurpiskes, about 10 km. southeast of the district administrative center Rasein. It is reasonable to assume that Girtegole Jews were among the victims in this grave.

In the 1990s a monument was erected on this mass grave with an inscription in Yiddish and Lithuanian. At the same time a stone monument was placed at the site of the Jewish cemetery with an inscription in Yiddish and Lithuanian: 'The old Jewish cemetery. Let the memory of the deceased be holy.'

The mass grave and the monument with the inscription in Yiddish and Lithuanian: "Here in this place, in 1941, the blood of about 1650 Jews - children, women and men - was spilled by Nazi murderers and their helpers, who cruelly murdered them."

Sources:
Yad Vashem archives, The Koniukhovsky collection 0-71, file 42
Di Yiddish Shtime, Kovno, 2.9.1919
Naujienos. Chicago, 11.6.1949

Grinkiškis (Grinkishok)

Grinkiskis (Grinkishok in Yiddish) is a town in central Lithuania, about 35 km. northwest of the district administrative center of Kedainiai, sprawling on the shores of the Susve River. An estate under the name Grinkiskis was mentioned in historical documents dating back to the sixteenth century. During the Russian rule (1795-1915), the town was included under the jurisdiction of the Vilna Province (*Gubernia*), and since 1843, in the Kovno *Gubernia*. In the middle of the nineteenth century, Grinkishok became a county administrative center. The town maintained its status during the period of Independent Lithuania (1918-1940). During that period, in addition to the county offices, thirty shops and ateliers were maintained by local business people. During World War I the town was almost totally destroyed by heavy military action.

Old documents of the seventeenth century mention a wooden synagogue in Grinkishok, proving that at that time there was already a Jewish community in this town. Jews made their living in commerce, crafts and agriculture.

The list of contributors for the victims of the famine in Persia in 1871-1872 included 67 names of Grinkishok Jews, as published in the Hebrew newspaper *HaMagid* (see **Appendix 1**).

On the list of contributors for The Settlement of Eretz-Yisrael, names of 33 Grinkishok Jews appear, as published in the Hebrew newspaper *HaMelitz* (see **Appendix 2**).

In 1886 there were 558 Jewish residents, and by 1897 the numbers had swelled to 924. In spite of impressive growth of the Grinkishok population in the second half of the nineteenth century, the economic situation of the Jews was difficult. A report published by a local man in *HaMelitz* in May 1883 stated that during the last two years there were no candles in the *Beth Midrash* and no heating fuel, and the *Gabaim's* efforts to raise money were fruitless because the "buyers" of the *aliyoth latorah* were not able to pay. The situation was so bad, that a policeman would collect the debts on behalf of the authorities.

A year before, the same newspaper announced that a *Gemiluth Hesed* society had been established in Grinkishok by the initiative of a young learned man Falek Kantorovitz.
The community had its own cemetery and a *Heder* as well as its own *Shohet* who also provided services to the nearby community of Beisagole (Baisogala).

Rabbi Aryeh-Leib Duber ben Tsevi-Hirsh HaLevi Volpert served in Grinkishok from 1872 until World War I. From 1934, the official rabbi of the town was Meir-Leib Matz. He was also the last rabbi of that community and was murdered by the Lithuanians in 1941.

In 1921, four years after the establishment of Independent Lithuania, there were 250 Jewish persons living in Grinkishok. In the elections for the first Seimas (Parliament) of Lithuania in 1922, 130 Grinkishok Jews cast their votes for the Jewish lists: 84 voted for the Zionists, 38 for *Akhduth (Agudath-Yisrael)* and 8 for the Democrats.

According to the first population census, conducted by the government in 1923, there were 972 residents in town, of whom 235 (24%) were identified as Jews.

During that period, just as before the war, Jews derived their livelihood from shopkeeping and trades. Commercial activities took place mainly on a Tuesday, which was the weekly market day. According to the Government survey conducted in 1931, Jews of Grinkishok owned seven shops: three textile shops, two butchers, one watchmaker and jeweler, and one shop selling Singer sewing machines. The Jews also owned two flourmills and a bakery. In 1937, there were eight Jewish tradespeople: four butchers, one baker, one barber, one tailor and one photographer.

In 1939, there were 20 telephone subscribers in Grinkishok; four of them were Jewish.

A segment of Grinkishok Jews were supporters of the Zionist movement.

The results of the elections to the Zionist congresses are given in the table below:

Cong No.	Year	Total Shek	Total Votes	Labor Party Z"S	Z"Z	Rev	Gen Zion A	B	Gros	Miz
16	1929	9	9	---	---	5	4	----	----	---
17	1931	8	8	---	---	7	---	----	----	1
18	1933	---	51	27		---	6	----	17	1
19	1935	---	22	12		---	---	9	---	1

Key: Cong No. = Congress Number, Total Shek = Total Shkalim, Rev = Revisionists, Gen Zion = General Zionists, Gros = Grosmanists, Miz = Mizrakhi

Among the Zionist youth organizations, *Benei-Akiva* is listed as an active one.

During the Soviet rule (1940-1941), Zionist activity was forbidden and several businesses were nationalized, including Jewish businesses.

When the German army invaded the Soviet Union on June 22nd, 1941, there were still twenty Jewish families living in Grinkishok. At the end of August 1941, armed Lithuanians led all the Jews to the nearby town of Krok (Krakes), and there, on September 2nd, 1941 (10th of Elul, 5701) they were murdered together with the Jews of Krakes and the surrounding areas.

Sources:
Yad Vashem archives, Jerusalem; M-9/15(6)
Gotlib - Ohalei Sheim, page 34
HaMelitz, St. Petersburg; 28.5.1883; 12.11.1884

The mass grave and the monument, near the village of Pestinukai about 1.5 km from Krakes

Appendix 1
A List of 67 Grinkishok donors for the victims of the Persian Famine in 1872 as published in *HaMagid* in 1872

(from Jewishgen Org.>Databases>Lithuania>HaMagid. Compiled by Jeffrey Maynard)

Surname	Given Name	Comments
BROIDA	Chaim Tzvi	Rabbi Gaon
HACOHEN	Eliezer Chaim	
HACOHEN	Yitzhok	
HALEVI	Zelig	
KAPLAN	Boruch	boy
KAPLAN	Meir ben Yoel	
KAPLAN	Toba bas Yuda Eliezer	woman
KAPLAN	Yehuda Eliezer ben Yoel	
KAPLAN	Yitzchok ben Y	
KAPLAN	Yosef ben Yoel	
KAPLAN	Zev	
KATZ	Meir ben Avraham	
KIRANEL	Yisroel	
KOBELUNA	Toba	
MILNER	Dovid ben Dov	
ROFE	Ari	
SANDLER	Aharon ben Yosef	
SANDLER	Dov	
SANDLER	Leib	
VILENTZIG	Shalom	
WEINER	Dovid	
WEINER	Meir ben Yitzchok	
WEINER	Reuven ben Yuda	
YAKOBZOHN	Yakov Noson	
ZAK	Moshe ben Shlomo	

Surname	Given Name	Comments
	Aharon ben Tzvi Yitzchok	
	Avraham Note ben Yisroel	
	Boruch ben Binyomin	
	Dov ben Yakov	boy
	Dov son of Rabbi Yechezkel	
	Dovid ben Yosef	boy
	Eli ben Meir	brother of Tzvi
	Eli ben Moshe	
	Eliezer ben Moshe	
	Eliezer ben Shlomo	
	Ita	woman
	Kalman ben Nachum	boy
	Leib ben Yitzchok	
	Meir ben Yehuda	father of Yehuda Leib
	Meir Tzvi ben Moshe	
	Menachem ben Avraham	
	Mordechai ben Yehoshua	
	Moshe ben Yakov	
	Nachum ben Yosef	
	Shalom Meir	nephew of Eli ben Meir
	Shimon ben Shalom	
	Shlomo ben Yehuda	
	Shmuel ben Yosef	
	Shraga Mordechai ben Eli	
	Tanchum ben Yehuda	
	Tzvi ben Meir	brother of Eli
	Tzvi Hirsh ben Nachum	s-i-l of the Rabbi
	Yakov Reuven ben Tzvi	
	Yakov Shraga ben Yuda	
	Yakov Yechiel ben Avraham	
	Yechezkel ben Shlomo	

Surname	Given Name	Comments
	Yechiel ben Shmariahu	
	Yehuda Leib ben Meir ben Yehuda	
	Yehuda Leib ben Tzvi	from Kairenai (Kiran)
	Yisroel Yehuda	Sha"tz & Shu"b
	Yosef Dov ben Moshe	
	Yosef Meir ben Yehuda	
	Yuda ben Yakov	
	Yuda Eliezer	wife of
	Zadok ben Yosef	boy
	Zalman ben Yakov	
	Zev ben Yechezkel	

Appendix 2

A List of 33 Grinkishok contributors for the benefit of Settlement of Eretz Yisrael, as published in *HaMelitz* in the years 1898-1902

(from Jewishgen Org.>Databases>Lithuania>HaMelitz. Compiled by Jeffrey Maynard) Note: Under "Source" all are from the publication "Hamelitz."

Surname	Given Name	Comments	Source	Year
KAPLAN	Boruch	in Johannesburg, SA	#102	1898
WOLPERT	Ari Leib	ravbbi gaon ABD	#137	1900
WOLPERT	Ari Leib	ravbbi gaon ABD	#137	1900
YAKOBZOHN	Shmuel Yitzchok	in Johannesburg, SA	#102	1898
YAKOBZOHN	Tzvi Hirsh	in Johannesburg, SA	#102	1898
BREGMAN	Moshe		#232	1902
BREGMAN	Zev		#232	1902
BRUK	Yisroel		#233	1902
COHEN	Moshe	from Gilwan	#233	1902
COHEN	Moshe husband of Chaya Lipshitz	wed 14 Elul in Grinkiskis	#232	1902
GLIK	Meir		#232	1902
GORDON	Avraham Yosef		#232	1902
HEILIGMAN	Gershon	shu"b	#232	1902
KAPLAN	B		#232	1902
KAPLAN	Shmuel Binyomin		#233	1902
KIRSHTEIN	Aharon		#232	1902
KIRSHTEIN	Miriam		#232	1902
KIRSHTEIN	Tuvia		#232	1902
LIPSHITZ	Chaya wife of Moshe Cohen	wed 14 Elul in Grinkiskis	#232	1902

Surname	Given Name	Comments	Source	Year
LUBIANTZKIN	Z	from Keidan	#233	1902
MAGID	Rochel		#232	1902
MARKAN	Sarah		#232	1902
MARKN	Avraham Yitzhok		#233	1902
MOLK	Yosef		#233	1902
PROK	Yosef		#232	1902
SANDLER	Matitiahu		#232	1902
WEIGER	Yisroel		#233	1902
WEINER	Leib		#232	1902
WEINER	Tzipa		#232	1902
WEINER	Yisroel		#232	1902
YAKOBSON	Mani		#232	1902
YOSELOWITZ	Yitzchok		#232	1902
YOTKIN	Zalkind Leib		#232	1902

Griškabūdis (Grishkabud)

Griskabudis (Grishkabud in Yiddish) was founded in 1697 in the woods of southwestern Lithuania, 14 km. southeast of the district administrative center Shaki (*Sakiai*).

Grishkabud was included in the Polish-Lithuanian Kingdom until 1795. According to the third division of Poland in the same year by the three superpowers of those times, Russia, Prussia and Austria, Lithuania was divided between Russia and Prussia. The part of the country on the left side of the Nieman (*Nemunas*) River, including Grishkabud, was handed over to Prussia. During the years from 1795 to 1807 the town was under Prussian rule. In 1797 the population of the town was 582, including just ten Jews.

A street in Grishkabud

During the years from 1807 to 1813 Grishkabud was under the auspices of the Great Dukedom of Warsaw. In 1813, after the defeat of Napoleon, all of Lithuania was annexed to Russia, and Grishkabud was included in the Augustowa Province (*Gubernia*) and in subsequent years in the Suwalk *Gubernia*. In the years of Independent Lithuania (1918-1940) Grishkabud was a county administrative center. There was a church that served the many farms of the vicinity. The town held twenty-four market days each year and occasional fairs, which largely provided the livelihood for the Jewish families.

In 1913, before World War I, about 30 Jewish families lived in Grishkabud. The first census, performed by the new Lithuanian government in 1923, counted 779 residents, including 92 Jews (12%).

According to the government survey of 1931 there were four Jewish-owned shops in town: tools and iron products, textiles, a sewing machine agency and a pub. In 1937 a Jewish butcher and a glazier worked in town. During these years the Jews were forced out of business by Lithuanian competitors, and most of the Jewish businessmen emigrated to America.

In 1936 a fire burned down 22 houses including the *Beth Midrash*. It was decided to modify the bathhouse that was under construction to include a *Beth Midrash*. Unfortunately there was not enough money to complete the project and so the community was left without either of them. There was a *Heder* but in the last years only five boys attended.

The market square in Grishkabud

In 1933 Grishkabud Jews participated in the elections for the eighteenth Zionist Congress. The General Zionist A list received 13 votes, the Labor party received 3 votes and the Mizrahi party received 2 votes.

No Jews were among the eight telephone subscribers in 1939.

In the summer of 1940 Lithuania was annexed to the Soviet Union and became a Soviet Republic. The Lithuanian Soviet regime ended with the invasion of the German army on June 22, 1941. On the first day of the war German soldiers entered Grishkabud. There are no details available about the life of the Jews there during Soviet rule and the few months of Nazi rule until September 13, 1941 (21st of Elul, 5701) when Grishkabud Jews were murdered together with the Jews of Shaki and the surroundings at the Baltiskiai Forest, 1.5 km north of Shaki.

The mass graves with the monument at Baltiskiai forest. The Yiddish inscription on the plaque reads: "In this mass grave lie four thousand innocent residents of Shaki and the surrounding district, who were murdered in the years 1941-1944 by the German Fascists and the Lithuanian Bourgeoisie nationalists. Their bright memory will be kept forever in the hearts of the patriots of our homeland."
Because this tablet was erected during Lithuanian Soviet rule, it does not specify that Jews were among the murdered.

Entrance gate to the site of the mass graves. The inscription in Yiddish, Lithuanian and Russian reads: "At this place in 1941-1944 the Hitler murderers and their local helpers murdered about 4000 Jews, men, women, children."

Source:
Folksblat, Kovno, 6.8.1936

Jieznas (Yezne)

Yezne (in Yiddish) can be found in the southwestern part Lithuania, near the road Alyte-Kovno (Alytus-Kaunas), about ten km. from the right-hand shore of the Nemunas River. An estate of the Lithuanian princes was already established in this place in the fourteenth century. In the seventeenth century the noble Patz family purchased the estate and erected a magnificent palace that for years was the glory of Yezne.

Before 1795 Yezne was included in the Polish-Lithuanian Kingdom. According to the third division of Poland the same year by the three superpowers of those times Russia, Prussia and Austria, Lithuania was divided between Russia and Prussia. As most of Lithuania, Yezne became a part of the Russian empire, first in the Vilna province (*Gubernia*) and from 1843 in the Kovno *Gubernia*.

Yezne suffered much during the war between Russia and Sweden at the beginning of the seventeenth century, and later during the battles of Koschusko in 1794 against the division of Poland and also during the Napoleon invasion into Russia 1812. In 1837 a large fire ruined totally the town including the palace. During the period of independent Lithuania (1918-1940) Yezne was a county administrative center in the Alite district.

Jews settled in Yezne in the first half of the nineteenth century. They established a cemetery in 1912 and until then they buried their dead at the Jewish cemetery of the nearby town Butrimantz (Butrimonys). In 1866, there were 170 Jews (31%) out of a total population of 553 .

Names of Yezne Jews appear in a list of donors for the settlement of *Eretz Yisrael* from 1903. The fundraiser was Yehudah-Zalman Zilber.

At the beginning of World War I, in the first months of 1915, the retreating Russian army exiled Yezne Jews into the inner parts of Russia. After the war and the establishment of the independent Lithuanian state most of the exiled returned to the town. Their economic situation was difficult and they received help from the *YeKoPo* organization.

In 1918 Lithuania became an independent state and following the Law of Autonomies for Minorities issued by the new Lithuanian government, the Minister for Jewish Affairs Dr. Menachem (Max) Soloveitshik ordered elections to community committees *Va'adei Kehilah* to be held in the summer of 1919. In Yezne a community committee of seven members was elected. This committee functioned from 1920 until the end of 1925 when the Law of

Autonomy was annulled by the Lithuanian government. In these years the committee was active in all aspects of the Jewish life in town.

According to the first government census of 1923, 989 residents were in town, 286 of them being Jewish (29%).

Yezne Jews made their livihoods in trade, crafts and agriculture. From the eighteen shops that were in town, sixteen belonged to Jews. Among them were several groceries, five textile shops, two leather shops and a few taverns.

In 1937 seventeen Jewish artisans worked in town: four bakers, three shoemakers, three butchers, one locksmith, one tinsmith, one carpenter, one photographer and one barber. Five families worked in agriculture. A branch of The United Company for Credit to Jewish Agrarians was active in Yezne.

The weekly markets and four or five yearly fairs were important factors in the economic life in town; the weekly fairs took place on Wednesdays. In 1939 thirteen telephone subscribers were in town, two of them in Jewish houses.

Before World War I the Jewish children in Yezne studied in a *Heder* and afterward in a *Heder Metukan*. During the period of independent Lithuania there was a Hebrew school from the Tarbuth chain in town in which about fifty children studied. There was a library in town with several hundred books in Hebrew and Yiddish. Many children continued their studies in Hebrew gymnasiums, mostly in Kovno.

Many of Yezne Jews were supporters of the Zionist movement and of all Zionist parties. In the elections for the first Lithuanian Seimas (Parliament) in 1922, Yezne Jewish voters gave the Zionist list 156 votes and the religious Akhduth list received 11 votes. In the elections for the Zionist Congresses Yezne Zionists voted as given in the table below:

Cong No.	Year	Total Shek	Total Votes	Labor Party		Rev	Gen Zion		Gros	Miz
				Z"S	Z"Z		A	B		
16	1929	22	19	3	6	9	1	----	---	---
18	1933	---	131	72		57	1	----	1	---
19	1935	---	88	86		---	1	----	---	1

Key: Cong No. = Congress Number, Total Shek = Total Shekalim, Rev = Revisionists, Gen Zion = General Zionists, Gros = Grosmanists, Miz = Mizrahi

Among the Zionist youth organizations *Beitar* and *Gordonia* were active in town. The youngsters of those organizations were the fund raisers for the National Funds (*KKL, Keren HaYesod*).

An old synagogue with an *Ezrath Nashim* at the second floor existed in Yezne. The house of the rabbi was near it. Among the rabbis who officiated in Yezne were:

Tsevi-Hirsh Ish Hurvitz-from 1884;
Mosheh Stol-from 1903;
Yits'hak Belitsky-from 1907;
Mosheh Litvak, the last rabbi of Yezne community, was murdered in1941 by the Lithuanians.

The rabbis made their living by selling yeast, and giving permission to slaughter poultry and cattle and from *Maoth Hitim* before Pesakh and from Hanukah Money that the community would donate.

A mass celebration at the market square in Jieznas 1930

There were welfare societies in town: *Hakhnasath Orkhim* that had a special building for accommodating travelers and refugees; *Mathan Beseter* - a charity fund that the rabbi held; *Bikur Holim, Hakhnasath Kalah* and *Hevrah Kadisha*.

Among the persons born in Yezne who became known were Dr. Yits'hak Peretz (1899-1967), educator and linguist, graduate of the Hebrew gymnasium in Kovno, studied Semitic linguistics in Germany, from 1934 teacher of the Hebrew language at the Levinsky teacher seminar in Tel Aviv , later the head of the Hebrew language class at Tel Aviv University, died in Tel Aviv; Yisrael Shwartsblat, rabbi in Odessa; Dov Aloni (Dubin), educator.

In June 1940, Lithuania was annexed to the Soviet Union and became a Soviet Republic. Following new rules, light industry enterprises owned by Jews were nationalized. The supply of goods decreased and, as a result, prices soared. The middle class, mostly Jewish, bore most of the brunt and the standard of living dropped gradually. All the Zionist parties were disbanded and the Hebrew school was closed.

Still before the invasion of the German army into Yezne on June 25, 1941, the Lithuanian nationalists organized and began to mistreat the Jews. They made searches of Jewish homes, robbed and murdered a few Jewish youngsters. The also took Jewish men for so-called work in order to mistreat and humiliate them. The first mass murder took place at August 16, 1941 (23rd of Av 5701). All Jews were ordered to gather in the market square and from them the Lithuanians selected 63 men and 26 women. These Jews together with Jews who arrived in five carts from Stoklishok, were led in the direction to Pren (Prienai) and were murdered there. On August 28, 1941 (5th of Elul, 5701) the Germans took a number of families, together about 70 persons, and transferred the to Alytus, where they were murdered together with the local Jews and buried in the mass graves there. The final liquidation of Yezne Jewish community occurred on September 9, 1941 (11th of Elul, 5701). On that day the women and children were concentrated in the Synagogue. There they were forced to undress down to their underwear and then they were led through the town to the lake and there, behind the fruit garden, near the village of Strazdiskes, they were shot and buried. The men who remained in town were forced to totally undress and then they were led through the town to the lake and there they were shot and buried in the same mass grave. That day 144 Jews were murdered. Of the eighteen Jews who managed to escape the massacre, only four survived: Yosef Gordon hid at the home of a Lithuanian peasant. After the war he came back to Yezne and lived there for two years (from July 1944 till May 1946); Meir Shador, Putchkarnik and Magulevitz. A few of them emigrated to Israel. The names of the Lithuanian rescuers are recorded in the archives of Yad Vashem.

Sources:
Yad Vashem archives, Jerusalem, M-1/Q-1313/134; Koniukhovsky collection 0-71, file 120
"On the Ruins of Wars and Riots." The records of the regional committee of *YeKoPo* 1919-1930 (edited by Moshe Shalit) (Yiddish), Vilna 1931
To the Memory of the Martyrs of the Yezne Community Who Perished in 5701 (Hebrew), (edited by Dov Aloni), published by the former Yezne Jews in Israel, Tel Aviv 1968
HaMelitz, St. Petersburg, 26.1.1882
Gimtasis Krastas (Homeland) (Lithuanian), # 2, 9.1.1992

The mass grave near the village of Strazdiskes and the monument with the inscription in Yiddish and Lithuanian: "In this place the Hitlerist assassins and their local helpers on September 3, 1941 murdered 144 Jews, men women, children."

The monument beside the path to the graves in Alytus with the inscription in Yiddish and Lithuanian: "Stop and think it over, this earth is saturated with blood of innocent people."

A broken Magen-David stands as a monument on the hill of the remembrance site

On March 19, 1993 a new metal monument was inaugurated in the Vidzgiris forest in the shape of a broken "Magen-David". The nine huge graves in which the bones of the murdered Jews were buried, were covered with a round black cover and on it there is a white pyramid. Near the path that leads to the hill a memorial plaque was erected that tells the story of the massacre in Yiddish and Lithuanian: "Here in this place in the years 1941-1944 the Nazis and their local helpers murdered tens of thousands of Jews children, women, men and old people, most of them from other countries. Let their memory last forever."

The architect of the site was Mrs. R. Vasiliauskiene and the sculptor was A. Smilingis

Kaltinėnai (Kaltinan)

Kaltinenai (Kaltinan in Yiddish) is located in the northwestern part of Lithuania, in the Zamut (*Zemaitija*) region, along the main Kaunas-Klaipeda road, about 50 km. to the northeast of the Tavrig (*Taurage*) district administrative center. The Kaltinan estate was first mentioned in the chronicles of the Prussian crusader order in the thirteenth and fourteenth centuries. In the sixteenth century a small town already existed beside the estate. In 1702 the town was granted permission to hold an annual fair.

Before 1795 Kaltinan was included in the Polish-Lithuanian Kingdom. According to the third division of Poland in that year by the three superpowers of those times, Russia, Prussia and Austria, Lithuania was divided between Russia and Prussia. As with most of Lithuania, Kaltinan became a part of the Russian Empire, first in the Vilna province (*Gubernia*) and from 1843 in the Kovno *Gubernia*. During the period of Independent Lithuania (1918-1940) Kaltinan was a county administrative center in the Tavrig district.

Jews settled in Kaltinan in the middle of the nineteenth century, having previously been forbidden to live there. The first Jew to receive permission was David Kaltinaner, who had been abducted as a child to serve in the army of Czar Nikolai I. He constructed a prayer house and a bathhouse in the town.

Eleven Kaltinan Jews are named in the Hebrew newspaper *HaMelitz* #121 in a list of donors for the settlement of *Eretz-Yisrael* dated 1900 (see **Appendix 1**).

In 1918 Lithuania became an independent state, and following the Law of Autonomies for Minorities issued by the new Lithuanian government, the Minister for Jewish Affairs, Dr. Menachem (Max) Soloveitshik, ordered elections to community committees (*Va'adei Kehilah*) to be held in the summer of 1919. In Kaltinan a community committee of five members was elected. This committee functioned from 1920 until the end of 1925 when the Autonomy Law was annulled by the Lithuanian government. In these years the committee was active in all aspects of the Jewish life in town.

According to the first government census of 1923, there were 660 residents, 130 of them being Jewish (20%).

During the first years of the new Lithuanian state the economic situation of Kaltinan Jews was difficult. They received aid from the *YeKoPo* organization for food and cultural needs, with access to a loan fund.

The government survey of 1931 showed that there were nine shops in Kaltinan, five of them being Jewish: two taverns, two textile shops and one leather shop. Jews also owned a wool-combing workshop and two flourmills.

In 1937 there were two Jewish butchers, a baker and a tinsmith. There were no Jews among the fourteen telephone subscribers listed in 1939.

In the elections for the eighteenth Zionist congress (1935) 28 Kaltinan Zionists voted as follows: twelve voted for the Revisionists, nine for the General Zionists A, six for the Labor party and one for *Mizrahi*.

Before World War II about 15 to 20 Jewish families lived in Kaltinan. Despite their small number, the community had a rabbi, Yits'hak-Eliezer Vishnevsky. He was murdered by Lithuanians in July 1941, together with his community.

With the annexation of Lithuania to the Soviet Union and its change of status to a Soviet republic in the summer of 1940, nationalization of factories and larger shops owned mostly by Jews, followed. All Zionist parties and youth organizations were disbanded, and Hebrew educational institutions were closed.

On the second or third day after the outbreak of war between Germany and the Soviet Union, June 23 or 24, 1941, following a battle with the retreating Red Army, the Germans entered Kaltinan. On June 29, 1941, S.S. men arrived in the town, and together with Lithuanians, they detained all Jewish males fifteen years old and older and transferred them to the work camp at Heydekrug (Silute). Jews from other towns including Vainutas and Laukuva were also brought to this camp. The prisoners were forced to work at digging drainage channels. The work mostly lasted from dawn till evening and the food was scanty; 300 grams of flavorless bread and half a liter of watery soup per day. The attitude of the German foreman towards them was vicious. In winter when the weather conditions precluded work on drainage, the Jews were sent to the railway station at Stonishken in East Prussia for the strenuous work of loading wagons.

In August 50 to 60 men, mainly the elderly and weak, were separated from the others. They were told that they would be returned home, but on the way they were murdered. In October and November 1941 further selections were made and those chosen were told as before that they would be sent home, but, as it was later discovered, they were murdered and buried in the ravines of Siaudvyciai.

At the end of July 1943 the men from the Heydekrug camp were transferred to Auschwitz. About 100 of them were annihilated there. The remainder of them were sent to the Warsaw ghetto after about two months in order to vacate the ruins. Many died in a typhus epidemic that broke out in Warsaw. In summer 1944 the survivors were transported to the Dachau concentration camp. No one from Kaltinan survived to be freed by the American army.

The women and children who remained in Kaltinan were put to work by the Lithuanians in different projects, mainly in agriculture. On September 16, 1941 (24th of Elul, 5701) they were all were brought to the Tubines Forest, to a place about 7 km. along the road to Silale, where they were murdered together with other Jews from the region. According to Soviet-Lithuanian sources two mass graves were later found to contain the bodies of 500 men and 700 women.

After the war a monument was erected on the graves: this was replaced in the 1990s.

The mass grave with the monument in the Tubines Forest

The tablet on the monument with the inscription in Lithuanian and Yiddish: "In this place the Hitler assassins and their local helpers in 1941 murdered 700 Jews, men, women, children."

The mass grave and the monument at the ravines of Siaudvyciai

Sources:
Yad Vashem archives, Jerusalem, M-9/15(6); 0-3/2580; Koniukhovsky
Collection 0-71, files 4, 13
YIVO, New York, Collection of Lithuanian Jewish Communities,
pages 69510-69516

Appendix 1
**List of 11 Kaltinan Jews donors for the settlement of Eretz Yisrael as
published in HaMelitz #121, in the year 1900**
(from JewishGen>Databases>Lithuania>*Hamelitz* by Jeffrey Maynard)

Surname	Given Name
AIZIKOWITZ	Tzvi Yehuda
BEKER	Aharon Leib
BERZ	Leib
FRIEDMAN	Moshe Leib
GOLDWASSER	Shimon
GRODNIK	Meir
KLEIN	Avraham
KOWKAIELER	Meir
MERKIND	Yitzchok
PAIURSH	Yitzchok
RUCHMAN	Tzvi Boruch

Kamajai (Kamai)

Kamajai (Kamai in Yiddish) is located in the eastern part of Lithuania, about 13 kilometers south of the district administrative center Rakishok (Rokiskis), on the banks of the Seteksna River. Forests, fields and villages surrounded the town. Its beginnings go back to an estate with the same name mentioned in historical sources from the sixteenth century.

Until 1795 Kamai was included in the Polish-Lithuanian Kingdom. At the time of the third division of Poland by the three superpowers of those times, Russia, Prussia and Austria, Lithuania was divided between Russia and Prussia.   As with most of Lithuania, Kamai became a part of the Russian Empire, first in the Vilna province (*Gubernia*) and Vilkomir district and from 1843 in the Kovno *Gubernia* and Novo-Alexandrovsk district. In the nineteenth century and the first half of the twentieth century Kamai was a county administrative center and this status extended to the period of Independent Lithuania (1918-1940), and then later in the Rakishok (Rokiskis) district.

The town held weekly markets and three annual fairs.

During World War 1, from 1915 to 1918, the town was under German military rule.

Jewish settlement before World War I
Jews began to settle in Kamai in the seventeenth century. In 1766 the town had 216 taxpayers. In 1847 there were 453 Jews in Kamai, and according to the all-Russian census of 1897, the population had risen to 1,105, of whom 944 were Jewish (85%).

The market place was in the center of the town, with four alleys branching out from it: the synagogue alley, the mill alley, the bridge alley and the Meshchansky alley that led to Panemunik (Panemunelis) where the railway station was located. Migrants to South Africa and America departed from this station. There was a tavern in the middle of the market.

At that time most Jews worked in trades. Some were shopkeepers, others engaged in the flax trade, in taverns and peddling. A few sold eggs, with a market extending to Riga. Jewish fishermen bought leases to fish in the lakes in the surrounding areas. A local Jew ran the post office, and a Jew owned the town pharmacy. There was no doctor, but a paramedic, Hayim Shalom, provided medical services. He was also able to prepare medications; this angered the town's pharmacist, Yoshe-Ber Garber, who informed authorities, and the paramedic was sent to jail. Garber later sold his pharmacy to a Lithuanian and emigrated to America.

Skilled workers in Kamai included three tailors, two glaziers, two shingle technicians, two blacksmiths and two shoemakers. People came to Rakishok to buy well-tailored suits. Only the barber was not Jewish. There were also musicians (*Klei Zemer*) who would travel to play at weddings.

In general the Jews were poor. Occasional fires exacerbated their poverty and only a few Jews remained prosperous.

The three annual fairs were major events in the life of the town. Because the majority of the population was Jewish, fairs were not organized on Sabbath days. This arrangement was supported by peasants from the region who wanted to trade with the Jews at the fairs. Many farmers, butchers, horse traders, rich and poor would come to the fairs. Jewish housewives made cakes and baked goods, and the income derived from these days enabled the Jews to earn a basic living.

Sometimes peasants caused disturbances in town, and the Jews feared pogroms. Christian hoodlums would get drunk and break windows in Jewish homes, and even assault Jews on the streets. Once a Jewish youngster challenged some hoodlums and inadvertently injured one of them. Panic broke out, and police from Rakishok arrived to investigate the case, but the shooter was not caught. On another occasion hoodlums from three neighboring villages arrived to instigate a pogrom against the Jews. The Jews called the Cossacks in from the nearby garrison to disperse the rioting crowd. On one occasion, Lithuanian leaders intervened in favor of the Jews, after receiving promises of support for their national and political activities.

Kamai suffered frequently from fires. The worst fire occurred in 1915 when almost the entire town burned down, and many Jewish families became homeless. Neighboring communities such as Rakishok sent aid to the victims. As a result of the fire most of the Jews left the town, and only ten families remained. After the war some of the former residents returned home.

Kamai Jews were divided between *Hasidim* and *Mithnagdim,* praying in different prayer houses. In addition, an old *Beth Midrash* accommodated worshipers during *Yamim Noraim* (the High Holy Days). For many years the building was left unfinished, without a roof and a floor.

From time to time there were interruptions in reading of the Torah in the prayer houses to collect money for heating from the worshippers. Another method for collecting money for the maintenance of the synagogue and the bathhouse was to take the men's *Tallithoth* on *Shabbath* in order to extract a pledge.

Before World War I a *yeshivah* was opened in town. The *yeshivah* was established by Rabbi Eliezer-Ze'ev Luft, the rabbi of the *Mithnagdim*, who also gave lessons, and Rabbi Yisrael-Zisl Dvoretz, who inherited the position of the town's rabbi after Rabbi Luft left. Rabbi Luft was a student of the Telz *yeshivah* and supporter of the *Musar* (Ethics) movement. More than fifty boys attended the *yeshivah*, which had "food days" – three meals a day at the home of a different wealthy family. The *yeshivah* became well known in the surrounding areas, and boys from the neighboring communities also joined it.

Zionism had its supporters in Kamai. There was one subscriber to the Hebrew periodical *HaTsefirah*. Rabbi Yisrael-Zisl Dvoretz was a delegate representing the *Mizrahi* party at one of the Zionist Congresses, and brought home a thermos flask, that caused a wondrous uproar in the town.

The 1905 revolution against the Czar was felt in Kamai. A clerical student, Jurgis Semeiskis (spelling uncertain), left his studies and organized a large meeting at the market square which had been decorated with red flags. The chief of the local police (*Pristav*) and three of his men were forced to remove their police hats and even to carry a red flag. A Cossack unit was rushed to Kamai to quash the riot. They looked for Semeiskis but he had disappeared, so they completely destroyed his house. With the establishment of Independent Lithuania, he returned to Kamai and became a headmaster of a school, but some time later he was assassinated for political reasons.

In 1915, when the German Russian front neared the town, most of the Jews left. Only ten Jewish families remained, and subsequently the German military sent them to perform forced labor on the railway line in Rakishok.

The rabbis who served in Kamai were:
Dov ben Avraham, in 1785
Bunim-Tsemakh Silver
Avraham Hirshovitz, from 1884
Eliyahu Gordon, from 1899, a learned man and a preacher, he wrote several books, later moved to Vilna. He was replaced by a young rabbi, a student of the Telz *yeshivah,* Eliezer-Ze'ev Luft (1871-?), the founder of the *yeshivah* in Kamai together with Rabbi Yisrael Zisl Dvorin, he arrived in Kamai in 1906, later emigrated to *Eretz-Yisrael.*
Meir Fain, emigrated to America.
Yehudah-Leib Siger, the last rabbi of the Kamai community, was murdered in the *Shoah.*

The *Hasidic* community had its own rabbi, Leib, the "Old One," born in Ponevezh. They also had a *Shohet*, Avraham-Leib Atlas who was a learned man.

Hasidic controversies arose often in Kamai.

During the period of Independent Lithuania (1918-1940)
After the war the Jewish community of Kamai needed aid. In 1919 the *YeKoPo* organization in Vilna spent 2,500 Marks on community support. At the beginning of 1920 the sum was increased to 9,000 Marks, and at the end of that year to 12,000 Marks. All this money was spent on food.

According to the first census performed by the new Lithuanian government in 1923, 336 Jews (153 males, 183 females) lived in the town.

Following the passage of the Law of Autonomous Minorities by the Lithuanian government, the Minister for Jewish Affairs, Dr. Menachem (Max) Soloveitshik, ordered elections to community committees *(Va'adei Kehilah)* to be held in the summer of 1919. In Kamai a *Va'ad* with five members was elected. The committee worked in all fields of Jewish life until the end of 1925.

At that time the Kamai Jews made their living mainly in the small trades. The weekly market days on Wednesdays and the three annual fairs still provided a source of income.

According to the government survey of 1931, there were eleven shops, all belonging to Jews: two butcher shops, two textile shops, two restaurants, one haberdashery shop, one flax business, one grocery, one leather shop and one sewing workshop.

In 1937, ten Jewish skilled workers provided services in Kamai: four shoemakers, three butchers, two tailors and one baker.

In 1939, eighteen telephones were listed; three were in Jewish homes.

The Hebrew school

At the beginning of this period Jewish children continued to study at a *Heder*, but later a mixed Hebrew school from the *Tarbuth* chain was established with about 50 to 60 students in five grades. The teachers were Miss Jeruzalem from Shavl (Siauliai) and Ya'akov Harit from Dusiat (Dusetos) who subsequently became the headmaster. The school taught arithmetic, Hebrew, Jewish history, nature, Jewish prayers and customs, Lithuanian history, singing and gymnastics. The school also had a performing choir. A large number of graduates continued their studies at the Hebrew gymnasiums in Ponevezh (Panevezys) or Vilkomir (Ukmerge).

The traditional *Heder* remained open with about twenty boys.

The Zionist movement was active and among others things, established a large library with Hebrew and Yiddish books. The local Zionists bought *Shekalim* and took part in the elections to the Zionist congresses as shown:

Cong No.	Year	Shek	Total Voter	Labor Party		Rev.	Gen. Zion	Gro	Miz
				Z"S	Z'Z				
16	1929	9	9	5	---	1	---	---	---	3
17	1931	19	15	12	---	---	1	---	---	2
18	1933	---	59	---		52	4	---	---	3
19	1935	---	98	---		92	---	1	5	---

Key: Cong No. = Congress Number, Tot Shek = Total Shkalim, Rev = Revisionists, Gen Zion = General Zionists, Gros = Grosmanists, Miz = Mizrakhi

The *Hashomer Hatsair* youth organization had an active branch in the town.

Among the personages born in Kamai were:
Professor Shemuel Atlas (1898-?), son of the *Shohet* of the *Hasidic* community Avraham-Leib Atlas, a graduate of the Slabodka and Ponevezh *yeshivoth* and the University of Berlin. He was also a lecturer of philosophy and Judaism in many institutes and universities, in Cambridge, Oxford, Cincinnati and New York; he published many books on philosophy including The Contemporary Relevance of the Philosophy of Maimonides (1964).

Rabbi Yitshak Agulnik, a graduate of the local *yeshivah*, he served as rabbi in Posvol.

Aharon Agulnik, his brother, head of the famous *yeshivah* in Novogrudek.
Rabbi Yisrael-Nisan Kark (1867-1938) served for forty years as a *dayan* (religious judge) in Kovno and as the chairman of the *Mizrahi* party in Lithuania until his immigration to *Eretz-Yisrael* in 1927; he was a delegate to the twelfth Zionist congress. He died in Tel Aviv.

Shemuel Her (1887-1950), writer and teacher, in *Eretz-Yisrael* in 1927, he published many books in Yiddish and Hebrew including The History of Talmudic Literature (Tel Aviv, 1937). He died in Tel Aviv.

Professor Shemuel Atlas

Rabbi Yisrael Nisan Kark

Shemuel Her

During World War II

In June 1940 Lithuania was annexed to the Soviet Union, becoming a Soviet Republic. Following new regulations, a number of shops belonging to Jews in Kamai were nationalized. All Zionist parties and youth organizations were disbanded. The Hebrew school was closed. Supply of goods decreased; as a result, prices soared. The middle class, mostly Jewish, bore most of the brunt, and the standard of living dropped gradually. At this time about 50 to 60 Jewish families still resided in the town.

The Germans entered Kamai on June 26, 1941, four days after the beginning of the war between Germany and the Soviet Union. Jews who owned transport tried to escape to Russia but most were stopped in Rakishok. There they suffered abuse and torture together with Rakishok Jews, and eventually were all murdered together with them.

Before the Germans entered Kamai, Lithuanian activists tried to take over the government institutions in town. The Soviet police resisted, and according to rumors, 15 Lithuanians were killed in the fight. This enraged the activists even more, and following the retreat of the Soviets, they instigated a pogrom against the Jews. They abused Jews badly and looted their property. Many of the Jews were beaten and tortured and a few were murdered before Germans were even seen in town.

With the Germans invasion, the situation of the Jews worsened. They were expelled from their homes and were told to gather at the *Beth Midrash*. There they were kept without food and water. By some miracle they managed to get some food. After a few weeks, the men were transferred to Rakishok. Women and children were sent to the Antanose village, about 5 km. from Obeliai where they were all murdered. Men were murdered in the Velniaduobe forest about 5 km. from Rakishok, together with Rakishok Jews and those of the surroundings towns. Mass murders took place between 15 and 27 August, 1941.

Only a few Jews survived, who had managed to escape to Russia at the beginning of the war.

The mass grave near Antanose village

The plaque on the monument carries an inscription in Yiddish and Lithuanian: "Here the blood of 1160 Jewish women, children and men was spilled, killed cruelly by the Nazi murderers and their local helpers in 1941."

The mass grave and the monument in the Velniaduobe forest

The inscription on the plaque of this monument, in Lithuanian and Yiddish, reads as follows: "On this site, on August 15-16, 1941 the Hitlerists and their local helpers murdered 3207 Jews, men, women and children. Let their memory live forever."

Sources:
Yad Vashem archives, Jerusalem, testimony of Bela Pasternak; testimony of David Cohen
YIVO, New York, Collection of Lithuanian Jewish Communities, file 1541, page 69755
Oshri, *Hurban Lite*, pages 321, 324
Bakaltshuk-Felin, Meilakh (Editor); Yizkor book of Rakishok and Surroundings (Yiddish), Johannesburg, 1952, pages 292-305
Gotlib, *Ohalei Shem*, page 142
Julius, Rafael, *Kamajai, Pinkas HaKehiloth-Lita* (Hebrew), Yad Vashem, Jerusalem 1996
Masines Zudynes Lietuvoje, Vol. II (Lithuanian), pages 213-214
Di Yiddishe Shtime, Kovno, 1.7.1932

Kražiai (Krozh)

Krazeiai (Krozh in Yiddish) is situated in the Zemaitija region in the northwestern part of Lithuania, about 40 km. northwest of Raseiniai (Rasein), the district administrative center. The Krazante River that flows nearby gave the town its name. The pine forest at the outskirts of the town served as a recreation place for the townspeople, besides provided wood and heating materials.

Krozh is one of the oldest settlements in Lithuania. In 1414, the great Prince Vytautas built a Catholic church in Krozh, and the town came under his ownership; there he formed a Benedictine monastery. Eventually he designated the town as a district center.

The Jesuit monks, who were expelled from England, built another big Catholic church in the town, and established a high school where local aristocracy schooled their children, thus making the school famous in the region. In 1846 the school was transferred to Kovno, removing the source of higher education for Krozh children.

In the mid-sixteenth century, King Stanislav August approved two weekly market days and three annual fairs in town. In the nineteenth century Krozh was designated a county administrative center.

During Russian rule (1795-1915) Krozh was included in the Vilna Province (*Gubernia*), and from 1843 belonged to the Kovno *Gubernia*.

In 1848 fire ravaged the town; consequently its economy declined and its population decreased. In 1880 when the road to Prussia was constructed through Kelm and the Libau-Romni railway was built, Shavl (Siauliai) and Kelm (Kelme) became the important trade centers, while Krozh continued to decline. The nearest railway station was in Nemoksht (Nemaksciai), 20 km. away.

In 1892 a serious dispute erupted between the residents and the administration, caused by a move by the authorities to convert the local Catholic Church into a Pravoslavic Church. Cossacks were brought in to suppress rebellion, resulting in many injuries and mass arrests, and people exiled to Siberia. In the history of Lithuania this event was called "the carnage of Kraziai".

During Lithuanian rule (1918-1940), Krozh once again became a county administrative center, affiliated with the Raseniai district administrative center.

In 1925, the first bus was acquired to replace horses and carts, and a round trip to Shavl could be accomplished in just one day.

In 1926, electricity was installed, and in 1927 sidewalks were paved and trees were planted in the streets of Krozh.

Jewish Settlement until World War I and afterwards
Jews probably began to settle in Krozh in the seventeenth century. The Krozh Jewish community was one of the oldest in Lithuania. During the period of *Va'ad Medinath Lita* (1623-1764) Krozh was included in the Keidan *Galil* (District), and it served as a meeting place for community leaders of the *Galil* area.
During the years 1675-1686 there were 40 Jewish houses in Krozh. During the "carnage of Kraziai" Jews managed to rescue quite a few of their Lithuanian neighbors from the wrath of the Cossacks.

According to an official poll, in 1766 there were 1,048 Jewish taxpayers in Krozh, while by 1888 the number increased to 1,125, or 31% of the total population of 3,375.

Krozh Jews made their living in commerce, trades and to a smaller extent in agriculture. In 1880, 192 Jewish trades people worked in 28 different occupations: 53 tailors, 30 brush makers, 25 shoemakers, 12 butchers, and other trades. There were also 129 merchants, 27 retailers, and 2 wholesalers; 18 horse merchants (who often traveled to Koenigsberg, Berlin and London on business). In addition, there were 15 farmers who leased plots for vegetable farms, and 12 farmers who grew fruit. There were also 12 liquor sellers, 3 tavern owners, 5 laundresses, 3 porters, 79 paid workers in various fields (60 of them worked at two pig bristle-processing workshops), and 2 peasants. There were also 12 *Melamdim,* 3 *Shamashim*, 2 teachers, 2 slaughterers, 1 paramedic, 1 rabbi, 1 doctor, 1 cantor. 29 persons were described as extremely poor.

Two Jewish men, Avigdor and Zalman, called "The Postmen," would ride once or twice a week to the nearby post office to provide mail service to the local population. The post office in Krozh was opened in the 1890s.

Before World War I, the pig bristle processing factory in Krozh owned by M. Falk employed a few hundred workers.

The big fire of 1848, together with the construction of the highway and the railway in 1880 which bypassed the areas near Krozh, caused a decline of the economic situation for Krozh Jews; many of them emigrated to America, South Africa and Australia.

At that time almost 120 Jewish children were enrolled in the *Heder* art institution. Some Jewish youngsters graduated to the Russian high school. Many of them continued their education in the bigger cities of Russia and Germany.

In 1888 a society named *Dorshei Zion* (Preachers of Zion) was formed in Krozh. It had about 60 members and its main purpose was to raise funds for *Eretz-Yisrael,* to be sent to J. M. Pines for Petakh Tikvah. Later, at the beginning of the twentieth century, representatives of *Hovevei Zion* visited Krozh on occasion, and the public would warmly welcome them.

In the Hebrew newspaper *HaMelitz* a list appeared of 17 Krozh Jews who contributed for the settlement of *Eretz-Yisrael* (see **Appendix 4**). A list of 24 Krozh Jews who donated money for the victims of the great famine in Persia in 1871-1872 was published in the Hebrew newspaper *HaMagid* (see **Appendix 2).**

The town had an old *Beth Midrash* with two *Shtiblakh* for prayers and Torah learning. In the middle of nineteenth century, a Synagogue was built where people would come to pray on *Shabbat* and holidays. Its arched ceiling was very high and the wooden *Aron Kodesh* was famous for its artistic carvings. Similar Arks could be found in Shukyan, Kelm, Yurburg and elsewhere.

Prior to the mid-nineteenth century the Krozh cemetery was used by the neighboring Jewish communities.

Krozh appointed its first rabbi at the end of the seventeenth century. Later, many famous rabbis provided services to the community of Krozh. For the list of rabbis see **Appendix 1.**

Many Torah study societies and aid associations were formed in the nineteenth century: *Gemara, Mishnah, Hayei-Adam, Ein Ya'akov, Midrash, Tehilim, Menorath Hamaor, Hafetz Hayim,* two *Hevroth Mikra, Nitei Sha'ashuim (*for book purchase for the *Beth HaMidrash), Tikun Sefarim* (book purchase for the school), *Pirkhei Shoshanim* (to support purchase of wood for heating the *Beth Midrash), Talmud Torah* (to support the *Melamdim* in the particular *Heder).*

The aid associations of Krozh were *Bikur Holim, Hakhnasath Orkhim, Hevrah Kadisha* and, *Beth Milveh* (later the *Gemiluth Hesed* society). The very needy could obtain loans from Hayim Neta Zaks. In 1879, a *Beth Hekdesh* (Poorhouse) was established by the *Hevrah Kadisha:* its members worked on a voluntary basis and their honoraria were donated back as contributions.

In 1915, the Russian military exiled most of the Lithuanian Jews deep into Russia, but Krozh Jews were not affected. Dozens of refugees from Tavrig and other places found shelter in Krozh at that time.

During the period of independent Lithuania (1918-1940)
With the establishment of the Independent Lithuanian state in 1918, the Jewish population of Krozh decreased to half its size before the war. According to the all-Russian census of 1897, the number of Jews in Krozh

reached 906, whereas the first census of the new Lithuanian government in 1923 counted only 470 Jews.

Following the Law of Autonomies for Minorities issued by the new Lithuanian government, the Minister of Jewish Affairs, Dr. Menachem (Max) Soloveitshik, ordered elections to community committees *(Va'adei Kehilah)* to be held in the summer of 1919. Of the 600 eligible voters, only 216 voted and 9 members were elected to the committee. In the elections of 1921 only 7 members were elected to the committee. According to the archives of the committee preserved at YIVO in New York, 52 documents demonstrate that its activity was very limited and came to a complete halt in 1923.

A street in Krozh 1927

Krozh Jews made their living in small business and trades. According to the government survey of 1931 there were 12 shops, 8 of them were owned by Jewish people.

Type of shop	Owned by Jews
Grocery and farm produce	1
Butcher's shops and cattle trade	2
Textile products and furs	2
Hardware	2
Radios, bicycles, sewing machines	1

According to the same survey Jewish people owned a sawmill, a candy factory, a shoe factory and a bristle-processing workshop.

At the end of 1930s, there were 54 merchants and shopkeepers, 4 unskilled laborers and 12 persons in liberal and religious occupations (*Klei Kodesh*). Several Jews leased and cultivated land. In 1925, the first Jewish dental clinic was opened in Krozh.

In 1937, 23 Jewish skilled tradespersons worked in Krozh: four tailors, four butchers, four shoemakers, two watchmakers, one milliner, one blacksmith, one tinsmith, one photographer and five others in skilled occupations.

In 1932, the Jewish popular bank (Folksbank) had 132 members and a *Gemiluth Hesed* was formed.

At the beginning of the 1930s, the Lithuanian Merchants' Association (*Verslas*) began its open propaganda against Jewish shops, and gradually Jews were pushed out of commerce. The economic situation for the Jews became worse and the numbers of poor families increased. Many relied on assistance from relatives abroad.

In 1929, before *Pesakh,* an attempt was made to defame Krozh Jews in a blood libel. In 1935 another anti-Semitic outburst occurred in the town.

In 1939 there were 22 telephones subscribers; one of them was the Jewish doctor Asher Shmidt.

At that time Jewish children studied at the Hebrew elementary school established in Krozh in 1921. There was also a *Heder*. In 1924 a library with Hebrew and Yiddish books opened and many would come to read newspapers and participate in cultural events organized at the library.

From 1928 Jewish students were accepted to the Lithuanian high school. In the school year of 1930/31, among the total of 179 students, 27 were Jewish (16 girls and 11 boys). During the years 1931-1933, eight Jewish students graduated this institution.

After World War I the Zionist youth organizations *Tseirei Zion* and *Tseirei Yisrael* (a Zionist religious movement) began to work in Krozh. Later *Hehalutz, HeHalutz HaTsair, Z"S* and *Betar* were active in regular fund-raising activities for the Jewish National Fund (*Keren Kayemeth*) and *Keren HaYesod*. In 1925, there were 61 KKL boxes (for small donations) in town. Aba Bunimovitz, a devoted Zionist activist, promoted fundraising. Sports activities were organized at the local branch of *Maccabi* which had 32 members at that time.

Many of Krozh Jews belonged to the Zionist camp and they voted at the Zionist congresses for most of the parties, as we can see in the table below:

Cong No.	Year	Total Shek	Total Votes	Labor Party		Rev	Gen Zion		Gros	Miz
				Z"S	Z"Z		A	B		
14	1925	8	----	----	---	---	---	---	---	---
15	1927	24	22	2	2	---	8	---	---	10
16	1929	65	38	19	---	---	4	---	---	15
17	1931	65	54	20	---	18	3	---	---	13
18	1933	---	180	84		79	4	---	---	13
19	1935	---	88	64		---	2	3	---	19

Key: **Cong No. = Congress Number, Tot Shek = Total Shekalim, Rev = Revisionists, Gen Zion = General Zionists, Gros = Grosmanists, Miz = Mizrahi, NB = National Block**

Before World War I, two prayer houses were open for the community. Jews, including artists, came to Krozh from all over Lithuania to marvel at the artistic carvings on the *Aron Kodesh* in the synagogue.

Some Torah Study Societies ceased their activities at that time, but a branch of the *Tiferet Bahurim* organization was formed instead. Its members were unmarried men who prayed in a special m*inyan,* studied the Bible together and listened to *Drashoth* (lessons).

A great celebration was organized for all Jewish residents on the occasion of the completion of the Talmud study. The celebration lasted a week in a specially arranged celebration area. It was a notable event involving all the surrounding towns.

For the list of the rabbis who performed rabbinical duties in Krozh during this period, refer to **Appendix 3.**

Most of the aid societies established before World War I continued their activities throughout this period. *Linath HaTsedek* society, providing medical help with overnight stay for the sick, was founded. All young people in the community participated in the work of this society.

Among the famous personages born in Krozh was H. A. Katz (born in 1905) who was active in the Lithuanian Communist party, and in 1942-1944 fought against the Nazis in the Lithuanian Division of the Red Army.

During World War II and afterwards

In June 1940 Lithuania was annexed to the Soviet Union and became a Soviet Republic. Under new laws, the majority of the factories and shops belonging to the Jews of Krozh were nationalized and commissars were appointed to manage them. All Zionist parties and youth organizations were disbanded and Hebrew educational institutions were closed. Supply of goods decreased and, as a result, prices soared. The middle class, mostly Jewish, was hit hard, and the standard of living dropped gradually. In 1941, 525 Jews lived in town.

On June 24, 1941, the third day after the invasion of the German army into the Soviet Union, a battle erupted near Krozh, and the whole town burned down, including the two prayer houses and the bank. The Jews who had fled to nearby villages at the beginning of the war, returned to the town and crowded together in the house of the town butcher, B. Z. Itskovitz, who had already managed to escape with his family to Russia. They gathered in the large yard, in the stable and the store houses while the Lithuanian auxiliary police brought in Jews from the surrounding villages as well.

On July 8, 1941 all Jews were ordered to take their belongings and gather at the market place. There the Lithuanians searched their pockets, body, shoes and baggage for valuables, money, watches and other property, taking everything away. Afterwards about 400 persons were ordered to go to the Sajukste farm, about one kilometer from the town. They were imprisoned in a barn which they named "The camp of the Jews". The Lithuanians allowed them to bring food that could be retrieved from the cellars of their burnt down homes. Every day a number of Jews would be taken out of the "camp" to sweep the streets and remove the debris.

After about two weeks, on 27th of Tamuz, Lithuanian police came with a list and took seventeen young men out of the camp, whom they transported by truck in the direction of Kelme. The men were told that they were going to work in Zhager. After a short time the truck returned and a bigger group of men and women was collected to go to work at the same place. On that day the truck made many trips until most of the Jews were removed from the camp. All were driven to the forest of Kupre, about 7 km. east of Krozh on the way to Kelme, and there, on July 25, 1941 (1st of Av, 5701), they were shot beside pits that were dug by that first group of the seventeen young men.

There were still 64 children under the age of thirteen left in the "camp," and also five adults, Rabbi Kremerman among them. Peasants from the nearby farms brought food for the children; they told the children that their parents were alive. A few of the peasants wanted to take the children with them but the rabbi ordered the children not to go with the peasants.

On August 2, 1941 (9th of Av, 5701) S"S men and Lithuanian police arrived at the camp and ordered the children and adults out of the "camp," leading them to the Medziokalnis forest about one kilometer northwest of Krozh. There they forced them to undress, pushed them into the freshly dug pit and shot them. Two girls and eight boys aged 10 to 14 somehow escaped from the massacre. The girls manage to go into hiding at a wealthy farmer's property not far from the town, where they stayed until the end of the war. After the war they were baptized and continued to live in the villages. The boys wandered from place to place, hiding in the forests. Most of them were caught and murdered; five were killed, their heads smashed with spades. Only three managed to survive, and emigrated to *Eretz-Yisrael* after the war. The names of the murderers and the names of the Lithuanians who made the rescues are preserved in the *Yad Vashem* archives.

In the early 1990s a monument was erected in Medziokalnis with an inscription in Lithuanian, Yiddish and Hebrew:
"On August 2, 1941 in this place, the Hitlerist murderers and their local helpers killed 71 Krozh Jews; 6 men and women and 65 children."

The mass grave and the monument in Medziokalnis

On the mass grave at the Kupre forest a monument was erected with the inscription in Lithuanian, Yiddish and Hebrew:
"On July 25, 1941, in this place the Hitlerist murderers and their local helpers murdered 370 Krozh Jews; men, women, children."

The mass grave and the monument at the Kupre forest

Sources:
Yahaduth Lita, (Hebrew) Tel-Aviv, Volumes 1-4
Lite, New-York 1951, Volume 1 (Yiddish).
The Small Lithuanian Encyclopedia, Vilnius 1966-1971 (Lithuanian).
The Lithuanians Encyclopedia, Boston 1953-1965 (Lithuanian).
Yad Vashem archives: M-9/15(6)
Koniuhovsky collection 0-71, files 51, 52, 161
Central Zionist archives: files 55/1701, 55/1788, 13/15/131, Z-4/2548
Moresheth archives, Givath-Havivah-A-401
YIVO, New York, Collection of Lithuanian Communities, files 1017, 1018, 1677
Abrahms B., *Ayarati Krozh* (My shtetl Krozh) (Hebrew), Barkai No.169, October-November 1952, pages 54-55
Gotlib, *Ohalei Shem* (Hebrew) page186
Yahaduth Lita (Hebrew) Vol. 1-4. Tel Aviv
Dos Vort, Kovno (Yiddish) 20.1.1935
Di Yiddishe Shtime, Kovno (Yiddish) 28.8.1919, 18.6.1929
Hamelitz, St. Petersburg, (Hebrew) 25.12.1878, 29.10.1883, 9.11.1889
Haintike Nais (Today's News), Kovno, (Yiddish) 1.8.1934
Folksblat. Kovno (Yiddish) 21.8.1935
Tsum Yugent (To the Youth) (Slabodka-Kovno), (Yiddish),
Tifereth Bahurim Movement, Mars 1928
Naujienos (News) Chicago (Lithuanian) 11.6.1949
Komunistu Zodis (Word of the Communists), Kelme, 11.6.1988

Appendix 1
A partial list of rabbis who served in Krozh until World War I

Ya'akov HaLevi, at the beginning of the eighteenth century
Yehudah-Leib Ziv, late eighteenth and early nineteenth century
Yehudah HaLevi Hurvitz, born 1821 in Krozh, moved to Vilna to become the teacher of the Gaon Rabbi Eliyahu's children.
Yom Tov Lipman, at the end of the eighteenth century
Mordehai Rabinovitz, at the beginning of the nineteenth century
Ya'akov son of Menakhem, born in Krozh, son of a poor laborer, officiated as rabbi for forty years, died in Jerusalem
Simhah HaLevi Horovitz, know as an active *Hovev Zion* and public worker, died in 1894
Zevulun-Leib Lipman, an ardent Hovev Zion, served during the mid-nineteenth century
Yits'hak Lipkin, son of Yisrael Salanter, was a distinguished sage and a famous orator.

Appendix 2
List of Krozh Jews donors for the victims of the great famine in Persia in 1872 as published in *Hamagid* #10, 1872 (from JewishGen Databases, by Jeffrey Maynard)

BERMAN	Shimon ben Zev	
HACOHEN	Raphel ben Meir	
MANDEL	Chaim Yitzchok	
ZAK"SH	Chaim ben Yakov	
ZAK"SH	Chaim Note	Rabbi
ZAK"SH	Eizik ben Yakov	
ZAK"SH	Moshe Shlome ben Chaim Note	
ZAK"SH	Tuvia ben Yakov	
ZAK"SH	Yitzchok ben Moshe	boy
ZILBERT	Dovid	
ZIV	Shrage Feiwes	
	Avraham ben Chaim	
	Binyomin ben Meir	
	Chaim ben Zelig	
	Eliezer ben Zevulun	bridegroom
	Leib ben Meir	
	Matitiahu ben Asher	
	Mordechai Yakov	
	Shlomo Zalman	son of the rabbi
	Tzvi Hirsh ben Yakov	
	Tzvi Yudil ben Shalom	
	Yechiel ben Boruch	Rabbi - teacher of Talmud society
	Yitzchok ben Avraham	
	Zevulun ben Eliezer	

Appendix 3
Partial list of rabbis who performed rabbinical duties in Krozh during the years of Independent Lithuania

Ze'ev Volf Turbovitz (1840-1921), served in Krozh for 36 years, from 1885 till his death in 1921. Published many books on religious issues, and articles on ethics in *HaMelitz* and *HaTsefirah*.

Josef Avigdor Lipman, emigrated to the USA in 1923.

Kalman Magid (1874-1941), rabbi in Krozh for a short time, member of the praesidium of the Association of Lithuanian Rabbis and one of the leaders of the *Mizrakhi* party.

Rabbi Kalman Magid   Rabbi Eliyahu-Mordehai Volkovsky

Eliyahu Mordehai Volkovsky (1874-1962), served in Krozh 1932-1934, emigrated to Eretz Yisrael in 1934; he was a member of the Rabbinate in Jerusalem and published his 11-volume work on the *Talmud*. He died in Jerusalem.

The last rabbi of Krozh was Eliyahu Kremerman, who served in Krozh since the middle of the 1930s; previously he was Head of a *Yeshivah* in Kelm, and was murdered in 1941 together with his community.

Appendix 4
A list of Krozh Jewish contributors to the settlement of *Eretz-Yisrael* as published in *HaMelitz* (from JewishGen> databases>by Jeffrey Maynard)

Surname	Given Name	Comments	Source	Year
AHRENSON	Shmuel		Hamelitz #122	1900
BEKER	Moshe Tzvi husband of Feige Hirshowitz	wed in Kroz 1 Nisan	#122	1900
BROIDA	Toibe wife of Mordechai Kriger	wed 4 Cheshvan in Omoli	#230	1895
DANELOWITZ	Leah wife of Kalman Magid from Kovno	wed 1897	# 206	1897
EDELMAN	Yisroel Leib		#122	1900
FRIDMAN	Yitzchok		#122	1900
GLOIN	Yosef		#122	1900
HIRSHOWITZ	Feige wife of Moshe Tzvi Beker	wed in Kroz 1 Nisan	#122	1900
KLEIN	Moshe		#151	1898
LIPMAN	Yitzchok		#122	1900
MILER	Yeshiyahu	government rabbi	#122	1900
RABINOWITZ	Mordechai		#69	1897
SHEINZON	Elchanan		#122	1900
YANKELOWITZ	Aharon		#122	1900
ZACHS	Gitl		#122	1900
ZACHS	Sheina		#122	1900
ZAKSH	Devorah wife of Nachman Abramowitz of Telziai	wed in Kraz	# 171	1893

Krekenava (Krakinove)

Krekenava (Krakinove in Yiddish) is situated in the northern part of Lithuania, on the right shore of the Nevezis River, 30 km. southwest of the district administrative center of Ponevezh (*Panevezys*).

The town of Krakinove was built in the sixteenth century next to an estate of the same name. In 1580 it was granted the privilege of running three annual fairs. As early as the seventeenth century a considerable number of merchants and trades people lived in the area, which became known for its production of tiles for stoves.

Until 1795 Krakinove was included in the Polish-Lithuanian Kingdom. According to the third division of Poland in the same year by the three superpowers of those times (Russia, Prussia and Austria), Lithuania was divided between Russia and Prussia. As most of the other towns of Lithuania, Krakinove became part of the Russian Empire, first under the auspices of the Vilna province (*Gubernia*) and from 1843 under the Kovno *Gubernia*.

In the seventeenth century and also during the years of independent Lithuania (1918-1940), Krakinove was a county administrative center.

Krakinove - General View

Jewish settlement until the period of post-World War I

It is probable that Jews began to settle in Krakinove at the end of the seventeenth century. In 1766, there were 344 Jewish taxpayers in Krakinove. Jews made their living in small trade, as peddlers and on leased farms. A few

Jews were in the limekiln fuel business. Several men moved to South Africa and sent money to their families back home, until enough was saved for the whole family to emigrate. At that time, an active <u>Association of Former Krakinovers</u> (*Landsmanshaft*) was formed in South Africa.

In 1881 a large fire broke out in Krakinove, and more than half of the homes, along with the *Beth Midrash*, under construction at that time, burned down. About 190 families became homeless and destitute. That year an appeal for help to the victims of the fire, signed by the son of the local rabbi Nathan-Neta Flaum and addressed to Baron Horace von Ginzburg of St. Petersburg, was published in the Hebrew newspaper *HaMelitz*. Consequently, donations were received from the Baron and from many communities in Lithuania. The rabbi from Memel, Dr. Yits'hak Rilf, also raised a considerable sum of money. Between 1882 and 1883 the *Beth Midrash* and the *Shtibl*, where poor people would come to pray, were both rebuilt. Krakinave also had another, smaller *Beth Midrash*, and a *Yeshivah*.

In 1897 two fires destroyed almost all the homes in Krakinove (about 270). In these fires the town also lost its great *Beth Midrash*, two small prayer houses and the two-storey *Talmud Torah* building.

According to the all-Russian census of 1897, the town population was 2,187, including 1,505 Jews (69%).

Rabbi Mosheh Haskin

The rabbis who served the community during that period were Mosheh-Mishel Luria, who served for 50 years beginning his service in 1800; his son, Nathan-Neta Flaum (Luria), who served for 35 years from 1860 until his death in 1895; Rabbi Mosheh Haskin (1874-1950), who lived in Krakinove during the period of 1900-1915, and was the founder and the head of the Krakinove *Yeshivah*; he later emigrated to Eretz Yisrael and died in Jerusalem.

The list of contributors for the *Agudath Yisrael Fund* includes seven names of Krakinove Jews.

The list of contributors for the settlement of *Eretz-Yisrael*, as published in the Hebrew newspaper *HaMelitz* includes the names of 190 Krakinove Jews (see **Appendix 1**). The fund raiser was David Gershater.

In 1915, during World War I, Krakinove Jews were exiled by the Russian rule deep into Russia and the whole town was burned down.

During the period of independent Lithuania (1918-1940)
At the end of the war and the establishment of the Lithuanian state, only a third of the Krakinove Jews returned home.

A street in Krakinove 1992
(Picture taken and presented by Joe Woolf, Ilaniah, Israel)

Following passage of the Law of Autonomies for Minorities by the new Lithuanian government, the Minister for Jewish Affairs, Dr. Menachem (Max) Soloveitshik, ordered elections to community committees *(Va'adei Kehilah)* to be held in the summer of 1919. In 1919 a *Va'ad (*community committee) with nine members was elected in Krakinove: four from the Mizrahi list, four were from the list of trades people and one was from independent. The committee was active in all fields of Jewish life until the end of 1925.

According to the first census performed by the new Lithuanian government in 1923, the population of the town was 1,048; 527 of them were Jews (50%).

At that time the Krakinove Jews were mainly engaged in trade and professional crafts. According to the government survey of 1931 there were twelve Jewish-owned shops:

Type of shop	Owned by Jews
Grocery and farm produce	2
Grains and Flax	1
Beverages	2
Textile Products and Furs	3
Leather and Shoes	1
Hardware	1
Medicines and Cosmetics	1
Radio, Sewing Machines	1

In addition, the town had two flourmills and a tar factory, all owned by Jews.

In 1937, thirty-seven skilled Jewish trades people worked in Krakinove: ten butchers, seven tailors, four shoemakers, three bakers, two blacksmiths, two needle trade workers, two knitters, two painters, one glazier, one milliner, one barber, one tinsmith and one potter.

A group of Krakinove Jews, August 1928
On the occasion of a wedding
(Courtesy of Naomi Musiker, from the Jewish Board of Deputies archive in Johannesburg, scanned by Barry Mann and Maurice Skikne)

The Jewish Popular Bank (*Folksbank*) with its membership of 62 persons in 1920 played an important role in the economic life of Krakinove Jews. By 1927 the membership increased to 215. In 1939, there were 28 telephone subscribers, 7 of them Jewish.

Relations between Jews and their Lithuanian neighbors were generally fair, but from time to time plots against Jews were instigated. In the summer of 1929, Lithuanian hoodlums attacked three Jewish merchants on the road near Krakinove. In 1936 a blood libel against Krakinove Jews was initiated, but thanks to the intervention of the authorities and the punishment meted out to the instigators, there were no casualties.

Jewish children of Krakinove acquired their elementary level education at the Hebrew school of the *Tarbuth* chain established in 1920. In 1922 a purpose-built school was constructed, thanks to the donation of a former Krakinover living in America. On average 170 students attended the school. A library with about 2,000 books in Hebrew and Yiddish was open for the residents of the town.

Many Krakinove Jews belonged to the Zionist movement. All Zionist parties were represented, and almost every home carried the blue *Keren Kayemeth* contribution box.

The results of the elections for the Zionist Congresses are given in the table below:

Cong No.	Year	Total Shek	Total Votes	Labor Party Z"S	Z"Z	Rev	Gen Zion A	B	Gros	Miz
16	1929	12	---	---	---	---	---	---	---	---
17	1931	17	11	---	9	---	---	---	---	2
18	1933	---	44	35		2	4	---	---	3
19	1935	178	177	85		---	35	2	29	26

Key: Cong No. = Congress Number, Total Shek = Total Shekalim, Rev = Revisionists, Gen Zion = General Zionists, Gros = Grosmanists, Miz = Mizrahi

Among the Zionist youth organization *HeHalutz, HeHalutz HaTsair, HaShomer HaTsair* and other groups were formed. Sport activities were organized at the local branch of *Maccabi*.

Krakinove had a synagogue, a *Beth Midrash* and a *Kloiz*. In addition, it had a *Yeshivah* with 30 students, and branches of religious youth organizations including *Tseirei Agutath Yisrael* and *Tifereth Bakhurim*. *Torah* study societies included *Lomdei Torah, Ein Ya'akov, Menorath HaMaor, Mishnah and Tehilim*.

The Synagogue

The community's welfare organizations included *Linath HaTsedek, Gemiluth Hesed, Hakhnasath Kalah, Hevra Kadisha* and more. Many Krakinove Jews were learned people and among them there were ordained rabbis who did not work in their field. The last rabbi to serve the community was Benyamin Movsha who was murdered together with his community.

Among the well known personages born in Krakinove were Rabbi Shaul Luria; Rabbi Eliezer-Yehuda Rabinovitz (1890-1941), who served in Memel for 19 years and was a member of the center of the Mizrahi party in Lithuania, and was murdered in Keidan in 1941; Rabbi Josef-Eliyahu Frid, who served as a rabbi in Shukyan for 16 years and later migrated to America; Aba Shaban (1908-1978), journalist and editor of the Yiddish newspapers in Johannesburg; Eliezer Molk (1913-1996?), in the 1970s was secretary of Haifa Workers Council.

Rabbi Eliezer-Yehudah Rabinovitz

During World War II and afterwards
In the summer of 1940 Lithuania was annexed to the Soviet Union and became a Soviet Republic. As in other places, factories, Jewish shops and Jewish flour mills of Krakinove were nationalized. All Zionist parties and youth organizations were disbanded. The Hebrew school became a Yiddish one.

When war broke out between Germany and the Soviet Union on June 22, 1941, Many Krakinove Jews tried to escape to Russia. They formed a long caravan of horse carts, but upon arrival at Ponevezh, well-organized Lithuanian nationalists stopped them, forcing them to return to Krakinove. Germans were already swarming the town, but the Lithuanians were still in power. They immediately detained all Jewish youths, imprisoning them in the jail beside the local police station. After several days of abuse the youths were divided into two groups. One group was brought to the "Priests' field" on the mountain while the other was herded to a field between the stone bridge and the Nevezis River. There they were forced to dig pits, and were then shot and buried in the pits they had dug. The murderers picked out the more beautiful girls and forcibly dragged them to a cellar, where they raped and tortured them to death.

After a short time, the remaining Jews were ordered out of their homes and imprisoned in the *Beth Midrash* without food or water. When one man attempted to escape, a Lithuanian guard produced a knife and stabbed him. A few days later most of the men were led to the road to Ponevezh, and forced to crack stones for road construction. Shortly afterwards, the men were murdered and buried in that location.

Women, children and a number of men who remained in their homes were ordered to the synagogue and into a few houses nearby, thus the place was proclaimed a ghetto. There, the Jews were deprived of food and drink until July 27, 1941, when they were ordered to pack their few belongings and told that they were to be transferred to a "Camp." They were then driven to an open airfield at Payust (Pajuoste), where they were thrown out of the carts, which quickly disappeared, loaded with their belongings. After days of torture without food or water they were murdered and buried in the pits that they themselves were forced to dig.

One Jewish man, who managed to survive the Krakinove massacre by hiding at a nearby Lithuanian farm, joined the Soviet police after the war, in an effort to avenge the murderers as best he could. However, after some time he was caught by opposition rebels and tortured to death.

After the war a mass grave was found on the shores of the Zeneparsa River, one kilometer from Krakinove, about 400 meters from Krakinove-Survilshok road. Two hundred men, women and children were buried there.

In 1991 a new metal gate was placed at the entrance to the old Jewish cemetery of Krakinove carrying an inscription in Lithuanian: "The old Jewish cemetery." Inside, a stone monument was erected with inscriptions in Yiddish, Hebrew and Lithuanian: "The old cemetery. Let the memory of the deceased live forever."

The Monument at a mass grave at the Pajuoste Forest. The inscription in Yiddish and in Russian states: Four mass graves of the Ponevezh Jews who were murdered by the German-Lithuanian Fascists in August 1941.

The monument on the mass grave near the Zenepersa River with the inscription in Yiddish and Lithuanian: "In this place the Hitlerist murderers and their local helpers in July and August 1941 murdered about 200 Jews, men, women, children."

The Monument at the mass grave at the Pajuoste Forest added later with an inscription in Lithuanian: "At this place the Hitlerists and their helpers killed about 8000 Jewish children, women and men in August 1941."

(Picture taken in 1996 and presented by Joe Woolf, Ilaniah, Israel)

Sources:
Yad Vashem archives, Jerusalem, O-3/3034; M-9/15(6)
Central Zionist Archives, Jerusalem: 55/1788; 55/1701; 13/15/131; Z-4/2548.
YIVO, New York, Collection of Lithuanian Communities, files 1022-1038
Kamzon T.D. (Editor) *Yahaduth Lita* (Hebrew), Mosad haRav Kook, Tel Aviv, 1959, pages 95, 102
Gotlib, *Ohalei Shem* (Hebrew), page188
Krakinovo 1901-1961 (English and Yiddish), published by Akhiezer d'Krakinivo in South Africa
Unzer Lebn (Yiddish), Kovno, 17.6.1938
Davar (Hebrew), Tel Aviv, 27.1.1943
Di Yiddishe Shtime (Yiddish), Kovno, 26.12.1920, 29.1.1922, 27.1.1928, 23.8.1929, 3.9.1931, 3.3.1936, 22.3.1936, 8.3.1938
HaMelitz (Hebrew) St.Petersburg, 7.6.1881, 21.6.1881, 7.2.1882, 7.11.1882, 14.5.1883, 15.6.1883, 23.2.1885, 19.1.1885, 7.4.1900
Folksblat (Yiddish), Kovno, 13.11.1940
Naujienos (Lithuanian) Chicago, 11.6.1949

Appendix 1
List of 190 Krakinove Jews, contributors to the settlement of *Eretz-Yisrael*, as published in *Hamelitz* in 1902-03
(from JewishGen.org>databases>Lithuania by Jeffrey Maynard)

Surname	Name	Comments	Source	Year
ABRAMOWITZ	Ephraim		#120	1903
ASHNEGORKE	M		#120	1903
BASERABIE	Hilell Noson		#120	1903
BEIER	Moshe		#120	1903
BENIAMIN	Chava		#120	1903
BERKOWITZ	Mordechai		#120	1903
BERMAN	Elke		#120	1903
BLA	Leib Abba		#120	1903
BLOCH	Chaya Hena		#120	1903
BLOCH	Malka		#120	1903
BODNIK	Pesach		#120	1903
BRENER	Fishel		#120	1903
BRUCHOWITZ	Sheine		#120	1903
CHAIMOWITZ	Aharon		#120	1903
CHAIMOWITZ	Chaim Tzvi		#120	1903
CHAIMOWITZ	Yosef		#120	1903
CHASKIN	Moshe	Rabbi - for victims of Bobruisk fire	#224	1902
DEMBA	Rivka		#120	1903
DISLER	Peia		#120	1903
DOBIANSKI	Roze		#120	1903
DOGOLER	Aba	from Vilna	#120	1903
DOVIDOWITZ	Leib		#120	1903
FEIWISH	Cheikil		#120	1903

Surname	Name	Comments	Source	Year
FRIDMAN	Chava		#120	1903
FRIDMAN	Rivka		#120	1903
FRIDMAN	Shmariahu Zev		#120	1903
FRIDMAN	Yakov Aharon		#120	1903
GARBER	Kalman		#120	1903
GEL	Boruch		#120	1903
GEL	Boruch		#34	1903
GEL	Moshe		#120	1903
GEL	Musha		#120	1903
GIRNON	Rivka		#120	1903
GOLDTZIN	Yosef		#120	1903
GOLOSKIN	Yakov		#120	1903
GREK	Uri		#120	1903
GRIN	Yakov		#120	1903
GROBOWETZKI	Freida		#120	1903
GROSKIN	Glika		#120	1903
HACOHEN	Henich		#120	1903
HACOHEN	Reuven		#120	1903
HACOHEN	Tzvi		#120	1903
HACOHEN	Yisroel ben Dovid		#120	1903
HANDELMAN	Tzvi		#120	1903
HAZAS	Moshe	Rabbi Gaon	#225	1902
HERMAN	Tzila		#120	1903
HERSHOTER	Dovid		#34	1903
HERSHOTER-ROKEACH	Chanah Leah wife of Dovid		#120	1903
HERSHOTER-ROKEACH	Dovid	for victims of Bobriusk fire	#224	1902

Surname	Name	Comments	Source	Year
HERSHOTER-ROKEACH	Dovid, husband of Chanah Leah		#120	1903
HESHILS	Dovid		#120	1903
HIRSHOWITZ	Mendel		#120	1903
HORWITZ	Riba Nita		#120	1903
HORWITZ	Sarah Etil		#120	1903
KATZ	Eliahu		#120	1903
KATZ	Sarah		#120	1903
KAPLAN	Beinish		#120	1903
KAPLAN	Yisroel		#34	1903
KEIDAN	Shneur		#120	1903
KIRIGER	Moshe Bentzion		#120	1903
KLIBANSKI	Shmuel		#120	1903
KLITONSKI	Chana		#34	1903
KLIWANSKI	Chana	from Mozg	#120	1903
KLIWANSKI	Yechezkel Yakov		#120	1903
KOIFMAN	Hade d-i-l of Shimon		#120	1903
KOIFMAN	Shimon f-i-l of Hade		#120	1903
KRAWITZ	Tzvi Mordechai		#120	1903
KRIGER	Beila		#120	1903
LEWIN	Ephraim		#120	1903
LEWIN	Yechezhel		#120	1903
LEWIN	Yitzchok		#120	1903
LEWIN	Zelig Aizik		#120	1903
LEWIT	Kalonimus Yechezkel Halevi		#120	1903
LEWIT	Leah	widow	#34	1903

Surname	Name	Comments	Source	Year
LEWIT	Leah wife of Abba		#120	1903
LEWITAN	Betzalel		#120	1903
LIBERMAN	Chava Chaya		#120	1903
LIBERMAN	Zev Zelig		#120	1903
LIDER	Leah		#120	1903
LIPMANOWITZ	Miriam		#120	1903
LIPSHITZ	Avraham		#120	1903
LIPSKI	Yisroel	for victims of Bobriusk fire	#224	1902
LUKMAN	Mordechai		#120	1903
MARKUS	Chaim Aizik		#120	1903
MARKUS	Gershon		#120	1903
MELAMED	Mordechai Shalom		#120	1903
MELAMED	Naphtali Moshe		#120	1903
MELER	Boruch		#120	1903
MELER	Feiwish		#120	1903
MENDELSON	Nisan	Shub	#120	1903
MER	Shmuel		#120	1903
MERGASHILSKI	Shmuel		#120	1903
MICHEL	Chaim		#34	1903
MICHEL	Risha		#34	1903
MICHEL	Shmuel		#34	1903
MIKALISHKAYA	Toiba		#34	1903
MIKALISHSKAIA	Leah		#120	1903
MILER	Betzalel		#34	1903
MILLER	Sarah		#120	1903
MILMEISTER	Rivka		#34	1903

Surname	Name	Comments	Source	Year
MINSK	Alte		#120	1903
MOLK	Aizik		#120	1903
MOLK	Chaya Gitl		#34	1903
MOLK	Mordechai		#120	1903
MOLK	Yakov		#120	1903
NACHUMOWITZ	Rivka		#120	1903
NODEL	Moshe Hacohen		#120	1903
OZWALK	Eliahu ben Yisroel Yehoshua		#120	1903
OZWALK	Yisroel Yehoshua, father of Eliyahu		#120	1903
PINCHOSEWITZ	Avraham Yitzchok		#120	1903
PINTZOK	Leib		#120	1903
POLOTINSKI	Mordechai		#120	1903
POSTER	Mendel		#120	1903
POTASHNIK	Mordechai		#120	1903
POTZ	Eli Zalman		#120	1903
RABINOWITZ	Elchanan		#120	1903
RABINOWITZ	Leah		#120	1903
RABINOWITZ	M A	for victims of Bobriusk fire	#224	1902
RABINOWITZ	Moshe Aharon		#120	1903
RABINOWITZ	Moshe Aharon husband of Ella Berman from Libau	wed 1 Nov 1902	#34	1903
REZNIK	Chaim Moshe		#120	1903
REZNIK	Dina		#34	1903

Surname	Name	Comments	Source	Year
REZNIK	Gershon		#120	1903
REZNIK	Mina		#120	1903
REZNIK	Moshe ben Michel		#120	1903
REZNIK	Moshe Lipman		#120	1903
REZNIK	Nachman	for victims of Bobriusk fire	#224	1902
REZNIK	Nachman		#120	1903
REZNIK	Tzipa		#120	1903
REZNIK	Yakov		#120	1903
REZNIK	Yechiel Michel		#120	1903
REZNIKOV	Menachem Mendil		#120	1903
REZNIKOW	Mendel		#34	1903
ROFF	Avraham Yitzchok		#120	1903
ROTMAN	Leib		#120	1903
ROTMAN	Zelig		#120	1903
RUBANENKA	Mendel	for victims of Bobruisk fire	#224	1902
SAPIRSHTEIN	Risa		#120	1903
SEGAL	Alter		#120	1903
SEGAL	Chana		#120	1903
SHALSKI	Zusman		#120	1903
SHAPIRO	Basia		#34	1903
SHAPIRO	Golde Rivka		#120	1903
SHAPIRO	Note	for victims of Bobruisk fire	#224	1902
SHAPIRO	Note Yakov		#120	1903

Surname	Name	Comments	Source	Year
SHAPIRO	Note Yakov		#120	1903
SHAPIRO	Note Yakov		#34	1903
SHARPONOWITZ	Shimshon		#120	1903
SHER	Avraham Eliezer		#120	1903
SHER	Bas Sheva		#34	1903
SHER	Dovid		#120	1903
SHER	Gitl		#34	1903
SHMIT	Nachum Zev		#120	1903
SHMUELOWITZ	Medel		#120	1903
SHOCH	Ester Gitl		#120	1903
SHOR	Ester		#120	1903
SLOWIANISHSKAYA	Riza		#34	1903
SOBON	Chaim		#120	1903
SOBON	Meir		#120	1903
SOLTOFSKI	Yosef	from Rogowe	#120	1903
STOLER	Aizik		#120	1903
TOBIANSKI	Figa		#120	1903
TOIB	Tzerna		#120	1903
TROKMAN	Meir Leib		#120	1903
TROKMAN	Meir Leib		#120	1903
TZIGON	Chaim		#120	1903
WALERSHTEIN	Getzil Zev		#120	1903
WALERSHTEIN	Pesa		#34	1903
WASERTZWEIG	Dovid		#120	1903
WEINER	Nachum		#120	1903
WINIK	Tzvi Asher		#120	1903
WISHNEWITZ	Freidel		#120	1903
WOLFOWITZ	Nechama		#120	1903

Surname	Name	Comments	Source	Year
WOLK	Shmuel Yosef		#120	1903
YAFE	Chava		#120	1903
YAFE	Yisroel		#120	1903
YAKOBSOHN	Hinda		#120	1903
YASHPAN	Meir	for victims of Bobruisk fire	#224	1902
YASHPAN	Meir		#120	1903
YASHPAN	Ruchama	widow	#34	1903
YERUCHAMOWITZ	Zalman Moshe		#120	1903
YONES	Meir		#120	1903
YUTER	Moshe		#120	1903
ZAKS	Zev		#120	1903
ZIW	Zev		#120	1903
ZOLK	Bluma Hade		#120	1903
	Moshe ben Binyomin		#120	1903
	Nechama Risa		#120	1903
	Shraga Yosef		#120	1903
	Zev ben Yehuda		#120	1903

Kuršėnai (Kurshan)

Kurshan (in Yiddish) lies 26 km. from the district administrative center Siauliai (*Shavl*). It is surrounded by hills and forests on the shores of the Venta River in the northwestern part of Lithuania in the Zemaitija region. The main part of the town was built along the right-hand shore of the river and a bridge connected it to neighborhoods on its left-hand side. A railway station on the Shavl-Mazheik-Libau (*Siauliai-Mazeikiai-Liepaja*) line was 4 km. away, and another station, Pavenciai, on the Shavl-Telz (Siauliai-Telsiai) line, was situated at a distance of 3.5 km. Roads to these towns also passed through Kurshan.

From the sixteenth century Kurshan is mentioned in historical documents, but the town began to grow alongside an estate of the same name at the end of the eighteenth century. The construction of the railway line to Liepaja (Libau) and the building of the Kurshan station in 1873 accelerated the town's development: big markets and fairs were active in the town and several light industries were established.

During 1795-1914, Kurshan was under Russian rule, first in the Vilna *Gubernia* (Province) and from 1843 in the Kovno *Gubernia*. During World War I, Kurshan was occupied by the German army which made it a district center, and during the years of Independent Lithuania (1818-1940) it was a county administrative center in the Siauliai district.

Jewish Settlement till after World War I

It is not known when Jews began to settle in Kurshan, but according to the Russian census of 1897, Jews comprised 48% of the total population of the town (1,542 Jews out of 3,189 residents). They traded in grains, flax, timber and cattle. Jewish farming families lived in surrounding villages: specifically there were six Jewish families who lived in the village of Kuzhi, about 15 km. east of Kurshan, until World War I. At the beginning of the war these Jews were accused of hiding German soldiers who had attacked Russian headquarters. This libel was one of the reasons that the Jews were exiled by the Russian army. Kurshan Jews also had to leave their town and abandon their property. During the war the town was destroyed, including its 255 Jewish houses. Before the war many Kurshan Jews had emigrated to South Africa and America.

In 1880 a *Talmud Torah* with 20 boys was established, where Bible and Hebrew grammar were taught. The older pupils were taught both the German and Russian languages three times a week.

Kurshan's synagogue was destroyed in one of the many fires, and thus, in 1879, a new synagogue was built, one of the most beautiful in Lithuania. But in 1915 this building too was burnt down, and in 1905 a large fire caused severe damage to one hundred Jewish houses.

For a partial list of rabbis who officiated in Kurshan during the years see **Appendix 1.**

During the period of Independent Lithuania (1918-1940)
After the war some of the exiled Jews returned to Kurshan. They rebuilt their houses and organized the community. Following the passage of the Law of Autonomies for Minorities by the new Lithuanian government, the Minister for Jewish Affairs, Dr. Menachem (Max) Soloveitshik, ordered elections for community committees (*Va'adei Kehilah)* to be held in the summer of 1919. In Kurshan a community committee with eleven members was elected: two from the *Tseirei Zion* list, five artisans, four independents. The committee was active in all aspects of Jewish life from 1919 till the beginning of 1926.

General view of Kurshan

According to the first census performed by the new Lithuanian government, there were 841 Jews in Kurshan in 1923.

During this period, Kurshan Jews made their living from trade and crafts. According to the government survey of shops and factories, in 1931 there were 55 shops, 50 (91%) of them Jewish owned. Their distribution is given in the table below:

Type of the business	Total	Owned by Jews
Grocery stores	9	8
Grain and flax	6	6
Butcher's shops and Cattle Trade	5	5
Restaurants and Taverns	4	3
Textile Products and Furs	9	9
Leather and Shoes	2	2
Haberdashery and domestic utensils	5	5
Medicine and Cosmetics	2	1
Building material and Furniture	2	2
Hardware products	3	3
Bicycles and electrical equipment	1	1
Timber and heating material	4	4
Stationery and Books	1	1
Others	2	0

There were 44 factories, 26 of them (59%) Jewish owned.

Type of Factory	Total	Jewish owned
Power Plants, Metal Workshops	4	2
Concrete products, Bricks, Tombstones	6	3
Textile: Wool, Flax, Knitting	7	1
Sawmills and Furniture	3	2
Flour mills, Bakeries, Food Production	16	12
Leather Industry: Production, Cobbling	2	2
Others	6	4

The Pres brothers owned a dairy, which produced cheese. In 1935 a Jewish doctor and dentist had clinics in Kurshan. The Jewish Popular Bank (*Folksbank*) played an important role in the economic life of the town, and had 345 registered members in 1927, which dwindled to 207 by 1932.

A Street in Kurshan

In 1937 there were 37 Jewish artisans: ten shoemakers, six tailors, six butchers, three tinsmiths, three barbers, two hatters, two knitters, two stitchers, one baker, one glazier, one leather worker.

Kurshan's Jewish artisans organized their own union and had a *Gemiluth Hesed* fund which was established and financed by membership fees and a donation from the *Ezrah* society. Its activities included courses for older members, where the Lithuanian language and arithmetic were taught.

In 1939 there were 84 telephone subscribers, 17 of them Jewish.

At the beginning of the 1920s a Hebrew elementary school was established, which joined the *Tarbuth* chain in 1927, with an average of 150 children studying there. Apart from the school there was a library with 500 books in Hebrew and Yiddish. In 1927 a Hebrew Kindergarten was opened, and in October 1932 a new school building was inaugurated.

Beginning in the mid-1930s, the number of Jews in Kurshan decreased gradually. The economic crisis in Lithuania and the open propaganda by the Association of the Lithuanian Merchants *Verslas* calling for the boycott Jewish shops caused many Jews to look elsewhere for their future. Many emigrated abroad, including to *Eretz-Yisrael*.

A class of the Hebrew School

(from the archive of the Association of Lithuanian Jews in Israel)
A class in the Hebrew school 1930

Many Kurshan Jews belonged to the Zionist movement, and all Zionist parties were represented in town. There was also a branch of WIZO. These were the Zionist youth organizations: *Hashomer Hatsair, Tseirei Zion, Betar* and others, as well as a *Hakhsharah* (training) group of *Brith HaKanaim*. Sports activities were carried out in the local *Maccabi* branch with its 48 members.

The results of the elections for the Zionist Congresses are given in the table below:

Cong No.	Year	Tot Shek	Total Votes	Labor Party		Rev	Gen Zion		Gros	Miz
				Z"S	Z"Z		A	B		
14	1925	107	----	----	----	--	----	----	----	----
15	1927	120	56	1	1	1	16	---	---	37
16	1929	178	92	5	2	29	34	----	----	22
17	1931	111	98	31	2	3	43	----	----	19
18	1933	----	288	119		28	31	---	37	13
19	1935	205	182	100		--	2	13	52	15

Key: Cong No. = Congress Number, Tot Shek = Total Shekalim, Rev = Revisionists, Gen Zion = General Zionists, Gros = Grosmanists, Miz =Mizrahi

(from the archive of the Association of Lithuanian Jews in Israel)
A Hanukah party at the school

Religious life was concentrated in two new prayer houses built in 1921 to replace the beautiful synagogue that was destroyed during the war. For the rabbis who officiated in Kurshan during this period see **Appendix 1.**

Among the active welfare societies there were *Ezrah, Bikur Holim and Gemiluth Hesed.*

Aryeh Kubovitsky-Kubovi (1896-1955) can be counted among the notables born in Kurshan. He was a lawyer and Zionist party worker, activist of the Jewish World Congress, a member of the Zionist executive and a delegate to Zionist congresses. He served as the Israeli ambassador to Czechoslovakia, later to Argentina, and was the chairman of Yad Vashem.

(from the archive of the Association of Lithuanian Jews in Israel)
The Halutsim in Kurshan at a party with the slogan "Troubles of father and mother" 1933

During World War II and afterwards

In 1940, Lithuania was annexed to the Soviet Union and became a Soviet Republic. Following new rules, the factories, most of them owned by Jews, were nationalized, as were Jewish shops and farms, and commissars were appointed to manage them. All Zionist parties and youth organizations were disbanded and the Hebrew school was closed. Supply of goods decreased and, as a result, prices soared. The middle class, mostly Jewish, bore the brunt of this situation and the standard of living dropped gradually

When war broke out between Russia and Germany on the 22nd of June, 1941, many Kurshan Jews tried to escape to Russia through Latvia, but only about 30 families succeeded. The majority returned because the border with Latvia was closed.

On the night of their entrance into Kurshan the Germans murdered two Jews. Lithuanian nationalists, already organized, forced the Jews to gather every day in the market place, whence they were led to various types of work, such as to bury dead Russian soldiers or the corpses of dead horses, or to move wrecked cannons and cars from the roads. No tools were supplied for these jobs, so work was very hard, made worse when they were abused and beaten. Some of these forced laborers fainted.

After a short time, all males aged 12 years and older were ordered to assemble in the great *Beth Midrash*. Ten invalids and mentally ill people were taken out and never seen again. Fifteen men were imprisoned in the local jail and from there they were taken to the Shavl prison.

A week later, 150 men were driven in trucks in the direction of Shavl, whence they were taken to a forest, about 3 km. from Kurshan. There, they were led in groups of twenty to a long pit that had been prepared before, and were shot. The remaining men, including the town's Rabbi Yerakhmiel Litvin, were murdered on July 16,1941 (21st of Tamuz, 5701).

For the women and children a so-called ghetto was established in two small streets in the town. The women were allowed to go out for one hour a day to buy food, but mostly they were cursed and chased away.

Padarbiu forest

אויף דעם אָרט האָבן ד־
היטלערישע רוצחים און
זייערע ערטיקע באהעלפער
דימ־ם־22.VII.1941 דערמאָרדעט
100 קורשאנער יידישע
מענער

The mass grave and monument with the inscription in Yiddish: "At this site Hitler's murderers and their local helpers murdered 100 Kurshan Jewish men on 22 July, 1941."

On August 15, 1941, all the women and children were transported to Zhager (Zagare). Before leaving, the women were searched for money and gold by two Lithuanian women volunteers. They were stripped, and the search was brutal and humiliating. All that they possessed was taken away from them. In Zhager they were then forced to do agricultural work for Lithuanian peasants. Later they were murdered together with Zhager Jews. The names of the Lithuanian murderers are listed in the Yad Vashem archives in Jerusalem.

Only one man and one woman, who were hidden by Lithuanian peasants, were privileged to see the liberation.

After the war, according to Soviet sources, a mass grave of 180 corpses of men was found in the forest of Padarbiai, 3.5 km. south-east from Kurshan, near the village Gaudziai.

The mass grave in the town park of Zhager where women and children from Kurshan were murdered, together with about 3,000 other Jews.
(Picture taken and supplied courtesy of Elkan Gamzu, July 2005)

Sources:

Yad-Vashem Archives: M-1/E-128/56,1670/1566; M-9/15(6)

Koniuchovsky Collection 0-71, Files 102, 111

Central Zionist Archives: 55/1788; 55/1701; 13/15/131; Z-4/2548.

YIVO, New York, Collection of Lithuanian Communities,
Files 923-942

Ish Shalom M. *BeSod Hotsvim uBonim* (Hebrew), Jerusalem 5749 (1989)

Kamzon T.D. (Editor) *Yahaduth Lita* (Hebrew), Mosad haRav Kook, Tel Aviv, 1959, pages162, 169

HaMeilitz (St. Petersburg) (Hebrew): 13.5.1879, 12.7.1881, 21.7.1884

Cohen Berl,. *Shtet, Shtetlach un Dorfishe Yishuvim in Lite biz 1918* (Towns, Small Towns and Rural Settlements in Lithuania till 1918) (Yiddish) New-York 1992.

From the Beginning to the End - The Book of the History of "HaShomer HaTzair" in Lithuania (Hebrew), Tel-Aviv 1986.

Folksblat, Kovno (Yiddish): 18.4.1939

Di Yiddishe Shtime (The Yiddish Voice) Kovno (Yiddish): 10.1.1922, 21.1.1922, 15.2.1922, 17.5.1922, 15.6.1928, 26.10.1932, 9.3.1938

Yiddisher Hantverker (Jewish Artisan) Kovno, (Yiddish): Nr.16, 1938.

Der Yiddisher Cooperator (Yiddish) Kovno, No. 2, 1927

Masines Zudynes Lietuvoje (Mass Murder in Lithuania) vol. 1-2, Vilnius 1941-1944 (Lithuanian).

The Book of Sorrow, (Hebrew, Yiddish, English, Lithuanian), Vilnius 1997.

Appendix 1
Partial list of rabbis who officiated in Kurshan

Until World War I:
Yehiel-Mihel HaCohen Gold, served in the years 1840-1880.
Shemuel-Mosheh Shapiro (1843-1908), in Kurshan from 1879.
Shelomoh-Nathan Kotler (1855-1945), was Rabbi and head of the Yits'hak Elhanan Yeshivah in New York, returned to Lithuania and became Rabbi in Kurshan. Later settled in Jerusalem. Published many books.

During Independent Lithuania
Yisrael Rif (1870-1941), very honored by the community, was murdered with his family in the Holocaust.
Yits'hak-Izik Fridman (1874-1944) served in Kurshan 1914-1924, wrote many articles and books. He was one of the founders of the Mizrahi party in Lithuania, and emigrated to Eretz Yisrael in 1935.

Rabbi Yits'hak Fridman

Rabbi Shelomoh Kotler

Appendix 2
List of 75 Kurshan Jewish donors for the victims of the Persian famine as published in Hamagid Nr. 15, 1872

(From Jewishgen.org>databases>Lithuania>by Jeffrey Maynard)

Surname	Given Name	Comments
BLUMBERG	Gershon	
BLUMBERG	Mordechai	
CHAYAT	Leib ben Shmuel	partner of Nechemiah
CHAYAT	Moshe ben Dovid	
CHAYAT	Yosef ben Tzvi	
EINBER	Mendel	
FRIDMAN	Takov	
GARBER	Mordechai HaCohen	Cohen
GLEZER	Eizik	
GLIK	Chaim	
HALEVY?	Dovid ben Shaul	Levy
HALEVY?	Dovid Tzvi	Levy
HESELZOHN	Getzel ben Eliezer Shmuel	

Surname	Given Name	Comments
HESELZOHN	Moshe	
HESELZOHN	Tzvi	brother of Yakov
HESELZOHN	Yakov	brother of Tzvi
HESELZOHN	Yakov Leib	
HIRSHZOHN	Ber	
KAZAV	Meir ben Yakov	
KOBELER	Yitzchok ben Tzvi	f-i-l of Leib ben Avraham
KOIFMAN	Ber	
KOIFMAN	Dovid Yitzchok	
KREMER	Dovid Tzvi ben Yehuda	
KREMER	Shmuel	
KREMER	Yosef ben Tzvi	
LIPSHITZ	Ber	
LIPSHITZ	Leib	brother of Yehoshua
LIPSHITZ	Mordechai	brother of Shaul
LIPSHITZ	Shaul	brother of Mordechai
LIPSHITZ	Yehoshua	brother of Leib
LOKNIKER	Eizik	
MALTZ	Avrohom	
MEGRADUS	Raphael	
MEYERER	Nechamiah	
NOTWEIZER	Meir ben Shmuel	
NUROK	Meir	
ORDONG	Naphtali	
PAWEKER	Yitzchok	
PELSER	Yitzchok	

Surname	Given Name	Comments
POPALSKER	Aharon	
ROZENGERMAN	Rachel	
SANDLER	Shaul ben Dovid HaCohen	boy
SHOHAM	Moshe ben Yisroel Yona	boy
SHOHAM	Shmuel Nachum	from Panevezys
SHOHAM	Yisroel Yona	
SHU"B	Lipman	
TAMINZSKER	Dovid	
TAMINZSKER	Leib ben Avraham	
WEGER	Aharon Moshe ben Yitschok	
YANISKE	Tzvi	
	Aharon ben Elchanan	
	Avraham ben Yakov	
	Chaikil ben Elchanan	bridegroom with his son
	Chaim ben Tuvia	
	Chaim Ber	
	Dovid ben Tzvi	
	Eli ben Sender	
	Eli ben Shimon	
	Isser ben Nechamiah	
	Leib ben Avraham	s-i-l of Yitzchok Kobeler
	Leib ben Ezriel	
	Leib ben Mordechai HaCohen	Cohen
	Meir ben Yakir	
	Mendil ben Yehuda	boy
	Neche m-i-l of Yakov Tzvi	woman

Surname	Given Name	Comments
	Nechemiah	partner of Leib Chayat
	Shabasai ben Kalonimos	
	Shimon Moshe	
	Shimon Yakov	
	Yakov Tzvi	s-i-l of Neche (woman)
	Yehuda Eliezer	
	Yisroel ben Yeshiahu	
	Yisroel Dov ben Tzvi	
	Yosef ben Matitiahu	
	Yosef ben Titzchok	

Appendix 3
List of 119 Kurshan Jewish donors for the settlement of Eretz Yisrael as published in HaMelitz.

(From JewishGen.org >Databases> Lithuania>by Jeffrey Maynard)

Surname	Given Name	Comments	Source in Hamelitz	Year
ADELZOHN	Chaim	Rabbi	#237	1897
ARONZOHN	Ber		#237	1897
BALKIN	Yisroel		#237	1897
BIKOWITZ	Eliezer		#237	1897
BLUMBERG	Mordechai		#237	1897
BODONES	Dovid Meir		#237	1897
BROINROIT	Avraham		#237	1897
CHAWKIN	Shlomo	from Zager	#237	1897
CHAZAN	Yehuda Eliezer		#237	1897
DONN	Dov Tzvi		#237	1897
FELDMANN	Yitzchok		#237	1897
FORMANN	Yakov Tzvi		#237	1897
GITELZON	Avraham		#237	1897
GLEZER	Aizik		#237	1897
GLEZER	Mordechai		#237	1897
GOLDBERG	Chaim		#237	1897
GOLDIN	Binyomin		#237	1897
GOLDWASER	Yehuda		#237	1897
GORDON	Abba	Shub	#237	1897
GROSBARD	Aharon		#237	1897

Surname	Given Name	Comments	Source in Hamelitz	Year
GROSBARD	Zusmann		#237	1897
GROZINSKI	Dov Tzvi		#237	1897
HESHILZOHN	Yakov		#237	1897
HIRSHZOHN	Ber		#237	1897
HIRSHZOHN	Shimon Yakov		#237	1897
HORWITZ	Dovid		#163	1897
HORWITZ	Dovid		#237	1897
HOTZ	Bentzion		#237	1897
HOTZ	Binyomin Zev		#237	1897
HOTZ	Micha Moshe		#237	1897
IZRALSHTAM	Shalom		#237	1897
KAPLAN	Chaim		#163	1897
KAPLAN	Moshe		#237	1897
KAPLAN	Yisroel		#145	1897
KARNOWSKI	Fane bas Yekil		#247	1895
KARNOWSKI	Sonie bas Yekil		#247	1895
KARNOWSKI	Yekil father of Fane & Sonie		#247	1895
KATZAV	Dov Zev		#237	1897
KIBOWILZKI	Shatz		#237	1897
KILEIA	Zusmann	wed 1897	#145	1897

Surname	Given Name	Comments	Source in Hamelitz	Year
	husband of Hende Nurok			
KITEIA	Yisroel		#163	1897
KITEIA	Zusman		#163	1897
KITEIA	Zusmann		#237	1897
KOHN	Leib		#237	1897
KOHN	Shaul		#237	1897
KOHN	Zalman		#237	1897
KOPIL	Bentzion		#237	1897
KORSH	Reuven		#237	1897
KRAWITZ	Avraham		#237	1897
KREMER	Dovid		#237	1897
KUBOZOITITZKI		Shatz	#145	1897
LEWI	Yakov		#237	1897
LEWITAS	Aizik		#237	1897
LEWITATZ	Yisroel		#237	1897
LEWITES	Y	son-in-law of Y Y Shagam	# 188	1893
LIFSHITZ	Aharon		#163	1897
LIFSHITZ	Leah bas Leib wife of Yesheyahu Tzukerman	wed 12 Av	# 181	1893
LIFSHITZ	Leib father of Leah		# 181	1893

Surname	Given Name	Comments	Source in Hamelitz	Year
LIFSHITZ	Tzvi		#237	1897
LIFSHITZ	Zalman		#237	1897
LIPOWSKI	Yisroel		#237	1897
LIPOWSKI	Yosef ben Eli		#237	1897
LIPOWSKI	Zev		#237	1897
LIPSHITZ	Aharon ben Tzvi		#145	1897
LIPSHITZ	Akiva		#237	1897
LIPSHITZ	Mordechai ben Yehoshua		#237	1897
LIPSHITZ	Yosef		#237	1897
LIPSHITZ	Zalman		#163	1897
LIPSHITZ	Zalman		#145	1897
LURIA	Mordechai		#237	1897
MARAM	Shimon Moshe		#237	1897
MARAM	Yakov		#237	1897
MEKOS	Chaim Tzvi		#237	1897
MIRNIK	Nechemiah		#237	1897
MITELZOHN	Aharon		#237	1897
NACHUMOWITZ	Shalom	from Kruk	#237	1897
NAFTALIK	Mendil		#163	1897
NAFTALIN	Mendil		#145	1897
NUROK	Henda wife of	wed 1897	#145	1897

Surname	Given Name	Comments	Source in Hamelitz	Year
	Zusmann Kileia			
NUROK	Yakov		#163	1897
NUROK	Yakov		#145	1897
ORDONG	Naphtali		#237	1897
PEKER	Zalman Meir		#237	1897
PROZ	Yitzchok Leib		#237	1897
ROZIN	Zev		#237	1897
RUBIN	Betzalel		#237	1897
RUBIN	Mordechai		#237	1897
SHAGAM	Y Y	f-i-l of Y Lewites	# 188	1893
SHAHAM	Yisroel Yona		#237	1897
SHAPIRO	Avraham son of the Gaon S M		#237	1897
SHAPIRO	Chaim Tzvi ben ha Gaon Shmuel Moshe		#247	1895
SHEFER	Gershon		#237	1897
SHIFMANN	Getzil		#237	1897
SHLOMOWITZ	Chaim		#237	1897
SHLOMOWITZ	Tzemach		#237	1897
SHNEIDER	Zalman		#237	1897

Surname	Given Name	Comments	Source in Hamelitz	Year
	Yosef			
SHTEIN	Yechezkel Mordechai		#237	1897
SHUSTER	Eliezer		#237	1897
TEPER	Michel		#237	1897
TEREN	Boruch Eliezer ben Yitzchok		#163	1897
TEREN	Boruch Eliezer	husband of Feiga Ita brother of Yitzchok Mendil	#145	1897
TEREN	Feiga bas Yitzchok		#163	1897
TEREN	Feiga Ita wife of Boruch		#145	1897
TEREN	Yitzchok father of Feiga & Boruch Eliezer	Deputy Government Rabbi	#163	1897
TEREN	Yitzchok Mendil		#237	1897
TEREN	Yitzchok Mendil	brother of Boruch Eliezer	#145	1897
TON	Shmuel		#237	1897
TON	Yakov		#237	1897
TZITRON	Feiwil		#237	1897

Surname	Given Name	Comments	Source in Hamelitz	Year
TZUKERMAN	Yesheyahu husband of Leah Lifshitz	wed 12 Av	# 181	1893
WEINER	Mordechai		#237	1897
WEINOWSKI	Zusmann		#237	1897
WEIS	Zelig		#237	1897
YANKELOWITZ	Yitzchok		#163	1897
YANKELOWITZ	Yitzchok		#145	1897
YODEIKIN	Moshe		#237	1897
YODEIKIN	Zalman		#237	1897
ZALTZBERG	Kalman		#237	1897
	Avraham Abba	son-in-law of Aizik	#237	1897

Laižuva (Laizeve)

Laizeve (in Yiddish) can be found in the northwestern part of Lithuania in the Zemaitija (*Zamut*) region, near the border with Latvia. It is 15 km. northeast of the district administrative center of Mazeikiai, near the Vadakstis River. Laizeve was mentioned in historical sources at the beginning of the seventeenth century. In 1713, it received permission to hold a weekly market day. By 1840, 62 families lived in Laizeve. At that time one could find several shops and taverns in Laizeve. At the second half of the nineteenth century, the Mazheik-Jelgava (Latvia) railway was built nearby, resulting in increased trade with Latvia. In the years 1855 and 1884, the town was heavily damaged by extensive fires.

Until 1795, Laizeve was included in the Polish-Lithuanian Kingdom. The same year, according to the third division of Poland by the three superpowers of those times, Russia, Prussia and Austria, Lithuania was divided between Russia and Prussia. As with most of Lithuania, Laizeve became a part of the Russian empire, first in the Vilna Province (*Gubernia*), and from 1843 in the Shavl district administrative center in the Kovno *Gubernia*. During independent Lithuania (1918-1940) Laizeve was a county administrative center. At the end of World War II the town was destroyed and set on fire by the retreating German army.

In Laizeve it was thought by the elderly people of the community that the first Jews settled in town in the first half of the eighteenth century, and during the first hundred years they buried their dead in the cemeteries of Vekshne and other nearby towns. In the 1860s a Jewish cemetery was established in Laizeve. The original synagogue collapsed and a new wooden Beth Midrash was built, which was used until World War II.

The *Beth Midrash* in Laizeve

The interior of the *Beth Midrash*

The first rabbi to serve the community was Azriel, who was subsequently replaced by Josef Grab and his son Yits'hak, and later by Tsevi Pshedmesky, who died in 1926 following his return from exile in Russia. The rabbis lived for the most part in the *shtibl* beside the Beth Midrash.

Most of the Jewish homes in Laizeve were built on land belonging to a local Jew named Zhager. He sold the land to a Polish estate owner named Zabielsky who forbade the tenants from making any changes without his permission, including important maintenance work. Many Laizeve Jews suffered extensively under his management policy. Jews also endured many hardships during the Polish rebellion in 1831, when the rebels forced the Jews to support them and to be loyal to them. A document of the time contains a loyalty statement addressed to the rebels, signed by Shelomoh Zalkind, Yisrael Volf and Azriel Ben Tsevi, the heads of the community of Laizeve.

Relations between the Jews and the non-Jews in Laizeve and the surrounding villages were satisfactory, and at times better than that. In July 1884 a large fire destroyed almost all the homes in town. Meir Joel Vigoder, a young scholar and son of a highly respected family, appealed to all the Jewish communities for help through the Hebrew newspaper, *HaMelitz*. This appeal was also signed by the local rabbi, Yits'hak Grab and the official (nominated by the authorities) rabbi, Nisan Levin. About a year later the same newspaper carried a report by Vigoder indicating that approximately 300 rubles were received from Jewish individuals and communities. An additional hundred rubles were received from "good and kind Christians," including Baron Nolken and the Lutheran priest, Bobe. The reporter also expressed gratitude to the Christian peasants of Kurland (Latvia) who left their work of plowing the fields to help with the restoration work.

Most Laizeve Jews made their living in the small trades and crafts. At the end of the nineteenth century Jews developed the pig bristle trade: part of the processing was completed in the nearby town of Akmyan (*Akmene*). The processed product was marketed in neighboring Kurland. Several families, including the Shif and Krofman families, succeeded in this business and became wealthy. Some of their children, along with other youngsters from Laizeve, emigrated to South Africa, United States and England, and a few to *Eretz Yisrael*. At that time a *Gemiluth Hesed* fund was established in town.

According to the all-Russian census of 1897, 931 residents lived in Laizeve, including 434 Jews (46%). During World War I, many Jewish families left Laizeve for different reasons. After the war about 35 families did not return to the town.

Following the passage of the Law of Autonomies for Minorities by the new Lithuanian government, the Minister for Jewish Affairs, Dr. Menachem (Max) Soloveitshik, ordered elections to community committees *(Va'adei Kehilah)* to be held in the summer of 1919. In Laizeve a *Va'ad (*community committee) with five members was elected. The committee worked for several years in all areas of Jewish life.

The first government census of 1923 recorded 845 residents in Laizeve, including 127 Jews (15%).

According to the government survey of 1931, the town had three Jewish-owned businesses: a butcher's shop, a textile shop and an iron products and tools shop. In 1937 three Jewish tradesmen worked in Laizeve; a locksmith, a carpenter and a knitter.

During this period of independent Lithuania, emigration from Laizeve to overseas countries continued and the numbers in the community decreased significantly. Public and cultural activities were restricted as well. Only 31 people voted in the elections for the nineteenth Zionist congress in 1935: 15 for the Labor party, 2 for the General Zionists A, 6-for the General Zionists B, 3 for the Grosmanists and 5 for Mizrahi.

At the beginning of the 1930s the Historic-Ethnographic Society of Lithuanian Jews maintained a correspondence with two elderly Laizeve men, Honeh-Mosheh Vald and the *shohet* Zalman-Reuven Rosenberg, on the history of the Laizeve Jewish community.

During Soviet rule (1940-1941) only thirteen Jewish families lived in the town. They were murdered, probably in Mazheik on August 9, 1941 ((*Shabbat,* 16th of *Av,* 5701) where they perished together with the Jews of Mazheik and the nearby towns of Akmyan (Akmene), Vieksniai (Vekshne), Zidikai (Zhidik), Tirksliai (Tirkshle), Pikeliai (Pikeln), Klykouliai (Klikol) and Siad (Seda).

The mass murder site near the Jewish cemetery

The monument at the entrance of the murder site with the inscription in Yiddish and Lithuanian: "At this site Hitler's murderers and their local helpers executed about 4000 Jews and people of other nationalities".

Sources:
Central Zionist archives-files 55/1701, 55/1788, 13/15/131, Z-4/2548
YIVO, New York: Collection of Lithuanian Communities, Files 542-549, 1526, 1666
Gotlib (Hebrew), page 93
Vigoder, Meyer-Joel: Sefer Zikaron, Dublin 1931
Vigoder, Meyer-Joel: My Life, Leeds 1935

Laukuva (Loikeve)

Laukuva (Loikeve in Yiddish) is situated in the Zamut (Zemaitija) region in western Lithuania, about 40 km. north of the district administrative center Tavrig (Taurage). Loikeve originally developed alongside an estate that is mentioned in historical documents from the thirteenth and fourteenth centuries. In 1778 it was granted the right to a weekly market day and two fairs per year.

Until 1795 Loikeve was included in the Polish-Lithuanian Kingdom. According to the third division of Poland in the same year by the three superpowers of those times, Russia, Prussia and Austria, Lithuania was divided between Russia and Prussia. As was the case with most of the other towns of Lithuania, Loikeve became part of the Russian Empire, first within the province (*Gubernia*) of Vilna and from 1843 in the Kovno *Gubernia*. During the period of Independent Lithuania (1918-1940) Loikeve was a county administrative center in the Taurage district.

Jews settled in Loikeve in the eighteenth century. The community grew and developed during Russian rule (1795-1915). According to the Russian census of 1897, the town had 753 residents, 418 being Jews (55%). During World War I Loikeve was occupied by the German army who controlled it from 1915 till 1918, at which time it was handed over to the new Lithuanian state.

After the establishment of Independent Lithuania its economic situation became difficult. The American Red Cross sent clothing to Loikeve for distribution amongst the needy, but the local priest refused to give any to Jews.

Following the passage of the Law of Autonomies for Minorities issued by the new Lithuanian government, the Minister for Jewish Affairs, Dr. Menachem (Max) Soloveitshik, ordered elections to community committees *(Va'adei Kehilah)* to be held in the summer of 1919. In Loikeve a *Va'ad* of seven members was elected, which was active for several years in all aspects of Jewish life.

The first census carried out by the new Lithuanian government in 1923, showed 724 residents in Loikeve, 305 of them being Jewish (42%).

During this period Loikeve Jews made their living mainly from trading. The main road from Kovno to Memel (Klaipeda), which passed through Loikeve, played an important role in the economy of the town. According to the government survey of 1931 there were then seven shops, six of them in Jewish hands (86%). The Jews also owned a wool combing workshop, a bakery, a sawmill and four flourmills. There were only a few Jewish artisans. In the surrounding villages four or five Jewish families earned their livelihood from agriculture.

Over the years the economic situation of Loikeve Jews deteriorated and many emigrated to South Africa, America and *Eretz-Yisrael*. In 1939 there were twenty telephone subscribers in Loikeve, of whom six were Jewish.

Jewish children received their education at a *Talmud Torah* and at the Hebrew school of the *Tarbuth* chain. Many of the graduates continued their studies at the *Yeshivah* or the Hebrew gymnasium in Telz or elsewhere. There was a library with about 500 books in Hebrew and Yiddish.

The number of Loikeve Jews who supported Zionist ideals increased during the 1930s. Their votes for Zionist congresses were as follows:

Cong No.	Year	Total Shek	Total Votes	Labor Party		Rev	Gen Zion		Gros	Miz
				Z"S	Z"Z		A	B		
15	1925	3	---	---	---	---	---	---	---	---
16	1929	17	---	---	---	---	---	---	---	---
18	1933	---	20	11		---	5	---	---	4
19	1935	---	112	40		---	4	2	---	66

Key: Cong No. = Congress Number, Total Shek = Total Shekalim, Rev = Revisionists, Gen Zion = General Zionists, Gros = Grosmanists, Miz = Mizrahi

There were branches of the *Mizrahi* party and of the Zionist youth organizations *Beitar* and *Hehalutz*. The community also maintained welfare societies, including *Gemiluth Hesed, Linath Hatsedek* and a women's society.

Religious life concentrated around the *Beth Midrash*. These rabbis, amongst others, officiated in Loikeve:

Eliyahu-Mosheh Zilbert, 1902-1910

Hayim-Zelig Kaplinsky, from 1911 until his death in the Holocaust in 1941.

In the summer of 1940 Lithuania was annexed to the Soviet Union and became a Soviet Republic. Following new regulations, factories owned by Jews were nationalized, as were some Jewish shops. All Zionist parties and youth organizations were disbanded and the Hebrew school was closed. Supply of goods decreased and, as a result, prices soared. The middle class, mostly Jewish, bore the brunt of this situation and the standard of living dropped gradually. At this time about 300 Jews lived in Loikeve.

On the evening of June 24, 1941, two days after the invasion of the USSR by the German army, German soldiers entered Loikeve. An immediate order was issued that all Jews who had escaped to nearby villages could return home, where they found their houses had been looted by their Lithuanian neighbors. The Jews were ordered to wear a yellow *Magen David* on their garments and were forced to bury Soviet soldiers who had died in battle, to remove dead horses, and to clean German vehicles as well as latrines and rubbish piles. Germans broke into Rabbi Kaplinsky's house and attempted to pluck out the rabbi's beard. The rabbi's daughters intervened and offered them scissors, so the Germans were satisfied with cutting off one edge of the beard.

On Sunday, June 29, 1941, the Germans together with Lithuanian auxiliary police, rounded up all Jewish males aged fifteen years and older. They thrashed them and forced them to assemble in the market place where they were made to hand over everything they had in their pockets. One man, whose pockets were empty, was beaten to death. All this was watched by passing Lithuanians on their day off, who found it entertaining.

Afterwards the men were transferred by trucks to the Mastubarn camp, about twenty kilometers from Heydekrug (now Silute). This camp was a section of the central working camp of Heydekrug. A week later other men who had just arrived in the town or were from nearby villages, were brought to this camp and forced to dig drainage channels. This work lasted from dawn till evening and the workers would receive 300 grams of stale bread and half a liter of watery soup per day. The German Meister treated them brutally. In winter, when drainage work was impossible, the Jews were sent to the nearby Stonishken railway station, where they had to load wagons.

The women and children and one old and poor man remained in the town. Every day new orders were imposed: they had to hand over the Lithuanian flags which they possessed; they were forbidden to leave the town or buy food from peasants; they had to hand over all books and Torah scrolls which the Germans then burned. Germans and Lithuanians would enter the Jewish houses and ask for clothes and money, ostensibly for the men in the camp, at the same time stealing everything they fancied.

On July 8, 1941 the women and children were rushed out of their houses and taken to the *Beth Midrash*. There they were kept for four days without food or water, in subhuman conditions. After that they were transferred by trucks to the Geruliai camp, about ten kilometers from Telz, where thousands of women and children from the surrounding towns had been collected. On Shabbath, August 30, 1941 (7th of Elul, 5701) the elderly women and the children were murdered. According to Soviet sources 1,580 men, women and children were buried in mass graves at this site.

The remaining women and girls were transported to the Telz ghetto and with the liquidation of this ghetto on December 24, 1941 (4th of Teveth 5701) they were murdered in Rainiai village, about six kilometers from Telz. According to Soviet sources 840 men, women and children were buried in this mass grave.

Seven women and one child survived, having been hidden by Lithuanian peasants.

In July 1943 the men of the Heydekrug camp were transferred to Auschwitz. On arrival one hundred of them were sent to the gas chambers. The others were taken to Warsaw two months later in order to evacuate the ruins of the ghetto. Several died in a typhus epidemic, and the remainder were sent to Dachau concentration camp. Only four Lithuanian Jews survived to be liberated by the American army. Josef Aharonovitz, who arrived in Dachau unconscious, was transferred to the sick room by a Kapo, where after two months of devoted care by a Frenchman, he recovered and survived.

The mass grave and the monument near the village of Rainiai

The monument at the mass grave at Rainiai

One of the mass graves at Geruliai

Another mass grave at Geruliai

Sources:
Yad Vashem archives, Jerusalem, M-1/E-1671; M-9/15(6)
Koniukhovsky collection 0-71, files 4, 8, 9, 34, 36, 37
Gotlib, *Ohalei Shem*, page 104
Di Yiddishe Shtime, Kovno, 27.8.1919

Leipalingis (Leipun)

Leipalingis (Leipun in Yiddish) lies in the southwestern part of Lithuania, high on the west bank of the Seira River, about 10 km. northwest of the resort town of Druskeninkai. Leipun was mentioned in historical sources dating from 1503 as a small estate belonging to the Lithuanian princes. A 1516 source mentions the small town that was beginning to be built. Over time the ownership of the estate passed through several noble families. In 1923, as a result of agrarian reform in Lithuania, the lands of the estate were divided among peasants and the main building became a school.

Until 1795 Leipun was included in the Polish-Lithuanian Kingdom. According to the third division of Poland in the same year by the three superpowers of those times, Russia, Prussia and Austria, Lithuania was divided between Russia and Prussia. The part of the country to the west of the Nieman (Nemunas) River, including Leipun, was handed over to Prussia. From 1795 to 1807 the town was under Prussian rule, and from 1807 to 1813 it fell under the auspices of the Great Dukedom of Warsaw. In 1813, after the defeat of Napoleon, all of Lithuania was annexed to Russia, and Leipun was included in the Augustowa province (*Gubernia*) and in subsequent years in the Suwalk *Gubernia*.

In the years of Independent Lithuania (1918-1940) Leipun was a county administrative center in the Sejny district. Until 1923 the residents of Leipun suffered attacks by armed Polish gangs who came from over the border.

Jews settled in Leipun at the first half of the nineteenth century. In 1847 a Jewish settlement was established on land granted by the Russian government. Jews from nearby Meretch (Merkine) settled there too. In time they erected a synagogue that became known for its beauty.

According to the all-Russian census of 1897, 1,314 there were residents in Leipun, 134 of them being Jewish (10%). 25 Jewish families made their living in agriculture.

On April 1, 1915 the retreating Russian army expelled Leipun Jews from their homes and their farms were badly damaged. In 1919 Jewish aid institutions carried out a survey of the Jewish farms in the vicinity: according to the survey half of the cattle and horses were lost and only eighteen families remained of those who had returned to the area. Eight families from Meretch joined the settlement, increasing the number to twenty-six. In 1919 and 1920 the Leipun Jewish community received help from *YeKoPo* that included food, cultural needs and heating fuel.

In 1920 a fire burned down twelve Jewish houses. As a result an all-Jewish volunteer fire brigade was established.

Leipun volunteer fire brigade 1934

According to the first government census of 1923, Leipun's population was 751 residents, 160 of them being Jewish (21%).

Following the passage of the Law of Autonomies for Minorities by the new Lithuanian government, the Minister for Jewish Affairs, Dr. Menachem (Max) Soloveitshik, ordered elections for community committees (*Va'adei Kehilah*) to be held in the summer of 1919. In Leipun a community committee was elected at the beginning of the 1920s. The committee was active until the end of 1925 in all aspects of Jewish life. The survey conducted in 1921 by the *Va'ad HaKehilah* recorded that 38 Jewish families lived there, comprising 119 persons including 33 children aged 7 to 13.

According to a survey carried out by the "Joint" in 1922, ten Jewish shopkeepers, six butchers, four fishermen, three coachmen, two peddlers, two tailors, two shoemakers, two glaziers and one carpenter lived in Leipun. Six families were landowners and five families cultivated rented lands.

The commercial activity of most of the Jews was based on the weekly market that took place on Thursdays and on the four yearly fairs.

The government survey of 1931 showed that in Leipun all shops were Jewish-owned: five groceries, three textile shops, one butcher shop, one tavern and one grain business. The same survey also showed that a wool combing workshop, a bakery, and a flourmill were owned by Jews. The power plant that supplied electricity to the town was also in Jewish hands.

A Jewish family outside a Jewish shop in Leipun

A Jewish coachman

In 1937 there were only seven Jewish artisans in town: three shoemakers, two butchers, one baker and one barber. Among the fourteen telephone subscribers listed in 1939, three were Jewish.

There was no Jewish school in Leipun and the children were sent to study in the nearby towns of Serey (*Seirijai*) and Meretch.

Many Leipun Jews were supporters of the Zionist movement. They purchased *Shekalim* and participated in the elections for the Zionist congresses. The table below shows how Leipun Zionists voted in the four Zionist congresses:

Cong No.	Year	Tot Shek	Total Votes	Labor Party		Rev	Gen Zion		Gros	Miz
				Z"S	Z"Z		A	B		
15	1927	10	---	---	---	---	---	---	---	---
16	1929	20	10	---	6	---	---	---	---	4
18	1933	---	8	5		---	---	---	---	3
19	1935	---	26	9		---	---	---	---	17
21	1939	12	12	3		---	---		N.B.9	

Key: Cong No. = Congress Number, Tot Shek = Total Shekalim, Rev = Revisionists, Gen Zion = General Zionists, Gros = Grosmanists, Miz = Mizrahi, N.B. = National Block

In addition to the cultural and political Zionist activities there was fund raising for the National Funds. For this goal a special committee was elected. Zionist youth organizations included a branch of *Gordonia* with 40 to 50 members and a branch of *Beitar*.

Stamp of the committee of *Keren Kayemeth LeYisrael* in Leipun

With the annexation of Lithuania by the Soviet Union and the change of its status to a Soviet republic in the summer of 1940, nationalization of factories and bigger shops owned mostly by Jews, followed. As a result all Zionist parties and youth organizations were disbanded and Hebrew educational institutions were closed.

On June 22, 1941, the German army invaded Lithuania. Leipun Jews tried to escape to the USSR but did not succeed and returned home. The Lithuanian activists had already taken control of the town and began to mistreat the returning Jews in a variety of ways. On September 9, 1941 (16th of Elul, 5701) 155 men, women and children were brought beside the Christian cemetery of Leipun, near the Seira River, and there they were shot and buried.

On the eve of *Rosh HaShanah* 5702 (September 23, 1941) the remaining Jews were taken by armed Lithuanians to the town Olkenik (*Valkininkai*) in the Vilna region and then they were led together with the Jews from this town and its vicinity to Eishishok (*Eisiskes*). On the way the Lithuanian guards shot two or three Jews every half-kilometer until by the end of the trek 70 Jews had been murdered. In Eishishok the Jews were locked in cowsheds and the abuse and torture came to its climax. All valuables, boots and good overcoats were looted. Women were raped. The abuse continued when the Jews were taken out of the cowshed and brought to the horse market in the town that was encircled by a high plank fence.

During the days until *Shabbath Shuvah* (September 29, 1941) groups of Jews were taken out of the market and murdered near the Catholic cemetery of Eishishok. Among the murdered was the last rabbi of the Leipun community, Aizik Stempner.

The names of the Lithuanian murderers are recorded at Yad Vashem in Jerusalem.

The mass grave beside the Christian cemetery in Leipun

The mass graves in Eishishok

**The monument on the mass graves with its inscription in Hebrew,
Lithuanian and English**

Sources:
Yad Vashem archives, Jerusalem, M-9/15(6); Koniukhovsky collection 0-71,
file 131
YIVO, New York, Collection of Lithuanian Jewish Communities, files 350-
353
The first Jewish district conference of YeKoPo for helping the victims of the
war (Yiddish), Vilna, 1920
Dos Vort, Kovno, 19.6.1939; 21.6.1939
Di Yiddishe Shtime, Kovno, 9.2.1923; 19.6.1939; 20.6.1939; 21.6.1939;
22.6.1939; 3.7.1939; 12.7.1939; 14.7.1939
Folksblat, Kovno, 20.6.1939; 18.7.1939
Dzuku Zinios, Lazdijaï, (Lithuanian) # 56, 25.7.1992

Liudvinavas (Ludvinove)

Liudvinavas (Ludvinove in Yiddish) is situated in the southwestern part of Lithuania, about 9 km. south of the district administrative center of Mariampol (Marijampole), on the banks of the Sesupe River and on the road to Alite (Alytus). It developed from a lodging place for hunters into a town and in 1719 it was granted the Magdeburg Rights for self-rule.

Until 1795 Ludvinove was included in the Polish-Lithuanian Kingdom. According to the third division of Poland in the same year by the three superpowers of those times, Russia, Prussia and Austria, Lithuania was divided between Russia and Prussia. The part of the country that lay to the west of the Nieman (Nemunas) River, including Ludvinove, was handed over to Prussia. From 1795 to 1807 the town was under Prussian rule. Between 1807 and 1813 Ludvinove was controlled by the Great Dukedom of Warsaw. In 1813, after the defeat of Napoleon, all of Lithuania was annexed to Russia, and Ludvinove was included in the Augustowa province (*Gubernia*) and in subsequent years in the Suwalk *Gubernia*. In the years of independent Lithuania (1918-1940) Ludvinove was a county administrative center. In World War I, in the first half of 1915, the town was on the front line between the Russian and the German armies and as a result it was totally destroyed by fire.

There were eight Jews in Ludvinove in 1662, but only after they were granted privileges from King August III on May 21, 1742, did Jews began to settle there. Most of them dealt in commerce and the others in agriculture. Their economic situation was then fair. In 1856, the population was 1,528 including 1,055 Jews (69%).

In 1886 a fire burned down half of the town including the synagogue and the *Beth Midrash* with their entire contents. On *Hol Hamoed Succoth* of 5649 (1888) a big fire destroyed about 300 houses. Wealthy people lost everything and needed aid from neighboring communities. On October 4, 1888 the Hebrew newspaper *HaMelitz* reported on the generous help that the Jewish community of Kalvarija gave to the victims of the fire.

According to the all-Russian census of 1897 the town's population had decreased, in particular the number and percentage of Jews: in that year there were 1,098 residents including 369 Jews (34 %).

Before World War I Rabbi Yehudah-Leib son of Rabbi Menakhem-Mendel Ostrinsky officiated in Ludvinove.

In a list of donors for the settlement of *Eretz Yisrael* the names of two families appear (see **Appendix 1**).

After the war and the establishment of Independent Lithuania in 1918, the number of Jews in the town decreased again. A number of those who escaped to Russia at the beginning of World War I did not return and others emigrated to overseas countries. The first census performed by the new Lithuanian government in 1923 counted 593 residents in Ludvinove, 85 of them being Jewish (14%).

The Jews who remained made their living in trade and farming. According to the government survey of 1931 there were two Jewish merchants in town: one sold meat and the other leather. A branch of The Society for Credit to Jewish Agrarians operated in the town.

In 1939 thirty-five telephone subscribers were in Ludvinove, six of them Jewish.

Next to the town was a farm owned by the Jewish Nun family. In 1940 a *Kibbutz Hakhsharah* for *Hekhalutz* youth who had escaped from Poland was established on this farm. Helped by the "Joint" a group of fourteen *Halutzim*, ten boys and four girls, was settled there. They worked in the vegetable garden that was allocated for them. This *kibbutz* continued during the Lithuanian-Soviet rule, until December 1940.

In June 1940 Lithuania was annexed to the Soviet Union and became a Soviet Republic. At the time there were 650 residents in the town, including about twenty Jewish families. According to Soviet economic policy some Jewish businesses were nationalized and the Jews' standard of living declined.

The Lithuanian Soviet rule ended with the invasion of the German army on June 22, 1941. On the first day of the war German soldiers entered Ludvinove. No details are available about the life of the Jews in the town during the Soviet rule and the few months of Nazi occupation until September 1, 1941 (9th of Elul, 5701). On that date Ludvinove Jews were murdered together with the Jews of Mariampol and the surrounding towns, and buried in mass graves behind the barracks on the bank of the River Sesupe near Mariampol (Marijampole).

A group of survivors at the massacre site on a commemoration in the 1970s

The site of the mass graves near the military barracks and the monument at the site. The inscription in Yiddish and Lithuanian reads: "Here blood was spilled of about 8000 Jewish children, women, men and of 1000 people of different nationalities, that the Nazis and their local helpers cruelly murdered in September 1941."

The monument on the mass graves

Sources:
Gotlib, *Ohalei Shem*, page 105
Bromberg, Kh, *Miklath Zemani BeLita* (A temporary shelter in Lithuania),
testimony, Ghetto Fighters House, Brochure # 5 (1992)
HaMelitz, St.Petersburg, 4.10.1888
Di Yiddishe Shtime, Kovno, 25.4.1938

Appendix 1
Two families from Ludvinove who donated money for the settlement of Eretz Yisrael on the occasion of their weddings as published in *HaMelitz*

(from JewishGen>Databases>Lithuania>Hamelitz - by Jeffrey Maynard).

Surname	Given Name	Comments	Town	Source	Year
LIFSHITZ	Nechemiah husband of Beile Rivka Finkelshtein of Shaki		Ludwinova, Lith.	#192	1893
WINTZBERG	Rochel Leah wife of Yosef Garbarski of Serhai	wed	Ludwinova, Lith.	#142	1898

Luokė (Luknik)

Luoke (Luknik in Yiddish) is in the northwestern part of Lithuania, in the Zamut (*Zemaitija*) region, 21 km. southeast of the district administrative center Telz (*Telsiai*). Luknik is mentioned in documents dating from the sixteenth century as an estate and a village that served as a county administrative center. From the middle of the seventeenth century the markets and the fairs of Luknik were known in the whole Zamut region. Until the middle of the nineteenth century the town belonged to the Bishops of Zamut and later to the noble Oginsky family.

Until 1795 Luknik was included in the Polish-Lithuanian Kingdom. According to the third division of Poland in the same year by the three superpowers of those times, Russia, Prussia and Austria, Lithuania was divided between Russia and Prussia. As was the case with most of Lithuania, Luknik became a part of the Russian Empire, first in the Vilna province (*Gubernia*) and then from 1843 in the Kovno *Gubernia*. From 1915 to 1918 the town was under German occupation. During the period of Independent Lithuania (1918-1940) Luknik was a county administrative center. In 1887 and 1934 fires destroyed almost the entire town.

Jewish settlement till World War II
Jews first settled in Luknik in the seventeenth century. In 1766 there were 556 taxpayers in the town. In the fire of 1887, seventy Jewish houses burned down within a few hours and about 170 Jewish families lost everything. The Jews from the neighboring towns sent carts filled with food and clothing to the victims. However for a long time afterwards many of the victims still depended on aid.

Around this time a wealthy Jewish merchant became known from Irkutsk, Siberia: Hayim Tsevi Golgot had been abducted at the age of fourteen, thirty years before, to serve in the army of Czar Nikolai I. Golgot was taken as a *Kantonist* and had been raised in a Christian family. He located his parents and family in Luknik and from then on sent money to his parents every month. He also donated money for the victims of the fire.

In 1847, there were 949 Jews in Luknik. According to the all-Russian census of 1897, the town's population was 1,626, 798 of them being Jewish (49%).

Before *Pesakh* of 1888 a blood libel rumor was spread in the town. The Jews were saved from a pogrom by miracle. However because of the bad economic situation, the fire and the feeling of insecurity, many Luknik Jews then emigrated to South Africa, America and *Eretz-Yisrael*.

In 1903 the *Dorshei Zion* (Preachers for Zion) society was established in Luknik.

In a list of donors for the settlement of *Eretz-Yisrael* published in the Hebrew newspaper *HaMelitz* during 1893, 1895 and 1903 twenty-nine names of Luknik Jews appear (see **Appendix 1).**

After the war and the establishment of the independent Lithuanian state in 1918 the Jewish community in Luknik shrank, as did its percentage of the total population. The first government census of 1923 counted 1,287 people, 513 of them being Jewish (40%).

Following the imposition of the Law of Autonomies for Minorities issued by the new Lithuanian government, the Minister for Jewish Affairs, Dr. Menachem (Max) Soloveitshik, ordered elections to the community committees *(Va'adei Kehilah)* to be held in the summer of 1919. In Luknik a *Va'ad* of nine members was elected. The committee worked for several years in all fields of Jewish life.

During this period Luknik Jews dealt in trade, crafts and light industry. Jews in nearby villages made their living in agriculture. In 1925 two Jewish doctors and a dentist practiced in the town.

According to the government survey of 1931 all six shops in Luknik were in Jewish hands: one grocery, two textile shops, one sewing machine shop, one pharmacy and one egg business. Other small shops were not included in the survey.

According to the same survey the Jews owned the power plant, a barbershop, a candy factory and a dyeing workshop. In adjacent villages within the county, Luknik Jews owned two flour mills, a spinning mill, a sawmill and a wool combing workshop.

In 1937 ten Jewish craftsmen worked in the town: six tailors, two shoemakers, one hatter and one barber.

The local Jewish People's Bank *(Folksbank)* was the center of economic life in the town. In 1927 it had 91 members.

In 1939 there were twenty-two telephone subscribers in town, seven of them Jewish.

The Jewish children received their elementary education at the Hebrew school that was part of the *Yavneh* chain. The town had a library with Hebrew and Yiddish books.

The Hebrew *Yavneh* school

The Zionist movement was very active in Luknik. The table below shows the distribution of votes for the Zionist congresses:

Cong No.	Year	Total Shek	Total Votes	Labor Party		Rev	Gen Zion		Gros	Miz
				Z"S	Z"Z		A	B		
14	1925	30	---	---	---	---	---	---	---	---
15	1927	13	---	---	---	---	11	---	---	---
16	1929	53	28	---	16	1	9	---	---	2
17	1931	21	16	---	3	3	9	---	---	1
18	1933	---	48	24		8	9	---	---	7
19	1935	---	114	39		---	32	7	11	25
21	1939	28	14	5		---	---		N.B. 9	

Key: Cong No. = Congress Number, Tot Shek = Total Shekalim, Rev = Revisionists, Gen Zion = General Zionists, Gros = Grosmanists, Miz = Mizrahi, NB = National Block

Zionist youth organizations included *Gordonia* with about 30 members, *Beitar,* and *Maccabi* with 32 members.

The religious life centered around the two *Batei-Midrash*; one of these was considered one of the most beautiful in Lithuania.

Among the rabbis who officiated in Luknik were:
Shemuel ben Yosef, who wrote an explanation of the book by the Vilna Gaon on Geometry and Algebra
Shelomoh-Zalman Zaksh (1814-1876)
Shelomoh-Nathan Kotler (1855-1945), was a rabbi in New York, in 1901 returned to Lithuania and officiated in Kurshan and Luknik. After World War I, he returned to America and was a rabbi in Detroit for seven years. Kotler emigrated to *Eretz-Yisrael* and settled in Jerusalem where he published several books on the Talmud. He died in Jerusalem.

Rabbi Shelomoh-Nathan Kotler

Shelomoh Kravitsky, the last rabbi of the community, was murdered in the Holocaust.

In September 1934 a fire that lasted for 24 hours burned down 100 Jewish houses, both *Batei-Midrash* and the Hebrew School, wooden buildings which had dried out from the summer heat. Even with help from fire brigades from the nearby towns the local brigade failed to extinguish the blaze. Only six Jewish houses were left intact. Lithuanian Jewry mobilized aid for the victims of the fire and organized collections of money. Within a year the school and one *Beth Midrash* were rebuilt.

The new Beth Midrash

Most of the Torah study and welfare societies that were common in the Lithuanian Jewish communities also existed in Luknik.

During World War II and afterwards

Following the annexation of Lithuania by the Soviet Union in summer 1940, the Jewish factories and most of the shops in Luknik were nationalized. All Zionist parties and youth organizations were disbanded and the Hebrew school was closed. At that time about 300 Jews remained.

When the German army invaded the Soviet Union on June 22, 1941, Luknik Jews escaped to the villages in the vicinity. About 25 families managed to escape to Russia, following the retreating Red Army. The Germans entered Luknik on the evening of June 25. The next day the Lithuanian nationalists took control of the town. The Jews returned home to find their houses had been entered and looted. Local Lithuanians abused their Jewish neighbors and took them away for forced labor. In particular they tortured the rabbi, Shelomoh Kravitsky. They cut off half his beard and forced him to run, soaking him with buckets with water.

A committee that the Lithuanians established to deal with the Jews, imposed a fine of 50,000 rubles on them. In order to insure that they would pay, the Lithuanians took three hostages, whom they released after the money was paid.

A few days later all the Jews were concentrated in the market square and from there they were led to the Gudiske estate, one kilometer east of the town. They were crowded into a barn and a local, not-very-bright carter was appointed as their guard. Every day Jews were taken out of the barn for different labor, such as burying the Russian soldiers who had died of untreated wounds, sweeping the streets and weeding. Many Lithuanians found it amusing to see their neighbors crawling on the ground and weeding.

Guards found that a family from a near village had a cushion covered with red cloth; the family was accused of intending to create a red flag from the cloth, and as a result they were cruelly beaten.

Jews were forbidden to talk to non-Jews. They could not receive any food or water; a guard was posted near the well to prevent the Jews from drawing water from it. The Jews were forced to take water from the nearby swamp. The Lithuanian auxiliary police threatened the young girls with death, then took them out of the camp at night and raped them.

On July 15, 1941, two S.S men on motorcycles appeared in the camp and ordered the Jews to bring all their belongings to the yard and to hand over their money and valuables. The women and children were returned to the barn and the men were made to stand in a line. The men were forced to run, and at the sound of a whistle blown by an S.S. man they had to fall and then stand up and keep running. Some who was not quick enough were beaten badly. Although wounded they were ordered to run to the barn and lie down there. That same night the strong and healthy men were taken out of the barn, supposedly to work in the peat fields. Instead they were led one kilometer from the barn and shot there. A day or two later the remaining men were murdered in the same place.

On July 17, 1941 the women and children were taken out of the barn and transported on carts to the Viesvenai camp where women and children from Riteve (*Rituva*) and other towns were already gathered. After about a week all the women and children were transferred to a larger camp in Geruliai, about ten kilometers from Telz (*Telsiai*). There many women and children from many other nearby towns were already concentrated. All were murdered at this place together with the women of Telz. Only a few survived, having been hidden by Lithuanian peasants.

According to Soviet sources a mass grave containing the bodies of 120 men was found in the village of Gudiske, one kilometer east of Luknik.

The mass grave in Gudiske

The monument with the inscription in Yiddish and Lithuanian: "In this place the Nazi murderers and their local helpers murdered a group of Luknik Jews in 1941."

The mass grave and the monument near the village of Geruliai

Sources:
Yad Vashem archives, Jerusalem, M-9/15(6); Koniukhovsky collection 0-71, Files 36, 38
YIVO, New York, Collection of Lithuanian Jewish Communities, file 1389
Kamzon Y.D., *Yahaduth Lita*, Tel Aviv, pages 46, 59
Dos Vort, Kovno, 13.9.1934; 16.9.1934; 7.11.1934; 4.2.1935
Di Yiddishe Shtime, Kovno, 1.12.1922
HaMelitz, St. Petersburg, 15.8.1879; 13.7.1880; 20.9.1881; 21.5.1883; 9.8.1887; 22.8.1887; 19.12.1887; 15.3.1888; 10.4.1888; 1.6.1888; 9.6.1889

Appendix 1
List of Luknik donors for the settlement of *Eretz-Yisrael* as published in *Hamelitz*
(from JewishGen>Databases>Lithuania>HaMelitz-by Jeffrey Maynard)

Surname	Given Name	Comments	Source	Year
ASHKENAZI	Chaim Zondil b-i-l of M E Reinwald & Y N Oshri of Birz		#46	1895
FEIWELOWITZ	Shmuel Moshe husband of Chana Tow	wed	#161	1895
GLIKMAN	T		#229	1903
GOLGIT	Z		#229	1903
GOLGOT	Ber Leib		#134	1900
GOLGOT	Chaya Rivka		#196	1893
GOLGOT	Sh		#229	1903
GOLGOT	Y		#229	1903
KAPLAN	Y		#229	1903
KERIL	A		#229	1903
LEWENZON	Ch Sh		#229	1903
LOS	Z	from Vilna	#229	1903
MELAMED			#229	1903
MOLINIK	P		#229	1903

Surname	Given Name	Comments	Source	Year
NAIK	Sh		#229	1903
OLSHWANG	Z		#229	1903
ORIASHOWITZ	Ch		#229	1903
ORIASHOWITZ	Ch B		#120	1893
POREGOWRA	Avraham Yitzchok		#229	1903
PROK	Z		#229	1903
PROS	A		#229	1903
PROS	Tz		#229	1903
REINWALD	M		#229	1903
REINWALD	M A		#120	1893
REINWALD	Moshe Eli b-i-l of h Z Ashkenazi & Y N Oshri of Birz		#46	1895
REINWALD	Y B		#229	1903
RODAK	Zlata fiancee of Avraham Yakov Hacohen of Vilna		#120	1893
TASMAN	Sh		#229	1903
TOW	Chana wife of Shmuel Moshe Feiwelowitz	wed	#161	1895

Miroslavas (Miroslav)

Miroslavas (Miroslav in Yiddish) is located in the southwestern part of Lithuania, about twelve kilometers to the southwest of the district administrative center of Alite (*Alytus*). Miroslav is mentioned in documents dating from the seventeenth century. In 1744 a wooden church was built there and by 1781 the town had its own monastery.

Until 1795 Miroslav was included in the Polish-Lithuanian Kingdom. According to the third division of Poland in the same year by the three superpowers of those times, Russia, Prussia and Austria, Lithuania was divided between Russia and Prussia. The part of the country to the west of the Nieman (*Nemunas*) River, including Miroslav, was handed over to Prussia. Between1795 and 1807 Miroslav was under Prussian rule. In 1800 the population of the town was 220.

From 1807 to 1813 Miroslav was controlled by the Great Dukedom of Warsaw. In 1813, after the defeat of Napoleon, all of Lithuania was annexed to Russia, and Miroslav became part of the Augustowa province (*Gubernia*) and in subsequent years belonged to the Suwalk *Gubernia*. In the years of Independent Lithuania (1918-1940) Miroslav was a county administrative center.

Jews most likely settled in Miroslav at the beginning of the nineteenth century. The synagogue was built in 1896. Among the rabbis who served in town were:

Mosheh Shapira
Shemuel-Aharon Plotkin
Shemuel Hatsor

According to the all-Russian census of 1897, the population of Miroslav was 485, including approximately 60 Jewish families.

Most Miroslav Jews made their living in the small trades and depended on the weekly markets, held on Wednesdays. About ten families worked in agriculture and ten others were engaged in skilled work.

During World War I, in April 1915, the retreating Russian army exiled Miroslav Jews to central Russia.

After the war and the establishment of Independent Lithuania in1918, not all of the exiled Jews returned. Following the passage of the Law of Autonomies for Minorities issued by the new Lithuanian government, the Minister for Jewish Affairs, Dr. Menachem (Max) Soloveitshik, ordered elections to community committees (*Va'adei Kehilah*) to be held in the summer of 1919. In Miroslav a *Va'ad* (community committee) with five members was elected. The committee was active in all fields of Jewish life until the end of 1925.

According to the first government census in 1923, 393 people lived in Miroslav; 124 of these were Jewish (32%).

During the period of Lithuanian rule the number of Jews in Miroslav decreased. Many young people emigrated to *Eretz-Yisrael* to become pioneers in *Emek Heifer* (The Heifer valley). The older people migrated to America.

By 1937 only two Jewish skilled workers remained in the town, a shoemaker and a knitter.

On July 5, 1939 a fire destroyed eight houses and ten other buildings. Most belonged to Jews and were not insured.

Many Miroslav Jews were supporters of the Zionist movement. They purchased *Shekalim* and took part in elections to the Zionist congresses. The results of their votes are given in the table below:

Cong No.	Year	Total Shek	Total Votes	Labor Party		Rev	Gen Zion		Gros	Miz
				Z"S	Z"Z		A	B		
16	1929	2	---	---	---	---	---	---	---	---
17	1931	7	7	---	---	2	4	---	---	1
18	1933	---	24	1		14	4	---	---	1
19	1935	---	15	---		---	---	16	---	2
21	1939	10	10	---		---	3		N.B.7	

Key: Cong No. = Congress Number, Tot Shek = Total Shekalim, Rev = Revisionists, Gen Zion = General Zionists, Gros = Grosmanists, Miz = Mizrahi, N.B. = National Block

The Zionist youth organization *Tseirei Zion* was active in the 1920s.

In the summer of 1940, Lithuania was annexed to the Soviet Union and became a Soviet Republic. Following new regulations, some Jewish shops were nationalized. All Zionist parties and youth organizations were disbanded. Supply of goods decreased, and as a result, prices soared. The middle class, mostly Jewish, bore the brunt, and the standard of living dropped gradually. At that time about 20 Jewish families lived in Miroslav.

The *Tseirei Zion* organization of Miroslav

On June 22, 1941 the German army invaded Lithuania. In a few days most of Lithuania, including Miroslav, was under Nazi occupation. Between August 13 and September 9 the Jews of Miroslav were murdered in the Vidzgiris Forest, most likely together with Jews from Alite and other neighboring towns.

The monument with memorial plaque by the path to the remembrance site

On March 19, 1993 a new metal monument in the shape of a broken *Magen David* was erected in the Vidzgiris Forest (see below). There are nine huge graves, where murdered Jews are buried; each has a circular black cover surmounted by a white pyramid. Near the path that leads to the hill, a memorial plaque now carries the inscription in Yiddish and Lithuanian: **"Here, in this place, the Nazis and their local helpers, in the years 1941-1944, murdered tens of thousands of Jews children, women, men and old people, most of them from other countries. Let their memory live forever."**

The architect of the site was Mrs. R. Vasiliauskiene and the sculptor A. Smilingis.

**A broken Magen-David stands as a monument on the hill
overlooking the remembrance site**

The graves with black circular covers surmounted with white pyramids

Sources:
Yad Vashem Archives, Jerusalem, 0-3/639
Lite, Vol. 1 (Yiddish), pages 1558-155, 1870
Folksblat, Kovno, 7.7.1939

Molėtai (Maliat)

Moletai (Maliat in Yiddish) is located in the eastern part of Lithuania, 28 km. southeast of the district administrative center Utyan (Utena) and 42 km. from the nearest railway station. At the southern edge of the town the Siesartis River flows, where summer vacationers came to relax.

Before 1795 Maliat belonged to the estate owned by the regional Catholic Bishop. Until 1795 Maliat was included in the Polish-Lithuanian Kingdom. According to the third division of Poland in the same year by the three superpowers of those times Russia, Prussia and Austria, Lithuania was divided between Russia and Prussia. As most of Lithuania, Maliat became a part of the Russian empire, first in the Vilna province (*Gubernia*) and from 1843 in the Kovno *Gubernia*.

At that time the estate was handed over to private ownership, and the town began to develop. In the second half of the nineteenth century many merchants settled in, and markets and fairs were organized. From then on, continuing through to the period of independent Lithuania (1918-1940) Maliat was a county administrative center.

Jewish settlement till World War II
Jews began to settle in Maliat in the eighteenth century. In 1765 there were 170 taxpayers. In 1847, 1,006 Jews had already settled in Maliat. According to the 1897 all-Russian census, the population of Maliat numbered 2,397 residents, of whom 1,948 were Jewish (81%). Most made their living in small trade and crafts. Jewish girls knitted socks for small shops in Vilna. Next to most homes, small auxiliary farms were maintained.

General View of Maliat

All the Jewish shops were located along the only street in town, extending one kilometer from the estate to the church.

In 1860 a large fire broke out in Maliat, and 130 houses burned down, including the prayer house with its ten *Torah* scrolls. Another fire in 1888 destroyed almost all the homes in the town. Only 40 of them were insured. After the fire of 1906 destroyed the majority of Maliat homes, the town was rebuilt over several years.

In the 1880s many Maliat Jews emigrated abroad, mostly to South Africa. At the cemetery on the Mount of Olives in Jerusalem at least five tombstones belong to Maliat Jews who emigrated to *Eretz-Yisrael* to live out their last days and be buried there.

In 1910 a Jewish elementary school was established, and there was also a *Talmud Torah*.

At the end of July 1915, in just four hours, Maliat Jews were exiled in sealed wagons to Penza in Russia. The retreating Russian army waged a pogrom against Maliat Jews: units of Cossacks robbed, murdered and raped.

Before World War I, in 1914 about 500 Jewish families (about 2,000 people) lived in the town. During the German occupation (1915-1918) the town's people were made to suffer through forced labor and confiscations instigated by the German army. Many families moved to Vilna at that time.

After the war, only two-thirds of the exiled people returned to Maliat. Helped by relatives from the United States and South Africa and by different institutions, they managed to restore their houses and businesses. In the years 1919-1920 the community received help from *YEKOPO* (The Jewish committee formed to help the victims of the war).

Following the passage of Law of Autonomies for Minorities by the new Lithuanian government, the Minister for Jewish Affairs,, Dr. Menachem (Max) Soloveitshik, ordered elections to community committees *Va'adei Kehilah* to be held in the summer of 1919. In Maliat a community committee of eleven members was elected: three from the ranks of General Zionists, four workers, and four independents. This committee functioned only until about the end of 1925 when the autonomy was annulled by the new Lithuanian government. For several years the committee was active in all aspects of the Maliat Jewish life. According to the first census performed by the government in 1923 there were 1,772 residents in Maliat, of whom 1,343 (76%) were Jewish.

At that time Maliat Jews made their living in trade, peddling, crafts and light industry. Fishing in the surrounding lakes and selling their catch in Utyan, Kovno and other towns, augmented their income. Important factors in the lives of Maliat Jews were the weekly markets and the two annual town fairs.

A Jewish Fisherman

According to the government survey of 1931 the town had 21 shops, 19 of them owned by Jews (90%). Their distribution according to the type of business is given in the table below:

Type of the business	Total	Owned by Jews
Grocery stores	3	3
Grain and flax	2	2
Butcher's shops and cattle trade	1	1
Restaurants and taverns	5	4
Textile products and furs	5	5
Leather and shoes	2	2
Medicine and cosmetics	1	1
Hardware products	1	1
Timber and heating material	1	0

According to the same survey 17 light industries were in town all Jewish owned.

Type of Factory	Owned by Jews
Metal Workshops	1
Textile: Wool, Flax, Knitting	6
Flour mills, Bakeries, Food Production	3
Leather Industry: Production, Cobbling	3
Barber Shops, Bristle Processing, Photographers	4

Cloth

UTENOS APSKR.

Aizin Necha, Malėtai, Vilniaus g.
Azbandas Elija, Labanoras.
Bermanas Bencelis, Utena, Viešoji g. 7.
Binderaitė Pezė, Anykščiai, Baranausko g.
Buividiškienė Šlovė, Malėtai, Vilniaus g.
Burginas Ruvelis, Malėtai.
Capienė Šeinė, Anykščiai.
Eidelmanas Faivis, Tauragnai.
Eidelmanas Ch., Reize Chave ir Kacienė Rocha
    Tauragnai.
Genkinienė Chasė, Vyžuonos.
Groisas Nochimas, Anykščiai, Baranausko g.
Kaganas Abramas, Malėtai.
Kaganas Berelis, Anykščiai.
Kopelovičius Leiba, Utena, Utenio A. 58.
Levinienė Feiga, Malėtai, Vilniaus g.
Levinas Mauša, Utena.
Macas Berelis, Utena.
Macas Todres, Utena, Utenio g. 47.
Portnoje Jankelis, Tauragnai.
Ručienė Agnė, Anykščiai, Baranausko a.
Ruvinas Kabas, Utena, Utenio g. 3.
Sacharas Mauša, Utena, Utenio g. 46.

Excerpt from the original survey where five Jewish cloth shops from Maliat appear

UTENOS APSKR.

Bakienė Genė, Tauragnai.
Bavarskis Alte-Chaja, Malėtai.
Čiobilienė Veronika, Utena, Basanavičiaus
    g. 59.
Savičienė Sara, Tauragnai.
Skopaitė Sara, Malėtai.
Šochas Dveise, Malėtai.

Excerpt from the survey where three Jewish knitting workshops from Maliat appear

In 1937, 80 Jewish trades people worked in Maliat : fourteen knitters, twelve tailors, ten bakers, nine butchers, four shoemakers, four tinsmiths, three carpenters, three leatherworkers, two felt boot makers, two milliners, two blacksmiths, two barbers, two potters, two watchmakers, two needle traders, one glazier, one etcher, one electrician, one book binder, one corset maker, one textile painter and one other.

An important role in the economic life of Maliat Jews was played by the Jewish Popular Bank (*Folksbank*) that had a branch in Alunta, 15 km. away, where 24 Jewish families lived. In 1927, the bank had 318 members, in 1929 the number increased to 322 members.

The Jewish Folksbank in Maliat-Management and Workers
Sitting from left: M.Calpuin, R.Shachar, D.Weinbren, ---, A.Flit, M.Margolis, A.Shapiro
Standing from left: ---, ---, E.Burgin, Z.Joselowitz, ---, H.Weinbren, Pockman
(Courtesy of Naomi Musiker, from the Jewish Board of Deputies archive in Johannesburg, scanned by Barry Mann and Maurice Skikne)

In 1939, the town had 22 telephone subscribers; 7 of them were Jewish.

The closure of the border with Vilna and its region which previously provided significant trade with Maliat, and the open propaganda of the Lithuanian Merchants Association (*Verslas*) urging people not to buy in Jewish shops, caused hardship to the town's Jews. The decision of the local authorities to foreclose 22 Jewish shops on the market square under the pretext that they were too old, aggravated the already pitiful situation. Following the destruction of 14 shops and three private homes in 1931 many Maliat Jews chose to emigrate to America, to Uruguay and in large numbers to South Africa, where an Association of Former Maliaters (*Landsmanshaft*) was active for many years.

The Jewish children of Maliat acquired their elementary education at the Yiddish school (established in 1910) and at the *Heder* (with 30 boys). During independent Lithuania the Yiddish school joined the *Kultur Lige* chain, and a Hebrew school of the *Tarbuth* chain was formed. On average 160 children studied in both schools. The teachers at the schools were A. Helfer, A. Shapiro, M. Pakman, G. Burgin, R. Gordon, A. Sudavsky, A. Shadkhan, Turetz, Zang, Vareis, Shapiro, Rozental, Reznik, Pilevsky, Kosover, Aizen.

In 1924 a Talmud Torah was also opened. Some of the students continued their studies in the Hebrew high schools of Vilkomir (Ukmerge), Utyan and Kovno. Maliat also had a library and a drama circle.

The Hebrew school
(Courtesy of Naomi Musiker, from the Jewish Board of Deputies archive in Johannesburg, scanned by Barry Mann and Maurice Skikne)

Religious life was concentrated at the four prayer houses. Among those who served as rabbis were the following religious authorities: Meir-Shalom HaCohen Guryon who worked in the 1820s and 1830s and died in Jerusalem in 1839; Yisrael-David Heilperin, died in 1883; Ya'akov-Meir Yaka served from 1901; Yits'hak-Aryeh Bilitsky (1887-1933) served in Maliat from 1920; his son, Neta-Hayim Bilitsky, the last rabbi of Maliat, who served from 1933 until 1941 and was murdered together with his community.

In 1891, before the Zionist movement was formed, Shimon Gordon from Maliat emigrated to *Eretz-Yisrael* and was one of the founders of *Haderah*. In 1898 the Hebrew newspaper *HaMelitz* (#173) mentioned two Jewish families, Helper and Shnipilishky, who donated money to the development of *Eretz-Yisrael*.

The Synagogue

In the 1920s and 1930s Zionist activities intensified, and most of the Zionist parties had their followers, as can be seen from the results of voting for the Zionist congresses in these years:

Cong No	Year	Tot Shek	Total Votes	Labor Party		Rev	Gen Zion		Gros	Miz
				Z"S	Z"Z		A	B		
15	1927	20	16	11	2	---	2	---	---	1
16	1929	62	34	27	1	1	4	---	---	1
17	1931	30	27	23	---	---	2	---	---	2
18	1933	---	163	144		11	4	---	1	3
19	1935	---	261	236		---	2	2	---	21

Key: Cong No. = Congress Number, Tot Shek = Total Shekalim, Rev = Revisionists, Gen Zion = General Zionists, Gros = Grosmanists, Miz =Mizrahi

Among the Zionist youth organizations *Gordonia* and *Beitar* had branches in Maliat. Also the Bund had an active membership together with a sport team. Sport activities were also organized by the Maccabi branch with its 30 members.

Shemuel Kagan was born in Maliat. He was the head of a Yeshivah in Slabodka for some time.

During World War II and afterwards

In summer 1940 Lithuania was annexed to the Soviet Union and became a Soviet Republic. Following new rules, the factories, mostly them owned by Jews, were nationalized, as were Jewish shops, and commissars were appointed to manage them. All Zionist parties and youth organizations were disbanded and the Hebrew school was closed. Supply of goods decreased and as a result, prices soared. The middle class, mostly Jewish, bore the brunt of this situation and the standard of living dropped gradually. At that time about 400 Jewish families lived in Maliat.

On June 26, 1941, several days after the German invasion of the Soviet Union, the German army entered Maliat. Prior to the invasion Lithuanian nationalists had taken over the town and arrested the supporters of Soviet rule; in particular they targeted the Jews. A short time later these Jews were murdered.

The first week, following the German invasion, 60 Jewish youngsters were shot and buried in the swamps of Babulka, 500 meters behind the old palace. Other Jews were herded to Utyan where they were murdered together with the local Jews.

On August 26, 1941 the Germans forced the remaining Jews, mainly women and children, to the *Beth Midrash* where they were kept for three days without food and water. On August 29, 1941 (6th of Elul, 5701) they were ordered out of the *Beth Midrash* and led to a place one kilometer out of town, 350 meters to the right of the road leading from Maliat to Vilna. There they were murdered and buried in a mass grave. In the early 1990s a monument was erected on the mass graves carrying an inscription in Yiddish and Lithuanian.

The mass grave and the monument

The inscription on the monument in Yiddish and Lithuanian:
"In this place on 9.8.1941 the Hitlerist murderers and their local helpers
murdered about 700 Jews, men, women and children."

After the war the grave was uncovered and 700 bodies of men, women and
children were found at this site of mass murder.

Several Jews who managed to escape the massacre sought shelter in the
surrounding areas but were caught by the Lithuanian auxiliary police and
murdered. A few survived, thanks to a few Lithuanians who hid them during
the war. Their names are preserved in the Yad Vashem archives.

Sources:
Yad Vashem archives, Jerusalem, M-33/985; Koniukhovsky collection 0-71,
file 95
Central Zionist Archives: 55/1788; 55/1701; 13/15/131; Z-4/2548.
YIVO, New York, Collection of Lithuanian Jewish Communities, files
1529,1667; pages 69585-86
Gotlib, *Ohalei Shem* (Hebrew) page105
Di Yiddishe Shtime (Yiddish), Kovno, 17.1.1922; 30.5.1930; 23.6.1931;
25.10.1933
Der Yiddisher Lebn (Yiddish). Kovno-Telz, 11.7.1924
Der Yiddisher Cooperator (Yiddish), Kovno, # 5(1928); # 11(1929)
Folksblat (Yiddish), Kovno, 7.8.1938; 27.9.1940

Nemakščiai (Nemoksht)

Nemaksciai (Nemoksht in Yiddish) is situated in central Lithuania, on the main Kovno-Memel (*Klaipeda*) road, about 24 km. to the northwest of Rasein (*Raseiniai*), the district administrative center. The town was first mentioned in 1386 in documents of the Prussian Crusader order. By 1590 markets were already established there. From 1785 weekly markets and tri-annual fairs were held in Nemoksht.

Until 1795 Nemoksht was included in the Polish-Lithuanian Kingdom. According to the third division of Poland in that same year by the three superpowers of those times, Russia, Prussia and Austria, Lithuania was divided between Russia and Prussia. As most of the other towns of Lithuania, Nemoksht became part of the Russian Empire, first in the Vilna province (*Gubernia*) and from 1843 within the Kovno *Gubernia*. In the years from 1915 to 1918 during World War I, Nemoksht was occupied by the German army. During the period of Independent Lithuania (1918-1940) Nemoksht was a county administrative center in the Raseiniai district.

Jewish settlement before World War II
Jews first settled in Nemoksht in the seventeenth century. In 1662 twelve Jews (seven men and five women, plus children who were not counted) were known to be living in the town. After King August III granted Nemokshst some privileges in 1742, its Jewish population increased. In 1847, there were 255 Jews. According to the all-Russian census of 1897, 1,180 people lived in Nemoksht, 954 being Jewish (81%). They made their living in trade, small trade and in agriculture.

The religious and social life of the Jews was centered around the *Beth Midrash*. On February 2, 1887 the Hebrew newspaper *HaMelitz* printed a complaint by Yekhezkel Furmansky against his co-residents who did not want to enlarge the *Beth Midrash*, stating that on *Shabatot* and holidays there was insufficient space for all the worshipers.

The welfare societies included *Gemiluth Hesed, Hevrah Kadisha* and *Linath HaTsedek*. Mutual aid was customary among the Jews, in particular the custom of sending food to the poor.

Zionism arrived at the end of the nineteenth century. In the years from 1895 to 1900 *HaMelitz* listed 96 Nemoksht donors for the settlement of *Eretz-Yisrael* (see **Appendix 1**). The fundraisers were: Yosef-Yits'hak Katz, Aba-Eliyahu Abelson and Eliezer-Yits'hak Zaksh.

During World War I the Russian army was not successful in exiling the town's Jews to Russia (as they had done in a great part of Lithuania) because the Germans preceded them and occupied the town. In 1917 a great fire burned down many houses.

In 1918 the Lithuanian state was established. Following the passage of the Law of Autonomies for Minorities by the new Lithuanian government, the Minister for Jewish Affairs, Dr. Menachem (Max) Soloveitshik, ordered elections to community committees *(Va'adei Kehilah)* to be held in the summer of 1919. In Nemoksht a *Va'ad (*community committee) with eleven members was elected. This committee was active in all fields of Jewish life until the end of 1925.

The first government census in 1923 counted 1,018 residents in Nemoksht, 704 them being Jewish (69%). In this period the number of the Jews in the town decreased as a result of emigration abroad and to *Eretz-Yisrael*.

Nemoksht Jews participated in the elections for the first *Seimas* (Parliament) that took place in October 1922. The Jewish votes were divided as follows: 240 for the Zionist list, 73 for the *Akhduth (Agudath Yisrael)* list and 6 for the *Demokrats*.

During this time the Jews made their living in small trade, cattle trade and crafts; there were also three farm owners. Most of the families maintained garden plots beside the houses and some others rented fruit gardens. However the opportunities for export decreased and this affected their living standards.

According to the government survey of 1931 there were fifteen businesses in Nemoksht, fourteen of them in Jewish hands (93%): one flax and grain shop, eight cattle trade businesses, two food shops, three textile shops. According to the same survey Nemoksht Jews owned a sawmill and two flourmills.

In 1937 sixty-four Jewish artisans were employed in the town: thirteen tailors, seven butchers, seven bakers, five shoemakers, two hatters, two glaziers, two barbers, two tinsmiths, one blacksmith, one knitter and four others.

The Jewish Popular Bank (*Folksbank*) played an important role in the economic life in town. In 1927 it had 159 members; by 1929 their number had decreased to 118. In 1939 there were twenty-five telephone subscribers, nine of whom were Jewish.

The Jewish children received their elementary education at the Hebrew *Tarbuth* school. The town had a library with Hebrew and Yiddish books.

The old *Beth Midrash* continued to serve as the main prayer place and the center of social and religious life. A new cultural center was erected with a donation from one of the Hering brothers, a Nemoksht-born philanthropist who had emigrated to America and supported the *Folksbank*. This was probably the only brick building in Nemoksht. It hummed with activity 24 hours a day. In it resided the bank, the *Tarbuth* school, the library, rooms for social and youth activities and a hall for sports and shows.

The rabbis who officiated during the years in Nemoksht were:
Uri-David Afrion (nineteenth century) was conversant in the Torah and many rabbis consulted with him.
Mosheh HaLevi Zaksh
Hayim-Tsevi Broide
Yehudah Ben Zion HaLevi Zaksh, 1905-1932, member of the *Yavneh* center and of the *Mizrahi* party center in Lithuania
Yisrael Krenitz, the last rabbi of Nemoksht, was murdered together with his community in summer of 1941.

Rabbi Uri-David Afrion

Many Nemoksht Jews were Zionists and all parties had supporters. The table below shows the voting for seven Zionist congresses:

Cong No.	Year	Total Shek	Total Votes	Labor Party Z"S	Z"Z	Rev	Gen Zion A	B	Gros	Miz
14	1925	45	---	---	---	---	---	---	---	---
15	1927	20	15	---	6	---	1	---	---	8
16	1929	40	18	8	4	---	---	---	---	6
17	1931	---	25	8	2	7	4	---	---	4
18	1933	---	52	33		---	8	---	---	11
19	1935	---	295	137		---	44	7	3	104
21	1939	---	71	3 8		---	1	---	30	2

Key: Cong No. = Congress Number, Tot Shek = Total Shekalim, Rev = Revisionists, Gen Zion = General Zionists, Gros = Grosmanists, Miz = Mizrahi

The Hebrew *Tarbuth* school, 1929

Zionist youth organizations included *HaShomer HaTsair* and *HeHalutz HaTsair* (from 1933). In 1934 an Urban Training Kibbutz (*Kibbutz Hakhsharah*) from *HeHalutz* movement operated. Under this scheme thirty Nemoksht youngsters emigrated to *Eretz-Yisrael*, included four from the Leizerovitz-Derori family.

Among the personages born in Nemoksht were:

Mosheh Markovitz (1855-1936), shoemaker and historian, published two volumes of the book *Shem Hagedolim HaShelishi* (Vilna 1810) about the rabbis of Lithuania, their lives and works and three books on the history of the Jewish communities in Rasein, Keidan and Novogrudek (published Warsaw 1813).

David-Matithyahu Lipman (1888-1941), pharmacist and historian of Lithuanian Jewry, initiator of the Historical-Ethnographic Society in Lithuania, published books and articles on this subject, murdered in 1941 in Tsaikishok (Cekiske).

William Siegal (Velvel Yits'hak Herzog) (1893-1966), a Yiddish actor and dramatist, lived in America from 1906.

Mosheh Markovitz

During World War II and afterwards

In summer 1940 Lithuania was annexed to the Soviet Union and became a Soviet Republic. Under the new regulations, factories owned by Jews were nationalized, as were some Jewish shops. All Zionist parties and youth organizations were disbanded and the Hebrew school was closed. Supply of goods decreased and as a result prices soared. The middle class, mostly Jewish, bore the brunt of this situation and their standard of living dropped gradually. At that time about 70 Jewish families lived in Nemoksht.

With the declaration of war between Germany and the USSR on June 22, 1941, Nemoksht was bombed and almost all of its homes were destroyed. The next day the Germans occupied the town. A month later all Jewish men aged fifteen years and older were taken for forced labor to the nearby town of Vidokle where they were imprisoned in the home of Ya'akov Fridman together with the local Jews. The Lithuanian guards entertained themselves by abusing and mistreating the Jews. They also forced them to do hard and menial labor and beat and humiliated them. Another torture they imposed was by forcing them to do 'gymnastics.' At the night they would break into the building, wake the Jews and shoot over their heads, to shock and terrify them.

On July 24, 1941 (29th of Tamuz, 5701) all men were taken out to bathe in the nearby lake. When they emerged naked from the lake, they were not permitted to dress, but were led in groups of ten to nearby pits and where they were shot and buried.

It is not exactly known where and when the women and children were murdered. Most likely they were murdered between August 18th and August 22nd. During this period, according to a German source, 1,926 Jews from the Rasein district were murdered.

The mass grave near Nemoksht

A Jewish youngster named Benyamin who returned to his hometown after the war, was murdered by his Lithuanian neighbor.

According to Soviet sources there is a mass grave 1.5 km from Nemoksht in which 543 bodies were found. At the beginning of the 1990s a stone monument was erected with the inscription in Yiddish: "Here the blood of Jews, men, women and children was spilled by the Germans and their helpers."

At the site of the Jewish cemetery a plaque was affixed with the inscription in Yiddish: "Here was the Jewish cemetery."

Sources:
Yad Vashem archives, Jerusalem, M-1/E-1655/1539; M-33/971;
Koniukhovsky collection 0-71, files 42, 52, 53; Testimony of Hanah Levy
(nee Leizerovitz), 0-57, file 50
YIVO, New York, Collection of Lithuanian Jewish Communities, file 1667
Gotlib, *Ohalei Shem*, page 129
Derori (Leizerovitz) Dov, Know from where you came; (Hebrew)
manuscript, Library of Yad Vashem
HaMelitz, St.Petersburg, 15.7.1879; 2.2.1887
Di Yiddishe Shtime, Kovno, 1.10.1920; 25.4.1938; 31.10.1938; 28.12.1938;
26.6.1939; 16.6.1940
Folksblat, Kovno, 2.1.1938; 21.8.1940
Der Yiddisher Kooperator, Kovno, 1927, #2
Dos Vort, Kovno, 17.12.1934

Appendix 1
List of 96 Nemoksht Jews, donors for the settlement of *Eretz-Yisrael* as published in HaMelitz
(from JewishGen>Databases>Lithuania>HaMelitz-by Jeffrey Maynard)

Surname	Given Name	Comments	Source	Year
ALT	Dovid		#121	1900
ALT	Shmuel Shlomo		#121	1900
BEKER	Shmuel		#170	1897
BEKER	Shmuel		#132	1898
BERLOWITZ	Aharon		#121	1900
BERMAN	Leib		#121	1900
BLOCH	Dov Ber		#121	1900
BLUM	Michel		#121	1900
BLUM	Yisroel		#121	1900
BORUCH	Shlomo		#121	1900
BROIER	Shmuel		#170	1897
BROIER	Shmuel		#132	1898
BROIER	Shmuel		#121	1900
COHEN	Yitzchok		#121	1900

Surname	Given Name	Comments	Source	Year
FIN	Ben Tzion		#121	1900
FRIEDMAN	Avraham Eli		#170	1897
FRIEDMAN	Avraham Eli		#121	1900
GEDREITZKI	Chaim Dovid		#121	1900
GEDREITZKI	Nochum		#121	1900
GEIZEROWITZ	Dov Yakov		#170	1897
GROSMAN	Eli		#121	1900
GROSMAN	Rochel Etil wife of Eliahu Bentzion Fin from Trishik	wed	#50	1899
GROSMANN	Eliahu		#132	1898
GROSSMAN	Eli		#170	1897
HALEVI	Eliezer Yitzchok		#132	1898
KATZ	Moshe		#170	1897
KLEIN	Zevulun		#121	1900
LEIBOWITZ	Dov Yakov		#170	1897
LEIBOWITZ	Shlomo		#121	1900
LEIBOWITZ	Tzvi		#121	1900
LEWITAN	Yakov		#170	1897
LEWITAN	Yakov		#132	1898
LIPMAN	Aizik		#170	1897
LIPMAN	Aizik son of the Gaon ABD Plungian		#132	1898
LIPMAN	Yitzchok Aizik		#121	1900
MAGELEWITZ	brothers		#121	1900
MANDEL	Leib Zundil		#121	1900
MEGELEWITZ	brothers		#132	1898
MEHL	Menachem Mendil		#132	1898
MEHL	Zev		#121	1900

Surname	Given Name	Comments	Source	Year
MEHL	Zev Wolf		#132	1898
MEIROWITZ	Eli		#170	1897
MEIROWITZ	Eli		#121	1900
MEIROWITZ	Eliahu		#132	1898
MEIROWITZ	Moshe Leib		#170	1897
MEIROWITZ	Moshe Leib		#132	1898
MEIROWITZ	Yosef Eli		#170	1897
MEIROWITZ	Yosef Eli		#121	1900
MEL	Zev		#170	1897
MIGELWITZ	Alechsander		#170	1897
MIGELWITZ	Pesach		#170	1897
NATKIN	Leib		#170	1897
NAWIAZSHKI	Moshe		#132	1898
OLSHWANGER	Roche daughter of Y R	born 1898	#132	1898
OLSHWANGER	Y R s-i-l of Rabbi Moshe Halevi Zachs		#132	1898
OLSHWANGER	Yakov Dovid		#170	1897
RATNOIUSKI	Moshe		#170	1897
REICHIL	Zev		#170	1897
ROTNOWSKI	Moshe		#121	1900
SHAPIRO	Chaim Tzvi ben haGaon from Kurshan		#170	1897
SHAPIRO	Chaim Tzvi son of the Gaon Shmuel Moshe from Kurshan		#132	1898
SHAPIRO	Chaim Tzvi son of the rabbi		#121	1900
SHMUELOWITZ	Avraham		#121	1900

Surname	Given Name	Comments	Source	Year
SHMUELOWITZ	Leib Yakov		#121	1900
SHMUELOWITZ	Mordechai		#121	1900
SHMUELOWITZ	Moshe		#121	1900
SHTER	Leib		#121	1900
TETZ	Yitzchok		#121	1900
WEINSHTEIN	Sh Sh		#121	1900
WOLF	Yehuda		#121	1900
YAKOBSOHN	Eliezer		#132	1898
YAKOBSON	Eliezer		#121	1900
YUDELOWITZ	Yechezkel		#121	1900
ZACHS	Bas Sheva bas Moshe wife of Yakov Dovid Olshwang of Taurage	wed	#201	1895
ZACHS	Eliezer Yitzchok son of the Gaon ABD Nemaksciai		#132	898
ZACHS	Eliezer Yitzchok son of the rabbi ABD		#121	1900
ZACHS	Moshe Halevi f-i-l of Y R Olshwanger	Rabbi Gaon ABD Av Beth Din	#132	1898
ZACHS	Moshe Halevi father of Bas Sheva	rabbi gaon ABD	#201	1895
ZACHS	Moshe Halevi father of Eliezer	Rabbi Gaon ABD	#170	1897
ZALTZBERG	Avraham Ben Tzion		#121	1900
ZALTZBERG	Avraham Bentzion		#121	1900
ZALTZBERG	Bentzion		#170	1897

Surname	Given Name	Comments	Source	Year
ZALTZBERG	Henich		#121	1900
ZALTZBERG	Kadish		#121	1900
ZALTZBERG	Yosef		# 132	1898
ZALTZBERG	Yosef Yitzchok		#170	1897
ZALTZBERG	Yosef Yitzchok		#121	1900
ZIW	Leib		#170	1897
ZIW	Leib		#121	1900
ZIW	Shlomo		#170	1897
ZIW	Shlomo		#132	1898
ZIW	Shlomo		#121	1900
ZIW	Yona		#170	1897
	Shlomo ben Shmuel		#132	1898

Onuškis (Anishok)

Onuskis (Anishok or Anushishok in Yiddish) lies in the northeastern part of Lithuania, about 5 km. from the Latvian border and about 20 km. northwest of the District Administrative Center Rakishok (Rokiskis).

Anishok is situated on a plain between forested hills which is very scenic. The lands of the town belonged to the Polish *Graf* Komar, to whom the Jews of the town and the farmers of the area paid rent. Wealthier Jews bought land from him on which they built their houses. The mansion of the *Graf* was situated near the town.

The square in the center of town was ringed with shops, and the town's water supply well stood in the middle of the square. From the square a narrow alley led to the winding road to Rakishok. Most houses were built of wood, except for the tavern that was more substantial. This belonged to the *Graf* until he sold it to a Jew named Fain.

Before World War I a tombstone from the mid-eighteenth century was found in the Jewish cemetery, which suggests that Jews had settled in Anishok by that time. In the nineteenth century the Jews were the majority in the town. Before World War I about 80 to 90 Jewish families lived in Anishok, but during the war years their number decreased to about 50 to 60 families.

Most Anishok Jews had shops selling tools, grocery, haberdashery, hats and women's clothing. One Jew had a business in dyeing textiles. Others dealt in timber, horses and cattle. Others grew fruit. There were Jewish craftsmen and peddlers. Most income was earned on Sundays and on the Christian holidays when hundreds of peasants from the district came to church and afterwards did their shopping. Their best customers were the nearby Latvians, because at this time there was no border between Lithuania and Kurland (Latvia).

Before World War I and until the establishment of the Lithuania-Latvia border, the economic situation of the Anishok Jews was fairly good. They all led traditional lives. The *Mithnagdim* and *Hasidim* attended separate prayer houses. There were *Hadarim* for the Jewish boys. Jewish children were sent to study in the Jewish schools of Rakishok, Vilkomir and Kovno, and a few attended the local Lithuanian pro-gymnasium.

At the beginning of the twentieth century the ideals of Zionism and *Haskalah* gained support in Anishok. The Jewish youth embraced the Zionist and revolutionary ideas that were popular at the time.

The names of many Anishok Jews appear in the published lists of donors for the settlement of *Eretz-Yisrael* for the years 1898, 1900 and 1903. The fund raisers were M. Kaplan, R. Kaplan and M. Fain.

In 1902 and 1905 a circle of active revolutionaries was established in Anishok. Hirsh Lekert (1879-1902) was a member of this circle; he attempted to kill the *Gubernator* of Vilna, Fon Wal. The *Gubernator* was only injured and Lekert was caught and hanged. This assault made a great impression all over Russia and in particular among the Jews. Authors wrote about this event and the best known was the drama "Hirsh Lekert" by the Yiddish writer H. Leivik, that was performed for the first time in Vilna in 1931.

Hirsh Lekert

With the outbreak of war in 1914, as the front moved toward Anishok many Jews escaped to Russia. A few returned home in 1922 and 1923, but many remained there. The returning Jews found the town plundered and desolate without any economic prospects. Many of them then chose to settle in the district center Rakishok or in Kovno.

After the establishment of the Lithuanian state in 1918 and following the Law of Autonomies for Minorities issued by the new Lithuanian government, the Minister for Jewish Affairs, Dr. Menachem (Max) Soloveitshik, ordered elections for Community Committees (*Va'adei Kehilah*) to be held in the summer of 1919. In Anishok a community committee with five members was elected in 1920. It received administrative and financial support from the Ministry for Jewish Affairs in Kovno. Letters from the Ministry to the committee were written in three languages: Lithuanian, Yiddish and Hebrew. The committee was active in all aspects of Jewish life from 1920 until 1924.

As stated above, the severing of the connection with markets in Latvia caused economic hardships in the town. The estate owners and the peasants, who lost their clients in Latvia, were forced take their produce to the district center in order to sell it, and they did much of their own shopping there. As a result of this many of the Jewish merchants in Anishok lost their livelihood.

A Jewish house in Anishok (1937)

According to the government survey of 1931 the Jewish businesses included a pharmacy and a general store. In 1937 there were fourteen Jewish artisans: five tailors, four shoemakers, two butchers, two bakers and one other.

In 1939 there were no telephones in the town.

The economic situation became worse from year to year and many, in particular the young, left town to build their future abroad. Also the elderly moved to Rakishok and Kovno or joined their families abroad.

All this led to a decrease in the number of the Jewish families in Anishok. Only about twenty-five families remained in town, mostly elderly who were supported by their children in America and South Africa.

Among the rabbis who officiated in Anishok were:
Yisrael-Iser Klatzkin (1844-1921)
Avraham-Dov Popel (1871-1923) who was among the builders of the Independence of Lithuania, later was Deputy Chairman of the *Nationalrat* (National Committee) of Lithuanian Jews, Chairman of the Association of Rabbis and a delegate to the Lithuanian *Seimas* where his speech against death penalty was printed in many newspapers around the world. Despite being active in the *Agudath Yisrael* party, he supported the funds for the settlement of *Eretz-Yisrael*. He died in Mariampol at the age of 52.

Tsevi-Nathan Kaplan, the last rabbi of the community, was murdered by the Lithuanians in 1941.

Rabbi Avraham-Dov Popel

Anishok Jews purchased *Shekalim* and took part in elections for the Zionist congresses. In 1927, 20 *Shekalim* were sold. In 1937, 55 Zionists voted for the nineteenth Zionist congress as follows: 20 for the Labor party, 24 voted for the General Zionists B, 6 for the General Zionists A and 5 for *Mizrahi*.

Jewish personages born in Anishok include:
    Hirsh Lekert, who is mentioned above;
    Yehoshua Bodzon (1858-1929), writer;
    Beinush Belek, a *melamed (teacher of a Heder)*. One of his sons, Leib Belek became a leader of the British Labor party and his second son Ben Zion was a leader of the leftist movement in Lithuania;
    Yehoshua Bodzon wrote many popular novels in Yiddish that were published in Vilna in the 1890s. He later became an accountant.

In 1940 Lithuania was annexed to the Soviet Union and became a Soviet Republic. Following new regulations some Jewish businesses were nationalized. All Zionist parties and some of the community institutions were disbanded. A number of Zionist activists were exiled to Siberia.

In 1941 the Jews of Anishok were murdered by the Germans and their Lithuanian helpers. The location of the murder site is not known. Nor is it known whether the atrocities took place in the town or if the Jews were transported to be murdered along with the Jews of Rakishok or Obeliai.

According to a Lithuanian source the pharmacist Antanas Truskis hid the Jewish doctor Kovalsky.

Sources:

Yad Vashem archives, Jerusalem, M-31/983; Koniukhovsky collection 0-71, files 88, 90

YIVO, New York, Collection of Lithuanian Jewish Communities, pages 4565, 4571, 4589

Bakaltchuk-Felin, Meilakh (Editor); Yizkor book of Rakishok and surroundings (Yiddish) Johannesburg, 1952, pages 366-369

Julius, Rafael; *Pinkas Hakehiloth-Lita*, Anishok, Yad Vashem, 1996

Folksblat, Kovno, 3.2.1935

Pašvitinys (Pashvitin)

Pasvitinys (Pashvitin in Yiddish) lies in northern Lithuania, about 42 km. northeast of the district administrative center Shavl (Siauliai).

Until 1795 Pashvitin was included in the Polish-Lithuanian Kingdom. According to the third division of Poland in that year by the three superpowers of those times, Russia, Prussia and Austria, Lithuania was divided between Russia and Prussia. As was the case with most other towns of Lithuania, Pashvitin became part of the Russian Empire, first within the province (*Gubernia*) of Vilna and from 1843 in the Kovno *Gubernia*. During this period and also during the period of Independent Lithuania (1918-1940) Pashvitin was a county administrative center in the Siauliai district.

Jewish settlement until after World War I
Jews probably first settled in Pashvitin at the end of the eighteenth century. They made their living in the small trades, peddling and crafts. In nearby villages Jews dealt in agricultural products. Among the Jewish craftsmen in the town were six shoemakers, six tailors, a number of glaziers and painters, a carpenter and a watchmaker. In addition there were carters, two or three *melamdim*, a teacher and a paramedic.

The weekly markets and the four fairs each year were important sources of income. Many of the town's Jews relied heavily on money sent by a former *Pashvitiner* from South Africa.

At the beginning of the 1860s a *Beth Midrash* was built in the town. In 1862 land was purchased for a cemetery, and a bath house was built. Previously the dead were buried at the Jewish cemetery of Yanishok (Joniskis).

According to the all-Russian census of 1897, there were 763 people in Pashvitin, 435 of them Jewish (57%).

Twenty-four Pashvitin Jews are named in the list of donors for the victims of the great famine in Persia in 1871-72.

The rabbis who officiated in Pashvitin included:
Mordehai Hilman (1868-1953), served in Pashvitin from 1841 to 1879, later was Rabbi in Glasgow and London, in 1934 emigrated to *Eretz-Yisrael* and became Head of the *Yeshivah Ohel Torah* in Jerusalem that had been established by his son-in-law, the Chief Rabbi of *Eretz-Yisrael* Yits'hak Halevi Herzog. Hilman published several books on the *Talmud* and the Rambam and died in Jerusalem.

Elhanan Cohen (1874-1941), served in Pashvitin 1898-1914, from 1926 was Rabbi in Dvinsk (Daugavpils), was murdered in Dvinsk in the Holocaust.

Rabbi Mordehai Hilman

In 1896 a *Heder Metukan* which taught Hebrew and the Bible was established in the town. This school was attended mainly by children from wealthier families. In 1899 a *Heder HaKolel* (Common *Heder*) in which the children of the affluent and the poor studied together was established in Pashvitin. This *Heder* was the first in its kind and served as an example for many *Hadarim* that were established in Zhager, Shavl and in other towns.

In June 1900 a blood libel developed into a pogrom against the Jews in Pashvitin that spread to neighboring towns. The windows of all the Jewish houses and the *Beth Midrash* were smashed and a few Jews were wounded. Until that time relations between the Jews and their Christian neighbors had generally been fair.

Pashvitin Jews were sympathetic to the ideals of *Hibath Zion*. As the first Zionist Congress approached a *Bonei Zion* (Builders of Zion) society was established in the town. Its members participated in all its activities and fund raising. Names of Pashvitin Jews appear in the list of donors for the settlement of *Eretz-Yisrael* from 1898. The fund raiser was Mosheh Plan.

On May 4, 1915, during World War I, the Russian military exiled Pashvitin Jews into the interior of Russia.

During Independent Lithuania (1918-1940)
After the war and the establishment of the Lithuanian state in 1918, only about half the exiled Jews of Pashvitin returned home. The returnees rebuilt their homes and organized the community. Following the Law of Autonomies for Minorities issued by the new Lithuanian government, the Minister for Jewish Affairs, Dr. Menachem (Max) Soloveitshik, ordered elections to community committees *(Va'adei Kehilah)* to be held in the summer of 1919. In Pashvitin a *Va'ad (*community committee) of seven

members was elected: three General Zionists, two from Tseirei Zion and two independents. The committee was active in all fields of Jewish life from 1921 until the end of 1925.

The first government census of 1923 counted 818 residents in Pashvitin, 274 being Jewish (33%).

During this period Pashvitin Jews made their living mainly in the small trades. According to the government survey of 1931 all nine shops in the town were Jewish-owned: one haberdashery, one iron products and tools, one textile, one butcher shop, one grocery, and three grain businesses and one other.

In 1937 only six Jewish artisans remained in Pashvitin: two tailors, two butchers, one baker and one blacksmith. The flourmill that for many years was in Jewish hands passed over to Lithuanians. A number of Pashvitin Jews relied upon aid from their relatives abroad. In 1925 the town had a Jewish dentist, Ogenia Rozenberg.

In 1939 two out of fifteen telephone subscribers in the town were Jewish.

Beginning in the mid-1930s, the Jewish community decreased gradually. The economic crisis in Lithuania and the open propaganda by the Association of the Lithuanian Merchants *Verslas* that called for the boycott of Jewish shops, caused many Jews to look elsewhere for their future. Many emigrated to South Africa, America and *Eretz-Yisrael*.

During this period the Jewish children received their elementary education at the government school in Pashvitin.

The Jewish cemetery in Pashvitin
(Courtesy of Naomi Musiker, from the Jewish Board of Deputies archive in Johannesburg, scanned by Barry Mann and Maurice Skikne)

The Blekher family
Rear: Hayah Golda and her husband Yisrael Pinhas Blekher
Front: Ethel, Hanah, Hirsh holding Yosef, Yits'hak, Matityahu.
(Courtesy of Naomi Musiker, from the Jewish Board of Deputies archive in Johannesburg, scanned by Barry Mann and Maurice Skikne)

Many Pashvitin Jews were Zionists and most of the Zionist parties had supporters in the town. The result of voting in the Zionist Congresses by Pashvitin Zionists is shown below:

Cong No.	Year	Tot Shek	Total Votes	Labor Party Z"S	Z"Z	Rev	Gen Zion A	B	Gros	Miz
15	1927	13	12	---	---	---	12	---	---	---
16	1929	25	12	---	2	---	10	---	---	---
17	1931	10	10	1	2	2	5	---	---	---
18	1933	---	27	9		15	3	---	---	---
19	1935	---	30	16		---	---	13	1	---
21	1939	24	24	2		---	---		N.B. 22	

Key: Cong No. = Congress Number, Tot Shek = Total Shekalim, Rev = Revisionists, Gen Zion = General Zionists, Gros = Grosmanists, Miz = Mizrahi, N.B. = National Block

The Zionist youth organization *HaShomer HaTsair* had a branch in the town.

The Yiddish poet and writer Leizer Leibovitz (1906-1972), whose work was published in the Jewish press in South Africa and from 1966 in Israel, was born in Pashvitin.

During World War II
With the annexation of Lithuania to the Soviet Union in the summer of 1940, some Jewish shops were nationalized. The Zionist parties and youth organizations were disbanded. At this time about twenty Jewish families remained in the town.

The war between Germany and the Soviet Union began on June 22, 1941. A few days later German soldiers entered Pashvitin. Lithuanian activists took control of the town and immediately began to mistreat the Jews.

A drunken German officer with two Lithuanians took hold of a Jewish girl. When her grandfather remonstrated with them he was shot.

The mass grave at the Narishkin Park
(Picture taken and supplied courtesy of Elkan Gamzu, July 2005)

A short time later the Jews were ordered to leave their homes. They were imprisoned in the old barn near the Stone Mill on the road to Zeimelis. From there they were taken out every day for farm work. One day they were loaded onto carts and driven to Zhager. It is believed that they were murdered together with Zhager Jews on the day after Yom Kippur 5702 (October 2, 1941). The names of the Lithuanian murderers are recorded in the archives of Yad Vashem in Jerusalem.

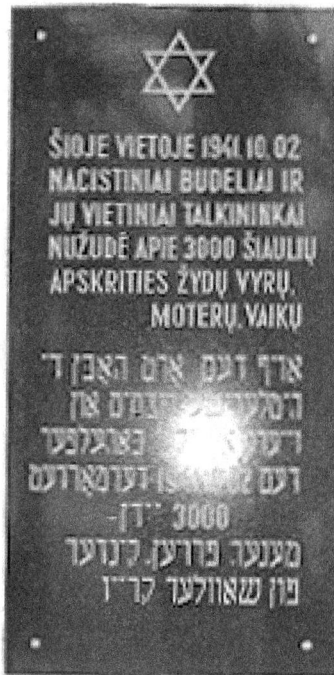

The inscription in Lithuanian and Yiddish on the monument: "At this site Hitler's murderers and their local helpers murdered about 3000 Jewish men, women, children from Shavl district on the 2nd of October 1941."

Sources:
YIVO, New York, Collection of Lithuanian Jewish Communities, files 837, 838, 1534
Nates A.: Days of Yesterday (Hebrew), Tel Aviv, 1981

Pikeliai (Pikeln)

Pikeln (in Yiddish) is situated in the northwestern part of Lithuania, in the *Zemaitija* region, 1 km. from the Latvian border. Pikeln was named after the nearby Pikelhof estate. Beside the town the Lusis River flows, and forested hills encircle it.

In the second half of the seventeenth century Pikeln became a town. In 1769 it received permission to maintain one weekly market and four yearly fairs. In particular the town developed at the second half of the nineteenth century. There were then in town about thirty shops, four workshops for processing leather, two liquor factories, and other workshops. Until World War I the town was an important center of trade with agricultural products. During the Russian rule (1795-1915) Pikeln was included in the Vilna province (*Gubernia*) and from 1843 in the Kovno *Gubernia* and Telzh district. During Lithuanian rule it was included in the Mazheik administrative center.

The first Jews probably settled in Pikeln at the end of the eighteenth century. Over time, two prayer houses and other community institutions were erected. A yeshiva operated in the town, directed by Rabbi Ze'ev-Volf Avrekh and later by Rabbi Hayim Nathanzon. Over the next hundred years, the number of Jews in town increased to more than a thousand and became two thirds of the total population. According to the all-Russian census of 1897, 1,758 residents lived in Pikeln, including 1,206 Jews (68%).

In the decades before World War I the number of the Jews in Pikeln decreased as a result of a strengthened emigration abroad, so that by 1914 only about 150 families remained in town.

In a list of donors for the victims of the great Persian famine in 1871-72 the names of 130 Pikeln Jews are given, as published in the Hebrew newspaper *HaMagid* (see **Appendix 1**).

The Zionist movement became popular in these years, and in the regional conference of the Lithuanian Zionists that took place in 1900 in Vilna, a delegate from Pikeln, Z. Zaks, participated. Twelve Pikeln Jews donated money in 1898 for the Settlement of Eretz Yisrael as published in the Hebrew newspaper *HaMelitz* (see **Appendix 2**).

Among the rabbis who officiated in Pikeln were Mosheh-Shimon Vizitz; Benyamin Rabinovitz (1812-1870) 1832-1842; Avraham Harif (?-1877); Ya'akov Vilentchik (?-1888).

Personages born in Pikeln included writer and translator Dr. Aba-Yits'hak Krim (1893-?), who lived in America from 1906; the brothers Robert and Albert Shif, known philanthropists from New York; Rabbi Marcus Shif from Cincinnati; Rabbi Eliyahu-David Rabinovitz-Teomim (1842-1905), in 1901 emigrated to Eretz Yisrael and was elected as the rabbi of Jerusalem.

He published many books on Judaism. The chief rabbi of Eretz Yisrael Avraham-Yits'hak Kook was his son in law.

Rabbi Eliyahu-David Rabinovitz-Teomim

At the beginning of World War I, by order of the Russian army, the Pikeln Jews were exiled deep into Russia. During the years 1915-1918 the town was under the German military rule.
The marking of the border between Lithuania and Latvia cut Pikeln Jewish traders off from the markets of Latvia and seriously reduced their livelihood. As a result they dealt now with small trade, peddling and crafts. Most of them maintained auxiliary farms next to their houses.

According to the government survey of 1931, three Jewish businesses operated in town: one grocery, one textile shop and one pharmacy. There were also two big flour merchants and two horse merchants in Pikeln. The Jews owned a bakery, a leather processing factory, a workshop for producing soap, two flour mills, one sawmill and two taverns.

In 1937 Pikeln had seven Jewish artisans: two bakers, two butchers, one glazier, one tailor and one shoemaker.

The Jewish Popular Bank (Folksbank), directed by Mosheh Nathanzon, played an important role in the economic life of Pikeln Jews. In 1927 it had 97 members. Other public institutions in Pikeln were *Bikur Holim, Gemiluth Hesed* fund, a library and a *Heder* where just seven boys studied before World War II.

The Leibovitz family with two German soldiers (1916):
First line from left: soldier, small boy, Hanah, Sonya
Second line: Hirsh, Ya'akov, soldier
(Courtesy of Naomi Musiker, from the Jewish Board of Deputies archive in Johannesburg, scanned by Barry Mann and Maurice Skikne)

During this period the rabbis who officiated in Pikeln were:
> Josef Ben Zion Fridman (1858-1920)
> Hayim Zalman Kron who in 1925 was the counselor for Jewish affairs in the Lithuanian Ministry of the Interior
> Yisrael Farber, the last rabbi, murdered by the Lithuanians in 1941.

Despite the falling Jewish population in Pikeln, the public and political activities continued. By 1940 about twenty Jewish families lived in town.

The table below shows how Pikeln Zionists voted for five Zionist congresses:

Cong No.	Year	Tot Shek	Total Votes	Labor Party Z"S	Z"Z	Rev	Gen Zion A	B	Gros	Miz
16	1929	13	6	---	---	---	3	----	----	3
17	1931	---	12	---	---	7	5	----	----	---
18	1933	----	45	10		32	2	---	1	---
19	1935	---	36	35		--	1	---	---	---
21	1939	10	10	7		---	2		N.B.	
									1	

Key: Cong No. = Congress Number, Tot Shek = Total Shekalim, Rev = Revisionists, Gen Zion = General Zionists, Gros = Grosmanists, Miz = Mizrahi, NB = National Block

In 1940 Lithuania was annexed to the Soviet Union and became a Soviet Republic. During the year of Soviet rule (1940-1941), Zionist activity was disbanded, as in all Lithuania, and there were great changes in their economic circumstances.

After the German army invaded the Soviet Union on 22 June, 1941 and Soviet rule ceased in Pikeln, Lithuanian nationalists took control of the town. During July 1941, Pikeln Jews suffered greatly from the abuse and oppression by their Lithuanian neighbors. On 5 August they were transferred to the Latz barns near Mazheik (Mazeikiai). The men were put to work digging pits, while the women and children were imprisoned in the barns together with the women from Mazheik and the surroundings, and kept there for four days under terrible conditions.

On August 9, 1941 (*Shabbat,* 16th of *Av*, 5701) all were taken to the same pits where a few days earlier the men were murdered, and there they too were killed in the most vile and cruel manner. Women were forced to undress. The children were thrown into a long ditch and many of them were buried under heaps of soil and lime while still alive. In the same place, together with the Mazheik Jews, Jews from the nearby towns of Akmyan (Akmene), Vekshne (Vieksniai), Zhidik (Zidikai), Tirkshle (Tirksliai), Pikeln (Pikeliai), Klikol (Klykouliai) and Siad (Seda) perished.

Sources:

Yahaduth Lita (Hebrew), Vol.1-4, Tel Aviv

Central Zionist Archives, Jerusalem, Files Z-4/2548, 13/15/131, 55/1788, 55/1701

JIVO, New York, Collection of Lithuanian Jewish Communities, Files 869-875

Gotlib, Ohalei Shem (Hebrew), page 155

Hamelitz (Hebrew), St.Petersburg, No. 120 (1893), No 29 (1894)

The mass murder site near the Jewish cemetery

The monument at the entrance of the murder site with the inscription in Yiddish and Lithuanian: "At this site Hitler's murderers and their local helpers executed about 4000 Jews and people of other nationalities".

Appendix 1
List of 130 Pikeln Jewish donors for the victims of the great Persian famine in 1871/72 as published in *HaMagid* #16, 1872
(From JewishGen>Databases>Lithuania>Hamagid, by Jeffrey Maynard)

Surname	Given Name	Comments
AKMOIANER	Leib	
BEITLER	Michel	
BROIDA	Shraga Feiwish	
BROIDA	Yakov Yitzchok	
BUCHMAN	Meir	
CHAYAT	Avraham Yitzchok	
CHAYAT	Dovid Yitzchok	
CHAYAT	Mendel	
CHAYAT	Yitzchok	
DALTAR	Shmuel	
FELSER	Shraga	
GARBER	Yitzchok	boy
GEITON	Yitzchok	
GERBER	Dovid	
HELMANN	Shmuel	
HENER	Shmuel	
HENES	Yitzchok	
HODES	Aharon	father of Meir & daughter Sheina
HODES	Avraham Segal	
HODES	Eliezer Yitzchok	
KATZ	Isser	
KATZ	Leib	
KATZ	Meir	

Surname	Given Name	Comments
KATZ	Moshe	
KATZ	Shneur	
KATZ	Uri	boy
KATZ	Yehuda ben Moshe	
KATZ	Yosef Eliezer	boy
LONG	Shlomo	
LONG	Yakov	
MAMARER	Yosef	
MASHOD	Simcha	woman
MELTZER	Chaim	
MILNER	Aharon	
NAMAKSES	Meir	
NEIAWADIL	Boruch Netanel	s-i-l of the rabbi
OHRMAKER	Dov	nephew of Falk ben Moshe Yom Tov
PARNFELD	Leizer ben Tzvi	
PARNFELD	Tzvi	father of Leizer
PIWANDENER	Dovid	
PLUNGIAN	Yechezkel	
RABIN	Eliahu	
REIN	Chaim	
REIN	Michel	
REIN	Yechezkel ben Michel	
SALANT	Kalman	
SALANT	Shraga	
SEGAL	Avraham	
SEGAL	Chaim Tzvi	boy
SEGAL	Kasil	bridegroom

Surname	Given Name	Comments
SEGAL	Moshe	
SEGAL	Moshe	brother of Shmuel Raphel
SEGAL	Shmuel Raphel	brother of Moshe
SEGAL	Tzvi ben Chaim	
SEGAL	Uri	boy
SEGAL	Yechezkel	
SHEMESH	Mendil	
SHTROL	Meir	
SHU"B	Eliahu	
TELZER		
WEKSNER	Avraham	
YELAK	Yakov	
ZELAK	Chai'	woman
ZOLOMON	Meir	
	Abba ben Yitzchok	
	Aharon Leib	
	Avraham	Rabbi Gaon ABD
	Avraham ben Aharon	
	Avraham ben Kadosh	
	Avraham Binyomin	
	Binyomin ben Eliahu	
	Boruch Zalman	
	Chaim ben Noson	
	Chaim ben Yoel	
	Ches ben Aharon	
	Dov ben Eliahu	

Surname	Given Name	Comments
	Dov ben Menachem	
	Dovid ben Yisroel	
	Dovid Yosef	boy
	Dvorah	woman
	Eizik ben Shmuel	
	Elchanan	
	Eliahu ben Yehuda	
	Eliezer Tzvi	
	Falk ben Moshe Yom Tov	uncle of Dov Ohrmaker
	Fruma	woman
	Leib ben Shlomo	
	Libe	woman
	Meir Aharon	
	Meir ben Nachum	
	Mordechai	s-i-l of Zev
	Mordechai ben Yehuda	
	Mordechai Leib	
	Moshe ben Yakov	
	Moshe ben Yehuda	
	Moshe ben Yitzchok	
	Moshe Meir	
	Moshe Meir	boy
	Moshe Yitzchok	
	Nachum	boy
	Nachum ben Aharon	
	Shalom ben Noson	
	Shalom Dov	

Surname	Given Name	Comments
	Shaul ben Yehuda	
	Sheima son of the Rabbi	
	Shlomo ben Yitzchok	
	Shmaya ben Shraga	boy
	Shmuel Eizik	
	Shmuel Moshe	
	Sima	woman
	Tzvi ben Elchanan	
	Tzvi ben Mordechai	
	Tzvi Dov	from Deselen
	Yakov ben Nachum	
	Yakov ben Shmuel	
	Yakov ben Yechezkel	
	Yakov ben Yechezkel	
	Yakov Menachem	
	Yekutiel ben Yitzchok	
	Yissachar Moshe	
	Yitzchok	boy
	Yitzchok ben Abba	
	Yitzchok ben Binyomin	boy
	Yitzchok ben Mordechai	
	Yitzchok Leib	
	Yosef ben Eliahu	
	Yoscf bcn Shraga	
	Zalkind	grandfather of Eidil son of his daughter
	Zev	boy
	Zev ben Moshe	boy

Appendix 2
List of Pikeln donors for the Settlement of Eretz Yisrael as published in *HaMelitz*
(From JewishGen.Org>Databases>Lithuania>Hamelitz, by Jeffrey Maynard)

Surname	Given Name	Comments	Town	Source: Hamelitz	Year
DONCHIN	B		Pikeliai	#107	1898
FRIDBERG		Doctor	Pikeliai	#107	1898
HARS	Fani fiancee of Avraham Segal of Shavel		Pikeliai	#201	1900
KOHN	Ch Y		Pikeliai	#107	1898
KWEIT	Dovid son of Rabbi Gaon Sh. Helman Kweit		Pikeliai	# 120	1893
NUROK	B		Pikeliai	#107	1898
NUROK	Z		Pikeliai	#107	1898
SHLEZ	L		Pikeliai	#107	1898
YELOWITZ	K		Pikeliai	#107	1898
ZAKS	N	husband of Devorah Sergei of Krotingen	Pikeliai	#156	1895
ZAKSH	Selig	at Chan Purim dinner in Vilna	Pikeliai	#77	1901
ZAKSH	Z	on occasion of Weisbord-Glemba wedding	Pikeliai	#185	1895

Plateliai (Plotel)

Plateliai (Plotel in Yiddish) lies along the western shore of Lake Plateliai in the Zamut (Zemaitija) region in Western Lithuania, about 50 km. northeast of the district administrative center Kretinga, and is one of the oldest settlements in Zamut. In 1572 it was granted the Magdeburg Rights for self rule and about two hundred years later permission was given to organize fairs twice a year. For many generations the noble Oginsky family ruled in this region.

Until 1795 Plotel was included in the Polish-Lithuanian Kingdom. According to the third division of Poland in the same year by the three superpowers of those times, Russia, Prussia and Austria, Lithuania was divided between Russia and Prussia. As most of Lithuania, Plotel became a part of the Russian Empire, first in the Vilna province (*Gubernia*), and from 1843 in the Kovno *Gubernia* where it became a county administrative center. This status remained during independent Lithuania, within the district administrative center of Kretinga.

The first Jews probably settled in Plotel at the end of the eighteenth century. They made their living in small trade, peddling and fishing in the nearby lake. The main community center was the *Beth Midrash*. Before World War I fifteen Plotel Jews belonged to the *Agudath Yisrael* party.

From the 1890s many Plotel Jews emigrated to America and South Africa.

Plotel in 1920

According to the all-Russian census of 1897, there were then 171 Jews (28%) in Plotel, out of a total population of 611.

During World War I, in the summer of 1915, Plotel Jews were exiled deep into Russia by the Russian army.

Rabbis who officiated in Plotel till World War I included Shelomoh Shkolnik, who served there for about fifty years from 1870, and Mosheh-Ze'ev HaCohen, who was elected Rabbi in 1911.

During the period of Independent Lithuania (1918-1940) the economic situation of Plotel's Jews deteriorated. In 1923 a fire burned down almost half of the town's houses, and as a result their economic situation worsened. In order to survive the town's Jews were helped by relatives from abroad and also by working the auxiliary farms, which they cultivated beside their houses.

A Jewish Family in the Thirties

According to the first census conducted by the new Lithuanian government in 1923, Plotel had 645 residents, 150 of them Jews (23%).

The government survey of 1931 showed two drapery shops, two flour mills, one iron products and tools shop and one grocery, all Jewish owned.

During this period Jewish emigration overseas continued and their numbers in the town decreased.

Most of Plotel's Jews were members of the Zionist movement. During the tenth anniversary festivities for Independent Lithuania in 1928, local Jews waved the blue and white flag with the *Magen David* in its center together with the national Lithuanian flag. In the elections for the nineteenth Zionist congress in 1935, a total of 41 Plotel Jews voted – 39 for the *Mizrahi* party and 2 for the General Zionists B.

A group of Plotel Jews

In the summer of 1940 Lithuania was annexed by the Soviet Union and became a Soviet Republic. Following new rules, Jewish mills were nationalized, as were Jewish shops. All Zionist parties and youth organizations were disbanded. At this time about 120 Jews (18 families) lived in the town, its rabbi being Nahum-Lipman Hananya.

War broke out between Germany and the USSR on June 22, 1941. A few days later the Germans entered Plotel. Lithuanian nationalists cooperated with the invaders, participating with the Germans in arresting about thirty Jewish men, who were murdered after several days and buried in sand pits at the foot of Mount Bokstakalnis, about half a kilometer from Plotel, along the road to Salant.

The women and children and the elderly, altogether numbering about 90, were left alone in the town for several weeks, but were murdered later in a grove near the village of Laumlenkai, south-east from the lake, about 3 km. from Plotel.

The mass grave and monument near Plateliai with an inscription in
Yiddish and Lithuanian: "Here the blood of 30 Jews - children, women
and men - was spilled by Nazi murderers and their helpers, who cruelly
murdered them. "

A wooden sculpture beside the mass grave

The monument on the mass grave near Laumlenkai with an inscription
in Yiddish and Lithuanian: "Here the blood of 90 Jews - children,
women and men - was spilled by Nazi murderers and their helpers, who
cruelly murdered them."

Sources:
Gotlib, *Ohalei Shem* (Hebrew), pages 155,368
Kamzon,*Yahaduth Lita* (Hebrew), pages137, 141
Masines Zudynes Lietuvoje, Vol. 2 (Lithuanian), page 397

Pumpėnai (Pumpyan)

Pumpenai (Pumpyan in Yiddish) lies in the northeastern part of Lithuania, about 24 km. north of the district administrative center Ponevezh (Panevezys). The town was mentioned for the first time in historical documents from 1556. Until the eighteenth century Pumpyan was included in the principality of Birzh that had five towns and thirty four estates. The Pumpyan estate was one of the largest owned by the noble Radzivil (Radvila) family. During the entire period of their rule Pumpyan Jews enjoyed good economic conditions and security.

Until 1795 Pumpyan was included in the Polish-Lithuanian Kingdom. According to the third division of Poland in the same year by the three superpowers of those times, Russia, Prussia and Austria, Lithuania was divided between Russia and Prussia. As most of Lithuania, Pumpyan became a part of the Russian Empire, first in the Vilna province (*Gubernia*) and from 1843 in the Kovno *Gubernia*. During the years 1915-1918 the town was under German occupation. During the period of independent Lithuania (1918-1940) Pumpyan was a county administrative center.

Jewish settlement until World War I and afterwards
Pumpyan was one of the oldest Jewish communities in Lithuania. Jews settled there in the middle of the seventeenth century. During the period of *Va'ad Medinath Lita* (1623-1764) Pumpyan was included in the Birzh district (*Galil*). In a list of Karaite taxpayers from 1704-05, residents of Pumpyan, who suffered from oppression and persecution, were mentioned. In the middle of the eighteenth century the Karaites moved elsewhere and Rabbinic Jews settled in their place. In 1766 there were 583 Jewish taxpayers in the town.

At the beginning of the nineteenth century a blood libel was directed at the Pumpyan Jews when they were accused of murdering a Christian boy for the *Pesakh*. A local Jew, Yisrael Pumpyansky, took the blame and so saved the lives of many other Jews who had been detained as suspects. The Christians burned Yisrael alive and he was buried at the yard of the synagogue. His grave was enclosed by a fence and a headstone was erected, and from that time Pumpyan Jews lived in the shadow of this blood libel.

In 1861 a fire destroyed most of the town's houses and the synagogue. Seven Jews died in the fire.

In 1881 the community acquired land near the old cemetery and fenced it. They bought building materials and erected a new synagogue on this site. They also renovated the bath house. These works were accomplished with the financial help of one wealthy man, Ben Zion Segal.

At this time the Hebrew newspaper *HaMelitz* reported that those responsible had overlooked the importance of having a *Talmud Torah,* and hadn't paid the salary of twenty rubles per year to the only teacher. Because of this the pupils of the *Talmud Torah* were not advanced enough in Bible studies and in Russian writing. It was also reported that a third *Shokhet* was appointed, who received unfair preference over the other two from the community funds.

By the end of the nineteenth century the Jews were in the majority in the town. According to the all-Russian census of 1897, the population was 1,480, of whom 1,017 were Jewish (69%). These included learned and intellectual men and also several wealthy and philanthropic people who cared for the needs of the community. Most Jews made their living in small trade, crafts, peddling and agriculture (auxiliary farms). Because of the hard economic conditions, many young people emigrated, mostly to South Africa.

In 1915, about six months after the outbreak of World War I, The Russian military authorities exiled all Pumpyan Jews to the central parts of Russia.

During independent Lithuania (1918-1940)
After the war and the establishment of the independent Lithuanian state in 1918, the exiled Pumpyan Jews returned to their town and found their property plundered and their homes burnt down. Many emigrated to America and South Africa. The Jewish community in Pumpyan became smaller and its percentage of the total population fell. According to the first government census of 1923, there were 1,137 people were in the town, 372 of them being Jewish (33%).

The Hebrew *Tarbuth* School 1929

Following the Law of Autonomies for Minorities issued by the new Lithuanian government, the Minister for Jewish Affairs, Dr. Menachem (Max) Soloveitshik, ordered elections to community committees *(Va'adei Kehilah)* to be held in the summer of 1919. In Pumpyan, with its 225 Jews, the elections took place in 1919. The right to vote was granted to citizens eighteen years and older. In Pumpyan 151 were eligible and 141 of them voted. A *Va'ad* (community committee) with seven members was elected: four from *Tseirei Zion*, two orthodox and one non-party man. The committee worked for several years in all fields of Jewish life.

The Jewish children received their elementary education at the Hebrew school of the *Tarbuth* chain. The *Tarbuth* association also organized evening courses. In 1922 just fifteen people participated in these courses.

Many Pumpyan Jews belonged to the Zionist camp. Most of the youth had hopes of emigrating to *Eretz-Yisrael* and some joined the *Kibutsei Hakhsharah* (training *Kibutsim*).

All Zionist parties had supporters in town and votes for the Zionist congresses were as shown:

Cong No.	Year	Total Shek	Total Votes	Labor Party Z"S	Z"Z	Rev	Gen Zion A	B	Gros	Miz
15	1927	14	14	3	6	---	4	----	---	1
16	1929	32	10	1	3	---	3	----	---	1
17	1931	10	10	---	6	1	2	----	---	1
18	1933	---	28	23		---	5	----	---	---
19	1935	---	83	38		---	14	24	1	6

Key: **Cong No. = Congress Number, Tot Shek = Total Shekalim, Rev = Revisionists, Gen Zion = General Zionists, Gros = Grosmanists, Miz = Mizrahi,**

In April 1933 there was a protest meeting against the persecution of the Jews in Germany, headed by Yehezkel Shtironi. The speakers at this meeting were Rabbi M. Y. Hayat, the *Gabai* Y. L. Zukh, the agronomist Y. Rasein and the teacher Sh. Glitsman.

In 1937 fourteen Jewish craftsmen worked in town: three shoemakers, three butchers, two bakers, a tailor, a hatter, a blacksmith, a barber, a cloth dyer and a watchmaker.

The Pumpyan-born poet B. Byalostotsky described the town thus: "There were deep swamps, particularly in autumn. The market place was shaped like a hand with five fingers that pointed in different directions; one finger pointed to the small town of Pushalot in which only a few dozen Jewish families lived; the second finger, in the direction to the town Posvol, that was seen by the Jews as an aristocratic and exclusive place; the third led to the town Vabolnik about which rumors were spreading that robbers and murderers were controlling it, which made Pumpyan Jews afraid to use this road; the fourth finger led to the big town of Ponevezh that was the ideal of every Pumpyan Jew; the fifth road was the shortest route to the *Beth Midrash* and the small *Shtibl* next door in which the *Hasidim* went to pray. Between the *Hasidim* and the *Mithnagdim* friendly and peaceful relations existed".

Pumpyan served as a center for study of Torah and was fortunate to appoint learned and well-known rabbis including:

Yits'hak ben Eliezer in the eighteenth century

Ya'akov from Shventsian

Yekhiel, whose headstone and that of his wife stood at the cemetery of Pumpyan

Mosheh Eliyahu

Shaul Shapiro (1797-1859)

Yehonathan Eliashberg (1850-1899), from 1875 in Pumpyan, one of the first rabbis of his generation to publish articles in newspapers; he was a fervent *Hovev Zion* and published a book of this subject along with other books on Judaism.

Aryeh Lipkin (1840-1902), in Pumpyan 1870-1878, published many books that were printed in Vilna, Jerusalem and elsewhere.

Hayim HaLevi Katz (1854-1932) in Pumpyan from 1889, was an excellent orator, preached for Zionism, published many books on Judaism.

Rabbi Hayim HaLevi Katz   **Rabbi Yohonathan Eliashberg**

During the period of independent Lithuania relations between the Jews and the Lithuanians in Pumpyan were generally good.

During World War II and afterwards
In summer of 1940 Lithuania was annexed to the Soviet Union and became a Soviet Republic. Following new regulations, the livelihood of many Jews was lost, including that of the rabbi. Some were even obliged to work for their living on the *Shabath*. All Zionist activity was forbidden and the Hebrew School was closed. At this time about 300 Jews (60 families) remained in Pumpyan.

On June 22, 1941 the German army invaded the Soviet Union. Five days later, on June 27, the Germans entered Pumpyan. Within a few days the Lithuanian activists together with the police, headed by the local Council chairman, began to take the Jews out for forced labor. They were mistreated and abused and robbed. On July 15, 1941, all Jews were forced to leave their houses and were crowded into a so-called ghetto surrounded by a barbed wire fence. The ghetto contained six Jewish houses, belonging to Shalom-Yits'hak Sandler, Mosheh Moierer, Mendl Kovalsky, Avraham Lurie, Moshe Kemer and Rabbi Hayat.

There they were kept in starvation and squalor until August 26. The Lithuanians accused the rabbi of swallowing golden coins and they tortured him to death in front of his wife and his three small children. On the same day, August 26, 1941 (3rd of Elul 5701) Pumpyan Jews were led to the Pajuoste forest, about 5 km. from Ponevezh, and there beside the long pits all were shot to death. The bodies were covered with earth despite some of the victims still being alive.

Several families were taken to Posvol (Pasvalys) and from there to Zadeikiai where they were murdered together with the Jews from the region.

The mass grave in the Zadeikiai forest

The monument and the tablet on it with the inscription in Yiddish and Lithuanian: "In this place the Hitlerist murderers and their local helpers on 26.8.1941 murdered 1350 Jews, men, women, children."

A group of survivors near the monument on the mass grave in Zadeikiai where the Jews from Posvol, Vabolnik, Salat, Pumpyan, Jonishkel and other places were murdered.

In the 1990s the plaque on the monument was replaced.

The last Jews of Pumpyan, the pharmacist Leib Lapolsky and his family were murdered in the town a few weeks later. All the murderers were Lithuanians from the surrounding area. Their names are recorded in the archives of Yad Vashem. In the early 1990s a new plaque was erected at the Jewish cemetery with the inscription in Yiddish and Lithuanian, "May they rest in their graves".

Sources:
YIVO, New York, Collection of Lithuanian Jewish Communities, file 839
Bardakh Y. (Hebrew); The Jews in the Birze princedom of the Radzivil family in the seventeenth and eighteenth centuries, Gilad #12 (1991), pages 23-44
Gotlib, *Ohalei Shem*, page149
Nehamah Borukhson-Kaufman, Pumpyan. *Pinkas HaKehiloth-Lita*, Yad Vashem, Jerusalem 1996
Di Yiddishe Shtime, Kovno, 31.8.1919; 15.3.1932; 25.3.1932;
HaMelitz, St.Petersburg (Hebrew), 8.3.1881; 7.11.1882
Folksblat, Kovno, 24.4.1933

Appendix 1:

A list of Pumpyan Jewish donors for the settlement of *Eretz-Yisrael* as published in *HaMelitz*
(from JewishGen>Databases>Lithuania>*HaMelitz* by Jeffrey Maynard)

Surname	Given Name	Comments	Source	Year
FRIDMAN	Yechezkel b-i-l of Rabbi Yehonason Eliasberg		#209	1893
LEWINZOHN	father of Nachman in Lodz		#4	1895
LEWINZON	Yehoshua Chaim		#132	1900
	Yosef ben Rabbi ABD Chaim		#132	1900
HALEVY	Chaim father of Shmaryahu	rabbi	#232	1902
HALEVY	Shmaryahu ben Chaim husband of Rivka	wed	#232	1902

Ramygala (Remigole)

Ramygala (Remigole in Yiddish) lies on the Ponevezh-Keidan (Panvezys-Kedainiai) road 25 km. south of the district administrative center Ponevezh. Remigole is mentioned in historical documents as early as the thirteenth century. In 1525 Remigole County was mentioned for the first time. In 1580 the town was granted the right to conduct three fairs per year as well as its large markets.

Until 1795 Remigole was included in the Polish-Lithuanian Kingdom. According to the third division of Poland in the same year by the three superpowers of those times, Russia, Prussia and Austria, Lithuania was divided between Russia and Prussia. As most of Lithuania, Remigole became a part of the Russian Empire, first in the Vilna province (*Gubernia*) and then from 1843 in the Kovno *Gubernia*. During the period of independent Lithuania (1918-1940) Remigole was a county administrative center in Ponevezh district.

Jews probably began to settle in Remigole at the end of the sixteenth century, according to gravestones at the old Jewish cemetery. In 1766, 225 Jewish taxpayers were living there. Their number increased by the second half of the nineteenth century. According to the all-Russian census of 1897 the population was 1,329 residents, 650 being Jewish (49%). It is known that in 1859 a synagogue already existed in the town.

In 1883 fire destroyed 35 Jewish homes. Sixty families became homeless and destitute and appealed for help from the Jewish communities in Lithuania.

In lists of donors for the settlement of *Eretz-Yisrael* published in the Hebrew newspaper *HaMelitz* during the years 1899 and 1900 the names of 91 Remigole Jews appear (see **Appendix 1).**

In Remigole the bibliographer Yits'hak ben Ya'akov (1801-1863) was born, whose main work was the book *Otsar HaSefarim* (Treasure of the Books). This was a detailed bibliography of 17,000 Hebrew books and manuscripts published up to 1863.

In May 1915, during World War I, the Russian military exiled Remigole Jews to the central regions of Russia. After the war only two-thirds of those exiled returned home.

In 1918 Lithuania became an independent state and following the Law of Autonomies for Minorities issued by the new Lithuanian government, the Minister for Jewish Affairs, Dr. Menachem (Max) Soloveitshik, ordered elections to community committees *Va'adei Kehilah* to be held in the summer of 1919. In Remigole a community committee of seven members was elected. This committee was active in all aspects of the Jewish life in the town from 1920 until the end of 1925 when the autonomy was annulled by the Lithuanian government.

A street in Remigole
Photograph courtesy of Joe Woolf, Ilania, Israel (1992)

Remigole Jews made their living in the small trades, peddling, crafts and agriculture. In 1929 there were thirty small shops owners, twenty-five orchard and farm tenants, twenty craftsmen and eight peddlers.

According to the government survey of 1931 four textile shops belonged to Jews; two flour mills in the area also belonged to Jews.

In 1937 eleven Jewish artisans worked in Remigole: three shoemakers, three butchers, two bakers, two blacksmiths and one tailor.

In summer of 1929 a fire destroyed 62 Jewish buildings. These included 27 dwellings, barns, stables and so on, as well as the *Linath HaTsedek* building, the library and the reading room, the *Beth Midrash* and the *Talmud Torah*. Only eleven houses were insured. All others victims of the fire required aid. This came in from the "Joint" organization and its subsidiary company "Foundation," local donations and government assistance with low-cost timber, which made it possible for uninsured house owners to rebuild their homes.

In the mid-1930s the Jewish population fell. The economic crisis in Lithuania and open propaganda of the Lithuanian merchants Association (*Verslas*) urging people not to buy in Jewish shops caused many to move elsewhere.

In 1939 there were ten telephone subscribers, of whom only one was Jewish.

At the beginning of the 1920s a Yiddish school was established in Remigole, but it was closed after a short time. Later the Jewish children studied at the Hebrew *Tarbuth* school. To replace the 600-book library that burned down in 1929, a new library was established in town; after a long dispute this was taken over in 1931 by the *Yiddishist Folkspartei*.

In January 1933 the community inaugurated the new *Beth Midrash* that was built where the original one had been burnt down. Now the town had two *Batei Midrash* and both held classes in *Talmud* and *Mishnah* every day, in the mornings and in the evenings. Remigole had quite a number of learned and intellectual men who also spoke Hebrew.

The tablet on the wall of the *Beth Midrash* with the inscription in Yiddish and Lithuanian: "Here stood the Beth Midrash. Now a community center."

Photograph courtesy of Joe Woolf, Ilania, Israel (1992)

The rabbis who officiated in Remigole included:
Shemuel-Mosheh Shapira (1843-1908), in Remigole from 1869
Joel Haitovsky, from 1892
Zisl Shteinfeld, the last rabbi, murdered together with his community in the Holocaust.

Many of the Remigole Jews were Zionists and supporters of most of the Zionist parties. The youth belonged to the *Tseirei Zion* organization. In the table below are given the results of the elections for three Zionist congresses:

Cong No.	Year	Tot Shek	Total Votes	Labor Party Z"S Z"Z	Rev	Gen Zion A B	Gros	Miz
18	1933	----	18	13	---	3	---	---	2
19	1935	---	68	46	---	1	2	---	19
21	1939	10	6	3	---	1		N.B.2	

Key: Cong No. = Congress Number, Tot Shek = Total Shekalim, Rev = Revisionists, Gen Zion = General Zionists, Gros = Grosmanists, Miz = Mizrahi, N.B. = National Block

In summer of 1940 Lithuania was annexed to the Soviet Union and became a Soviet Republic. Under the new regulations, the Jewish flour mills and some of the shops were nationalized. All Zionist parties and youth organizations were disbanded and the Hebrew school was closed. Supply of goods decreased and as a result, prices soared. The middle class, mostly Jewish, bore the brunt of this situation and the standard of living dropped gradually. At that time about 350 Jews lived in Remigole. The Soviet rule lasted for one year until June 22, 1941 when the German army invaded Lithuania.

Even before German soldiers were seen in Remigole, Lithuanian nationalists organized themselves and began to abuse the Jews.   One Jews was immediately shot and another who resisted was buried alive with his feet protruding from the ground. Rabbi Zisl Shteinfeld was tied to a cart harnessed to a horse and was dragged through the streets until he died. When the Germans entered the town the Lithuanians began to snatch Jewish girls. The Germans and the Lithuanians abused the girls, cutting their bodies with knives, while the Jews were forced to attend and watch the horror. After two months of this torture the Jews were ordered to assemble in the *Beth Midrash* in order to be transferred to Ponevezh where they were told they would live and work. The old and ill were left in the *Beth Midrash* which was set on fire and burnt down with the people inside it.

On August 24 and 25, 1941 (1st and 2nd of Elul 5701) the remaining Jews were led by foot in the direction to Ponevezh and were murdered in the Pajuoste Forest, about 8 km. east of Ponevezh. The names of the Lithuanian murderers are recorded in the archives of Yad Vashem.

The monument in the Pajuoste forest with the inscription in Lithuanian: "In this place the Hitlerists and their helpers in August 1941 murdered about 8000 Jewish children, women and men."

In 1992 a monument was erected with an inscription in Yiddish and Lithuanian in the place where the Jewish cemetery once was.

One of the few intact tombstones at the cemetery:
"Our dear mother, the modest and great Rabanith Shasha daughter
of Pinhas who died on the 5th of Iyar 5685 (1925)"

Sources:
Yad Vashem archives, Jerusalem, M-9/15(6)
YIVO, New York, Collection of Lithuanian Jewish Communities, Files
1130-1148, 1349, 1546
Gotlib, *Ohalei Shem*, page 378
Di Yiddishe Shtime, Kovno, 19.4.1922; 23.7.1929; 29.7.1929; 31.7.1929;
14.1.1931; 8.5.1931; 1.7.1931; 9.1.1933
Der Yiddishe Kooperator, Kovno, #10, 12, 1929
HaMelitz, St. Petersburg, 9.11.1883; 25.3.1889
Folksblat, Kovno, 2.10.1935

Appendix 1
List of 91 Remigole donors for the settlement of *Eretz-Yisrael* as published in *HaMelitz*
(from JewishGen>Databases>Lithuania>*HaMelitz* by Jeffrey Maynard)

Surname	Given Name	Comments	Source	Year
BERKLEIN	Cheikel		#56	1900
BERKLEIN	Cheikil		#121	1899
BERKLEIN	Shmuel		#121	1899
BERKOWITZ	Aba Shlomo		#56	1900
BERKOWITZ	Gronm		#121	1899
BERKOWITZ	Nachum		#121	1899
BERKOWITZ	Nochum Yona		#56	1900
BERKOWITZ	Yakov		#56	1900
BERMAN	Yakov Dov		#121	1899
BINYAMINOWITZ	Shlomo		#56	1900
CHATOFSKI	Chaim Leib		#121	1900
CHATOFSKI	Yoel	rabbi gaon ABD	#121	1900
CHOTOFSKI	Yoel	Rabbi Gaon ABD	#56	1899
COHEN	Avraham Aba		#56	1899
COHEN	Michel Mordechai		#56	1899
DAVIDOWITZ	Shaul		#56	1899
DAVIDOWITZ	Shimon		#56	1899
DAWIDOWITZ	Shaul		#121	1900
DAWIDOWITZ	Shimon		#121	1900
ELIASH	Menachem Mendel		#121	1900
ELIASHEWITZ	Avraham Aba		#121	1900
ELIASHEWITZ	Zusman		#121	1900
ELIASHOWITZ	Avraham Aba		#56	1899

Surname	Given Name	Comments	Source	Year
ELIASHOWITZ	Chaya Henia		#56	1899
ELIASHOWITZ	Sarah		#56	1899
ELIASHOWITZ	Zusman		#56	1899
FISHER	Eliezer Yehuda		#121	1900
FROM	Kalman		#121	1900
FROM	Pinchos		#121	1900
GANTZER	Yakov		#121	1900
GATMAN	Yosef		#121	1900
GOLFE	Chaim	rabbi	#121	1900
GOTTLER	Moshe		#56	1899
GRIN	Avraham		#121	1900
HEILPERN	Chaim	Rabbi	#56	1899
KATZ	Alte		#56	1899
KATZ	Eli		#56	1899
KATZ	Eli		#121	1900
KATZ	Nachman Tzvi		#121	1900
KATZ	Yitzchok		#56	1899
KAGAN	Alte		#121	1900
KOTLER	Moshe		#121	1900
KOTLER	Noson Note		#121	1900
KRAWITZ	Binyomin Aba		#121	1900
KRAWITZ	Dovid Benyomin		#56	1899
KRAWITZ	Kopil		#56	1899
KRIGER	Moshe		#56	1899
KRUK	Freida		#56	1899
KRUK	Freida		#121	1900
KRUK	Shmuel		#121	1900

Surname	Given Name	Comments	Source	Year
KRUK	Yehuda Zondil		#56	1899
KRUK	Yehuda Zundel		#121	1900
LEIBOWITZ	Elchanan		#56	1899
LEINT	Yitzchok Dov		#121	1900
LEWEMSHTEIN	Mordechai		#56	1899
LEWENSHTEIN	Sarah Dobra		#121	1900
LEWINSHTAM	Yitzchok		#56	1899
LEWINSHTEIN	Yakov		#56	1899
LEWINSHTEIN	Yakov		#121	1900
LEWINSHTEIN	Yitzchok		#121	1900
LIBERMAN	Tzvi		#56	1899
LICHTENSHTEIN	Leib		#121	1900
LICHTENSHTEIN	Nechemiah		#121	1900
LIEBERMAN	Yehuda		#56	1899
MAWSHOWITZ	Moshe		#121	1900
MEHLNER	Yehuda		#56	1899
MILER	Yitzchok Dov		#121	1900
NAWISHERTZ	Reuven	from Boiski	#121	1900
NAWISHERZ	Reuven		#56	1899
PDOM	Kalman		#56	1899
PIKSHER	Dov Ber		#56	1899
PIKSHER	Moshe Yitzchok		#56	1899
PROM	Nechemiah		#56	1899
PROM	Shraga Feiwil		#56	1899
PROM	Yocheved		#56	1899
RAMIGOLSKI	Leib		#56	1899
RONEN	Yitzchok Aizik		#56	1899

Surname	Given Name	Comments	Source	Year
SEGAL	Reizel		#121	1900
SHKLAR	Aharon		#121	1900
SHKLIAR	Aharon		#56	1899
SHMILG	Mordechai		#56	1899
SHMIT	Shlomo		#56	1899
SHMIT	Shlomo		#121	1900
SHTEIN	Hinda Leah		#121	1900
SHTOKER	Lipman		#56	1899
SHTOKINA	Lipman		#121	1900
WOLFOWITZ	Mordechai		#56	1899
WOLFOWITZ	Pesach		#56	1899
YAFE	Chaim		#121	1900
YAFE	Yehuda Leib		#121	1900
YANKELOWITZ	Meir		#56	1899

Raseiniai (Rasein)

Rasein (in Yiddish) lies in the center of Lithuania, near the main road between Kaunas and Klaipeda (Memel), about 73 km. northwest of Kovno. Rasein is one of the oldest towns in Lithuania, being mentioned in historical documents dating from 1253.

One of the first Catholic churches was built there in 1421. At the end of the fifteenth century Rasein was granted the Magdeburg rights, which gave it the status of a town, and during the sixteenth century it was the most important town in Zamut (Zemaitija). In 1580 the nobility of the region assembled in Rasein to elect its delegates to the Warsaw *Seim,* and in 1585 it became the permanent site of the regional *Seim,* the *Seimik.*

Until 1795, Rasein was a part of the Polish-Lithuanian Kingdom. That same year, when Poland was divided up for the third time by the three superpowers of those times (Russia, Prussia and Austria), Lithuania was split between Russia and Prussia. Like most of Lithuania, Rasein became a part of the Russian Empire, first in the Vilna province (*Gubernia*) and from 1843 as a district administrative center in the Kovno *Gubernia.*

In 1812 Napoleon's army passed through the town, and almost totally destroyed it. During the Polish rebellion of 1831 the town suffered badly. In 1848 and again in 1893 cholera epidemics raged in Rasein, causing hundreds of deaths.

Vilna Street in Rasein

Ships sailing on the Dubysa (about 8 km. from the town) and the Neman (Nemunas) rivers were able to establish contact with Kovno by 1912. During the period of independent Lithuania (1918-1940), Rasein remained a district administrative center, but because of its distance from the railway line (about

17 km.) and the lack of a paved road (which was not constructed until 1939), it suffered economically and its population decreased.

Jewish settlement until after World War I

Jews settled in Rasein in the seventeenth century, and in 1662 there were at least 111 Jews (50 men, 61 women), excluding children. Rasein's Jewish community was one of the first in Lithuania and was known as *Yerushalayim D'Zamut*. During the period of the autonomy of Lithuanian Jews, *Va'ad Medinath Lita* (1623-1764), Rasein was included in the Keidan *Galil* (District).

A Street in Rasein

In the middle of the nineteenth century, Jews constituted the majority of Rasein's population. In 1857, out of a total of 8,516 residents, about 5,000 (about 59%) were Jews.

In 1876, Rasein's population was 10,889, including 8,481 Jews (78%). Trade was almost exclusively in Jewish hands, and there were also many Jewish artisans: 45 tailors, 30 shoemakers and six watchmakers. However, due to the many restrictions that the Czarist rulers imposed upon the Jews, their economic situation deteriorated, and as a result many emigrated, mainly to South Africa.

The Russian census of 1897 showed 7,455 residents in Rasein, 3,484 of them being Jews (47%).

In 1865, and again in 1883, fires caused great damage. On the eve of *Pesakh* 1886, fire broke out and more then 200 Jewish families were left roofless and destitute. Help was received from former Rasein citizens in South Africa. In 1888, 50 Jewish houses burned down. Muraviov, the *Gubernator* (head of the *Gubernia*) transfered 800 rubles from the government to help victims of the fire.

During World War I, Rasein Jews stayed in town and traded with the German occupation army. At this time many wholesale businesses opened, supplying goods all over Lithuania.

Religious life centered around the many prayer houses: the Great Synagogue, the *Beth Midrash* and the *Kloizim - Hayei Adam,* Blakhes, of Dr. Shemuel Gavrilovitz, of Hosid, of the hatters and of the pedlars.

The alley of the synagogue

Among the rabbis who officiated in Rasein during this period, many were well known for their scholarship and public service: Avraham Lisker who lived in the middle of the seventeenth century; Mosheh Tseitlin (1812-1857), served in Rasein 1848-1856; Avraham-Shemuel Rabinovitz (1809-1869), published many books and was known as a community worker; Alexander-Mosheh Lapidoth, (1819-1906) Rabbi in Rasein for forty years 1866-1906, an ardent preacher and *Hovev Zion,* who published books and many articles in newspapers, engaging in polemics with the young intellectuals Yehudah-Leib Gordon and Mosheh-Leib Lilienblum. The official rabbi nominated by the authorities, who served for 39 years, was Avraham (Abali) Yofe, who died in 1902.

In 1913, sixteen Rasein Jews were supporters of the *Agudath Yisrael Fund*. During the years of famine 1869-1871, a committee was established to help the poor. Long tables for 1,500 people were placed alongside the *Beth Midrash*, and every needy person received half a kilogram of bread per day. The *Tomkhei Aniyim* (Supporters of the Poor) society also donated 500 rubles, a large sum, to the Central Help Committee in Memel.

Despite this situation, a list of 74 Rasein Jews, who in 1871 donated money for victims of the great famine in Persia, was published in the Hebrew newspaper *HaMagid* in that year (see **Appendix 2**).

In 1878, a hospital was built, supported by former Raseiners in America and by the local municipality. In 1879, the *Bikur Holim* society was organized, and in 1880-81 the *Gemiluth Hesed* society was established, with 500 rubles as a starting fund, supplying free meals to forty families. Bread and heating materials for the needy were sold at low prices and seventy pairs of shoes were distributed among them. In 1883 the *Hakhnasath Orkhim* society built a house for passing travelers, where they were provided with accommodation and food. In 1907, a *Moshav Zekeinim* (Home for the Aged) was established by the community, helped by a bequest from the native-born Soloveitchik.

A cholera epidemic caused the death of many Jews in 1903. The community, headed by the two rabbis, supplied free medical help.

In 1853, a school directed by Rabinovitz was established, but most Jewish children were educated at the Talmud Torah (which had about 100 boys in 1883), where, in addition to Torah, Russian and arithmetic were also taught. In 1888, a School for Teaching Crafts to Jewish Children was opened in Rasein. The school budget was based mostly on the meat tax (*Karobka*).

Many learned people who knew Hebrew, were active in spreading knowledge of subjects such as general history and natural sciences by translating and teaching foreign languages.

A Hebrew library was established in 1910, in addition to the Yiddish one that already existed. In 1835, the Hebrew writer, Avraham Mapu (1808-1867) arrived in Rasein, and lived there for seven years. His Hebrew love story, "*Ahavath Zion*", was the first ever written, and made a great impression on the entire Jewish world.

Zionist activity in Rasein began in the 1880s and consisted of propaganda and the collection of money for the settlement of *Eretz-Yisrael*. In 1884, fifty pictures of Mosheh Motefiori, used to promote fundraising, were sold locally.

In 1886, a branch of *Hovevei Zion* movement was active in town. At the end of the nineteenth century Rasein Jews acquired 130 shares in the bank of the Zionist organization *(Otsar Hityashvuth HaYehudim)*, and several hundred Rubles were collected for the settlement of *Eretz-Yisrael*. At this time, courses for studying Hebrew and the Bible were opened in town, with about forty girls participating. A society named *Daughters of Zion and Evident Language* was created for this purpose, making efforts to teach Hebrew to local Jewish girls. This initiative can be attributed to Nehamah Lapidoth.

In 1899 a delegate from Rasein took part in the regional conference of Zionist Societies which took place in Vilna.

Names of 234 Rasein Jews appear in lists of donors for the settlement of *Eretz-Yisrael*, as published in the Hebrew newspaper *Hamelitz* in 1893-1903 (**see Appendix 3**), and thirteen names appear in a list from 1907. Among the fundraisers were Yehudah Vigodsky, Hayim-Yisrael Zaks, Avraham-Aba Klivansky and Yits'hak Agushevitz.

In 1902, 162 *Shekalim* were sold in Rasein. And in the same year a Society of Hebrew Speakers, whose members were obliged to speak only Hebrew during their meetings, came into being. Zionist youths founded a library with books in Hebrew, Yiddish and Russian. The *Bund* party also had much influence in the Jewish community, which sometimes led to confrontations between its members and the Zionists.

Among those born in Rasein who emigrated to *Eretz-Yisrael* in the 1880s and 1890s were: Rabbi Eliezer HaCohen who, arriving in Jerusalem in 1884, refused to make his living as a rabbi and instead repaired shoes in the old city; his son Mihal, who was one of the editors of the Hebrew periodicals *HaLevanon* and *Ariel* and a founder of *Nahalath Shivah*, a neighborhood in Jerusalem; another son, Eliyahu-Shaul, a doctor in the Galilee and in Petakh Tikvah; Yehoshua Berman arrived in the land in 1876 and was a *Shohet* in Jerusalem; Yits'hak-Aizik Ben-Tovim (Bendet) arrived in the 1890s and became the head of *Hovevei Zion* in Yafo and one of the first activists of the *Mizrahi* party in *Eretz-Yisrael*.

Mosheh ben Shelomoh-Zalman Markovitz (1867-1936) was born in Nemoksht (Nemaksciai), but lived most of his life in Rasein. He was a shoemaker and learned to read and write later in life. Despite this, Markovitz published several biographies of rabbis and other Jewish personages. His books, including *Shem HaGedolim Ha Shelishi* (The Third Book of The Names of the Great), Vilna 5670 (1910), concentrated mainly on their works, which had been partly lost but thus became known again.

Mosheh ben Shelomoh-Zalman Markovitz with his book

During World War I, in May 1915, when the Russian rulers published an order exiling all Jews from the Kovno *Gubernia*, Rasein's Jews remained in the town.

During the Period of Independent Lithuania (1918-1940)
Society and Economics

Although the independence of Lithuania was proclaimed on February 16, 1918, the German army ruled in Rasein until the autumn of that year. As German rule waned, the local authority, where Jews played an important role, took over. The municipal council consisted of twelve members, five of them Jews. (Adv. M. Levi, the merchant Kaplan, the tinsmith Katz and two others, Yehudah and David whose surnames are not known). A local youngster named Avraham Mogilevsky, later an officer in the Lithuanian army, excelled in the temporary auxiliary police force, which numbered sixty men. In the printing press of a local Jew named Kadushin, postage stamps of the town Rasein were printed, long before the government post office began to issue stamps. Lazar Sudak, a Jewish student, published a newspaper in Lithuanian entitled *Zemaitija* for several months, in which news and announcements of local rules were printed.

According to the first census performed by the new Lithuanian government in 1923, 5,270 residents lived in Rasein, 2,035 (39%) being Jews.

A Street in Rasein

Following the Law of Autonomies for Minorities issued by the new Lithuanian government, the Minister for Jewish Affairs, Dr. Menachem (Max) Soloveitshik, ordered elections to community committees, *Va'adei Kehilah,* to be held in the summer of 1919. In Rasein, a community committee was elected at the end of 1919, which functioned until about the beginning of 1926, when the autonomy was annulled by a new Lithuanian government. In 1921 the committee consisted of fifteen members: four from *Tseirei Zion,* one from *Akhduth (Agudath Yisrael),* one from the General Zionists, one non-party and eight independent. During its existence the committee collected taxes according to law and looked after all aspects of Jewish life. Sub-committees were used to collect taxes, for appeals, for the bath house, for culture and education, for the administration of the community's property, for social aid and for inspection (control). Gedalyah Halperin was elected chairman of the committee.

For the elections to the first Lithuanian *Seimas* (Parliament) in October 1922, Rasein's Jews voted as follows: the Zionist list received 493 votes, *Akhduth* 136 and the Democrats 182.

The 1921 municipal council elections resulted in seven Jews being elected, out of seventeen council members. The elections of 1931 brought five Jews to the council of twelve: Max Levy, Noakh Yisrael, Mosheh Ziv, Gedalyah Halperin and Meir Zusmanovitz. However the elections of 1934 showed only three Jews among the twelve members elected. For some time a local Jew named Leibovitz served as deputy mayor.

Rasein Jews made their living during this period in trade, industry and crafts, with a few in agriculture. In 1924 the Association of Jewish Retailers and the General Association of Jewish Merchants were established. The Retailers

Association established a purchasing cooperative in response to a Lithuanian association which held a monopoly for the wholesale trade of sugar, salt, herring and kerosene.

According to the government survey of 1931, Rasein had 116 shops, 90 Jewish owned (78%). The business distribution of these is given in the table below:

Type of business	Total	Owned by Jews
Grocery store	12	11
Grain and flax	10	9
Butcher shop and cattle trade	22	14
Restaurant and tavern	7	4
Food products, eggs	8	8
Beverages	2	2
Textile products and furs	13	12
Leather and shoe store	6	6
Haberdashery and house utensils	7	6
Medicine and cosmetics	5	4
Watches, jewels and optics	2	2
Hardware products	6	6
Bicycles and electrical equipment	2	1
Heating materials and cattle food	1	1
Machines, transportation	3	2
Stationery and books	4	1
Other	6	1

The main income of most of the Jews was on the weekly market days, which took place on Mondays and Thursdays.

Of the 40 light industrial businesses, 27 (67%) were owned by Jews.

Type of Factory	Total	Jewish owned
Headstones, glass, bricks	3	0
Printing press, binderies	1	1
Textile: wool, flax, knitting	3	0
Sawmills and furniture, tar production	6	3
Flour mills, bakeries, beverages, candies	14	11
Dresses, footwear	6	5
Leather industry: production, cobbling	3	3
Other: barbers, photographers, jewelers	4	4

In 1925 there were two Jewish doctors, one dentist and two Jewish dental practitioners.

Eighty-nine Jewish artisans could be found in the town in 1937: twenty tailors, fourteen butchers, twelve shoemakers, six stitchers, four hatters, four barbers, three bakers, three locksmiths, three tinsmiths, three watchmakers, two knitters, two painters, two cloth dyers, two seamstresses, an electrician, a book binder, a printer, a carpenter, a blacksmith, a photographer and three others.

The Jewish Popular bank (*Folksbank*) played an important role in the economic life of Rasein's Jews. In 1920 it had 191 members, in 1927 there were 560 and in 1929, 504.

In the mid-1930s the economic situation of the Jews began to deteriorate. One reason was the blatant propaganda of the <u>Association of Lithuanian Merchants</u> (*Verslas*), which campaigned against buying from Jewish shops. The Lithuanians established consumer cooperatives competing with Jewish trade. Jewish exporters of eggs, flax, grains and timber lost their living. The livelihood of Jewish artisans also declined, because Lithuanian artisans moved away from villages and settled in town. In 1934 Jews were attacked physically. During these years many Jews emigrated to America, South Africa and Mexico, with some youths emigrating to *Eretz-Yisrael*.

By 1939 there were 149 telephone subscribers, 46 of them in Jewish homes and businesses.

Education and Culture
During this period a Hebrew Kindergarten, a Hebrew elementary school of the *Tarbuth* chain (directed by Levinson, Aba Yofe), a Hebrew elementary school of the *Yavneh* chain (the director was Kirsh) and a Hebrew gymnasium (High School) also of the *Tarbuth* chain, were established in Rasein. Youngsters from the Tavrig and Keidan districts also studied in this gymnasium, which opened in 1922. During the first years about 180 pupils attended the school. The gymnasium had its own building, the ground floor being occupied by the government elementary school. Many of its graduates continued their studies at Kovno University.

With the decline of the economic situation of Lithuanian Jewry in general and of Rasein Jews in particular, the number of pupils in the gymnasium declined, numbering less than a hundred by the end of the 1930s. High tuition fees that many families could not afford, and the difficulties that the Lithuanian examiners placed in the way of Jewish students at matriculation examinations were among the reasons for this. More and more Jewish youngsters began to study at the government high school, where tuition fees were minimal but some teachers were anti-Semitic.

The Hebrew Gymnasium (1930)

Directors of the Hebrew gymnasium included: Dr. Josef Levinzon; Dr. Refael Rabinovitz, who was also the deputy head of the community; Dr. Tsevi Rolnik; Dr. Yisrael Mehlman (died in Jerusalem in 1990); Dr. Tuviyah Arieli (Leibovitz); Y. Salomon; Dr. Avraham Berkovitz. The last director was Dr. Dov Zilber. Some teachers would converse with students on Fridays evening or on *Shabbath* afternoon on subjects of correct behavior or on present-day problems concerning world Jewry and *Eretz-Yisrael*. These included the poetess Leah Goldberg, Dr. Batyah Rabinovitz and Tsevi Levin.

The gymnasium housed a Hebrew library in addition to the big community library named after *Mendele Mokher Sefarim* (pseudonym of the writer Shalom Ya'akov Abramovitz), with its hundreds of Yiddish and Hebrew books. During its existence the gymnasium was supported by the *Folksbank* and by the local *Hevrah Kadisha*. It was closed down after Lithuania became annexed to the Soviet Union in the summer of 1940.

The fourth group of the evening lessons (of Hebrew) in Rasein

Zionist and other activities

During the years of the autonomy, the leftist parties *Bund* and *Poalei Zion Smol* had great influence among Rasein's Jews. They established the *Kultur Lige* (Culture League) and organized evening courses for children and adults. In the course of time only the *Folkist* (Peoples) movement, which fostered the use of Yiddish and opposed Zionism, remained from the Yiddish speaking camp. Its official propaganda organ was the Yiddish daily newspaper *Folksblat* which was published in Kovno. At this time the Zionist movement with all its variations conquered the Jewish public, and all Zionist parties had branches in Rasein. Many participated in the elections for the Zionist congresses. The table below reveals the division of the votes for each party:

Cong No.	Year	Tot Shek	Total Voter	Labor Party		Rev.	Gen. Zion		Gro	Miz
				Z"S	Z'Z					
14	1925	34	----	----	----	--	----	----	----	----
15	1927	142	43	18	5	11	5	----	----	4
16	1929	164	62	27	9	14	4	----	----	8
17	1931	159	23	35	23	56	6	----	----	3
18	1933	---	428	246		166	11	----	18	37
19	1935	---	783	405		---	37	99	76	166

Key: Cong No. = Congress Number, Tot Shek = Total Shkalim, Rev = Revisionists, Gen Zion = General Zionists, Gro = Grosmanists, Miz = Mizrakhi

A branch of WIZO headed by Mrs. Roza Ziv was also active in town, as were the Zionist youth organizations *HaShomer HaTsair, Beitar, Gordonia, HeHalutz, HeHalutz HaMizrahi, Berith HaKanaim, HaNoar HaZioni,* and *Benei Akiva.*

Sports activities were carried out in the Maccabi branch with its 54 members, as well as the Y.A.K. (*Yiddisher Arbeiter Klub*) of the Yiddishists. There were active *Kibutsei Hakhsharah* (Training Kibutsim) of *HeHalutz* and *Berith HaKanaim* (from 1933), and some Jewish youth belonged to the Communist underground.

A group of Hashomer HaTsair in Rasein, 1924

Religion and Welfare

The eight prayer houses which existed in Rasein before World War I continued to serve the community during this period too. These were the rabbis who officiated: Yehoshua-Mordehai Klatskin (1862-1925); Mosheh Soloveitshik (1878-1941) from 1908 in Rasein, and from 1931 head of the Rabbi Yits'hak–Elhanan *Yeshivah* in New York. He was one of the leaders of the Rabbinic Association of America and Canada, and died in New York. The last Rabbi of Rasein, Aharon-Shemuel Katz (1871-1941), who published several books on the *Talmud*, was murdered in the Holocaust.

Rabbi Mosheh Soloveitshik

During all these years there was a *Small Yeshivah* headed by Rabbi Roz and later by Rabbi Goldshlag, as well as branches of *Agudath Yisrael* and of the religious women's organization *Beth-Ya'akov* headed by pharmacist Mrs. Volpert. There was also a branch of the religious boys' organization *Tifereth Bakhurim*, headed by Eliyahu Alinik and a *Ben Zakai* society where gymnasium students were taught *Talmud,* as well as other societies for studying Judaism, such as *Talmud, Mishnah* and *Ein Ya'akov.*

The *Ezrah* society, which was active instead of the closed Community Committee, operated the Bath House, the Home for the Aged and the Jewish Hospital. Other welfare societies were the Society for Helping Poor Women in Confinement, headed by Mrs. Blokh, *Hakhnasath Orhim* and *Hevrah Kadisha.*

For a list of personages born in Rasein see **Appendix 1.**

During World War II and afterwards
In June 1940 Lithuania was annexed by the Soviet Union, becoming a Soviet Republic. Following new rules, the majority of factories and shops belonging to Jews in Rasein were nationalized and commissars were appointed to manage them. All Zionist parties and youth organizations were disbanded, several of the activists being detained. Hebrew educational institutions were closed. About twenty families whose businesses were nationalized were exiled to Siberia and elsewhere. A Jewish kindergarten with 64 children and a drama circle were established by the new rulers.

On June 23, 1941, the second day of the German invasion of the Soviet Union, Rasein was bombed by German planes. Most of the Jews left town and dispersed in the fields and villages. During the night a heavy battle between the German army and the Red Army ensued, and the next morning,

June 24, the German army entered Rasein. The Jews returning to the town found most of the houses, including all prayer houses, ruined. Those that were left intact had been ransacked by their Lithuanian neighbors and the returning Jews crowded into those houses. Every day Lithuanian police would take out Jews for various types of work, such as burying dead soldiers of the Red Army, collecting weapons scattered in the fields and roads, cleaning streets and latrines, and so on. The police abused the Jews, hitting them with whips and sticks and forcing them to roll empty barrels over a distance of 15 km. Educated Jewish women would be sent to wash floors in institutions and in the houses of Lithuanian and German officials. They did not receive any food and were already beginning to exchange various items and garments for food.

During the third week of the war, restrictions were imposed on the Jews: the obligation to wear a white patch on the right side of the chest, banning them from walking on the sidewalks, buying products in the market, or leaving their houses during the hours of darkness, and so on.

A week later an order was issued to all Jewish men and women from the age of 15 to 45, to congregate in a monastery half a kilometer from the town on the road to Yurburg. This was a two-storey house with a big yard with stables, pig sheds and barns. The place was encircled by a barbed wire fence and forty Lithuanian guards were stationed around it in order to prevent Jews from escaping. Family members who were not obliged to go to the monastery were allowed to join their families. In a single day about 1,500 Jews were imprisoned here, making it a so-called Labor Camp. The next morning, July 27, 1941, all Jewish men were forced to cut their beards and shave. Later, five cars with ten Germans arrived. The Lithuanian commander read out names from a list which had been prepared the day before, and ordered those named to stand in rows. Some were given shovels and all were led towards Yurburg by sixty armed Lithuanians. Those remaining in the camp were sure that they had been selected for some hard work. But the truth was that the 393 men on the list and another 100 Jews who were brought from the jail were led to a sand quarry, about 5 km. from the town, where pits had been prepared. There they were shot and buried. The murderers were Lithuanians, the Germans standing alongside to observe.

That same evening Lithuanian police arrested the Jewish intelligentsia, among them lawyers Levy and Fridland, Rabbi Katz and others, the sick and the old, and all were brought to the camp in the monastery. On July 29, this group was led to the same pits and murdered there. Before the murders the Lithuanians forced some Jews to write notes to their wives in the camp or in town, asking them to send money, gold and diamonds by way of the police. And indeed some women believed the message with regard to the money and gave the murderers their valuables.

One day the residents of the camp were told that they may go to their families in town and to be ready to be transferred together with their entire family to the camp. They were allowed to bring everything they wanted. The unfortunate Jews collected their possessions which had been accumulated over generations. Their Lithuanian neighbors offered to store things with them for safe keeping till the end of the war.

After their arrival in the camp, crowding became unbearable. From time to time small groups of people would be taken out by the Lithuanians and they would disappear without a trace. At night the Lithuanians would burst into the camp, stealing everything they fancied and raping the young women. The camp at this time housed about forty men and more than a thousand women and children.

In the second half of August 1941 an order was issued to all Jews remaining in Rasein and the villages in the vicinity, to move to the estate of Bilevitz, about 5 km. from Rasein, by August 27. An estimated 2,000 people, mostly women and children, arrived at the estate.

On August 29, 1941 (6th of Elul, 5701) trucks with armed Lithuanians appeared. The women and children were put on to the trucks, group by group, and transported in the direction of Girtegole (Girkalnis). About 2 km. from the town, near the village of Kalnujai, pits had been prepared. The victims were made to stand at the edge of the pit, and were shot and buried in these pits. A Lithuanian eye-witness who hid in a tree, reported later that the women were forced to undress completely before they were shot. The children were thrown in to the pits alive or their heads were shattered on tree trunks. The garments of the murdered were divided up among the murderers and residents of the town.

The mass grave and the monument at the Kalnujai Castle Hill

**The monument with the inscription in Yiddish and Lithuanian:
"In this place the blood of 1877 Jews, children, women and men,
was spilled by the Nazi murderers and their local helpers on
29.8.1941"**

Only a few Jews managed to hide with Lithuanian peasants, and survived.
Some peasants were murdered for hiding Jews. In the summer of 1941
several Jewish youngsters managed to escape to Russia, from where they
tried to get to *Eretz-Yisrael* but were detained by the authorities.

According to Soviet sources, mass graves of the Jews of Rasein and the
surroundings were found in two places: beside the town of Girkalnis, about
1,600-1,650 Jews are buried about 10 km. south-east from Rasein, and a further
1,677 victims are buried near Kalnujai Hill, about 6 km. south-west of Rasein.

After the war, monuments were erected on these mass graves. At the beginning
of the 1990s a monument was erected on the Kalnujai mass grave, with an
inscription in Yiddish and Lithuanian. Also a wooden tablet was fixed where the
Jewish cemetery in Vytautas Street had been, with an inscription in Yiddish and
Lithuanian saying: "This was the site of the Jewish cemetery."

According to the 1990 cartographic survey of Jewish cemeteries in Lithuania,
one cemetery was found in the village Uzdubysis in the Rasein district.

Sources:

Yad Vashem archives, Jerusalem, M-9/13(2); M-1/Q-1219/69; M-1/E761/625: M-9/15(60); M-21/5/267

Koniukhovsky Collection; 0-17, files 42-45, 152, 3785/33

YIVO, New York, Lithuanian Communities Collection, files 1149-1184, 1447, 1553, 1554, 1647, 1678

Gotlib, *Ohalei Shem* (Hebrew), pages 198, 377

Markovitz Mosheh, *LeKoroth Ir Rasein VeRabaneha* (The History of the town Rasein and its Rabbis), Warsaw, 5673 (1913)

Unzer Lebn (Our Life) (Yiddish), Kovno, 9.10.1938

Kamzon, *Yahaduth Lita* (Hebrew), pages 145, 147

Barkai, South Africa, September 1969, pages 83-84

Dos Vort, (Yiddish), Kovno,13.11.1934, 7.3.1938

Di Yiddishe Shtime (Yiddish), Kovno, 1.11.1919; 22.3.1929; 11.10.1929; 2.5.1930; 22.5.1930; 22.8.1930; 22.1.1931; 5.5.1931; 3.7.1931; 9.5.1935; 11.9.1938;

Di Tsait (Yiddish) Shavl, 7.5.1923; 10.4.1924

HaMelitz (Hebrew), St.Petersburg, 18.7.1870; 19.1.1879; 19.8.1879; 8.5.1881; 21.6.1881; 13.5.1883; 18.6.1883; 25.6.1883; 5.10.1883; 17.12.1883; 18.1.1884; 29.2.1884; 25.4.1884; 7.2.1886; 30.4.1886; 18.1.1887; 15.6.1887; 31.10.1887; 11.7.1888; 11.12.1890; 2.1.1891; 17.2.1891; 23.1.1893; 12.3.1893; 19.5.1902; 25.12.1902; 8.8.1903

Tog (Yiddish) Kovno, 10.6.1926; 1.7.1926

Yiddisher Hantverker (Jewish Artisan), Kovno, # 5

Folksblat (Yiddish), Kovno, 11.8.1935; 5.10.1937; 6.4.1939; 11.5.1939; 5.11.1940

Funken Kovno, 15.5.1931

Naujienos (News) (Lithuanian) Chicago,11.6.1949

Zukas K. Zvilgsnis; *I praeiti* (A look in the past) (Lithuanian), Chicago, 1959

Appendix 1
A partial list of personages born in Rasein

Emanuel Soloveitchik lived in the nineteenth century, was a doctor in the Russian Navy and together with Pinsker established the periodical *Zion* (in Russian).

Meir-Faivel Getz (1853-1932), director of the Hebrew high schools in Moscow and Riga, published books and organized pedagogic courses for *Tseirei Yisrael* and for teachers of the *Yavneh* chain in Kovno.

Yisrael-Yits'hak Volf (1861-1926), publisher of Zionist periodicals in the United States.

Eliezer-Lipman Zilberman (1819-1882), founder of the modern Hebrew press, established the *HaMagid* newspaper and published it till 1880.

Adolf Landau (1841-1902), established the monthly *Voskhod* (Sunrise) and the weekly *Cronika of Voskhod*, published nine volumes of the *Hebrew Biblioteka* in Russian, and more.

Hayim Rafalovitz (1882-1928), publisher and writer, editor of the Yiddish periodical *Unzer Tsait* (Our Time), activist of the *Yiddishists Folkspartei* in Kovno, established the publishing firm *Likht* (Light), wrote a few plays.

Yehezkel-Faivel Rotshtein – lived in the nineteenth century, a teacher and writer in Germany.

Yosef Cohen (1890-?), lawyer, legislator in Quebec Province in Canada, active in Jewish issues.

Rabbi Menahem-Mendel Aharonson, one of the activists of *Mizrahi* in South Africa.

Rabbi Josef Yehudah Blokh (1849-1930), Rabbi of Telz and head of its *Yeshivah*.

Dr. Tsemakh Tsemerion (Halperin), writer, educator, researcher. Died in Haifa in 1988.

Emanuel Fortuna, Engineer in Chemistry and Physics, one of the pioneers of the chemical industry in Israel, was a director of the military physical industry, also a member of the delegation of industrialists to the reparations agreement with Germany.

Appendix 2
List of 47 Rasein Jews, donors for the victims of the Persian famine in 1871 as published in Hamagid # 47-1871
(JewishGen>Databases>Lithuania>Hamagid, By Jeffrey Maynard)

Surname	Given Name	Comments
ABELMAN	Yakov	
ANZIL	Abba	
ASHER	Simcha	
ASHER	Yosef	
AVKAWSKI	Yehuda Leib	
BERMAN	Shlomo Zalman	
BERMAN	Zev	
BLOCH	Moshe son of Rabbi M	
BLUMBERG	Mordechai Eliezer	
BLUMBERG	Binyamin	

Surname	Given Name	Comments
BOMHAN	Nechama	woman
BROIDA	Boruch	
DOVIDOW	Aharon	
FEIN	Yerechmiel	
FRIDMAN	Mendil	
GAR	Eliahu	
GAVRIELOWITZ	Shmuel	
GAVRILOWITZ	Tzvi	
GEIWIDEL	Beinish	
GETZ	Shimon	
GIN	Moshe	
GORDON	Eliezer	
GRINBERG	Shmuel Yosef	
GRINBERG	Yosef	
GRINBERG	Zalman	
GRINBERG	Zondil	
GRINBLAT	Yisroel Katz	
GROSMAN	Tzvi	
HELMAN	Nachum	
KAPLAN	Avraham Zev	
LANDA	Zalman	
LAPIDOS	Shalom Yakov	
LEWIN	Dov Ber	
LEWIN	Nachum	
LEWINSKI	Leib	
LUNZ	Eliezer Getzel	
LUNZ		Doctor
LURIA	Moshe	boy
MANISHEWITZ		

Surname	Given Name	Comments
MANKOWSKI	Yakov	
MERKIL	Moshe	
MILDET	Etil	woman
NADIL	Mordechai Meir	
PA"TZ	Yakov Asher	
PLUNGIANER	Tzvi	
RACHAWITZKI	Eliezer	
RACHAWITZKI	Malka	woman
RACHAWITZKI	Yosef	
ROZENFELD	Nechemiah	boy
SHA"TZ	Yisroel Isser	
SHAMSHINAWITZ	Yosef Meir	
SHAPIRO	Meina	
SHASHKALSKI	Moshe	Rabbi Gaon
SHMATRITEL		
SHOHAM	Reuven	
SHU"B	Ari	
SHU"B	Gershon Mendil	
SHU"B	Yosef	
SHULMAN	Moshe	
TERESPOLSKI	Yehuda Yitzchok	
TRACHTENBERG	H	businessman visiting Riga
WARSHAWITZKI	Shmuel Leib	
WEINBERG	Lima	
YERUZLIM	Moshe Yakov	
	Ever ben Yona	
	Meir ben Chaim	
	Mina Mere	woman

Surname	Given Name	Comments
	Moshe son of Rabbi B	
	Shalom Tuvia	
	Shaul son of Rabbi H	
	Shlomo ben Tzvi	
	Yakov ben Chaim	
	Yakov son of Rabbi y tz"a Galeis	
	Yehuda ben Tzvi	

Appendix 3 234 Rasein Jewish donors to the settlement of *Eretz-Yisrael* listed in *Hamelitz*

(JewishGen>Databases>Lithuania>HaMelitz, By Jeffrey Maynard)

Surname	Given Name	Comments	Source	Year
AGUSHEWITZ	Yitzchok		Hamelitz #80	1901
AKS	Yisroel Chaim		#27	1901
ANUSHEWITZ	Yitzchok		#27	1901
ANUSHEWITZ	Yitzchok		#80	1901
ARENZOHN			# 224	1903
ARONSON	Aba		#80	1901
ARONSON	Yehoshua		#80	1901
ATZORKIN	Yechezkel		#80	1901
AVROMSOHN	Heshel		#80	1901
BEHR	Fishel		#80	1901
BEHRMAN	M		# 218	1901
BEILOWITZ		government teacher	# 218	1901
BEKER	Olga		#80	1901
BERGSHTEIN	M		# 218	1901
BERLOWITZ	Dovid		#80	1901

Surname	Given Name	Comments	Source	Year
BERNSHTEIN	Moshe		#80	1901
BIRMAN	Yisroel		# 224	1903
BLAT	Yosef		# 224	1903
BLAT	Yosef		#27	1901
BLECH	Chaya bas Shlomo wife of Chaim Avraham Shailski	wed	#288	1897
BLECH	Mirl wife of Shlomo	wed	#288	1897
BLECH	Shlomo husband of Mirl father of Chaya		#288	1897
BLOCH	Leib		#80	1901
BLOCH	Pinchos		#80	1901
BLOCH	Yakov		#80	1901
BLOCH	Yakov Antzel		#80	1901
BLOCHER	Nechemiah		# 224	1903
BRUCHZOHN			# 224	1903
BUATZ	Boruch		#27	1901
CHANOCH		lawyer	# 218	1901
CHWEIDAN	Z		#80	1901
COHEN	Yakov		#80	1901
DAWIDOWITZ	Y		#80	1901
DAWIDOWITZ	Yosef		#27	1901
DORFMAN	L		# 218	1901
DORFMAN	Sh		# 218	1901
DORFMAN	Shmaya		#80	1901
FEIBUSH	Yitzchak husband of Feiga Goldberg	wed 1901	# 218	1901
FEIN	A		# 218	1901
FEIN	Aharon		#80	1901
FEIN	Avraham Aba		# 224	1903

Surname	Given Name	Comments	Source	Year
FEIN	Brocha		# 224	1903
FEIN	Yerachmiel		#80	1901
FISH	Meir		#80	1901
FLOIM	Yona husband of Nechama Leibowitz	wed in Shavel	#27	1901
FRIDMAN	Chaim Tzvi	in N(G?)irtenole	# 218	1901
FRIDMAN	Chaim Tzvi		#27	1901
FRIDMAN	Nochum		#80	1901
FRIDMAN	Sh K		# 218	1901
GALIBRODSKI	Heshil		#80	1901
GEL	Yakov		#80	1901
GIN	Yosef Chaim		#80	1901
GOLDBERG	A		# 218	1901
GOLDBERG	A		#27	1901
GOLDBERG	Avraham father of Feige	in Tzitenan	# 218	1901
GOLDBERG	Elchanan		#203	1900
GOLDBERG	Elchanan		#27	1901
GOLDBERG	Elchanan		#80	1901
GOLDBERG	Elchanan nephew of Avraham Goldberg		# 218	1901
GOLDBERG	Feige wife of Yitzchak Feibush	wed 1901	# 218	1901
GORDON	Yisroel		#80	1901
GRINBERG	Ester bas Zalman wife of Yitzchok Markus	wed 1903	# 224	1903
GRINBERG	Mordechai		# 224	1903
GRINBERG	Zalman		#80	1901
GRODNIK	Y		# 218	1901
GROFMAN	Tz		# 218	1901

Surname	Given Name	Comments	Source	Year
HENOK		doctor	#80	1901
HERTZMAN	Chaim Halewi		#197	1895
HERTZMAN	Chaim husband of Ester Horwitz of Taurage	wed 21 May in Taurage	# 120	1893
HERTZMAN	Sh		# 218	1901
ISERLIS	Zalman		#80	1901
KALMANOK	Anna wife of Moshe Yafe		#247	1895
KAMBER	Yakov Zondil		# 224	1903
KAMBER	Yitzchok		# 224	1903
KAMBER	Yitzchok		#80	1901
KAPLAN	B		#214	1895
KAPLAN	Leib		#27	1901
KAPLAN	Leib		#80	1901
KAPLAN	Pinchos		#80	1901
KAPLAN	Shmaryahu		#80	1901
KARNOWSKI	Note		# 224	1903
KATZAV	Dov Leib		#80	1901
KATZAV	Eli Menachem		#80	1901
KATZAV	Mordechai Yakov		#80	1901
KATZAV	Pesach		#80	1901
KATZAV	Shmuel		#80	1901
KATZAV	Yisroel Leib		#80	1901
KLEIN	Eta wife of Mordechai Shoboshewitz	wed 1903 in Kapshtat, South Africa	# 224	1903
KLIBANSKI	Aba nephew of Aharon Shtreibman		#27	1901
KOHN	Y		# 218	1901
KOHN	Y		# 218	1901

Surname	Given Name	Comments	Source	Year
KRASNASTOW	Yakov		#80	1901
KRASTANOW	Yakov		# 224	1903
KRAZER	Yitzchok		#80	1901
LEIBOWITZ	Nechama wife of Yona Floim	wed in Shavel	#27	1901
LESHEM	Rivka Rochel ben Mordechai wife of Yosef Yuzl Magilnitzki	wed Philadelphia (America) 10 Sivan	# 147	1893
LESHEM	Shachna ben Mordechai		# 147	1893
LEWI	Maks		#80	1901
LEWIASH	Boruch		#80	1901
LEWIN	Shlomo Zalman husband of Fruma Rik	wed 1903	# 224	1903
LEWINSKI	Ephraim Yehuda		#80	1901
LEWITAN	Alter		#208	1895
LEWITAN	Alter		#72	1899
LEWITAN	Alter		#204	1900
LEWITAN	Alter husband of Devorah Rosenfeld	wed	#27	1901
LEWITAN	Alter husband of Devorah Rosenfeld		#80	1901
LEWNER	Boruch		#80	1901
LEWNER	Chaim Bune		#27	1901
LIPSHITZ	Menachem		#80	1901
LIUBIN	Yehudis		# 224	1903
MAGILEWSKI	Heshil		#130	1900
MAGILEWSKI	Yehoshua		#27	1901
MAGILNITZKI	Yosef Yuzl husband of Rivka Rochel Leshem	wed Philadelphia (America) 10 Sivan	# 147	1893

Surname	Given Name	Comments	Source	Year
MAITZ	Zelig		#80	1901
MAKS (ZAKS?)	Hinde		#229	1902
MANKOWSKI	L		#80	1901
MANKOWSKI	Yosef		#80	1901
MANKOWSKI		doctor	#80	1901
MARKUS	Gitel		# 224	1903
MARKUS	Sh		# 224	1903
MARKUS	Yakov		# 224	1903
MARKUS	Yehoshua		# 224	1903
MARKUS	Yitzchok husband of Ester Grinberg	wed 1903	# 224	1903
MEIROWITZ			# 224	1903
MICHELEWITZ	Ch		# 224	1903
MILER	M		#80	1901
MOGILEWSKI	Heshil		#80	1901
MOHILEWSKI	H		# 224	1903
MOHILEWSKI	Y		# 218	1901
MOTZ	Moshe father of Shmuel		# 218	1901
MOTZ	Shmuel ben Moshe		# 218	1901
MOW	Tzvi Yakov		#80	1901
NETANELIS	Sfia wife of Shmuel Sudak	wed 1903	# 224	1903
NETANELIS	Yosef		# 224	1903
NOBAWSKI	Rochel		# 224	1903
OLIAN	Chana Gitl wife of Aharon Rubinshtein	wed 1 Marcheshvan in Libau	#214	1895
OLSWANG	Yehuda Dovid	Rabbi Gaon in Koltinen	# 218	1901
PAK	Shlomo		#187	1900

Surname	Given Name	Comments	Source	Year
PARIZ	W		# 224	1903
PASEL	Avraham Eliahu		#27	1901
PERLMAN	Sh R		# 218	1901
PERLOW	Mordechai		#80	1901
POSEL	A Y		# 218	1901
PRESS	Pinchos		# 224	1903
PULEROWITZ	A		#214	1895
RABINOWITZ	Tzadok		#80	1901
REMEZ	Yehoshua		#80	1901
RIK	Fruma bas Reiza wife of Shlomo Zalman Lewin	wed 1903	# 224	1903
RIK	Reiza		# 224	1903
ROSENFELD	Devorah wife of Alter Lewitan	wed	#27	1901
ROTSHTEIN	Meir Yosef		#27	1901
ROZENBLUM	A P T		# 224	1903
ROZENBLUM	Dovid		#27	1901
ROZENBLUM	Dovid	apothecary	#80	1901
RUBINSHTEIN	Aharon husband of Chana Gitl Olian	wed 1 Marcheshvan in Libau	#214	1895
SADOWSKI	Boruch		# 224	1903
SADOWSKI	Boruch		#80	1901
SEGAL	Eliezer		#80	1901
SEGALOWITZ	Dov Ber husband of Reina Shamshanowitz	wed 1903	# 224	1903
SHABASHEWITZ	A Y		# 224	1903
SHABASHEWITZ	E		# 224	1903
SHABASHEWITZ	Nochum		#80	1901
SHABASHEWITZ	Tzvi		#80	1901

Surname	Given Name	Comments	Source	Year
SHAGAM	Moshe		# 224	1903
SHAGAM		Mrs.	# 218	1901
SHAILSKI	Chaim Avraham ben Mordechai husband of Chaya Blech	wed - from Yanova	#288	1897
SHAMSHANOWITZ	Reina wife of Dov Ber Segalowitz	wed 1903	# 224	1903
SHAPIRO	A		# 218	1901
SHAPIRO	Shmuel		# 224	1903
SHAPIRO	Yosef		#80	1901
SHEINFELD	Dov	Rabbi	#80	1901
SHEMESH	Dovid		#80	1901
SHINDELBEKER	Tzvi		#80	1901
SHNITKIN	Yakov Meir		#80	1901
SHOBOSHEWITZ	Mordechai husband of Eta Klein	wed 1903 in Kapshtat, South Africa	# 224	1903
SHOGAM	Moshe		# 224	1903
SHOGAM	Yisroel		# 224	1903
SHROLOWITZ	Yakov		#80	1901
SHTILMAN	Tzvi		# 218	1901
SHTREIBMAN	Aharon father of Chanah uncle of Aba Klibanski		#27	1901
SHTREIBMAN	Chanah bas Aharon wife of Mlatdowitz	wed 10 Teves	#27	1901
SHUB	Ezriel		# 218	1901
STRASBURG	Meir		# 224	1903
SUDAK	Eliahu		# 224	1903
SUDAK	Shmuel husband of Sfia Netanelis	wed 1903	# 224	1903
TANOR	Chaim Hillel		#80	1901

Surname	Given Name	Comments	Source	Year
TELEM	Gavriel		#80	1901
TELM	Gavriel		# 218	1901
TEREMPOLSKI	Tzvia		#80	1901
TERESPOLSKI	Dov		# 218	1901
TERESPOLSKI	Yechiel		# 224	1903
TOIBMAN	Chaim		#27	1901
TOIBMAN	Kopil		#80	1901
TOW	Tz Y		# 218	1901
TZIMANT	Chaim		#80	1901
WIGODSKI	Yehuda		#27	1901
WIGODSKI	Yehuda		#80	1901
WILENTZIK	M L		# 224	1903
WILENTZIK	Yosef		# 224	1903
WINIK	Yitzchok		#80	1901
WINNIK	Yitzchok		#27	1901
WINOK	Yisroel	in N(G?)irtenole	# 218	1901
WOLF	Yisroel Yitzchok	in Louisville, America	#85	1899
WOLFE	Avraham		#80	1901
WOLFE	Tzemach		# 218	1901
WOLFE		Mrs.	# 218	1901
WOLK	W		#80	1901
WOLPE	Avraham		#27	1901
YABLONSKI	Miriam		# 224	1903
YAFE	Avraham	government rabbi	#80	1901
YAFE	Avraham father of Moshe	government rabbi	#247	1895
YAFE	Moshe ben Avraham husband of Anna Kalmanok	wed 9 Marcheshvan	#247	1895

Surname	Given Name	Comments	Source	Year
YASHPE	Avraham		#80	1901
ZACHER	Uriah		#80	1901
ZACHS	Yisroel		#137	1900
ZACHS	Yisroel		#137	1900
ZAKHEIM	Chaim Tzvi		#27	1901
ZAKHEIM	Chaim Tzvi		#80	1901
ZAKHEIM	Noson		# 224	1903
ZAKS	Chaim Yisroel		#229	1902
ZAKS	Chaim Yisroel		#285	1900
ZAKS	Chaim Yisroel		#27	1901
ZAKS	Chaim Yisroel		#80	1901
ZAKS	Chaim Yisroel		#80	1901
ZAKS	Shalom		#229	1902
ZAKS	Shalom		#80	1901
ZAKS	Yitzchok		#80	1901
ZALTZBERG	Boruch		#80	1901
ZALTZBERG	P		# 224	1903
ZIW	Yissachar		#80	1901
ZIW	Yitzchok		#80	1901
ZIW	Zalman	from Kelm	# 218	1901
	Chanoch Zondil ben Moshe Betzalel husband of Elka Margolis of Wishnewe	wed	#142	1898
	Moshe Betzalel father of Chanoch Zondil	Rabbi Gaon ABD	#142	1898

Rietavas (Riteve)

Rietavas (Riteve in Yiddish) is located in northwestern Lithuania along the banks of the Jura River, near the Kaunas-Klaipeda road. Riteve is first mentioned in historical documents dating from 1253. The town was owned by the Great Prince of Lithuania from 1527. In 1590 King Zigmunt Vaza granted Riteve permission to hold two weekly market days and one annual fair. After 1767 the number of annual bazaars was increased to four. In 1792 the town obtained the Magdeburg Rights of self-rule.

Before 1795 Riteve was included in the Polish-Lithuanian Kingdom. According to the third division of Poland the same year by the three superpowers of those times, Russia, Prussia and Austria, Lithuania was divided between Russia and Prussia. As was the case with most of Lithuania, Riteve became a part of the Russian Empire, first in the Vilna province (*Gubernia*) and from 1843 in the Kovno *Gubernia*.

From 1812 to 1909 the land of the town and the nearby estate was owned by nobleman Oginsky's family. In 1892 the family built a power station on their estate, and in 1909 Riteve became the first town in Lithuania to have electricity. During the period of Independent Lithuania (1918-1940) Riteve was a county administrative center. In 1915-1918 the town was under German occupation and during World War II it was almost totally destroyed.

Jewish settlement until after World War I
Jews began to settle in Riteve in the second half of the sixteenth century. In 1662 the Jewish population was 421 (200 men, 201 women, 9 boys and 11 girls).

During the years of *Va'ad Medinath Lita* (1623-1764), Riteve was included in *Galil* Keidan.

Jews made their living in the small trades and peddling and were based mainly at the markets and fairs. For a long time, flax trade was the most important occupation for Jewish merchants. The town had tailors and shoemakers who worked very long hours to sustain their families.

In the 1870s a dispute broke out between landlord Oginsky and Jewish homeowners about rent for the land on which their homes were built. Most of the Jews were poor and could ill afford their rent. In retaliation Oginsky cleared out the *Beth Midrash* and herded pigs and cattle inside. Later, he converted the building into living quarters for his servants. Only after World War I, the heirs of the Oginsky family ordered demolition of the building and the return of the land to the Jews.

In the late 1880s many infants fell ill following their *Brith Milah* (ritual circumcision). It became obvious that the local *Mohel* was incompetent, and the *Mohel* from Plungyan was asked to replace him.

Most of the Jewish boys attended the *Heder*. Children from poor families studied at the *Talmud Torah* located in the attic of the *Beth Midrash*. Supporters of the Zionists brought in a teacher who opened up a *Heder Metukan* (Improved Heder), however only a few families sent their children to this school. Some of the Jewish girls studied at the Russian elementary school, but most of the boys were content with religious education. Twice a week a private teacher taught them to write Russian and Latin lettering.

The *Hibath Zion* movement had supporters in Riteve. In 1898 a society of *Banoth Zion* (Daughters of Zion) was formed. The women who belonged to this society promoted the *Shekel* and the stamps of *Keren Kayemeth LeYisrael*. Most of the Riteve Jews perceived members of this society as heretics. When Theodore Herzl died and the Zionists wanted to say *Kadish* in his memory at the synagogue, the public objected and the idea had to be abandoned.

The names of 89 Riteve Jews were included in three lists of contributors for the settlement of *Eretz-Yisrael* during the years 1898, 1899 and 1900, as published in the Hebrew newspaper *HaMelitz,* (see **Appendix 2**). The fundraisers were Elhanan Ahronson, Shemuel Zachs, Peretz Jochelson and G.H. Klenitsky. A delegate from Riteve participated in the conference of the Zionist Societies of Kovno and Suwalk *Gubernias* organized in the Kovno *Gubernia* during the fall of 1909. In 1891 Barukh Marcus from Riteve emigrated to *Eretz-Yisrael*. Some time later, he became the Rabbi in Haifa.

The list of contributors for victims of famine in Besarabia in 1909 includes names of 109 Riteve Jews. The *Agudath Yisrael* party had six contributors from Riteve in 1913.

At the end of the nineteenth and the beginning of the twentieth century many Riteve Jews emigrated to South Africa while others chose *Eretz-Yisrael*. Some later returned, having saved some money abroad.

During the drought in the summer of 1911 a fire broke out in the town destroying all of the wooden homes in the area.

Religious life centered around the synagogue and the *Beth Midrash*. Almost every Jew, if able, took part in evening Torah study groups offered by local societies.

Among the rabbis who served in Riteve were:
   Naftali-Hertz (1783-1828), born in Riteve, had several books on Torah issues published in Warsaw and Vilna.

Avraham-Aharon Burshtein (1867-1926), served in Riteve for five years, emigrated to *Eretz-Yisrael* in 1924, served as the head of the *yeshiva Merkaz Harav* in Jerusalem until his death. His son Aryeh was a journalist and general secretary of the *Tseirei Zion* party in Lithuania. His second son Reuven Barkat was the secretary of the Israeli Labor party and for some time the Israeli ambassador in Norway.

Yits'hak Eliyahu Gefen (?-1920), was head of a *yeshivah* in Slabodka before his term in Riteve.

Rabbi Avraham-Aharon Burshtein

According to the all-Russian census of 1897, 1,750 people lived in Riteve; 1,397 of them were Jewish (80%).

When World War I began a battalion of Cossacks arrived to defend the town against the Germans, but the Jews were the first to be attacked on the streets. In the spring of 1915 the German army occupied Riteve before the Russians were able to carry out the order to exile the Jews to Russia.

The Germans who controlled the town until 1918 introduced a Compulsory Education Law, and all Jewish children went to the German school that had been opened in the town. However, during the German occupation there were food shortages and the youngsters were enlisted to carry out forced labor.

During the period of independent Lithuania (1918-1940)
After the war and the establishment of the independent Lithuanian state in 1918, the Jewish community in Riteve dwindled and so did its percentage of the total population. According to the first government census of 1923, the population of Riteve was 1,720 people, 868 of them Jewish (50%). Before the war the percentage was 80%, and after the war it had decreased to 50%.

Following the passage of the Law of Autonomies for Minorities by the new Lithuanian government, the Minister for Jewish Affairs, Dr. Menachem

(Max) Soloveitshik, ordered elections to community committees *(Va'adei Kehilah)* to be held in the summer of 1919. In Riteve a *Va'ad (*community committee) was elected in 1919, despite the objections of different *Gabaim*. The committee worked for many years in all fields of Jewish life.

During the years when the currency was still the *Ostmark*, the town experienced economic prosperity. Merchants earned well but soon their funds were devalued, and when the Lithuanian *Litas* currency was introduced, the merchants were left with piles of worthless banknotes. Emigration intensified, and many Riteve Jews joined their relatives in South Africa. A few managed to obtain entry visas to America and to *Eretz-Yisrael*.

During that period, Riteve Jews worked in the trades and as skilled workers, while others engaged in agriculture by leasing orchards. Although many were tailors and shoemakers, there were also Jewish plasterers, carpenters and blacksmiths.

A view of Riteve

According to the government survey of 1931, Riteve had eighteen shops, fifteen of which belonged to Jews (83%) as shown below:

Type of business	Total	Owned by Jews
Butcher's shops and cattle trade	2	2
Restaurants and taverns	2	2
Food products	1	0
Textile products and furs	7	7
Medicine and cosmetics	1	0
Sewing machines and electric equipment	1	1
Watchmakers and jewelers	2	2
Other	2	1

Jews also owned a flourmill, a sawmill, a barbershop, a photography shop and a leather factory. Two Jewish doctors and two midwives offered services to the townspeople.

In 1937, twenty-one skilled Jewish workers worked in Riteve: six butchers, three shoemakers, two bookbinders, two tailors, two milliners, two watchmakers, one glazier, one barber, one tinsmith and one photographer.

The Jewish Popular Bank (*Folksbank*) played an important role in the economic life of Riteve Jews. In 1927 the bank had 193 members, in 1935 the numbers had decreased to 150. In 1939, there were 41 telephone subscribers, 15 of them Jewish.

In the middle of the 1930s the economic situation of Riteve Jews gradually deteriorated because of open propaganda against Jewish stores by the Lithuanian Merchants' Association (*Verslas*). At a regional conference of the Association in January 1939 calls against Jewish "parasites" were heard, with public announcements urging the boycott of the Jewish shops. The rise of the Nazis in neighboring Germany and the deterioration of commercial relations with Lithuania aggravated the situation.

In 1919 the Hebrew school in Riteve was opened to students. Later the school affiliated to the *Yavneh* chain.

The land returned to the community by the Oginsky family housed a modern *Talmud Torah* building and the Rabbi's residence. The funding for these projects was provided by the Riteve-born Mr. Kroskal, who lived in Frankfurt-on-Main.

Almost all the students in the school were girls. Although the boys studied at the *Talmud Torah* (40 boys in 1935), later they would attend the local *yeshivah* (10 boys in 1935). Some of the young students continued their studies at the Telz *Yeshivah* or the Hebrew gymnasium. The community had a library of about 1,300 books in Hebrew and Yiddish. The library also served as a meeting place for youths. From time to time, amateur groups would perform shows there.

During this period the Zionist movement had many supporters in Riteve, particularly among the youth. All Zionist parties were active and their supporters and members took part in the elections for the Zionist Congresses, as follows:

Cong No.	Year	Shek	Total Votes	Labor Party		Rev.	Gen. Zion		Gros	Miz
				Z"S	Z'Z					
14	1925	30	---	---	---	---	---	---	---	---
15	1927	114	75	9	30	2	22	---	---	12
16	1929	152	59	5	20	5	19	---	---	10
17	1931	93	77	4	29	17	20	---	---	7
18	1933	---	82	47		12	11	---	---	12
19	1935	---	255	142		---	11	1	---	101
21	1939	155	120	108		---	5		N.B 7	

Key: **Cong No. = Congress Number, Tot Shek = Total Shekalim, Rev. = Revisionists, Gen Zion = General Zionists, Gros = Grosmanists, Miz = Mizrakhi, N.B. = National Block**

Donations for *Keren Kayemeth LeYisrael* were often collected in the synagogues on the eve of Yom Kippur, where a large table held in bowls for donations to different societies. In the school the *Keren Kayemeth* stamps and the Blue Box were promoted. Fundraising for *Keren HaYesod* was organized once a year following the election for an emissary from the center in Kovno. During all these years the local fundraiser was Eliezer Prisman.

Among the Zionist youth organizations the most active were *HaShomer HaTsair, HeHalutz* and later also *Beitar*. *Kibbutz Hakhsharah* (Training Kibbutz) of *HeHalutz* was active for several years. A dozen Jewish youngsters from Riteve emigrated to *Eretz-Yisrael*. Sports activities were run by the local branch of Maccabi which had about 45 members.

The synagogue and the *Beth Midrash* were centers of religious life. The *Beth Midrash* also served as a learning center where almost all men would come in the evenings to study a chapter of the *Mishnah, Ein Ya'akov* or a page of the *Gemara*. The rabbi who served during this period (after 1926) was Shemuel Ponideler. In 1927 he emigrated to *Eretz-Yisrael* where he served as the director of a men's *Kolel* (a *yeshivah* community). In 1929 he returned to Riteve. He was murdered together with his community in the summer of 1941.

Rabbi Shemuel Ponideler

Welfare societies in Riteve, included *Linath HaTsedek,* whose members would stay overnight with sick people or watch their children during the day, *Bikur Holim*, which offered medical help, *Hevrah Kadisha, Ma'oth Hitim* and other societies.

See **Appendix 1** for a partial list of well-known personages born in Riteve.

During World War II and afterwards
In June 1940 Lithuania was annexed to the Soviet Union, becoming a Soviet Republic. Under new regulations, the majority of factories and shops belonging to Jews in Riteve were nationalized, and commissars were appointed to manage them. All Zionist parties and youth organizations were disbanded. Hebrew educational institutions were closed. Supply of goods decreased; as a result, prices soared. The middle class, mostly Jewish, bore the brunt, and the standard of living dropped gradually. At this time about 500 Jews still resided in the town.

With the invasion of the German army into the territory of the Soviet Union on June 22, 1941, Riteve Jews left the town looking for shelter in the neighboring villages. The next day the Germans entered the town. After heavy fighting with the retreating Russian army, fires broke out. The Lithuanian nationalists immediately organized and took over the town. In a short time they issued an order for all Jews to return to their homes. The order also caused the confiscation of property of any Lithuanian peasant who hid a Jew. The returning Jews found their houses burnt down. The majority of Jewish people were herded into animal stalls on Lithuanian peasants' farms and forced to sleep together with the cattle on layers of manure that covered the ground. Every day a few Germans and the Lithuanian guards would victimize the men, they made them run in a circle and sing while they themselves were bashing them with wooden bars. On July 1, all the Jews were transferred to another place where they were crowded into one building. The Lithuanian guards did not allow food, and the Jews were starving. A few times they were given moldy bread and herring left in storage by the Red Army. The starving people ate the food and became sick with diarrhea. The men were forced to clean toilets and streets. Women worked in laundries and washed the floors of the Lithuanian guards.

One day a Lithuanian guard murdered four Jewish young men suspected of being communists: Felix Radiskansky (aged 20), Heshel Gerber (29), and Nachman Smalle were executed by firing squad.

Thefts of clothing and valuables became a daily event. During the first days of the German occupation, when Jews worked at the Oginsky estate, Lithuanians harnessed Rabbi Shemuel Ponideler to a cart and forced him to pull, while they lashed him with whips. The rabbi succumbed to a heart attack and died shortly afterwards.

Later, Jews were threatened again, ordered to hand over money, gold and silver jewelry as well as other valuables to the guards. The frail elderly and the sick were transferred by carts to Telz together with their belongings. Others traveled 40 kilometers to Telz by foot in two and a half days. The Lithuanian guards escorting the walking convoy were even more cruel than their Germans counterparts. Riteve Jews were brought to the Rainiai camp where Telz Jews had already gathered. From there, all were transferred to the Viesvenai estate, about four kilometers from Rainiai. Jewish men, women and children from Vorne (Varniai), Tver (Tverai), Naveran (Nevarenai), Zharan (Zarenai), Alsiad (Alsedziai), along with women and children from Loikeve (Laukuva) were brought to this place. In Viesvenai they were forced to stay in five barns. The hunger, lice and filth were unbearable. The women were taken to work at the local farms, and the men were victimized by Lithuanians who forced them to perform so called "gymnastics." During the torture several Jews died or were shot.

On July 15, 1941, just before dusk, a truck with armed Lithuanians and a few Germans arrived at the camp. They led the 13-year-old boys to a nearby grove and murdered them. The next day they took older children and murdered them at the same place. The clothes of the victims were brought to the yard of the camp to be sorted. The women forced to sort the clothes recognized the belongings of their own loved ones, and found their documents and photos scattered near piles of clothing.

The mass grave near Viesvenai

The mass grave in Geruliai

On August 29, 1941 all the surviving women and children were transferred to the Geruliai camp where other women and children from Telz were held. On Shabbath, August 30 (7th of Elul, 5701) all were murdered. A few women survived, hidden by Lithuanian peasants. Several managed to make their way to the Shavl ghetto.

The ringleaders among the Lithuanian murderers were Stasys Ramaskis, Kazis Ramaskis, Olis Jokubaitis and others.

According to Soviet sources a mass grave with about forty families was found about two kilometers from the Viesvenai estate.

At the Holocaust Cellar on Mount Zion in Jerusalem a memorial plaque for the Riteve community was erected. At the Martyrs Forest on the Jerusalem Hills there is a grove of trees in memory of Riteve community.

Sources:
Yad Vashem archives, Jerusalem, M-1/Q-1322/136; M-1/E-1694/1562; M-9/15(6); Koniukhovsky collection 0-71, files 36, 37
Kamzon Y.D., *Yahaduth Lita*, page 60
Rituva *Yizkor* Book. Published by the Association of Former Rituva Jews in Israel, Tel Aviv, 1975
Yiddishe Shtime, Los Angeles, 25.7.1941; 8.1.1943; 26.2.1943; 4.6.1943; 6.8.1943; 14.7.1944; 11.8.1944; 25.8.1944; 15.12.1944; 12.1.1945
Einikait (Unity) (Yiddish), New York, December 1944
Di Yiddishe Shtime, Kovno, 13.5.1923; 22.5.1935; 29.7.1936; 24.7.1938; 24.1.1939
HaMelitz, St. Petersburg, 30.10.1878; 25.7.1879; 21.10.1879; 12.7.1881; 25.6.1883; 18.2.1888; 25.8.1889
Folksblat, Kovno, 23.12.1935
Naujienos, Chicago, (Lithuanian) 11.6.1949
Zemaitis; Plungyan county newspaper (Lithuanian), 24.6.1992
Saulute; Plungyan county weekly (Lithuanian), 20-27.11.1922

Appendix 1
A partial list of personages born in Riteve
Ze'ev Volf Avrekh (1845-1922), Yeshivah head in several towns of Lithuania.
Aharon-Shelomoh Zalmanovitz (1870-1941), was rabbi in several towns of Lithuania, in 1924 emigrated to Canada and was rabbi in Montreal till his death.
Barukh Markus (1870-1961), established and directed the yeshivah *Or Hadash* in Jerusalem for fourteen years together with Haim Zonenfeld. In 1906 settled in Haifa and was rabbi in the town for fifty five years. He was member of the Head Rabbinate Council.
Getsel (Georg) Zelikovitz (1863-1926), orientalist and researcher, lecturer of Egyptology at the University of Pennsylvania, published books and articles in different languages in the Jewish press in Russia and America.
Menahem-Mendel Serhey (18?? – 19??), a learned man and doctor in Riga, published a famous book on the laws on the *Milah* (Circumcision).
Aharon Ben Zion Shurin (1913-?), Rabbi in New York and Brooklyn, published many articles in Hebrew and Yiddish in the religious press and in the Yiddish newspaper Jewish Daily Forward.

Gavriel Grad (1890-1951), a music teacher in Kovno who emigrated to *Eretz-Yisrael* in 1926 and composed more than 500 musical compositions, 160 of which were published. He also composed melodies to many Hebrew songs and a few operas. He excelled as a musical educator in Israel.

Appendix 2
List of 89 Riteve donors for the Settlement of Eretz Yisrael as published in *HaMelitz*
(from Jewishgen>Databases>Lithuania>*HaMelitz*-by Jeffrey Maynard)

Surname	Given Name	Comments	Source	Year
AHARONZON	Elchanan		#56	1899
AHRONZON	Elchanan		#121	1900
AWERBACH	Moshe		#132	1898
AWERBACH	Nachman		#132	1898
AWERBUCH	Moshe		#56	1899
AWERBUCH	Moshe		#121	1900
AWERBUCH	Nachman		#121	1900
AWERBUCH	Yeshiyahu Mishel		#121	1900
BABUS	Shmuel		#56	1899
BORSHTEIN	Avraham Aharon	Rabbi Gaon ABD	#132	1898
BRITZ	Leib husband of Tzerna Friedman		#173	1898
COHEN	Meir		#56	1899
COHEN	Meir		#121	1900
EITZIKOWITZ	Moshe		#132	1898
EITZIKOWITZ	Moshe		#56	1899
EITZIKOWITZ	Moshe		#121	1900
FRIEDMAN	Moshe Zev brother of Yakov Dovid & Tzerna	wed	#173	1898
FRIEDMAN	Tzerna sister of Y D & M Z wife of Leib Britz	wed	#173	1898

Surname	Given Name	Comments	Source	Year
FRIEDMAN	Yakov Dovid brother of Moshe Zev & Tzerna		#173	1898
FRIEDMANN	Moshe Zev		#132	1898
FRISMAN	Yehoshua Kalman	rabbi	#121	1900
GEFEN	Avraham		#56	1899
GOREN	Yeshiyahu		#121	1900
GRAF	Yitzchok		#132	1898
HACOHEN	Avraham		#121	1900
HACOHEN	Ephraim Shmuel		#132	1898
HENDLER	Nachshon		#132	1898
HENDLER	Nachshon		#56	1899
HENDLER	Nachshon		#121	1900
KAMOWITZ	Moshe		#56	1899
KAPLAN	Yakov	has brother in Africa	#56	1899
KLAGMAN	Shalom		#132	1898
KLEIN	Moshe		#56	1899
KLENITZKI	G D		#132	1898
KLENITZKI	R		#132	1898
LASOWSKI	Meir		#56	1899
LEWINZOHN	Dovid		#132	1898
LEWITA	Dov		#56	1899
LEWITA	Dov		#121	1900
LEWITA	Eli		#56	1899
LEWITA	Eli		#121	1900
LEWITA	Mordechai Dov		#56	1899
LEWITA	Yakov		#121	1900
LOSONSKI	Meir		#121	1900
MARKOWITZ	Tuvia		#121	1900

Surname	Given Name	Comments	Source	Year
MARKUS	Yisroel		#56	1899
MARKUS	Yisroel		#121	1900
MAWSHOWITZ	Yosef ben Yehuda Leib		#56	1899
MEGOREL	Mordechai		#121	1900
MISHUB	Yosef ben Dovid		#121	1900
MOZESZOHN	Moshe Yitzchok		#132	1898
MOZESZOHN	Moshe Yitzchok		#56	1899
MOZESZON	Moshe Yitzchok		#121	1900
ODWIN	Shraga		#121	1900
ORWIN	Shraga		#56	1899
POLUKAST	Yitzchok		#56	1899
POLUKSHT	Yitzchok Leib		#121	1900
RIK	Moshe Aharon		#137	1900
RIK	Moshe Aharon		#137	1900
SEGAL	Moshe		#56	1899
SEGAL	Yosef		#121	1900
SHAPIRO	Boruch		#132	1898
SHAPIRO	Boruch		#121	1900
SHAPIRO	Dovid		#121	1900
SHAPIRO	Elchanan		#132	1898
SHAPIRO	Yisroel Dov		#132	1898
SHAPIRO	Yisroel Dov		#121	1900
SHAPIRO	Yitzchok		#132	1898
SHATIN	Ezriel		#121	1900
SHOZREROWER	Chaim		#56	1899
TZELKE	Aharon	Rabbi	#56	1899
TZELKER	Aharon	Rabbi	#121	1900
YAVETZ	Moshe Dovid		#132	1898

Surname	Given Name	Comments	Source	Year
YAVETZ	Shmuel		#56	1899
YEBATZ	Feige Leah		#121	1900
YOCHELSOHN	Katrial		#132	1898
YOCHELSOHN	Peretz		#132	1898
ZACHS	Aharon		#121	1900
ZACHS	Eli		#56	1899
ZACHS	Eli Yehoshua		#121	1900
ZACHS	Nachman		#132	1898
ZACHS	Shmuel		#121	1900
ZACHS	Shmuel Dovid		#56	1899
ZACHS	Simcha		#121	1900
ZACHS	Yakov		#56	1899
ZACHS	Yakov		#121	1900
ZACHS	Yitzchok		#56	1899
ZACHS	Yitzchok Dov		#121	1900
ZINGER	Micha		#132	1898

Seda (Siad)

Seda (Siad in Yiddish) is located in the northwestern part of Lithuania, in the Zamut (Zemaitija) region, about 26 kilometers southwest of the district administrative center Mazheik (Mazeikiai). The Varduva River flows through the town, connecting to a small millpond. A settlement by the name of Seda was mentioned in historical sources dating back to the thirteenth century. In 1508 a Catholic church was built in Seda, but during the second half of the sixteenth century it was converted into a Calvinist center. In 1638 the lands of Seda were purchased by the Sapiega family, town developers who turned it into a center of economic activity. A weekly market and four annual fairs were conducted in Seda.

Until 1795 Seda was included in the Polish-Lithuanian Kingdom. According to the third division of Poland in the same year by the three superpowers of those times, Russia, Prussia and Austria, Lithuania was divided between Russia and Prussia. As most of the other towns of Lithuania, Seda became part of the Russian Empire, first under the auspices of the Vilna province (*Gubernia*) and from 1843 under the Kovno *Gubernia* in the Telz district. At that time Seda became a county administrative center with its own schools and other government institutions. Commercial buildings were erected at the market place. At the end of the nineteenth century the town boasted forty stores, twenty pubs and restaurants, a flour mill and a post office.

At the end of 1918, during the struggle for a Lithuanian state, the Bolsheviks (Communists) seized power in Seda and surrounding areas, keeping control for several months.

Seda continued to preserve its status as a county administrative center in the Mazheik district during the period of Independent Lithuania (1918-1940) and during Soviet rule (1940-1941), continuing through the years of the Nazi occupation (1941-1944).

Jewish settlement before World War I
Jews most likely began to settle in Seda in the middle of the eighteenth century. Decades later the Jewish community grew to be the largest in the region. In 1847, 1,729 Jews lived in Seda, and according to the all-Russian census of 1897, there were 1,384 Jews out of a total population of 2,015 (69%). Jews made their living in trade, crafts and small-scale agricultural activities.

About 40 families maintained agricultural farms and residences covering an area of about 100 hectares in a village near the town. The neighbors called that place *Zydu Dvaras* (Jewish Farm).

During the Polish rebellion in 1831, Siad Jews suffered at the hands of both the rebels and the Cossacks who were sent in to quell the rebellion. On 8

June, 1831 the Jewish community of Siad received an edict from Captain Borisovitz, the commander of the rebels, stating that every Jew seen on the road at a distance of a hundred feet from the town would be shot, and the community would pay the Polish army 333 Polish guilders and ten groschen (cents) for not controlling trespassers. On June 17, Borisovitz warned the Jews about spying activities, telling them that a Jew by the name of Yits'hak ben David Dukhin, who worked at a bar of the Yankovsky tavern, had been hanged for espionage.

Siad - a view near the pond

At that time most intellectual and social activities concentrated around the *Beth Midrash*, the synagogue and other religious institutions.

The *Gemiluth Hesed* fund played an important role in the community, supported by Eliezer Ordongin and Shimon-Aba Gordon and others. Donations were also received from a former resident of Siad, the wealthy businessman Leib Perl from St. Petersburg.

On the eve of *Pesakh* of 1886, a huge fire broke out in Siad that destroyed 200 homes and numerous buildings, most of them belonging to Jews. Five people lost their lives in the fire, and 255 families, numbering about 1000 people, became homeless and destitute.

The Rabbi issued an urgent appeal to nearby towns. Soon Siad was inundated with parcels of *Matsoth*, meat and other foods for the holiday season. Shelomoh-Mosheh Levenberg from Mazheik and other rabbis from the nearby communities published an appeal for help in the Hebrew newspaper *HaMelitz*. Two aid committees were organized to work on receiving and distributing the goods among the needy. One committee was headed by the pharmacist A. Kahan with the assistance of L. Tiger and A. Zax. The second was led by Count Plater (who himself donated 200 rubles and grain, bread and other foods), nobleman Oginsky and other high-ranking government officials. Donations designated to rebuild a new *Beth Midrash* were received from America. Despite all the efforts, the restoration work took several years, and in the meantime many Jews emigrated overseas, resulting in significant decrease in the Jewish population of Siad.

The list of contributors for the settlement of *Eretz-Yisrael* between the years 1897-1900 includes 53 names of Siad Jews, as published in *HaMelitz* (see **Appendix 1**).

Before World War I the rabbis who served in Siad were:
Joel-Yits'hak Katsenelbogen
David Regensberg
Moshe-Barukh HaLevi Hurvitz, *Dayan*
Yisrael-Ezra HaLevi Levin (1892-1903)
Mordehai Graf, from 1912

Among the personages born in Siad were:
Ya'akov Geri (Hering), who later became the Minister for Commerce and Industry in the Israeli Government
The journalist Yits'hak ben David (Binder)
The poetess Leah Kaplan, burned to death in the Kovno ghetto in 1944
Professor Benyamin Ziv (1879-1947), from 1936 in *Eretz-Yisrael*, became Head of the Faculty of Law and Economics at the Hebrew University in Jerusalem.

Professor Benyamin Ziv

During Independent Lithuania (1918-1940)
Due to social and economic difficulties, emigration of Siad Jews continued. The birth rate was very low. In 1920 there were twenty-four deaths but only nine births and four weddings, strongly indicating that the number of the Jews was dwindling.

Following the passage of the Law of Autonomies for Minorities issued by the new Lithuanian government, the Minister for Jewish Affairs, Dr. Menachem (Max) Soloveitshik, ordered elections to community committees *(Va'adei Kehilah)* to be held in the summer of 1919. In 1920 a *Va'ad (*community committee) with eleven members was elected in Siad. The committee worked in all fields of Jewish life until the end of 1925. By its initiative several social and religious institutions including the *Talmud Torah, Linath Hatsedek, Lehem Aniyim* and *Malbish Arumim* became active again. A Hebrew School was opened as well, accommodating 65 students.

A street in Siad

In the elections for the first *Seimas* (Parliament) in Lithuania in 1922, Siad Jews cast 289 votes for the Zionist list, 88 votes for the religious *Akhdut* and only 2 votes for the democrats.

According to first census performed by the new Lithuanian government in 1923 the Siad population was 1,851, with 815 of them Jewish (44%).

Siad Jews made their living in trade, crafts and auxiliary farms. Jewish shops were located in two large buildings in the market square. Weekly market days on Mondays and Wednesdays and the three annual fairs provided opportunities for trade.

According to the government survey of 1931 there were 31 active businesses in Siad, 29 of them in Jewish hands (93%) as shown:

Type of business	Total	Owned by Jews
Grocery stores	1	1
Grain and flax	2	2
Butcher's shops and cattle trade	5	4
Restaurants and taverns	3	3
Food products	2	2
Textile products and furs	7	6
Leather and shoes	4	4
Haberdashery and house utensils	1	1
Medicine and cosmetics	1	1
Hardware products	3	3
Bicycles and electrical equipment	1	1
Timber and heating material	1	1

According to the same survey the town had fifteen factories, six of them owned by Jewish persons (40%).

Type of Factory	Total	Jewish owned
Power plants, metal workshops	1	0
Textile: wool, knitting	5	2
Dresses and shoes	1	0
Sawmills and furniture	4	2
Flour mills, bakeries, food production	3	1
Other	1	1

In 1927, the Jewish People's Bank (*Folksbank*) of Siad, directed by Izidor Kahan, had 154 members and exerted a commendable influence on the economic life of Siad Jews. A branch of the United Credit Association for Jewish Agrarians also provided services in Siad.

In 1939, there were 37 telephones listed in the town, 14 of them in the homes and business of Jews.

Rabbi Mordehai Rabinovitz served in Siad from 1935 until he was murdered in the summer of 1941 together with his community.

A library with many books in Yiddish and Hebrew formed by the Yiddishist association *Libhober fun Vissen* (Fans of Knowledge) was open for readers in Siad.

Many Siad Jews belonged to the Zionist camp and took part in the elections for the Zionist congresses. The results of their votes are given in the table below:

Cong No.	Year	Shek	Total Votes	Labor Party		Rev.	Gen. Zion	Gro	Miz
				Z"S	Z"Z				
15	1927	27	25	4	6	4	3	----	----	8
16	1929	68	32	15	6	9	---	----	----	2
17	1931	81	71	34	7	20	2	----	----	8
18	1933	---	164	143		7	4	----	4	6
19	1935	---	215	160		---	---	1	27	27
21	1939	76	60	38			5	---	16	1

Key: Cong No. = Congress Number, Tot Shek = Total Shkalim, Rev = Revisionists, Gen Zion = General Zionists, Gros = Grosmanists, Miz = Mizrakhi

Many of the Jewish youth spoke very good Hebrew and belonged to Zionist organizations such as *HaShomer HaTsair*. Sports activities were organized by *Maccabi* and *HaPoel* which had 60 members.

During World War II and afterwards

In June 1940 Lithuania was annexed by the Soviet Union, becoming a Soviet Republic. Following new regulations, the majority of Jewish factories and shops were nationalized, and commissars were appointed to manage them. All Zionist parties and youth organizations were disbanded, and Hebrew educational institutions were closed.

That year 2,087 people lived in Siad, of whom 400 (about 110 families) were Jewish.

On June 23, 1941, the day after the German invasion into the Soviet Union, the first German soldiers entered Siad. However, before their invasion, Lithuanian nationalists organized under the leadership of Kamaitis and Stankus were already murdering Jewish youths. Their first victims were the Binder brothers, Kon and other boys. The murders intensified, and among victims who were subject to torture was Rabbi Mordehai Rabinovitz. Soon all Jews were herded into the nearby "Jewish Farm" where they were kept without food and water for several days. On July 3, 1941 (8th of Tamuz 5701) armed Lithuanians took the men out, murdered them and buried them at a site near the Jewish cemetery.

The mass grave and the monument near the Jewish cemetery in Siad

The women and children were taken to the site of the Jewish cemetery in Mazheik on August 9, 1941 (15th of Av 5701), where they were murdered together with Jews from the surrounding towns. Horrific details of the last moments of the murdered Jews emerged later, as recounted by one of the murderers during his trial by the Lithuanian Soviet authorities on October 2, 1958.

The mass grave with the monument at the entrance to the site in Mazheik

The monument at the entrance to the murder site with the inscription in Yiddish and Lithuanian: "At this site Hitler's murderers and their local helpers executed about 4000 Jews and people of other nationalities."

The names of the murderers are recorded at the archives of Yad Vashem in Jerusalem.

At the beginning of the 1990s a monument was built at the place where the old Jewish cemetery of Siad had been, carrying an inscription in Hebrew and Lithuanian "The old Jewish cemetery; let the memory of the deceased live forever."

Sources:
Yad Vashem Archives, Jerusalem, M-1/E-1670/1555, 1771/1637;
Koniukhovsky Collection 0-71, file 21
YIVO, New York, Collection of Lithuanian Jewish Communities,
files 675-684
Gotlib, *Ohalei Shem*, page 201
Fridman A.A. Memories Book (Hebrew), pages 114-115
Kamzon Y.D. *Yahaduth Lita*, pages 75-76
Levin Dov, Seda (Siad), *Pinkas Hakehiloth-Lita* (Hebrew), Yad Vashem,
Jerusalem 1996
Unzer veg (Yiddish) Kovno, 2.7.1925
Di Yiddishe Shtime, Kovno, 2.8.1929; 26.5.1933
HaMelitz; St.Petersburg, 29.3.1881; 10.5.1881; 13.6.1885; 18.4.1886;
4.6.1886; 27.4.1887; 2.6.1903
Janulaitis Augustinas, *Zydai Lietuvoje* (Jews in Lithuania) (Lithuanian),
Kaunas, 1924, pages 139-140
Vicas J., S.S *Tarniboje* (In the S.S. service) (Lithuanian), Vilnius 1966,
pages 48-49
Masines Zudynes Lietuvoje (mass murder in Lithuania) (Lithuanian), Vol. 2,
Page 399

Appendix 1
**List of 53 Siad Jewish donors for the settlement of *Eretz-Yisrael* as
published in *HaMelitz***
(From JewishGen>Databases>Lithuania>Hamelitz-by Jeffrey Maynard)

Surname	Given Name	Comments	Source	Year
ABRACH	Done		Hamelitz #191	1900
ALECHSANDER	Sarah		#191	1900
BAII	Chaim		#191	1900
BAII	Chanah	widow	#191	1900
BAII	Sarah		#191	1900
BEINKO	Avraham		#191	1900
BLOCH	Sarah		#191	1900
BORBEITZKI	Dovid		#191	1900
BORBEITZKI	Ester		#191	1900

Surname	Given Name	Comments	Source	Year
BORBEITZKI	Zlote		#191	1900
COHEN	Sheine	widow	#191	1900
EDELSHTEIN	Breine		#191	1900
GOPERSHTOK	Rochel		#191	1900
HELPER	Sarah		#191	1900
KOCHMISTER	Tzvi husband of Alte Zachs	wed in Shad	#191	1900
KOLK	Chaim husband of Mina Zalkower	wed 1897	#145	1897
LEWIN		rabbi's wife	#191	1900
MARKOWHEWITZ	Toiba		#191	1900
ORDONG		sisters	#191	1900
PREIS	Frume		#191	1900
RITOWA	Ch		#191	1900
RUBIN	Aharon		#191	1900
RUBIN	Zalman Boruch		#191	1900
SEGAL	Chaya		#191	1900
SHAPIRO	Toibe		#191	1900
SHIF	Dov		#191	1900
SHIF	Ester		#191	1900
TIGER	Devorah		#191	1900
TIGER	Mina		#191	1900
TIGER	Miriam		#191	1900
WEINROCH	Rochel		#191	1900
WEINSHTEIN	Gitl		#191	1900
WOLFOWITZ	Tzvi fiance of widow Gordon of Koshedori	engaged	#56	1899
YOFE	Reize		#191	1900

Surname	Given Name	Comments	Source	Year
ZACHS	Alte wife of Tzvi Kochmister	wed in Shad	#191	1900
ZACHS	Chanah		#191	1900
ZAKS	Aharon father of Rochel Nechama		#198	1900
ZAKS	Rochel Nechama bas Aharon		#198	1900
ZALKOWER	Aharon father of Mina		#145	1897
ZEINGER	Ester		#191	1900
ZELIKOWITZ	Zara Roza		#191	1900
ZEWIL	Chaya		#191	1900
ZEWIL	Chaya Leah		#191	1900
ZILBERT	Sarah		#191	1900
ZIW	Ephraim		#191	1900
ZIW	Ephraim		#285	1900
ZIW	Hane		#191	1900
ZIW	Meir husband of Sarah		#285	1900
ZIW	Rochel Leah		#191	1900
ZIW	Sarah wife of Meir		#285	1900
ZIWAN	Sarah		#191	1900
ZUSMANOWITZ	Sarah		#191	1900

Šeduva (Shadeve)

Seduva (Shadeve in Yiddish) is situated in the center of Lithuania, about 42 kilometers west of the Ponevezh (Panevezys) district administrative center. Shadeve was first mentioned in archival documents dating back to the fifteenth century. In the sixteenth and seventeenth centuries its growth can be attributed largely to the construction of nearby Kovno-Riga commercial road. In the second half of the seventeenth century the town acquired the status of a county administrative center and became a commercial town with storefronts, shops and taverns. In 1654 Shadeve was granted the Magdeburg Rights of self-rule and a permit to run one weekly market day and four annual fairs.

Until 1795 Shadeve was included in the Polish-Lithuanian Kingdom. According to the third division of Poland in the same year by the three superpowers of those times, Russia, Prussia and Austria, Lithuania was divided between Russia and Prussia. As most of Lithuania, Shadeve became part of the Russian Empire, first under the jurisdiction of Vilna province (*Gubernia*) and from 1843 in the Kovno *Gubernia*.

In 1798, Baron T. von Ropp bought Shadeve and the surrounding areas. The railway, constructed two kilometers away between 1871 and 1873, encouraged the local export trade of grains, flax and seeds to Liepaja in Latvia.

During the years of Independent Lithuania (1918-1940) and after, Shadeve retained its status of a county administrative center. In 1924 Shadeve acquired the title of a town with self-rule.

Jewish settlement until after World War I
Jews lived in Shadeve dating back to the fifteenth century. Rabbi Mosheh "*HaGolah*" was born in Sheduve in 1449 and lived there until he was 31 years old. At the beginning of the eighteenth century, on the initiative of Chartorisky, the deputy Chancellor of Lithuania, many Jews settled in Shadeve. In 1766 there were 508 Jewish taxpayers. They worked in the small trades, crafts and agriculture. By the end of the 1780s, there were 43 shops, probably all Jewish. Jews rented land upon which they cultivated vegetables and fruits that they sold to the merchants of Riga and St. Petersburg.

During the Polish rebellion of 1831, Shadeve Jews found themselves "between a hammer and a sword" and they suffered at the hands of both the rebels and the Cossacks who were brought in to suppress the rebellion. Cows and horses confiscated from the estates and from the rebels were herded to the camp of the Russian General Tolstoy. On July 2, 1831 seven Jewish merchants escorted by a policeman (*Ispravnik*) went to the camp of the Russian army intending to purchase the cattle. On the way a small group of rebels attacked the merchants, robbed them of their money and hanged them in the Pakalnishki Forest, in the vicinity of Shadeve. Only the policeman managed to escape.

In 1847, the Jewish population of the town was 1,211. In 1880 the Jewish population increased to 2,386 (63%) out of a total population of 3,783.

In the 1880s, during the great emigration of Russian Jews overseas (mainly to America), many Jews had to cross the border to Germany with assistance of smugglers. In Shadeve some Jews participated in the smuggling of emigrants over the border and were known not always to have treated the migrants fairly.

During the years of famine between 1868 and 1870, Shadeve Jews suffered considerably, consequently getting help from the Aid Committee in Memel. In 1871 and 1872, in spite of their own difficulties, 128 Shadeve Jews donated money to the victims of the great famine in Persia, and the Hebrew newspaper *HaMagid* presented the list of 128 contributors from the town (see **Appendix 4).**

Jewish boys received their education in *Heder*-like institutions. In 1879 a four-year grade school opened, and local Jews undertook to raise a fixed sum for its annual support. Rabbi Yosef-Leib Blokh, later the head of the Telz *Yeshivah*, established a *Yeshivah* in Shadeve. In 1910, following his move to Telz, Rabbi Aharon Baksht replaced him. Approximately fifty young men studied in this *Yeshivah*. Rabbi Baksht also formed the Shadeve *Yeshivah Ketanah.*

The great fire of 1871 destroyed 150 houses, and 300 Jewish families became homeless and destitute. In 1884 another fire affected 200 Jewish families reducing them to poverty. Zamut Jews, in particular Keidan (Kedainiai) Jews, donated considerable amounts of money to the victims. Having realized the gravity of the situation, Baron von Ropp, who owned the town and the surrounding areas, helped many Jews by providing building materials and funds for home reconstruction.

Public life centered on the synagogue and a few small prayer houses. In 1866, the *Hevrah Kadisha* inaugurated a beautiful synagogue in Shadeve. One of the most beautiful *Aron Kodesh* in Lithuania was added in 1895. Since 1902 a *Somekh Noflim* society, was formed; its task was to grant small interest-free loans to be repaid in small installments. Also the Zionist movement was active and had a mandate to raise funds for the settlement of *Eretz-Yisrael*. The list of contributors for the settlement of *Eretz-Yisrael* between 1883 and 1900, as published in the Hebrew newspaper *HaMelitz* lists names of 57 Shadeve Jews (see **Appendix 3**). The Bund party was active in the underground until World War I.

For a partial list of the rabbis who served in Shadeve before World War I see **Appendix 1.**

According to the census of 1897, the population of Shadave was 4,474 of which 2,513 were Jewish (56%).

At the beginning of World War I Shadeve was almost completely burnt down.

During the period of independent Lithuania (1918-1940)
Economy and Society:
Following the end of German occupation Shadeve Jews began to re-establish their businesses and social life. According to the first census carried out by the new Lithuanian government in 1923, the number of the Jews in town was only 916 (29%) out of a total population of 3,186, compared to 56% before the war.

General View of Shadeve

Following the passage of the Law of Autonomies for Minorities by the new Lithuanian government, the Minister for Jewish Affairs, Dr. Menachem (Max) Soloveitshik, ordered elections to community committees *(Va'adei Kehilah)* to be held in the summer of 1919. In 1920 a *Va'ad (*community committee) with eleven members was elected in Shadeve: two from *Tseirei Zion*, one from the *Mizrahi* list and eight non-party men. The committee worked in all fields of Jewish life until the end of 1925.

In the elections for the municipal council of 1931 two Jews were elected among its nine members (Leizer Melamed and Berl Peim).

During that period the Shadeve Jews made their living in trade, crafts, light industry and agriculture. According to the government survey of 1931 there were 36 shops in the town, 31 of them owned by Jews (86%).

The distribution according to type of business is given in the table below:

Type of business	Total	Owned by Jews
Grocery stores	1	1
Grain and flax	1	1
Butcher's shops and cattle trade	6	6
Restaurants and taverns	1	0
Food products	7	7
Beverages	1	1
Textile products and furs	5	5
Leather and shoes	2	2
Haberdashery and household utensils	2	2
Medicine and cosmetics	2	0
Watches and jewelry	1	1
Hardware products	2	2
Bicycles and electrical equipment	2	1
Timber and heating material	2	2
Stationery and books	1	0

According to the same survey there were industrial 20 enterprises, 13 of them Jewish-owned (65%).

Type of Factory	Total	Jewish owned
Power plants, metal workshops	1	1
Dresses, shoes, furs, hats	3	2
Textile: wool, flax, knitting	3	2
Sawmills and furniture	1	1
Flour mills, bakeries, food production	10	6
Other	2	1

In 1925, a Jewish doctor and a Jewish dentist provided services to the population. In 1937 thirty-seven Jewish trades people worked in Shadeve: eight shoemakers, seven tailors, six butchers, three barbers, two milliners, two tinsmiths, two needle trade people, one baker, one glazier, one bookbinder, one locksmith, one painter, one photographer and one saddler.

At the annual conference of the Trade Association held in February 1938, Y. Kolektor was elected chairman of the branch, Shimon Segal as the secretary and Lipa Pamuz as the treasurer.

The Jewish Popular Bank (*Folksbank*) played an important role in the economic life of the Shadeve Jews. Upon its establishment in 1927 there were 266 members, however in 1929 there were only 216 members.

The workers of the Folksbank

The economic crisis of Lithuania and the open propaganda against Jewish shops organized by the Association of Lithuanian Merchants (*Verslas*) resulted in deterioration of the economic situation of Shadeve Jews. A large number of community members needed support from their relatives abroad.

Two orphans who emigrated overseas became financially very successful. After a time one of them, Shemuel Bar, returned to Shadeve to donate generously to community institutions and to everybody who turned to him and, of course, to his relatives who had raised him as a child.

During these years many Shadeve Jews emigrated to America, South Africa and *Eretz-Yisrael*. One of these migrants was Reuven Shnaider who became one of the founders of *Kefar Malal* (named after Moshe Leib Lilienblum).

In 1939, there were 47 telephones listed, 17 of which belonged to Jews.

Relations between the Jews and the Lithuanian population were generally good, but deteriorated at that time. Often the Lithuanians would mock and make scornful comments on the Jews. From time to time attacks on Jews were instigated and there were libels against Jews. A few Shadeve Jewish men were known to react strongly to such incidents.

A market day in Shadeve

In December 1931 a blood libel against Shadeve Jews was instigated because a Lithuanian boy pretended to have disappeared. After the Nazis took control in the neighboring Germany and after the annexation of the Memel region in 1939 to Germany, the situation became worse. Attacks against Jews were reported in January 1940.

Education and Public activities:

Schools in Shadeve included a *yeshivah*, two *Heder* schools for boys and a Hebrew school of the *Tarbuth* chain. Its last headmaster was the teacher Fish. The Jewish public library had hundreds of books in Hebrew, Yiddish, German and Russian. A few youngsters studied at the Hebrew High Schools in Kovno, Ponevezh and Shavl. A few others were enrolled at the Ponevezh *yeshivah* while students with high grades studied at the public high school. All youngsters were able to speak and write Hebrew. From time to time cultural activities were organized. In 1935 a public performance of the 1907 play *Got fun Nekome* (God of Revenge) by the Yiddish writer Sholem Asch was organized.

A group of *Hashomer HaTsair* Scouts in Shadeve, 1923

Many Shadeve Jews belonged to the Zionist camp and all Zionist parties were supported. The results of the elections for the Zionist Congresses are given in the table below:

Cong No.	Year	Tot Shek	Total Votes	Labor Party		Rev	Gen Zion		Gros	Miz
				Z"S	Z"Z		A	B		
14	1925	40	---	---	---	---	---	---	---	---
15	1927	35	---	---	---	---	---	---	---	---
16	1929	60	25	13	4	3	4	---	---	1
17	1931	48	35	6	6	14	3	---	---	6
18	1933	---	135	96		---	10	---	3	25
19	1935	281	255	132		---	15	45	16	47
21		92	68	44			5		N.B 19	

Key: Cong No. = Congress Number, Tot Shek = Total Shekalim, Rev = Revisionists, Gen Zion = General Zionists, Gros = Grosmanists, Miz = Mizrahi, N.B. = National Block

Among the Zionist youth organizations were *HaShomer HaTsair* with about 76 members and *HeHalutz* with 9 members (1932). In 1934 an urban Training Kibbutz of *HeHalutz* was formed in Shadeve. Sport activities were organized in the local branch of Maccabi with about 42 members.

Religious life centered on the old synagogue which held an *Aron Kodesh* with artistic carvings, also the new *Beth Midrash* and the smaller prayer houses. Shadeve had the oldest *Sefer Torah* (Torah Scroll) in Lithuania.

The religious youth belonged to the *Tifereth Bahurim* and *Beth Ya'akov* movements (established in 1931).

The rabbis who served at that period were Aharon Baksht, who was murdered in the Holocaust and Ben-Zion Notelevitz (served from 1926). The last rabbi of Shadeve was Mordehai-David Henkin, who was murdered together with his congregation.

For a partial list of personages born in Shadeve see **Appendix 2.**

A group of *Hashomer HaTsair* Scouts around the camp table, 1924

During World War II and afterwards

In summer of 1940 Lithuania was annexed to the Soviet Union and became a Soviet Republic. Under the new regulations, the Shadeve factories, owned mostly by Jews, were nationalized. Jewish shops were also nationalized and in many cases the former owners were appointed to manage them. All Zionist parties and youth organizations were disbanded, and the Hebrew school was closed. Supply of goods decreased and, as a result, prices soared. The middle class, mostly Jewish, bore the brunt of this situation and the standard of living dropped gradually.

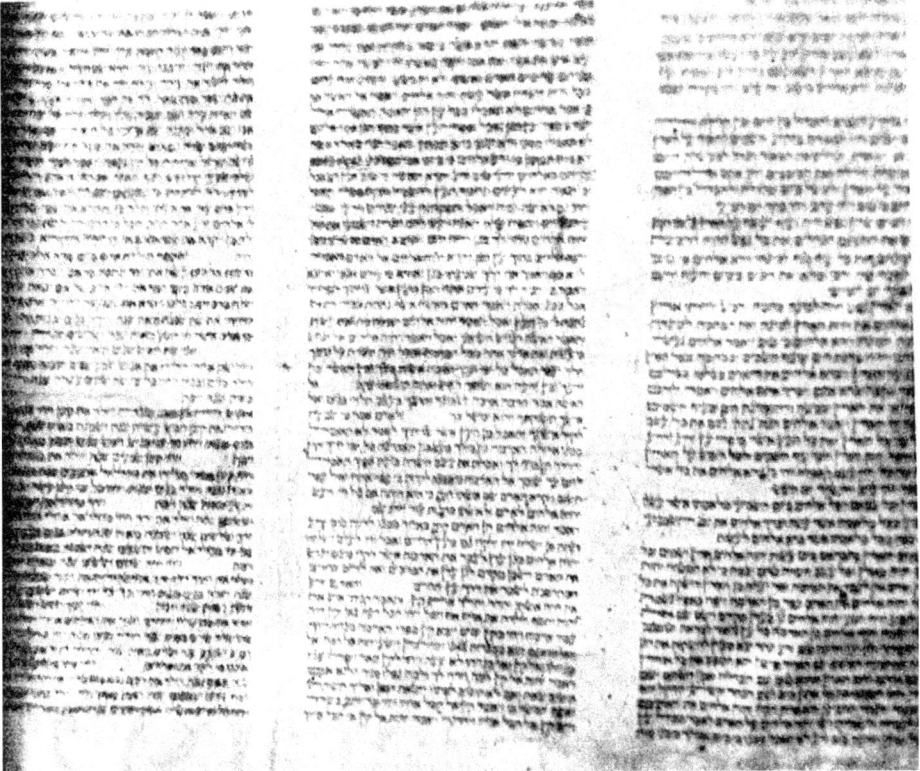

A fragment of the oldest Sefer Torah in Lithuania

When the German army invaded the Soviet Union on June 22, 1941, Shadeve Jews tried to escape to Russia in carts and by foot. The Lithuanian nationalists, who were already organized and armed, robbed and sometimes murdered the refugees on the roads. Within a few days most of the refugees had returned home.

The Germans entered Shadeve on June 26, 1941 and the Lithuanians received them joyfully and with flowers. The German army moved forward into Russia and several Germans remained in Shadeve. The Lithuanians, headed by the teacher Grinius, took control of the town, and forced the Jews to wear a white band with a yellow Magen David stitched on the sleeve. Refugees from other places who happened to be in Shadeve were forced to return to their homes. Youngsters who were assigned duties during the years of Soviet rule were detained and murdered. Jews who were employed in clearing the debris of the arms factory in Linkaiciai blown up by the Soviets before their retreat, were accused of stealing grenades and were shot. The railway station where great quantities of food, ammunition and building materials were stored by the Soviets, engaged Jews as laborers. Jews also swept the streets and cleaned the market square. All the work was done under the guard of armed Lithuanians who would abuse and maltreat the workers.

In the middle of July an order was issued for all the Jews to lock and leave their homes, after pasting a note on the door with the name of the owner. They were then ordered to gather in the market square. They were allowed to take a small parcel and were told to hand over keys of their homes to the police.

They were then transported, heavily guarded, passing a few stations on the way, and in the middle of the night they arrived at the village Pabarstyciai, about five kilometers from Shadeve. There, they were crowded into two unfinished wooden structures with no water and no light that the Soviets had intended to use as barracks; it had a low barbed wire fence with a guard stationed at it. Twenty-five Jewish youngsters who had worked at nearby farms were brought to this camp as well. They had wounds from blows inflicted by the Lithuanian guards. The only Jewish doctor present at the scene was Dr. Patorsky, who tended the wounded.

The camp inmates were provided with small amounts of food that guards had collected from the deserted Jewish homes.

The day the Jews were taken out of their homes amid death threats, they were forced to hand over money, gold and other valuables in their possession. On August 3, 1941 the Lithuanians took ten more men out of the camp for "labor" activities. On the way to Radvilishok (Radviliskis) they were shot near lime pits, and their bodies covered with lime. In the middle of August the Lithuanians took twenty-seven Jews out of the camp, including Rabbi Mordehai-David Henkin, and led them to the neighboring village of Kauliskiai where they were shot dead. Thirty-five Jews who worked on the farms at the Raudondvaris estate, a few kilometers away, were also murdered and buried at the same place.

On August 25, 1941 (2nd of Elul, 5701) the last Shadeve Jews were loaded on trucks, and driven to the Liaudiskiai forest, about 10 kilometers to the southwest of Shadeve, where all were shot. According to Soviet sources two mass graves were found containing the bodies of 664 men, women and children. After the murders, the murderers held an all-night drinking feast.

Three families, which included Dr. Patorsky, and the Nul and Kuper families who were fighters in the Lithuanian battles of independence were allowed to remain in the town six further weeks, but were shot later. Only Shulamith, the wife of Nul, managed to survive by hiding at a peasant's farm all the years until the liberation.

Mass grave near the village Pakutenai (one of two massacre sites). The inscriptions on the tablet are in Yiddish, Hebrew and Lithuanian.

The names of the Lithuanians who robbed and murdered the Jews are recorded at the archives of Yad Vashem in Jerusalem.

After the war monuments were erected at mass graves.

According to the census of 1970 and 1979 one Jew lived in Shadeve. In 1985 not one Jew remained in the town.

The second massacre site near Pakutenai village. The burial site of the six Jews who managed to escape from the camp in Pabarstyciai village. In August 1941 all of them were tortured to death by the Lithuanian Nazi collaborators.

The massacre site in Liaudiskiai forest
The inscriptions in Yiddish, Hebrew and Lithuanian state: "In this place, on August 25, 1941, the Hitlerist murderers and their local collaborators murdered about 800 Seduva Jews, men, women, children."

Sources:
Yad Vashem archives, Jerusalem, M-33/975; Koniukhovsky collection 0-71, files 61-64
YIVO, collection of Lithuanian Jewish Communities, files 1207-1211, pages 56688-56835
Lipman M.D., The history of the Jews in Kovno and Slabodka (Hebrew), Pages 25-33
Kamzon Y.D., *Yahaduth Lita* (Hebrew), pages 95, 100
HaMelitz, St. Petersburg (Hebrew), 28.11.1867; 1.1.1879; 5.8.1879; 31.5.1881; 25.4.1884; 30.6.1884; 21.7.1884; 24.2.1887; 6.3.1887; 13.2.1888; 21.2.1888; 27.6.1888; 15.11.1899; 23.7.1902
Di Yiddishe Shtime, Kovno (Yiddish), 13.11.1931; 17.12.1931; 25.3.1932; 22.6.1932; 1.3.1938; 12.2.1939
Dos Naie Vort, Kovno (Yiddish) 22.7.1934
Folksblat, Kovno (Yiddish) 16.41937; 28.2.1938
Der Yiddisher Kooperator, Kovno (Yiddish) # 8-9, 1929
Dos Vort, Kovno (Yiddish) 13.12.1935
Yiddisher Hantverker, Kovno (Yiddish) # 16, 1939
Kovner Tog (Yiddish) 8.6.1926
Naujienos, Chicago (Lithuanian) 11.6.1949
Augustinas Janulaitis; *Zydai Lietuvoje* (Jews in Lithuania) (Lithuanian), Kaunas, 1923

Appendix 1
A partial list of rabbis who officiated in Shadeve till World War I
Gershon Kremer, cousin of the Rabbi Eliyahu, Gaon from Vilna, served in Shadeve 1831, wrote several books.
Eliezer-Simhah Rabinovitz (1832-1911), was active in public issues.
Noakh Rabinovitz (1832-1902), in Shadeve from 1890, preached for the settlement of *Eretz-Yisrael*, published several books.
Simhah HaLevi Hurvitz, in Shadeve from 1871.
Yehudah-Leib Rif, from 1886.
Avraham-Aharon Burshtein (1867-1926), in Shadeve 1901-1902.
Yosef Kanovitz, from 1903.
Yosef-Yehudah-Leib Blokh (1849-1930), in Shadeve 1905-1910, moved to Telz where he became the rabbi of the town and the head of the famous Yeshivah.

Rabbi Yosef Yehudah Leib Blokh   **Rabbi Eliezer Simhah Rabinovitz**

Rabbi Aharon Baksht

Appendix 2
A partial list of personages born in Shadeve

Rabbi Mosheh ben Ya'akov-Moshe (*HaGolah*) (1449-1520), studied in Istanbul, returned to Shadeve in 1495 where he wrote his book *Sodoth Shoshan* (in the steps of the Rambam), later was Rabbi in Krim, where he died.

Shemuel-Yits'hak Hilman (1868-1953), was Rabbi in Berezino, Glasgow and London. In 1934 emigrated to *Eretz-Yisrael* where he became headmaster and director of the *Yeshivah Or HaYashar* in Jerusalem. He published twenty volumes of his book on the *Talmud*.

Hayim-Mordehai Kotz (1894-1930), was active in the *Yavneh* movement and in the establishment of the preparatory class of the Telz *Yeshivah*. In 1940 arrived in America where he together with A.M. Blokh established the Cleveland *Yeshivah*.

Yisrael Mah-Yafith (Ma Yofis) (1897-1930), authorized rabbi, writer and poet, translated popular poems of Kh. N. Bialik into Yiddish and the allegories of Krilov into Hebrew and Yiddish. For ten years he wrote for the Yiddish newspaper *Di Yiddishe Shtime* that was published in Kovno. A selection of his writings in Hebrew and Yiddish was published in a book in Tel Aviv in 1970, by *Menorah* publishers.

Yisrael Mah-Yafith

Appendix 3
List of 57 Sheduva Jews, donors for the Settlement of *Eretz-Yisrael*, as published in *HaMelitz* 1893-1900
(From JewishGen>Databases>Lithuania>*Hamelitz*, by Jeffrey Maynard)

Surname	Given Name	Comment	Source	Year
AMALS	Tanchum	in Johannesburg, SA	#2	1897
AMALSKI	Tanchum		#137	1900
AMALSKI	Zalman		#137	1900
BERGMAN	Shlomo Elihu		#35	1900
BRET	Akiva		#35	1900
DIMONT	Shmuel		#10	1897
FLEISHMAN	Mordechai		#10	1897
FRANK	Dovid		#35	1900
FRANK	Noson		#35	1900
FRIDGUT	Avraham Yakov		#10	1897
FRIDLAND	Boruch Tzvi		#35	1900
FRIDLAND	Meir Yona		#35	1900
FRIDLANDER	Yehoshua ben Yehuda Leib	born 1896/7	#10	1897
FRIDLANDER	Yehuda Leib father of Yehoshua		#10	1897
GODIN	Yisroel		#35	1900
GUTMAN	Asher	returned from Africa	#35	1900
KAHANOWITZ	Mordechai		#35	1900
KALIAN	Yakov		#10	1897
KANTOR	Moshe		#56	1899
KANTOR	Shacna	Shatz	#56	1899
KAPLAN	Eliezer Arieh		#35	1900
KARL	Kalman grandfather of baby boy	from Riga	#10	1897
KRIGER	Osher husband of Bertha Yossel	wed	#56	1899
LEWIATAN	Yeshiahu		#10	1897

Surname	Given Name	Comment	Source	Year
LICHTENSHTEIN	Eliezer		#35	1900
LIPSHITZ	Yona		#10	1897
LIPSHITZ	Yosef		#35	1900
LURIA	Shmuel		#10	1897
MAWSHOWITZ	Aba Moshe		#35	1900
MEIROWITZ	Yakov		#35	1900
MEIROWITZ	Yakov		#247	1895
MER	Chaim		#137	1900
NEWIAZKE	Elke		#35	1900
NISAN	Avraham		#10	1897
OLEIZKE	Avraham		#35	1900
OLEIZKE	Dovid		#35	1900
POLB	Zalman		#10	1897
RABINOWITZ	Bebe bas Noach wife of Ephraim Nisan of Droia	wed 13 Elul	#204	1893
RABINOWITZ	Noach father of Bebe	Rabbi Gaon	#204	1893
RABINOWITZ	Rivka		#56	1899
RABINOWITZ	Zev		#63	1895
RAPOPORT	Dovid		#35	1900
SEGAL	Yosef		#10	1897
SHAPIRO	Avraham	Rabbi	#35	1900
SHAPIRO	Chaim		#10	1897
SHAPIRO	Nisan	Shatz	#35	1900
SHEIN	Leib	returned from Africa	#35	1900
TANOR	Rochel		#35	1900
YAFT	Moshe		#10	1897
YOSSEL	Bertha wife of Osher Kriger	wed	#56	1899
ZACHS	Aharon		#35	1900
ZEGALL	Yosef		#56	1895

Appendix 4
List of 128 Shadeve Jews, donors for the victims of the great famine in Persia in 1871-72 as published in *HaMagid*
(From JewishGen.>Databases>Lithuania>*HaMagid*, by Jeffrey Maynard)

Surname	Given Name	Comment	Source	Year
ABRAHAM	Yakov ben Yeshi		#9	1872
ABRAHAM	Yeshei father of Yakov		#9	1872
BEITLECHEM	Mordechai		#9	1872
BENA	Eli		#9	1872
BERMAN	Avraham		#9	1872
BERMAN	Avraham	father of Tzvi	#25	1871
BERMAN	Tzvi		#9	1872
BERMAN	Tzvi ben Avraham		#25	1871
FATZTER	Zalman		#9	1872
FREED	Tsvi		#9	1872
FRIDGOT	A Y		#9	1872
FUNKEL	Moshe		#9	1872
GARBER	Yehuda		#9	1872
GOMPIL	Yosef		#9	1872
HOROWITZ	Yosef ben Simcha Halevy		#9	1872
KA"TZ	Moshe		#9	1872
KA"TZ	Yitzchok Meir		#9	1872
KALIBANSHKI	Shmuel		#9	1872
LEVI	Kalman ben Shimon		#9	1872
LEVITA	Chaim		#9	1872
LEVITAN	Yitschak	Hagvir	#9	1872
LEWINTHAL	Yitzchok		#25	1871
LIPSHITZ	Avraham		#9	1872
LIPSHITZ	Avraham		#25	1871
MAHAR	Yehuda		#9	1872

Surname	Given Name	Comment	Source	Year
MAKLEBANSHIK	Moshe		#9	1872
MALCHHAS	Aharon		#9	1872
MAN	Menachem		#9	1872
MANOSH	Yitschak		#9	1872
MELMAN	L		#9	1872
MELMAN	Leib		#25	1871
MER	Avraham		#25	1871
MER	Chaim ben Eli		#9	1872
MER	Chaim ben Eli		#25	1871
MER	Dov		#25	1871
MER	Eli	father of Chaim	#9	1872
MER	Sarah	widow	#9	1872
MER	Tzvi		#9	1872
MER	Eli	father of Chaim	#25	1871
MERSHAN	Avraham		#9	1872
MIPRASITZTZ	Yehuda		#9	1872
MORDECAI	Yitschak		#9	1872
POLOK	Yosef		#9	1872
RABINOWITZ	Natan Neta		#9	1872
SANDLER	Neta		#9	1872
SEGAL	Dov		#9	1872
SEGAL	Moshe Yakov		#9	1872
SEGAL	Yosef ben Yona		#9	1872
SHADINER	Shmuel		#9	1872
SHAWLANER	Natan		#9	1872
SHLAPABERSKI	Chaim Titzchok		#25	1871
SHLAPEBERSKI	Baruch ben D		#9	1872
SHLAPEBERSKI	Ch"ai	Hagvir	#9	1872
SHLAPEBERSKI	Dovid		#9	1872

Surname	Given Name	Comment	Source	Year
SHMID	Shmuel		#9	1872
SHMID	Yisroel		#9	1872
TALPIOS	A		#9	1872
TALPIOS	Avraham		#25	1871
WABELE	Eizik		#9	1872
WEINMAN	Aharon Yakov		#25	1871
WOLPE	Mordechai Leib		#9	1872
YAKOV	Yisroel		#9	1872
YEHONATAN	Boruch		#9	1872
YENTES	Shmuel	son in law of Shmuel ben Tzvi	#9	1872
ZALIMAN	Yakov		#25	1871
	Abba ben Moshe		#9	1872
	Avraham ben Kalman		#9	1872
	Avraham Chaim		#9	1872
	Avraham Yitzchok ben Nechamiah		#9	1872
	Avraham Yona		#9	1872
	Bena ben Shmuel		#9	1872
	Bentzion	son in law of Shraga	#9	1872
	Bentzion ben Tzvi		#9	1872
	Bentzion Yudel		#25	1871
	Binyamin Ari		#9	1872
	Dov	son in law of Avraham Mershan	#9	1872
	Dov ben Moshe		#9	1872
	Eizik ben Eliezer		#9	1872
	Eizik ben Moshe		#9	1872
	Elazar ben Eliezer		#9	1872

Surname	Given Name	Comment	Source	Year
	Eli ben Boruch		#9	1872
	Ephraim ben Leib		#9	1872
	Heshil ben Micha		#9	1872
	Leib ben rabbi A		#9	1872
	Leib ben rabbi D		#9	1872
	Leib ben Yakov		#9	1872
	Leib Yakov ben A		#9	1872
	Leizer Micha		#9	1872
	Meir	Eliezer son in law of Avraham Yona	#9	1872
	Meir	son in law of Shraga Yakov	#9	1872
	Meir Eliezer		#25	1871
	Mordechai ben Moshe		#9	1872
	Moshe ben Shmuel		#9	1872
	Nechamiah ben D		#9	1872
	Nechamiah ben Moshe		#9	1872
	Noson Note ben Rabbi M		#25	1871
	Pesach ben Eizik		#9	1872
	Pesach ben Ephraim Meir		#9	1872
	Rase	woman	#25	1871
	Reuven ben Shmuel		#9	1872
	Rivka	woman	#25	1871
	Rivka bas Eli		#9	1872
	Shmuel ben Dovid		#9	1872
	Shmuel ben Moshe		#9	1872
	Shmuel ben Tzvi		#9	1872

Surname	Given Name	Comment	Source	Year
	Shraga ben Dov		#9	1872
	Shraga ben Manish		#9	1872
	Shraga Yakov ben Dovid		#9	1872
	Yakov	son in law of Menachem Man	#9	1872
	Yakov	Rabbi Gaon m"tz ABD	#25	1871
	Yakov ben Alexander		#9	1872
	Yakov ben Avraham		#9	1872
	Yakov ben Avraham		#25	1871
	Yakov ben Ephraim		#9	1872
	Yakov ben Tzvi		#9	1872
	Yakov ben Leib		#9	1872
	Yehiyahu ben Yehuda		#25	1871
	Yeshei ben Binyamin		#9	1872
	Yisroel Yakov		#25	1871
	Yitzchok Ari		#9	1872
	Yitzchok Menachem		#25	1871
	Yochanason	son in law of Abba	#9	1872
	Yona ben Yechiel		#9	1872
	Yosef	son in law of Avraham Berman	#25	1871
	Zalman Yitschak		#9	1872
	Zev ben Ari		#9	1872
	Zev ben Eliahu		#9	1872

Seredžius (Srednik)

Seredzius (Srednik in Yiddish) is situated on the right high shore of the Neman (*Nemunas*) River, where its estuary, the Dubysa,joins it. Srednik is 38 km. northwest of the district administrative center of Kovno (Kaunas). In documents dating from the sixteenth century Srednik is mentioned as a village next to the estate of the Grand Prince of Lithuania. At the turn of the seventeenth century many merchants and craftsmen lived there. In 1762 the town was granted permission to operate markets and fairs.

Until 1795 Srednik was included in the Polish-Lithuanian Kingdom. According to the third division of Poland during that year by the three superpowers of those times, Russia, Prussia and Austria, Lithuania was divided between Russia and Prussia. As with other towns in Lithuania, Srednik became part of the Russian Empire, first under the auspices of the Vilna province (*Gubernia*) and from 1843 under the Kovno *Gubernia* in the Kovno district. At that time Srednik became a county administrative center, maintaining this status during the period of Independent Lithuania (1918-1940). In 1829 the town was flooded by the Neman River and many buildings were destroyed.

Jewish settlement until after World War I

Jews settled in Srednik at the beginning of the eighteenth century, making their living in the timber trade, peddling and crafts. A few worked on rafts on the Neman River for German timber merchants. The timber was brought from the Kovno and Vilna *Gubernias*.

There were two *Batei Midrash* and a *Hasidic Shtibl* established by Jews from Belarus, who had come to Srednik in order to trade in timber.

Among the rabbis who officiated in town during this period were Hayim Lifshitz who died in 1866, and his son Ze'ev-Dov Lifshitz, who officiated in Srednik from 1866 until his death in 1900.

Several Srednik Jews were named in the 1895 list of donors for settlement of *Eretz-Yisrael*.

In 1847, the town's population numbered 1,090 residents. By 1897 the all-Russian census reported 1,648 people living there, of whom 1,174 (71%) were Jewish.

At the beginning of World War I, in the spring of 1915, the Russian military exiled Srednik Jews to central Russian territories. After the German army conquered Lithuania, some of them returned. They found their possessions had been stolen and their property burnt, including the two *Batei Midrash* and the *Shtibl*. From the end of the nineteenth century until 1914 many Srednik Jews emigrated to America and South Africa and the Jewish population decreased to two-thirds of its previous size. By 1914 only about 800 Jews remained in town.

During independent Lithuania (1918-1940)
After the end of the war and the establishment of the independent Lithuanian state in 1918, only half of the exiled Jews returned home. With the assistance of the "Joint" organization they rebuilt their houses and businesses.

Following the passage of the Law of Autonomies for Minorities issued by the new Lithuanian government, the Minister for Jewish Affairs, Dr. Menachem (Max) Soloveitshik, ordered elections to community committees *(Va'adei Kehilah)* to be held in the summer of 1919. In 1921 a *Va'ad (*community committee) with seven members was elected in Srednik: two from the *Tseirei Zion* party, two from *Mizrahi*, two craftsmen and one independent. The committee was active in all fields of Jewish life until the end of 1925.

Srednik; the bridge on the Dubysa River

During this period Srednik Jews made their living from commerce, peddling, crafts and agriculture. Because the Polish army cut the Vilna region off from Lithuania in 1920, export of timber to Germany was reduced and many of the raft workers lost their jobs.

The first government census of 1923 showed 931 residents, 449 of them Jewish (48%).

According to the government survey of 1931 there were twelve shops and businesses, all Jewish owned. The distribution according to type of business is given in the table below:

Type of the business	Total
Butcher shops and cattle trade	1
Barrooms and restaurants	3
Textile products and furs	4
Flax and grains	1
Medicine and cosmetics	1
Iron products and tools	1
Other	1

According to the same survey there were two wool combing workshops, two bakeries and a small factory making men's hats, all Jewish owned.

In 1937 twenty-eight Jewish craftsmen worked in Srednik: ten tailors, five shoemakers, three bakers, three barbers, two butchers, two photographers, one hatter, one tinsmith and one stitcher. There were also five or six carters.

Most of the Jews of Srednik owned their own houses, with a small plot of land where they grew vegetables and fruit. Others rented fruit gardens from the surrounding Lithuanian peasants. Some Jews dealt in river transport, because the only access to Srednik was by boat on the Neman River. After the construction of the Kovno-Yurburg road which passed through Srednik, their livelihood was restricted. Generous aid to the town's Jews was extended by relatives who had emigrated to America and sent them money and parcels. The Jewish Popular Bank (*Folksbank*) played an important role in their economic life, and by 1927 some 172 members had registered in this institution. In 1939 there were twenty-two telephone subscribers; nine of them were Jewish houses and businesses. A slight improvement in their economic situation happened in the late 1930s when the building of barracks for the army began and many workers came into the town.

From the middle of the 1930s the number of Jews decreased, as the Lithuanian economic crisis and the open incitement of the Lithuanian Merchants Association (*Verslas*) to boycott the Jewish shops caused Jews to look for their future in other places. A slight improvement in their economic situation took place in the second half of the 1930s when building began on an army barracks and employed many workers in the town.

At this time there was also a Hebrew school from the *Tarbuth* chain with about 150 pupils.

Religious life concentrated around the synagogue, which had been built after the war. These were some of the rabbis who officiated in Srednik:

> Yisrael HaCohen Kaplan (1878-1926), who served in Srednik from 1901-1920, and was active in religious education and one of the heads of the Mizrahi party, and the first military rabbi in the Lithuania army, from 1920. In 1925 he was a delegate to the fourteenth Zionist Congress as well as to the international Mizrahi conference in Vienna.
> Mosheh-Yonah Katz, in Srednik from the 1920s until his death in 1936.
> Zalman Karbuz, the last rabbi of Srednik, murdered by Lithuanians in the summer of 1941.

Linath HaTsedek and the *Gemiluth Hesed* Fund were among the local welfare societies.

Many Srednik Jews belonged to the Zionist movement, with many members in all Zionist parties, as can be seen by their votes for Zionist congresses in the table below:

Cong No.	Year	Total Shek	Total Votes	Labor Party Z"S	Z"Z	Rev	Gen Zion A	B	Gros	Miz
14	1925	40	---	---	---	---	---	---	---	---
15	1927	11	10	4	---	---	3	---	---	3
16	1929	23	13	4	5	1	1	---	---	2
17	1931	---	13	2	7	1	1	---	---	2
18	1933	---	75	62		---	2	---	8	3
19	1935	---	218	136		---	3	15	42	22

Key: Cong No. = Congress Number, Tot Shek = Total Shekalim, Rev = Revisionists, Gen Zion = General Zionists, Gros = Grosmanists, Miz = Mizrahi, NB = National Block

Zionist youth organizations included *Tseirei Zion, Hashomer HaTsair* and *Hehalutz* with its 100 members. Sports were organized by the local *Maccabi* branch.

Srednik-born personages included:

> Rabbi Dov-Aryeh Levintal (1864-1952). He emigrated to America in 1891 and officiated as rabbi in Philadelphia. Levintal was one of the founders of the Yits'hak-Elhanan Yeshiva in New York and of the Association of Orthodox Rabbis in America and Canada. He was the delegate of American Jewry at the peace conference in Versailles after World War I.
> Meir Yelin (1910-19??), a writer who published many books in Lithuanian and Yiddish, mostly against the background of the Shoah.

During World War II and afterwards

In June 1940 Lithuania was annexed by the Soviet Union, becoming a Soviet Republic. Under the new regulations, some shops and workshops belonging to Jews in Srednik were nationalized. All Zionist parties and youth organizations were disbanded, and Hebrew educational institutions were closed.

The supply of goods decreased and as a result, prices soared. The middle class, mostly Jewish, bore most of the brunt and the standard of living dropped gradually.

At this time the town had 1,200 residents, about 500 of them being Jews (about 42%).

On June 22, 1941 the German army invaded the Soviet Union. Several days later the Germans entered Srednik. As there were no survivors from Srednik, there are no details relating to their fate and the destruction of this community. Relying on testimonies from neighboring towns it can be assumed that with the appearance of the Germans, the Lithuanian authorities imposed discriminatory regulations against the Jews. Single men and small groups of men were murdered and probably all Jews were concentrated in the local synagogue.

It is known that the Jewish men were murdered on August 28, 1941 in the Pakarkles Forest near Vilki (Vilkija). The women and children were murdered on September 3, 1941 (11th of Elul, 5701) in the village of Skrebenai, two kilometers away.

After the war the Soviet authorities uncovered a mass grave at this location and found the remains of 193 victims.

In 1992, at the site of the Jewish cemetery, a stone monument was erected with an inscription in Yiddish and Lithuanian: "The old Jewish cemetery. Sacred is the memory of the deceased."

The mass grave and monument at the Pakarkles forest near Vilki

Sources:
Yad Vashem archives, Jerusalem, file 3785/55
YIVO, New York, Collection of Lithuanian Jewish Communities, file 700
Gotlib, *Ohalei Shem*, Page143
Folksblat, Kovno, 8.8.1935

Šiluva (Shidleve)

Siluva (Shidleve in Yiddish) is located in the western part of Lithuania, in the Zamut (Zemaitija) region, about 20 km. northeast of the Rasein (Raseiniai) district administrative center. The town was built on a hill surrounded by forests and was regarded as a resort town. In historical documents dating back to the fifteenth century Siluva was mentioned as a rural settlement. Subsequently, in the sixteenth century it acquired the status of a town. In 1612 the Catholic priests began to spread a story of a so-called miraculous happening in the area. In 1768 the Pope confirmed that the event was indeed a miracle and from then on every year thousands of pilgrims would come to pray and ask the "Holy Mother of Siluva" for forgiveness.

Until 1795 Shidleve was included in the Polish-Lithuanian Kingdom. According to the third division of Poland in the same year by the three superpowers of those times, Russia, Prussia and Austria, Lithuania was divided between Russia and Prussia. As with most of Lithuania, Shidleve became a part of the Russian Empire, first in the Vilna province (*Gubernia*) and after 1843 in the Kovno *Gubernia* as a county administrative center. During the years from 1915 to 1918 the town was under German occupation. During the period of Independent Lithuania (1918-1940) Shidleve retained its status of a county administrative center.

Jews probably began to settle in Shidleve in the eighteenth century. The town had a Jewish prayer house in the nineteenth century. In 1854 a Jewish settlement near Shidleve named Preni was built on land granted by the Russian government. In 1847, 245 Jews resided in the town. According to the all-Russian census of 1897, 1,215 people lived in Shidleve, of whom 506 were Jewish (42%).

After World War I and the establishment of the independent Lithuanian state in 1918, the Jewish community in Shidleve declined and so did its percentage of the total population. According to the first government census of 1923, 992 residents lived in the town; 365 of them were Jewish (37%).

Following the passage of the Law of Autonomies for Minorities by the new Lithuanian government, the Minister for Jewish Affairs, Dr. Menachem (Max) Soloveitshik, ordered elections to community committees *(Va'adei Kehilah)* to be held in the summer of 1919. In Shidleve a *Va'ad* (community committee) of five members was elected, which was active between 1920 and 1924 in all fields of Jewish life. Shidleve Jews took part in the elections to the first Lithuanian *Seimas* (Parliament) held in October 1922. They voted as follows: 124 votes for the Zionist list, four votes for *Akhduth* (*Agudath Yisrael*) and one vote for the Democrats.

Shidleve Jews made their living mainly in the trades and crafts, while a few others were engaged in agriculture. Market days were an important element of the economic life of the town as was the annual fair which lasted a week and carried a religious component.

General view of Shidleve

According to the government survey of 1931 seven of the town's eleven shops had Jewish owners. The distribution according to type of business is given in the table below:

Type of business	Total	Owned by Jews
Butcher shops and cattle trade	2	0
Restaurants and taverns	1	1
Food products	1	0
Textile products and furs	2	2
Medicine and cosmetics	1	0
Sewing machines and electric equipment	1	1
Tools and steel products	2	2
Heating materials	1	1

According to the same survey in the Shidleve county, Jews owned a sawmill and two flourmills.

In the 1930s the economic situation of Shidleve Jews deteriorated. One reason for the decline was the open propaganda run by the Association of the Lithuanian Merchants (*Verslas*), which urged Lithuanians to boycott the Jewish stores. The rise of the Nazis in neighboring Germany contributed to the suffering of Shidleve Jews who became targets of more frequent anti-Semitic activity. One instance occurred in January 1928, when Lithuanians broke into a Jewish home demanding the return of a Christian child that the Jews had allegedly abducted. They broke windows and doors in the neighboring homes. The blood libel was prompted by a woman who five years earlier murdered her illegitimate child and was subsequently sentenced. A pogrom atmosphere lingered, but the police gained control of the situation. During that period many Shidleve Jews emigrated to South Africa.

Jewish children in Shidleve received their elementary schooling at three schools: the Hebrew school of the Tarbuth chain, the Hebrew school of the Yavneh chain and the Yiddish school. Some graduates continued their studies at the Hebrew gymnasium in Rasein. The community had a library containing books in Hebrew and Yiddish.

Many Shidleve Jews supported the Zionist ideology. In 1899 a Zionist Society was formed in town, and the 1899, 1900 and 1903 lists of contributors for the benefit of *Eretz-Yisrael* contained many names of Shidleve Jews. **Appendix 1** names fourteen contributors as published in *HaMelitz* in 1903. The fundraisers were Eliezer-Aryeh Kaplan, Ya'akov Meirovitz, Mosheh Movshovitz and Neta Shain. Among Shidleve Zionists there were supporters of all Zionist parties, as shown by the number of votes cast during the elections to the Zionist congresses, presented in the table below:

Cong No.	Year	Total Shek	Total Votes	Labor Party Z"S	Z"Z	Rev	Gen Zion A	B	Gros	Miz
18	1933	---	37	23		1	3	---	---	10
19	1935	---	53	16		---	3	8	---	26
21	1939	44	36	8		---	2		N.B. 26	

Key: Cong No. = Congress Number, Tot Shek = Total Shekalim, Rev = Revisionists, Gen Zion = General Zionists, Gros = Grosmanists, Miz = Mizrahi, NB = National Block

The *Beth Midrash* of Shidleve was a large and beautiful building. It was renovated at the end of the 1930s, thanks to a donation by a former Shidleve Jew living in South Africa.

Among the rabbis who served in town were:
Tsevi-Hirsh ben Avraham Abele, died in 1856.
Ben-Zion-Ya'akov Levitan who served in Shidleve for 36 years, from 1903 until his death in 1939.
Yosef Pagramansky, the last rabbi, who was murdered in the Holocaust together with his community.

Aharon Frank (1889-1945), a writer, teacher and educator was born in Shidleve. He published many stories and articles. Frank was one of the founders of the first Hebrew gymnasium in Virbalis. He died in the concentration camp of Dachau after being transferred from the Shavl (Siauliai) ghetto.

Aharon Frank

Following the annexation of Lithuania by the Soviet Union in the summer of 1940, and its subsequent transformation into a Soviet republic, the Jewish factories and most of the shops in Shidleve were nationalized. All Zionist parties and youth organizations were disbanded and Hebrew schools were closed. Supply of goods decreased and, as a result, prices soared. The middle class, mostly Jewish, bore the brunt, and the standard of living dropped gradually. At that time approximately 80 Jewish families still lived in the town.

On June 24, 1941, two days after the outbreak of the war between Germany and the Soviet Union, the Germans entered Shidleve. All the Jews of Shidluve were immediately transferred to nearby Ribuk (Ribukai) village where they were imprisoned in barns. The men were taken to the railway station Lidevyan (Lyduvenai) where they were forced to perform hard labor amid abuse by the Lithuanian guards.

At the beginning of August 1941 a group of 100 people that included Jews from the nearby villages, was taken out of the barns and led to the village of Padubysis, about six kilometers from Lyduvenai. There they were murdered and buried in mass graves. The remaining Shidleve Jews were murdered on August 21, 1941 (28th of Av, 5701) and buried in sand pits near the Ribuk village, about one kilometer northeast of Lyduvenai.

Three Jews, Mosheh Fainshtein, Berl Mehr and Yeshayahu Medinetz, were warned about what was going to happen by a Lithuanian friend and they managed to escape and hide at a Lithuanian peasant's farm for some time. When they became aware of the existence of the Shavl ghetto, they managed to infiltrate the ghetto with the help of the same peasant.

The list of mass graves which appears in the book Mass Murder in Lithuania Vol. II includes these two locations:
1. The Padubysis village, 6 km. from Lyduvenai, on August 15-16 of 1941; the victims numbered about 115 to 120.
2. In the sands of the Ribukai village, 1 km. from Lyduvenai, in August 1941; the victims numbered about 300.

The mass grave near the village of Padubysis

At the beginning of the 1990s a monument was built at the Jewish cemetery carrying an inscription in Yiddish and Lithuanian: "The old Jewish cemetery. Let the memory of the deceased be sacred."

Sources:
Yad Vashem archives, Jerusalem, 0-3/2580; M-9/15(6)
YIVO, New York, Collection of Lithuanian Jewish Communities, files 1311-1315
Gotlib, *Ohalei Shem*, page 204
Di Yiddishe Shtime, Kovno,11.1.1938; 12.1.1938; 20.12.1938;
Naujienos, Chicago, 11.6.1949
Mass Murder in Lithuania Vol. II

The mass grave in the Ribukai village

Appendix 1
A List of 19 Shidleve Jewish donors for the benefit of the settlement of
Eretz-Yisrael, **as published in** *HaMelitz* **#224 in 1903**
(From JewishGen>Databases>Lithuania>*HaMelitz* by Jeffrey Maynard)

Surname	Given Name	Comments
CARMEL	M	
FRIDLANDER	B Tz	
FRIDLANDER	Dov Avigdor husband of Gitel Lichtenshtein	wed 1903
FRIDLANDER	G	
GOTHELP	M	
LEWITAN	B Y	Rabbi ABD
LICHTENSHTEIN	A	
LICHTENSHTEIN	Gitel wife of Dov Avigdor Fridlander	wed 1903
LICHTENSHTEIN	R	
MEDNITZ	Y	
MEHR	A	
MEHR	M	
MEHR	P Z	
MEHR	Yisroel Tzvi	

Surviliškis (Survilishok)

Surviliskis (Survilishok in Yiddish) is situated in the north of Lithuania, in the Zamut (Zemaitija) region, about 19 km. north of the Keidan (Kedainiai) district administrative center. Its beginning can be traced back to the sixteenth century in a village which belonged to noble families and the bishop of Zamut. For a long time the town retained the status of a county administrative center with big market fairs.

In 1796, 344 residents lived in Survilishok, but following epidemic outbreaks the number decreased and in 1873 its population was only 250.

Most likely, Jewish settlement in Survilishok developed at the beginning of the nineteenth century. Jews made their living in shopkeeping, peddling and crafts. Their economic situation was difficult; thus craftsmen had to change their professions and look for other means of support. Survilishok had a wooden *Beth Midrash*, a *Heder* for children and some other community institutions.

Between 1905 and 1914 the community was served by Rabbi Hayim-Meir Feldberg.

The *Beth Midrash*

Following the Law of Autonomies for Minorities issued by the new Lithuanian government, the Minister for Jewish Affairs, Dr. Menachem (Max) Soloveitshik, ordered elections to community committees, *Va'adei Kehilah*, to be held in the summer of 1919. In Survilishok a community committee of five members was elected: two craftsmen, one from the

General Zionists Party, one from the *Mizrahi* and one from *Akhduth*. The committee worked for several years in most fields of Jewish life and was supported by the ministry of Jewish affairs in Kovno.

Despite the religious leanings of most of the Jews, votes cast in the elections for the ninth Zionist congress in 1935 gave 19 to the Labor Party and only two to the Mizrahi Party.

A Jewish family In Survilishok 1937

During this period the economic situation of Survilishok Jews was difficult. According to the government survey of 1931, there was one grain shop, one textile shop and one bakery owned by Jews.In 1939 there were twelve telephone subscribers in town, but none of these were Jewish families, who at that time numbered only twenty-five.

The rabbis who served during that period were:
> Ya'akov-Gershon Rabinovitz: two of his three sons, Meir and Kalman, were rabbis in Lithuanian communities and Mihal-Yits'hak was a well-known writer in Jerusalem until his death in 1948
> Elhanan-Yehudah Burland (1931)
> Aharon Yelnivitz (1931-1932)
> Yehudah-Leib Nemyatin (from 1934).

During World War II a small number of Jews remained in the town. All were brutally murdered, in similar fashion to the other Jews of the Keidan area.

The mass grave In Keidan (Kedainiai)

The tablet of the monument with the inscription in Yiddish and Lithuanian: "In this place the Hitler murderers and their local helpers on 28.8.1941 murdered 2076 Jews."

Sources:
YIVO, New York - Collection of Lithuanian Jewish Communities, file 674
Gotlib - *Ohalei Shem*, page 204
Kamzon Y.D. - *Yahaduth Lita*, page 123

Suvainiškis (Suveinishok)

Suvainiskis (Suveinishok in Yiddish) is situated along the shore of the Nereta River, which marks the northern border of Lithuania with Latvia. It lies about 15 km. north of the county administrative center of Panemunis and about 30 km. northwest of the district administrative center of Rokiskis. The village and the estate that bore the same name are mentioned in historic sources from the eighteenth century. After the third division of the Polish Lithuanian Kingdom in 1795, Suveinishok, like almost all of Lithuania, became part of the Russian Empire. Suveinishok was first included in the Vilna province, and from 1843 in the Novo-Alexandrovsk (Zarasai) district of the Kovno province (*Gubernia*). In 1856 there were 14 houses and 53 residents, but during the second half of the nineteenth century the town's population multiplied.

According to the Russian census of 1897 there were then 855 residents, of whom 684 were Jews (80%). A new road connected Suveinishok with Riga, Latvia's capital, the main market town for its products. The merchants and peddlers of Suveinishok also made their living from the market in the Latvian town of Nereta, attended by many peasants from the region.

Suveinishok's market square was in the center of the town and four streets branched out from it. During the German occupation (1915-1918) the town was connected to nearby Skopishok by a narrow gauge railway.

The Beth Midrash

After the establishment of independent Lithuania in 1918, and the subsequent delineation of the border with Latvia, travel across the border to Riga and Nereta became more difficult.

The first Jews probably settled in Suveinishok at the end of the eighteenth century. Public life was concentrated around the *Beth Midrash*. The children studied in a *Heder* and there were several of this kind in town.

Most of the Jews made their living by trading in grains, timber, cattle and furs. During World War I Suveinishok Jews were exiled deep into Russia by the Russian army.

The Jewish cemetery

After the war, when independent Lithuania was established, exiles returned to find most of their houses had been ruined and their property stolen. With help from the *Joint*, economic life was partly rehabilitated.

Following the Law of Autonomies for Minorities issued by the new Lithuanian government, the Minister for Jewish Affairs, Dr. Menachem (Max) Soloveitshik, ordered elections for community committees (*Va'adei Kehilah*) to be held in the summer of 1919. In Suveinishok a five-member community committee was elected, which was active during 1922-1925 in all fields of Jewish life. At this time a Hebrew elementary school of the *Tarbuth* chain was established, with about forty pupils, and another fifteen boys studied in a *Heder*. Some youths continued their studies in the Lithuanian gymnasium in Rakishok (Rokiskis) or in the *Yeshivah* there.

In 1921 the town had a population of 250 Jews (60 families).

Because of traffic limitations to Riga and Nereta, the activities of Jewish merchants were restricted. Some subsisted on small trade with agricultural products and horses, others smuggled goods over the border. More prosperous Jews were the owners of the flourmill, the sawmill and cloth workshops.

Celebration of the volunteer fire brigade of Suvainishok

According to the government survey of 1931 in Suveinishok, there were two horse traders, one butcher's shop, one restaurant and three mixed goods shops owned by Jews. In 1937 there were eleven Jewish artisans: six butchers, three tailors, a glazier and a watchmaker. In 1939 only one Jew, a member of the Ginzburg family which owned the flourmill, possessed a telephone, out of a total of eight telephone subscribers in the town.

As a result of the decline in the opportunities to make a living, many Surveinishok Jews emigrated to America and South Africa or to *Eretz-Yisrael.*

The following table shows the involvement of Surveinishok's Jews in politics and how they voted for four Zionist congresses:

Cong No.	Year	Total Shek	Total Votes	Labor Party		Rev	Gen Zion		Gros	Miz
				Z"S	Z"Z		A	B		
15	1927	28	10	---	7	---	3	---	---	---
16	1929	22	---	---	---	---	---	---	---	---
18	1933	---	3	1		---	2	---	---	---
19	1935	---	94	57		---	---	27	9	1

Key: Cong No. = Congress Number; Tot Shek = Total Shekalim; Rev = Revisionists; Gen Zion = General Zionists; Gros = Grosmanists; Miz = Mizrahi

In addition to the few educational and cultural institutions there was a *Bikur Holim* society and also a *Gemiluth Hesed* fund.

Rabbis who officiated in Suveinishok included Hayim-Yonah Itkin (1882-?) from 1905 in Suveinishok; Yehoshua haCohen Kaplan (1873-1941) in Suveinishok 1920-1926, murdered in Vidukle together with his community in 1941; Avraham-Mihal Viner, the last rabbi of Suveinishok, murdered by the Lithuanians in the summer of 1941.

After Lithuania was annexed to the USSR in 1940 and became a Soviet Republic, several Jewish owned shops and factories were nationalized and their owners dispossessed. Some of them integrated into the administrative and economic institutions of the new regime. The Hebrew school was closed and all Zionist activities were forbidden. At this time there were about fifty Jewish families.

The Germans entered Suveinishok in the first week of the war between Germany and the USSR which began on June 22, 1941. On August 15-16, 1941 all Suveinishok Jews were brought to the Velniaduobe Forest, 5 km. from Rokiskis, where they were murdered together with Jews from the surrounding towns.

The mass grave and monument in the Velniaduobe Forest

The inscription on the tablet of this monument, in Lithuanian and Yiddish, reads as follows: "On this site the Hitlerists and their local helpers murdered 3207 Jews, men, women and children, on 15-16.8.1941. Let their memory endure forever."

Sources:
Central Zionist Archives: 55/1788; 55/1701; 13/15/131; Z-4/2548.
Yahaduth Lita (Hebrew), Tel Aviv
YIVO, New York, Collection of Lithuanian Communities, files 1300-1309
Gotlib, *Ohalei Shem*, page 97
Yizkor Buch Rakishok (Yiddish), pages 362-365
Levin, Dov: *Suveinishok, Pinkas haKehilot Lita*, Yad Vashem, Jerusalem, 1996

Svedasai (Svadushch)

Svedasai (Svadushch in Yiddish) lies in northeastern Lithuania, between the Alausas and Svedasas lakes and surrounded by pine forests, 26 kilometers northwest of the district administrative center Utyan (Utena).

Svadushch is first mentioned in documents from 1503. Military documents from 1567 mention an estate named Svedasai that belonged to the Radzivil (Radvila in Lithuanian) family. In 1645 it was already a considerable settlement. It was built around a square with houses on all sides. In the center of the great plaza stood the church, and a well. Seven roads radiated from the plaza to nearby villages. The buildings of the estate were situated to the southwest of the town.

From the eighteenth century onward, great markets and two yearly fairs were held in the town. At the end of the eighteenth century the estate was administered by the Morikonis family.

In 1863 Svadushch residents were involved in the rebellion against the Czar's rule. By the end of the nineteenth century the town had grown to contain 64 courtyards, a church and the offices of the county headquarters. The farmers of the county grew mainly flax, that was processed locally.

Until 1795 Svadushch was included in the Polish-Lithuanian Kingdom. According to the third division of Poland in the same year by the three superpowers of those times, Russia, Prussia and Austria, Lithuania was divided between Russia and Prussia. As most of Lithuania, Svadushch became a part of the Russian Empire, first in the Vilna province (*Gubernia*) and from 1843 in the Kovno *Gubernia* in the Vilkomir (Ukmerge) district.

In 1904 a great fire destroyed almost the entire town. In 1905 there were uprisings against the Czar's rule. In 1915 during World War I the front line between the invading German army and the defending Russian army stopped for seven weeks at the lakes near the town. Later Svadushch was occupied by the Germans who ruled there till the end of the war and the establishment of the independent Lithuanian state in 1918.

In the eighteenth century an organized Jewish community already functioned in Svadushch. In 1766, the Jewish population was 154 in the town and 75 more in the district. Before World War I many Jews rented their land from the landowners, but subsequently they acquired them and became the owners.

According to the all Russian census of 1897 there were 1,423 residents in Svadushch, 528 of them Jewish (37%).

During World War I, in 1915 many Svadushch Jews moved to Russia and only a fraction remained in the town. After the war, in 1920, most of them returned home.

Relations between the Jews and non-Jews in the town were generally harmonious. Almost all the houses of the Jews who left for Russia were saved intact and not looted. The local priest continued to preach for good relations between the two communities.

During the period of Independent Lithuania (1918-1940)

Following the passage of the Law of Autonomies for Minorities issued by the new Lithuanian government, the Minister for Jewish Affairs, Dr. Menachem (Max) Soloveitshik, ordered elections to community committees *Va'adei Kehilah* to be held in the summer of 1919. In Svadushch a community committee of five members was elected. This committee functioned until about the end of 1925 when the autonomy was annulled by the Lithuanian government. For several years the committee was active in all aspects of the Jewish life in town.

The first census conducted by the government in 1923 recorded 1,146 residents in the town, 245 of them being Jewish (21%).

The government survey of businesses of 1931 counted nine Jewish shops in Svadushch: three textile shops, one grocery, one leather shop, one restaurant, one bakery, one sewing machines shop an one pharmacy. The remaining businesses were timber and flax merchants, carters, peddlers and fruit growers.

In this period fifteen Jewish artisans worked in Svadushch: five butchers, three tailors, three shoemakers, two metal workers and one baker. There was one customs agent. Of the thirteen telephone subscribers in town, only one was Jewish.

Svadushch Jews were either *Hasidim* from the *Habad* movement or *Mithnagdim*. The *Habad* men were acknowledged as the erudites in town and they sent their boys to study in Lubavitch. There were two *Batei Midrash*, one for the *Hasidim* and one for the *Mithnagdim,* but they shared one rabbi and one *shohet*. The rabbi would pray one week with the Hasidim and one week with the *Mithnagdim.*

Most Svadushch men went to the *Beth Midrash* after work in order to learn with one of the Torah societies such as *Talmud, Mishnah* or *Ein Ya'akov* or to read and study the *Tehilim* (Psalms).

The wealthier people in the town sought literate husbands for their daughters; thus the *Haskalah* movement (Jewish enlightenment in the 18th and 19th centuries that was influenced by European intellectuals and sought to offer secular education to European Jews) arrived. One man, Mosheh Ya'akov Farber, sent his daughter to study medicine and after she qualified she worked as a doctor in Svadushch. Her husband was a dentist who also worked there. With the arrival of the Germans in June 1941, both committed suicide.

Before World War I the Jewish children received their education in *Hadarim* and then in *Yeshivoth*. Only a few, mainly girls, attended the Russian school.

After the establishment of the Lithuanian state, the community committee looked for a licensed teacher for the planned school. A suitable teacher arrived and wanted to establish the school, but he could not find an appropriate building for it. So the teaching was done in the *Ezrath Nashim* (the women's section in the synagogue) that was empty on weekdays. However the orthodox group, headed by the rabbi, opposed this and expelled the teacher and the children with some violence and unpleasantness. The children's parents, mostly craftsmen, fought back.

A Hebrew school of the *Tarbuth* chain was opened with about 60 pupils. Some of its graduates continued their studies in the Hebrew high schools in Utyan and Ponevezh. Besides the school a library and a drama circle operated. Profits from its shows were donated to the *Keren Kayemeth Le'Yisrael* fund.

Many Svadushch Jews belonged to the Zionist camp. Branches of the General Zionists, the Revisionists and the Zionists Socialists (Z.S.) parties were established, as was a branch of the youth organization *Hehalutz HaTsair*. Zionist activists included the pharmacist Ya'akov Stolov, in whose house the elections for the 21st Zionist Congress took place, and Shemuel Gafanovitz.

The results of the elections in Svadushch for five Zionist congresses are given in the table below:

Cong No.	Year	Tot Shek	Total Votes	Labor Party		Rev	Gen Zion		Gros	Miz
				Z"S	Z"Z		A	B		
16	1929	10	8	---	1	---	7	---	---	---
17	1931	35	26	14	---	2	8	---	---	2
18	1933	---	62	36		9	5	---	9	3
19	1935	---	89	43		---	7	1	10	28
21	1939	25	24	15		---	3		N.B.6	

Key: Cong No. = Congress Number, Tot Shek = Total Shekalim, Rev = Revisionists, Gen Zion = General Zionists, Gros = Grosmanists, Miz = Mizrahi, N.B. = National Block

The elections committee for the nineteenth Zionist congress (1935)

Many young people went to *Kibbutsei Hakhshrah* (Training *Kibbutsim*) and later emigrated to *Eretz-Yisrael*. Among the first to do so were Zalman Berzon, Havivah Finkel, Yosef Gafny and Mosheh Stolov. Others migrated to South Africa.

Rabbis who officiated in Svadushch included:
  Shemuel ben Hayim (?-1822)
  Yehoshua-Heshl ben Iser
  Yehoshua-Mordehai Klatskin (1862-1925)
  Aba Shlomovitz
  Yosef-Hayim Urinson (1880-?)
  Mosheh-Yits'hak Veichik
  Yosef Shakhnovitz, the last rabbi of the community, murdered in the
  Holocaust.

Before World War I the *shohet* Nathan Fridman taught *Gemera* in the *Beth Midrash.*

During World War II

On June 15, 1940 the Red Army entered Lithuania and the state was annexed to the Soviet Union to become a Soviet Republic. Following new regulations, the bigger Jewish businesses were nationalized. All Zionist parties and youth organizations were disbanded and the Hebrew school was closed. Supply of goods decreased and, as a result, prices soared. The middle class, mostly Jewish, bore the brunt of this situation and the standard of living dropped gradually. At that time about 400 Jews (100 families) lived in Svadushch. Soviet rule lasted for one year until June 22, 1941 when the German army invaded Lithuania.

On June 25, German soldiers appeared outside the town and the next day they entered Svadushch and took it over. But even earlier there had been fights between the Soviet militia, in which several Jewish youngsters served, and the Lithuanian nationalists who intended to take control of the town. One of activists was a young Jew, Yits'hak Aras. The Germans placed a reward of 10,000 Marks on his head and his photograph was publicized. But he managed to escape to the Soviet Union, fought in the Red Army against the Germans and was badly wounded. After the war he made his way to *Eretz-Yisrael*. The Lithuanians hanged his father, the blacksmith, in his shop.

The local Lithuanian activists began to abuse the Jews, in particular the wealthier ones. Two brothers, Jonas and Juozas Rimkus, were excessive in their cruelty. They rounded up the prosperous Jews, imprisoned them in the blacksmith's shop and tortured them into handing over their money and valuables or revealing where they were hidden.

Many Jews were murdered in the town, while others including the rabbi Yosef Shakhnovitz were transported to Rakishok (Rokiskis) under the pretext that they were to work there. On August 10 and 20, 1941 (17th and 27th of Av, 5701) they were murdered together with the Jews of the surrounding areas.

The mass grave near Svadushch with the monument

The mass grave with the monument at Velniaduobe

The monument with the inscription in Lithuanian and Yiddish:
"In this place the Hitlerists and their local helpers on 6-15.8.1941 cruelly murdered 3,207 Jews, children, women, men. Let their memory be sacred."

The monument with the inscription in Yiddish: "In this place the Nazi murderers and their local helpers in 1941 murdered a group of Svadushch Jews."

On the way to the murder site the Lithuanians tried to rape Jewish girls, who resisted and were shot on the spot. The wounded were thrown in the pits alive. A young Jew named Sheftl, who had previously been a friend of the murderers, they saved till last as a 'gesture of friendship'. He asked them, "Why do you want to shoot me? Let me live." The answer was, "What would you do all alone in the town?" He tried to escape but his so-called friends shot him in the back. Two men, David and Leib Pakovitz managed to hide, but some time later they were caught and murdered.

Near the town several mass graves are marked:
1. At the Grove of the Priest eighteen of the more prosperous Jews were buried.
2. At the Jewish cemetery Yeshayahu Shapira, his wife and their four children were murdered and buried.
3. A mass grave behind the town on the way to Ushpol.

Sources:

Yad Vashem archives, Collection of Lithuanian Jewish Communities, 0-57, testimony of Yits'hak Aras
YIVO, New York, Collection of Lithuanian Jewish Communities, files 1296-1299, 1549
Bakaltchuk-Felin, Melakh (Redactor), Yizkor Book of Rakishok and surroundings (Yiddish), Johannesburg, 1952, pages 356-361
Julius, Rafael, Svedasai (Hebrew), *Pinkas HaKehiloth-Lita*, Yad Vashem, Jerusalem 1996
Tsait, Shavl #12, 9.5.1924

Troškūnai (Trashkun)

Troskunai (Trashkun in Yiddish) is located on the Juosta River in central Lithuania, about 35 kilometers southeast of the Ponevez (Panevezys) district administrative center. The town was two kilometers from the nearest railway station.

Trashkun is first mentioned in historical documents dating back to 1512. The town began to develop quickly after the king granted permission to hold weekly markets in 1748, which encouraged settlement of merchants and craftsmen. In 1869 there were fifty houses in Trashkun.

Until 1795 Trashkun was included in the Polish-Lithuanian Kingdom. According to the third division of Poland in that year by the three superpowers of those times, Russia, Prussia and Austria, Lithuania was divided between Russia and Prussia. As with most other towns of Lithuania, Trashkun became part of the Russian Empire, first under the auspices of the Vilna province (*Gubernia*) and from 1843 under the Kovno *Gubernia* in the Vilkomir district. At that time and during the period of independent Lithuania (1918-1940) Trashkun was a county administrative center.

In 1904 a fire destroyed almost all the homes in Troshkun.

Jewish settlement until after World War I

The Jewish community in Trashkun began to form at the end of the eighteenth century. Two synagogues were opened; one adhered to the *Mithnagdim* tradition and the other to the *Hasidic* tradition. Between 1883 and 1890 Rabbi Benyamin Gitelzon (1851-1932) served the congregation. He published several books. One was printed in New York in 1898 and another in Jerusalem in 1904; both dealt with religious issues.

In 1885 Hayim Yosefovitz from Trashkun praised the Polish Nobleman Komar in the Hebrew newspaper *HaMelitz* for his donation of a large quantity of wheat to bake *Matsoth* for *Pesakh*.

At the end of the nineteenth century Jews made up the majority of the town's population. The all-Russian census of 1897 counted 1,221 people in Trashkun, 779 of them Jewish (64%). Their economic situation was tough, and the community institutions faced difficulties as well. In the 1890s the rabbi's pay was reduced from four Rubles per week to two Rubles. To improve his low wages he was offered a position as an Official Rabbi. This resulted into great communal controversy that created disagreement among the authorities. The story was published in *HaMelitz* at that time.

Before World War I there were forty-four Jewish tradesmen in the town: twelve shoemakers, seven builders, six tailors, six butchers, three carters, two carpenters, two tile workers, one milliner, one binder, one watchmaker, one blacksmith, one barber and one tinsmith. Three Jews practiced liberal professions.

During World War I, on July 13, 1915, Cossacks from the Russian army instigated a pogrom against Trashkun Jews and exiled them deep into Russia; their properties were looted and twenty-eight homes were totally destroyed.

During Independent Lithuania (1918-1940)
After the war and the establishment of an independent Lithuanian state in 1918, most of the exiles returned home and the Jewish community in Trashkun was rebuilt, but their numbers had decreased and so did the their percentage of the total population. According to the first government census of 1923, 877 people lived in the town, 424 of them being Jewish (48%).

Following passage of the Law of Autonomies for Minorities by the new Lithuanian government, the Minister for Jewish Affairs, Dr. Menachem (Max) Soloveitshik, ordered elections to community committees *(Va'adei Kehilah)* to be held in the summer of 1919. In 1921 a *Va'ad (*community committee) with seven members was elected in Trashkun. The committee worked in all fields of Jewish life until March 17, 1926 with the support of the Ministry of Jewish Affairs in Kovno. The chairman of the committee was Shelomoh Kovnovitz and its members were Rabbi Y. M. Shmukler, G. Shalomon, N. Haimovitz, Ts. Shefshelevitz and Y. Vinik.

According to the government survey of 1931 a total of seven shops and other businesses belonged to Jews at that time, including two heating fuel shops, one grocery, one leather shop, a wool combing workshop, a flour mill and an alcohol factory. Commercial activities were organized on Tuesdays, which was the weekly market day of Troshkun.

Seventeen people received financial support from the committee and twelve families received aid from their relatives abroad.

In the 1920s thirty Jews made their living in trade and twenty-eight (representing twelve families) were engaged in skilled work: five shoemakers, five tailors, five builders, four tile workers, two carpenters, two carters, two butchers, one watchmaker, one binder and one tinsmith. Some Jews were farmers.

According to the 1937 survey of the Association of Jewish Craftsmen there were forty-two skilled workers in Trashkun: thirteen shoemakers, six oven builders, three butchers, three carpenters, two tailors, two knitters, two barbers, two tinsmiths, one felt-boot maker, one watchmaker, one needle trade worker, one wood etcher, one milliner and four others. There was also a practicing Jewish doctor, Guta Zalk.

A street in Trashkun

The Jewish Popular Bank (*Folksbank*) played an important role in the economy of Trashkun Jews. In 1929 it counted 96 members. For many years it was chaired by the local rabbi Mosheh-Ya'akov Shmukler. Later he moved to the Kovno suburb of Shantz (Sanciai) and during Nazi rule he was a member of the *Judenrat* in the Kovno ghetto until his death. He was replaced by Eliezer Sheinkman as rabbi of Troshkun. The United Jewish Agrarian Credit Society ran a branch in the town as well.

In 1939 there were sixteen telephones listed: four of them belonged to Jewish trades people, and one was in the home of doctor Shtukarevitz.

The cultural life of Trashkun Jews centered around the Hebrew *Tarbuth* School and the library.

Cultural activities among the youth were run by the Youth Society, the Yiddishists Circle, the Z.S. (Zionists Socialists), by *Hashomer HaTsair*, *Hehalutz* and others.

One famous personage born in Trashkun was Avraham Kotliarek (1857-1943) who migrated to America in 1888. He was the pioneer of Hebrew parody and satire in America.

Many Trashkun Jews were Zionists. Almost all Zionist parties had their supporters in the town. The table shows how the local Zionists voted in elections for the Zionist congresses:

Cong No.	Year	Total Shek	Total Votes	Labor Party Z"S	Z"Z	Rev	Gen Zion A	B	Gros	Miz
17	1931	28	22	18	---	---	2	---	---	2
18	1933	---	51	48		---	2	---	---	1
19	1935	---	116	95		---	---	1	---	20
21	1939	---	24	23		---	---		N.B. 1	---

Key: Cong No. = Congress Number, Tot Shek = Total Shekalim, Rev = Revisionists, Gen Zion = General Zionists, Gros = Grosmanists, Miz = Mizrahi, NB = National Block

During World War II and afterwards

In June 1940, Lithuania was annexed to the Soviet Union and became a Soviet Republic. Following new regulations, light industry enterprises owned by Jews were nationalized. The supply of goods decreased and, as a result, prices soared. The middle class, mostly Jewish, bore the brunt and the standard of living dropped gradually. All the Zionist parties were disbanded and the Hebrew school was closed. A Jew named Shemuel Kovanovitz served as secretary of the local Communist party.

In 1940 about 90 Jewish families resided in Trashkun.

Following the German invasion into Lithuania on June 22, 1941 many Trashkun Jews tried to escape to the Soviet Union, but only a few succeeded.

After a few days control of town was taken over by local armed Lithuanian nationalists. They began to rob and murder their Jewish neighbors. Jewish youngsters were taken to the Jewish cemetery and ordered to dig pits. Immediately after they had finished, they were shot and buried in these pits. Several Jews, Asher Shmidt, Perl and Hayim Shumakher, Feige and Menahem Krasovsky, tried to resist their murderers and were killed. In July the Jews were ordered to leave their homes and move into the small homes near the bathhouse where the poorest people had lived.

On August 21 or 22, 1941 all Trashkun Jews were led by heavily armed Lithuanian guards to the Pajuoste Forest, not far from Ponevezh. In this forest was the murder site of all Jews from the surrounding areas; the mass murder took place on August 23, 1941 (30th of Av 5701).

Only a few Jews survived. Some managed to escape to the Soviet Union in the first days of the war and joined the Red Army.

After the war a monument to the Jews murdered in summer of 1941 was built. In the early 1990s a new monument was erected with the inscription in Yiddish and Lithuanian: "In this place in 1941, the Hitler murderers with their local helpers murdered Trashkun Jews, men, women and children." Below, an inscription in Lithuanian follows: "Let their memory be sacred." At the old Jewish cemetery in Trashkun a monument was built with the inscriptions in Yiddish and Lithuanian: "The old Jewish cemetery. Let the memory of the deceased be sacred."

The monument at the Jewish cemetery

The Jewish cemetery in Trashkun

The monument in Pajuoste

Sources:
Yad Vashem archives, Jerusalem, Koniukhovsky collection 0-71, files
145,147
Oral History Division of the Contemporary Jewry Institution, the Hebrew
University of Jerusalem. Interview #12/104
YIVO, New York, Collection of Lithuanian Jewish Communities,
files 466-472
Levin, Dov, Trashkun, *Pinkas Hakehiloth-Lita*; Yad Vashem, Jerusalem
1996
HaMelitz, St. Petersburg; 18.3.1885; 11.11.1885; 16.12.1886
Dos Vort, Kovno; 26.12.1934
Folksblat, Kovno;18.4.1939;19.11.1940

Tryškiai (Trishik)

Tryskiai (Trishki in Yiddish) is a small town in the northwestern part of Lithuania, spreading along the shores of the Virvyte River, about 54 km. from the Shavl (Siauliai) district administrative center to the northwest. The Tryskiai estate and the village itself were mentioned in historical documents dating back to 1538. In 1792, the town was granted the Magdeburg rights of autonomy. After the third division of the Polish Lithuanian Kingdom in 1795, Trishki, like almost all of Lithuania, became part of the Russian empire. Initially Trishki was included in the Vilna province; however, in 1843 it fell under the jurisdiction of the Kovno Province (*Gubernia*).

Since the middle of the nineteenth century, Trishki was considered a county administrative center, with public markets and fairs. Trishki preserved its status as a county administrative center during German occupation in World War I (1915-1918), and during the period of independent Lithuania (1918-1940).

Jewish settlement till World War II
A few Jewish families settled in Trishki at the end of the seventeenth century, but a community was formed only at the end of the eighteenth century. In 1848, seventeen Jews died during a pandemic of cholera which ravaged the town. During the famine of 1869-1872, Trishki Jews were helped by the Help Committee of Memel. Famine notwithstanding, some Trishki Jews were motivated and able to send money for the victims of the great famine of Persia in 1871-72. The list of contributors for the benefit of the victims was published in the Hebrew newspaper *HaMagid* in 1872 and included names of 62 Trishki Jews (see **Appendix 1**).

In the fall of 1887 a fire destroyed all the houses in town, including the synagogue and it's Torah scrolls. About 200 families lost shelter and were stricken by poverty. On September 1, 1887, the Hebrew newspaper *HaMelitz* published a moving appeal for help on behalf of the victims of the fire, signed by the local rabbi Hayim Pun. At the end of the nineteenth century, the economic situation deteriorated, and many Trishki Jews emigrated.

Nevertheless, Trishki Jews donated money to the Jewish National Fund to buy land in *Eretz-Yisrael*. The list of contributors for the years of 1899, 1903 and 1909, includes the names of fourteen Trishki Jews (see **Appendix 2**).

According to the all-Russian census of 1897, 1,971 people lived in Trishki, of whom 681 (34%) were identified as Jews.

A *Talmud Torah* was formed and the *Bikur Holim* society provided medical care and medication free of charge. At its beginning in 1903 the society was headed by Ya'akov-Hanokh Grinberg and the teacher Mosheh-Ze'ev Rakovchik.

Following the Law of Autonomies for Minorities issued by the new Lithuanian government, the Minister for Jewish Affairs, Dr. Menachem (Max) Soloveitshik, ordered elections to community committees *(Va'adei Kehilah)* to be held in the summer of 1919. In 1921 a *Va'ad (*community committee) with seven members was elected in Trishki: four were from the General Zionist list, one from *Tseirei Zion*, one from *Akhduth* and one from the artisans list.

The *Va'ad* worked for several years in all areas of Jewish life. In the elections to the first Lithuanian *Seimas* (Parliament) in October 1922, Trishki Jews cast 122 votes for the Zionists, 72 votes for *Akhduth (Agudath Yisrael)* and none for the Democrats.

A street in Trishki

15 Trishki families made their living in manual occupations, in particular in the tanning trade, while five families worked in agriculture and the remainder in trades. The weekly markets and the monthly fairs were their main source of income.

According to the government survey of 1931 there were 13 shops, all owned by Jewish families: five textile shops, two grain stores, one grocery shop, one butcher's shop, one leather shop and one timber and fuel business.

According to the same survey, Trishki Jews owned eleven factories including five shoe manufacturers, two leather processing ateliers, one flour mill owned by Kaganton who also supplied electricity, a bakery, a textile business and a felt factory. Later, the Cohen family opened another flourmill in the area.

In 1937, ten Jewish people worked in various trades: three shoemakers, a baker, a tailor, a milliner, a blacksmith, a tinsmith, a butcher and a needle trade specialist.

The Jewish Popular Bank (*Folksbank*) played an important role in the economic life of Trishki Jews. It was established in 1926 with 97 members, and in 1929 it gained the recognition of the *Folksbanks*.

Council of the Jewish Folksbanks 1938
from left: speaker Agr. Kelzon, Dr.Gregory Volf, Leib Gorfinkel,
Gedalyahu Halperin, Adv. H.Landoi, Fain, ---, Katz

In 1939, the town had 25 telephone subscribers, 10 of them Jewish.

Jewish children were schooled at the Hebrew elementary *Tarbuth* School, which had an average of 30 students. A number of its graduates continued their studies at the *Telz Yeshivah* or at the local Hebrew gymnasium or in Shavl (Siauliai). A library with about 400 books in Yiddish and Hebrew was open for the public. Social life was busy in the branches of *Mizrahi, Beitar, Z.S.* and *Maccabi.*

Before the beginning of the 1930s, the relations between Jews and the non-Jews were more or less acceptable. The situation worsened when open propaganda of the Association of the Lithuanian Merchants-Verslas urged people not to buy in Jewish stores. As a result, many Trishki Jews, in particular the youth, had to seek opportunities in bigger Lithuanian towns and abroad. Later some of them began to support their relatives who stayed in Trishki. The Association of Former Trishki Jews in Chicago was continually sending money to support the poor people of their town (*Maoth Hitim* for *Pesakh*, for fuel in winter, and so on). On the initiative of the *Gabai* of the synagogue and the people who worked in the public sector, a society was formed to deal with social issues of the Trishki Jews.

In 1939 a fire broke out and eight buildings burned down, including four residential homes, the *Folksbank* building and the Hebrew school as well as other homes.

Many Trishki Jews supported the Zionist camp. All Zionist parties were represented in the town's political structure. The table below shows how Trishki Zionists voted for five Zionist congresses:

Cong No.	Year	Tot Shek	Total Voter	Labor Party		Rev.	Gen. Zion	Gro	Miz
				Z"S	Z'Z				
15	1927	11	---	---	---	---	---	---	---
16	1929	15	10	1	1	5	2	---	1
17	1931	---	7	1	1	4	1	---	---
18	1933	---	31	10		---	12	5	4
19	1935	---	124	42		---	1	39	42

Key: Cong No. = Congress Number, Tot Shek = Total Shekalim, Rev = Revisionists, Gen Zion = General Zionists, Gros = Grosmanists, Miz = Mizrahi, NB = National Block

The rabbis who served Trishki during these years included Shemuel-Mosheh Shapiro (1843-1908) who lived in Trishki from 1874; Hayim Pun (?-1903), between 1891-1897; Yisrael-Yehoshua Segal, from 1898; Eliyahu-Ben Zion Pun, 1922-1941, later murdered by the Lithuanians.

Among the personages born in Trishki were Ze'ev Volf Kaplan (1826-1888), a writer, who published his works under the name ZKN, and Mosheh-Yits'hak Svitz (Shayevitz 1896-1939), a writer who lived in South Africa.

During World War II and afterwards
With the annexation of Lithuania to the USSR in 1940 and its transformation into a Soviet Republic, most of the Jewish-owned shops and factories were nationalized. Trades people organized into cooperatives (known as *Artels*). The Hebrew school was closed. Following the closure of the *Telz Yeshivah*, a number of its students moved to Trishki to continue their studies there. After the invasion by the German army into the USSR on June 22, 1941, the *Yeshivah* students joined the retreating Red Army heading towards Russia. Many of them later arrived in America, where they established the *Telz Yeshivah* in Cleveland.

The Germans entered Trishki on June 25, 1941, three days after the war began. The Lithuanian nationalists immediately took control. They began by bursting into Jewish homes, beating everybody inside and robbing the families. The Jews were fearful and did not dare to go outside. At that time one of the most respected members of the community, Kaganton, passed away. The *gabai* of *Hevrah Kadisha* was courageous and decided to bury the deceased in the Jewish cemetery, but he was shot by Lithuanians and buried together with Kaganton.

The mass grave and the monument at the murder site of Trishki Jewish men

In the middle of July the Jews were ordered to leave their houses and they were led to the estate of Graf Plater, where they were crammed in a barn. A barbed wire fence was placed around the barn and Lithuanian guards were stationed around.

Later, three Germans arrived and ordered 70 Jewish men out of the barn. Lithuanians who knew these men prepared a list of names. Everyone was called by his name and profession to make it appear that he was called to work outside. These men were taken to the shores of the Virvyte River where the Kaganton's flourmill stood, about 300 meters from the road to Telz. They were ordered to undress and led in small groups to prepared pits. There they were shot and buried.

Women and children were kept in the barn longer. Money and valuables were taken from them and in exchange they received small rations of food. Hungry and weak, they walked around in circles inside the closed barn. When the women inquired about the fate of their husbands they were told that the men were working and would soon return home.

The mass grave and the monument at the town park in Zhager

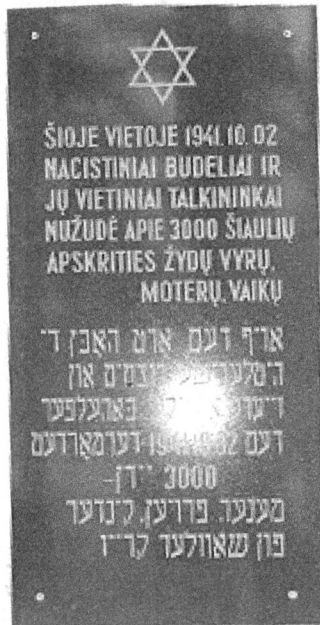

The inscription on the monument in Lithuanian and Yiddish states:
On 2.10.1941, here Hitler's murderers and their local helpers murdered
3000 Jews, men, women, children from the Siauliai district.

At the beginning of August the women were told that they would join their husbands, but in fact they were led to Gruzd (Gruzdziai) and there, they were left in an open field without any shelter from the burning sun, wind or rain, and suffered abuse by the Lithuanian guards.

A week later, in the middle of August, they were brought to the Zhager ghetto. On October 2, 1941 (11th of Tishrei, 5702) they were murdered in the city park (Narishkin estate) together with 3,000 Jews from Zhager and the surrounding towns.

Sources:
Yad Vashem archives, Koniukhovsky collection: 0-71, files 68, 102
Central Zionist archives: files 55/1701, 55/1788, 13/15/131, Z-4/2548
Yahaduth Lita (Hebrew) Vol. 1-4, Tel Aviv
YIVO New York, Collection of Lithuania Jewish Communities, pages 757-761
Di Yiddishe Shtime (Yiddish) Kovno, 19.7.1939
Der Yiddisher Cooperator (Yiddish) Kovno, #7-8 (1928); #10 (1929)
HaMelitz (Hebrew) St.Petersburg: 8.6.1883; 22.8.1883; 30.8.1887; 1.9.1887; 30.1.1893; 15.2.1893
Folksblat (Yiddish) Kovno, 19.7.1939

Appendix 1
List of 62 Trishki Jewish contributors to the victims of the great Persian famine in 1871/72 as published in *HaMagid* page 94, 1872
(From JewishGen.org>Databases>Lithuania>Hamagid, by Jeffrey Maynard)

Surname	Given Name	Comments
BAR	Chenich	
GREENSHTEIN	Hoshea	
KA"TZ	Zondil	
KURSHAN	Getzil	
PEZER	Shalom	
RABINOWITZ	Sheftel	
RADNAZER	Avraham ben Kadish	
RADZANER	Kadish	father of Avraham

Surname	Given Name	Comments
ROZE	Hoshea	from Pabalve (Pavolne)
RUBIN	Shimon	
RUBIN	Yosef	
SEGAL	Mordechai ben Sh	
SHAPIRO	Levi	
STOKMIANER	Shlomo	
WEINBERG	Tzvi ben K	
ZILBERT	Shraga	
ZIV	Shlomo	
ZUSMAN	Tzvi	
	Abba ben Getzil	brother of Meir
	Abba ben Tzvi	
	Ari bn Binyomin	
	Ber ben Leib	
	Binyomin Zev	
	Chaim Shalom son of the rabbi	
	Daniel ben Yakov	
	Dov ben Y	
	Dov ben Zev	
	Dovid ben Hillel	
	Dovid Yakov ben Eli	
	Eli ben Shraga	
	Ephraim ben Shraga	
	Gedalia ben Avraham	
	Leib ben Dov	
	Manesh ben Shmuel	
	Meir ben Getzil	brother of Abba
	Meir ben Zelig	

Surname	Given Name	Comments
	Mordechai ben Dov	
	Mordechai ben h"k Tzvi	
	Moshe ben Meir ben Moshe	
	Moshe ben Tzvi	
	Moshe ben Yosef	
	Nachum ben Shraga	
	Reuven ben Y	
	Shlomo ben Ari	
	Shlomo ben Nachman	
	Shlomo ben Shraga	
	Shraga ben Don	
	Tzvi ben Boruch	
	Tzvi ben Shlomo	
	Yakov ben Aharon	
	Yakov ben Zusman	
	Yakov Yosef ben Tzvi	
	Yehoshua ben Sh	
	Yisroel ben Chaluna	
	Yisroel Yitzchok ben Yehuda	
	Yitzchok ben Dovid	
	Yitzchok ben Tzvi	
	Yitzchok ben Y	
	Yoel ben Yakov	
	Yosef Zev ben m"r	
	Zev ben Chaim	
	Zev ben G	

Appendix 2

On the occasion of the wedding of Ben Zion, the Fin family donated some money for the settlement of *Eretz-Yisrael*, as published in *HaMelitz* # 50, 1899.

(From JewishGen.org>Databases>Lithuania, by Jeffrey Maynard)

Surname	Given Name	Comments	Town	Source	Year
FIN	Chaim father of Eliahu Bentzion	Rabbi ABD	Tryskiai, Lith.	Hamelitz #50	1899
FIN	Eliahu Bentzion ben Chaim husband of Rochel Etil Grosman from Nemakst	wed	Tryskiai, Lith.	Hamelitz #50	1899

Tytuvėnai (Tsitevyan)

Tytuvenai (Tsitevyan in Yiddish) is situated in central Lithuania, in the Zamut (Zemaitija) region, about 24 kilometers north of the district administrative center Rasein (Raseniai). The town is surrounded by forests and lakes and people visited it as a resort. The name of the town, Tytuvenai, appears on a map of Europe that was published in the second half of the fifteenth century. In 1724 the town was granted a permit to hold a yearly fair.

Until 1795 Tsitevyan was included in the Polish-Lithuanian Kingdom. According to the third division of Poland in the same year by the three superpowers of those times, Russia, Prussia and Austria, Lithuania was divided between Russia and Prussia. As was the case with most other towns of Lithuania, Tsitevyan became part of the Russian Empire, first within the province (*Gubernia*) of Vilna and from 1843 in the Kovno *Gubernia*. During this period and also in the period of independent Lithuania (1918-1940) Tsitevyan was a county administrative center in the Raseiniai district.

Jewish settlement until World War II

The first Jews probably settled in Tsitevyan in the nineteenth century. Before World War I about 60 Jewish families lived in the town and they made their living in agriculture and the small trades. Jews dealt also in the production of tar from timber.

One Tsitevyan donor for the settlement of *Eretz-Yisrael* was named in the Hebrew newspaper *HaMelitz* in 1898 (see Appendix I).

During World War I, in 1915, Tsitevyan Jews were expelled from the town by the Russian rulers, but most returned home the same year. After the war many migrated to South Africa and a few migrated to *Eretz-Yisrael*.

After the war and the establishment of the Lithuanian state in 1918, the new Lithuanian government passed the Law of Autonomies for Minorities. The Minister for Jewish Affairs, Dr. Menachem (Max) Soloveitshik, ordered elections to community committees *(Va'adei Kehilah)* to be held in the summer of 1919. In Tsitevyan a *Va'ad (*community committee) with five members was elected. The committee was active for several years in all fields of Jewish life.

Tsitevyan Jews took part in the elections for the first Lithuanian *Seimas* (Parliament) in October 1922. From the three Jewish lists that participated, the Zionists received 23 votes, while *Akhduth (Agudath Yisrael)* and the Democrats received three votes each.

During this period most of the Tsitevyan Jews (70%) were farmers, the remainder were shopkeepers, peddlers and craftsmen. An important source of livelihood was the multitude of visitors who came each summer to vacation in the nearby forests.

The first government census in 1923 counted 1,164 residents in Tsitevyan, 221 being Jewish (19%).

According to the government survey of 1931 three textile shops and one heating fuel shop were in Jewish hands. The same survey showed that Tsitevyan Jews owned a wool combing workshop in the town and a flourmill and a sawmill in the county.

Jewish girls in a field of Tsitevyan

In 1937 thirteen Jewish artisans were employed in the town: four butchers, three potters, two bakers, one glazier, one tailor, one shoemaker and one other.

The Jewish Popular Bank (*Folksbank*) had 49 members in 1920, but closed after a few years.

Jewish boys received their elementary education at the local *Heder* and continued their studies at the *Yeshivoth* in the nearby towns. The girls studied at the Hebrew *Yavneh* school. The town had a library with Hebrew and Yiddish books. An active *Ezrah* welfare society was run by the Jewish women.

Many Tsitevyan Jews were Zionists and included supporters of almost all the Zionist parties. From the 85 Zionists who voted for the nineteenth (1935) Zionist congress, 42 gave their votes for the Labor party, 4 voted for the

General Zionist A, 12 voted for the General Zionist B, 8 voted for the *Grosmanists* and 19 voted for the *Mizrahi* party.

There were a synagogue and a *Beth-Midrash* in the town. One of these was built in the 1880s.

Among the rabbis who officiated in Tsitevyan were:
Tsevi-Ya'akov Openheim (1854-1926), served in Tsitevyan 1881-1882, published several books on the *Talmud*.
Avraham-Aharon Burshtein (1867-1926) at the age of twenty-four became the rabbi in Tsitevyan, where he served for a short time. From 1924 he lived in *Eretz-Yisrael* and was the head of the *yeshivah Merkaz Harav* in Jerusalem.
Shelomoh-Ya'akov Shein
Eliezer-Ya'akov Levin
Yosef Zif until 1913

Rabbi Avraham-Aharon Burshtein   Rabbi Tsevi-Ya'akov Openheim

Ya'akov Kamenetzky, from 1926 in Tsitevyan, later head of the *Yeshivah Torah veDa'ath* in New York
Yisrael-Yehoshua Segal
Shelomoh-Efraim Kravitzky
Avraham-Azriel Medin, in Tsitevyan from 1938, murdered in 1941 together with his community.

Tsitevyan Jews were proud of the *Gaon* and *Tsadik* rabbi Leib Tsigler (Leib Hosid) from Vertyan who lived in their town and was also accepted by the secular Jews. He died at the age of 70 and it is believed that 12 rabbis and 4,000 people from the region attended his funeral.

Zerakh Barnet (1843-1935) was born and grew up in Tsitevyan. In 1872 he emigrated to *Eretz-Yisrael* and was one of the founders of Petakh Tikvah and the Neve Shalom quarter in Yaffo.

Zerakh Barnet

During World War II
With the annexation of Lithuania to the Soviet Union in summer 1940, some Jewish shops and other businesses were nationalized. The Zionist parties and youth organizations were disbanded. The Hebrew schools were closed. At this time about 50 Jewish families lived in the town.

On June 22, 1941 the German army invaded the Soviet Union, and on the very next day they entered Tsitevyan. Local Lithuanian activists immediately began to abuse the Jews. They murdered several Jewish men and buried them in the nearby forest about two kilometers from the town; this was called the Shapiro Forest after the doctor Shapiro, who promoted this forest as a place for healing and recreation. After a few days the Lithuanians burned all the religious books from the *Beth Midrash* and also the private library of the local rabbi Avraham-Azriel Medin. They detained several Jewish men together with the rabbi and took them away to the prison in Rasein where they were murdered.

Until August 12, 1941, the Jews remained in their houses and were taken out for various work. A Lithuanian resident warned his Jewish acquaintances to leave everything and escape to the Shavl ghetto, because all local Jews were to be murdered, but nobody believed him. They thought that he wanted to steal their property.

One night, apparently on August 12, 1941 (19th of Av 5701) the Lithuanian auxiliary police arrived in the town. They forced all the Jews from their homes, crowded them into trucks and drove them to the Shapiro Forest where they were murdered and buried. A few managed to escape the massacre and made their way to the Shavl ghetto. Their fate was ultimately that of the other ghetto Jews.

According to Soviet-Lithuanian sources the bodies of 140 men, women and children were found in the mass grave.

After the war a monument was erected on the mass grave. In the early 1990s a new monument was built with the inscription in Yiddish, Hebrew and Lithuanian: "In this place the Hitlerist murderers and their local helpers murdered 140 Jewish men, heroes ,on June 25, 1941."

The mass grave and the monument to the Tsitevyan men

The monument on the mass grave of the men

The mass grave of the elders, women and children

Sources:
Yad Vashem archives, Jerusalem, M-1/E-1700/1568; M-9/15(6);
Koniukhovsky collection 0-71, file 54
Di Yiddishe Shtime, Kovno, 22.8.1930
Yiddisher Lebn, Kovno-Telz, #162,3.6.1938

Appendix 1
One donor from Tsitevyan for the settlement of Eretz Yisrael as published in HaMelitz #68 in 1898
(from Jewishgen>Databases>Lithuania>HaMelitz-by Jeffrey Maynard)

Surname	Given Name	Comments	Town	Source	Year
SHEIN	Shlomo Yakov father of Aba Heshil of Taurage	Rabbi Gaon ABD	Tytuvenai, Lith.	Hamelitz #68	1898

Vabalninkas (Vabolnik)

Vabalninkas (Vabolnik in Yiddish) is situated in the north of Lithuania, about 24 km. south of the Birzai (Birzh) district administrative center. The settlement is mentioned in historical documents dating back to 1554. In 1619 Vabolnik received permission to conduct markets. Between 1709 and 1712 an epidemic ravaged the town, and three-fourths of its population succumbed to it. In 1775 Vabolnik was granted the Magdeburg rights for self-rule.

Until 1795 Vabolnik was included in the Polish-Lithuanian Kingdom. According to the third division of Poland in the same year by the three superpowers of those times: Russia, Prussia and Austria. Lithuania was divided between Russia and Prussia. As with most of Lithuania, Vabolnik became part of the Russian empire, first under the auspices of the Vilna province (*Gubernia*) and from 1843 the Kovno *Gubernia*.

During World War I (1915-1918) the town was under the military rule of the Germans. During the years of independent Lithuania (1918-1940) Vabolnik was considered a county administrative center in the Birzh district.

Jewish settlement till after World War I
According to a document from 1667, the first Jew settled in Vabolnik around that time. With the passing years the number of Jews increased, but in 1717 they were expelled from the town. After several years Jews returned to live in Vabolnik. In 1738, there were fifteen Jewish families among its total of 160 residents.

In 1741 the Bishop of Vilna granted the Jews permission to build a synagogue. At that time all shops and stores were owned by Jews.

It is said that in 1818, Russian Czar Alexander I passed through Vabolnik with his entourage, and one of the carts broke down. A local Jew named Tsevi repaired the cart and later received a considerable sum of money for his work.

In 1858 there were 545 Jews (46%) living in Vabolnik, among a total population of 1,178.

The Hebrew newspaper *Hamagid* #17 of 1872 presented a list of 41 Vabolnik Jews who donated money for the benefit of the victims of the great famine in Persia (see **Appendix 1**).

In the 1880s the economic situation of Vabolnik Jews was difficult and many of them were very poor. In 1881 at *Hanukah,* a meeting was organized in town, and participants pledged to donate money every month as they were able. This money was to be spent on rye flour for bread that would be sold to the poor at half price.

In 1883 a huge fire rendered 200 families homeless. The synagogue and the four *Batei Midrash* burned down as well.

According to the all-Russian census of 1897, 2,333 residents lived in Vabolnik, of whom 1,828 were Jews (78%).

From 1901 a *Linath HaTsedek* society was actively involved in the lives of Vabolnik Jews; its task was to support the needy and the frail and to supply medicines free of charge.

As was usual in those times, some children studied at a *Heder* and others in a Russian public school. In 1886 five out of the seventy-two students were Jewish.

Jews of Vabolnik began to emigrate to *Eretz-Yisrael* before the *Hibath Zion* movement was established. At the old cemetery on *Har HaZeitim* (Mount of Olives) in Jerusalem at least five tombstones belong to Vabolnik Jews who died there in the second half of the nineteenth century.

The list of contributors to the settlement of *Eretz-Yisrael* dating back to 1900 contains many names of Vabolnik Jews. Another list from 1914 gives the names of twenty Vabolnik Jews.

During World War I, in July 1915, retreating Cossacks instigated a pogrom against Vabolnik Jews: they plundered property, raped women and left many families destitute. The Russian army exiled the Jews far into Russia, and the town with its four prayer houses and its *Pinkasim* and books was set on fire. Only the *Sifrei Torah* were saved, because the people who were forced into exile took the books with them.

During the German rule of 1915-1918 some Jews returned to Vabolnik, and managed to renovate the remaining *Kloiz of the Shamashim* which was more solidly built.

During Independent Lithuania (1918-1940)
With the establishment of independent Lithuania some Vabolnik Jews began to return home. The first census taken by the new Lithuanian government in 1923 confirmed that only one-fourth of the Jewish population who had lived in Vabolnik before World War I returned; i.e. 441 Jews, or 32% of its total 1,361 residents.

Following the Law of Autonomies for Minorities issued by the new Lithuanian government, the minister for Jewish Affairs, Dr. Menachem (Max) Soloveitshik, ordered elections to community committees *(Va'adei Kehilah)* to be held in the summer of 1919. In 1920 a *Va'ad (*community committee) with five members was elected in Vabolnik, and was active in all fields of Jewish life from April 1920 until the end of 1923.

A street in Vabolnik

In the autumn of 1920 recruits of the Lithuanian army began to riot in town; they smashed windows in Jewish homes and robbed Jews. Following a complaint by a community committee to the Ministry of Jewish Affairs, fourteen of the rioters were charged.

At that time Vabolnik Jews made their living in small trade, crafts, light industry and agriculture.

According to the 1931 government survey there were ten stores in Vabolnik, seven of them owned by Jewish persons. There were also small shops. A Jewish doctor was first mentioned by name in 1925.

The distribution according to type of business is given in the table below:

Type of the business	Total	Owned by Jews
Grocery stores	1	0
Textile products and furs	3	2
Leather and shoes	1	1
Medicine and cosmetics	1	0
Radios, sewing machines	1	1
Iron products and tools	1	1
Other	2	2

According to the same survey, Jews owned eleven light industry factories: three flour mills, two bakeries, two wool-combing workshops, one spinning mill, one leather factory, one felt factory and a power plant.

In 1937, sixteen Jewish tradesmen worked in Vabolnik: three needle trade workers, two bakers, two shoemakers, two metal workers, two butchers, one glazier, one painter, one book-binder, one watchmaker and one tailor.

The Jewish Popular Bank (*Folksbank*) played an important role in the economic life of the Vabolnik community and numbered 97 members in 1927. In 1939 there were twenty-two telephone subscribers in town, six of them Jewish.

Following the great fire, the *Beth Midrash*, with its solid structure, remained with only its walls intact, and was renovated in 1931. As previously mentioned, The *Kloiz of the Shamashim* was renovated during the German rule. The other two prayer houses, the *Kloiz* of the Grocers and the *Kloiz* of the Craftsmen, with its two buildings, were never rebuilt. Not all of the *Sifrei Torah* removed by the people who were exiled were returned.

Many Vabolnik Jews belonged to the Zionist movement and most of the Zionist parties had supporters, as seen by the results of voting in the Zionist congresses:

Cong No	Year	Tot Shek	Total Votes	Labor Party Z"S	Z"Z	Rev	Gen Zion A	B	Gros	Miz
15	1927	14	13	2	7	---	---	---	---	4
16	1929	28	10	1	7	---	---	---	---	2
17	1931	---	12	2	5	---	1	---	---	4
18	1933	---	17	14		---	3	---	---	---
19	1935	---	93	81		---	1	1	---	10

Key: **Cong No. = Congress Number, Tot Shek = Total Shekalim, Rev = Revisionists, Gen Zion = General Zionists, Gros = Grosmanists, Miz = Mizrahi**

Among the rabbis who served in Vabolnik were:
Mosheh Harif (?-1874)
Shalom-Elhanan Yofe (1858-?), born in Vabolnik, was the rabbi from 1889. Following his emigration to America he served as a rabbi in St. Louis and Brooklyn. He published many books on religious issues.
Yehudah-Leib Furer, served in Vabolnik from 1907
Zalman Rokhlin from 1934.

The most active Zionist youth organization was Gordonia with 40 to 50 members.

Among the personages born in Vabolnik were Shemuel Yatskan (1874-1936), journalist, editor and publisher, who published articles in the Hebrew newspapers *HaMelitz* and *HaTsefirah*; he also founded the Yiddish *Haint* (Today) newspaper in Warsaw and later the *Pariser Haint.*
Benyamin Kremer (1887-1942), educator and writer, was a literature teacher in the Krinsky gymnasium of Warsaw and published articles in the Hebrew and Yiddish press; *Pinhas Shukyan* (1856-?), *Hovev Zion* and a Zionist activist, who published articles in *HaMelitz.*

During World War II and later
In the summer of 1940 Lithuania was annexed to the Soviet Union and became a Soviet Republic. Following new rules, the Vabolnik factories and shops, mostly owned by Jews, were nationalized. All Zionist parties and youth organizations were disbanded. Supply of goods decreased and, as a result, prices soared. The middle class, mostly Jewish, bore the brunt and the standard of living dropped gradually.

On June 27, 1941, five days after the German invasion into the Russia, the German army entered Vabolnik. The local Lithuanian nationalists immediately detained every person with ties to the Soviet rule. Among them were many Jews who did not have anything to do with the Soviets. All the detainees were transferred to Kupishok (Kupiskis) and murdered. The Lithuanian nationalists walked the streets armed, looting Jewish homes. 86 Jews were murdered in the market place.

About three weeks after the war broke out, the Jews were ordered to leave their homes, bringing the most necessary possession, and settle in a small alleyway where poor Lithuanians lived. The Lithuanian residents who lived in this alley moved to the empty Jewish homes. The alley, which became the so-called ghetto, was not fenced, but a few armed Lithuanians guarded it. The Jews were ordered to prepare a detailed list of all the residents of the ghetto under the pretext that the names were needed to prepare a correct supply of food for ghetto residents. In fact, they needed the list to prevent escape of the Jewish people from the ghetto. The list named 600 persons including a number of refugees from other places. Every day the Jews would be ordered to perform different jobs, such as sweeping the streets or washing the floors in town offices. They would buy food at peasants' farms or in exchange for clothes.

On August 18, 1941 the Jews were ordered to gather at the *Beth Midrash* and the *Shulhoif* and bring along food for three days. There, they were ordered to deliver their money and valuables. Many preferred to throw out the money in the washrooms instead of handing it over to the murderers. After a short time they were transferred by trucks to Posvol (Pasvalys). The transfer continued the next day as well.

Approximately forty Jews detained in the local school escaped, thanks to the efforts of teachers Sheine and Hayim Gertner who managed to convince one of the Lithuanian guards, also a teacher, to release the prisoners. Only three of them survived.

A local priest came to the ghetto and offered to convert the Jews to Christianity so that they could be rescued from imminent death. After a difficult inner struggle and referring to Rambam and other *Geonim*, seventy agreed to convert. It is not clear if they managed to become baptized. For some time these converts were kept apart from the other Jews, but their fate was the same as that of the other Jews in Posvol.

Jews from Posvol, Vabolnik, Salat and Jonishkel were kept alive until August 26, 1941 (3rd of Elul 5701). On the morning of that day all Jews were ordered on big trucks and taken to the Zadeikiai forest, about 4.5 km. from Posvol. There all were shot and buried in prepared pits. On that day 1,349 Jewish men, women and children were buried in these pits.

After the war survivors of Posvol and other towns built a monument at the site of the mass grave. In the 1990s another monument was erected with inscriptions in Yiddish and Lithuanian.

A local Lithuanian photographer, J.Daubaras, saved 134 photo negatives of Vabolnik Jews. A number of these were presented in an exhibition in Vabolnik in October 1990 organized by the State Jewish Museum of Vilna.

The monument on the mass grave of the victims of Posvol, Vabolnik, Salat and Jonishkel with a group of survivors from these towns.
[Erected during the Soviet rule. Inscription only in Lithuanian.
Indicated with white arrows are Hayim and Sheine Gertner]

The mass grave with the new monument in Zadeikiai forest

The monument with the inscription in Yiddish and Lithuanian: "In this place on 28.8.1941 the Hitlerist murderers and their local helpers murdered 1,349 Jews - men, women, children."

Sources:
Yad Vashem archives, Jerusalem, O-33/1125; O-3/3680; M-45/1
Koniukhovsky Collection 0-71, files 70, 71
YIVO, New York, Lithuanian Jewish Communities Collection, files 162-177, 1513; pages 8544-9008, 69422/23
Gotlib, *Ohalei Shem* (Hebrew), page 49
Kamzon J.D., *Yahaduth Lita* (Hebrew), Tel Aviv page 95
Shakhar-Gertner, Sheine; How did they fight with the Satan (Hebrew), Tel Aviv 1985
Yiddisher Lebn (Jewish Life), (Yiddish), Kovno 11.7.1934
Di Yiddishe Shtime (The Jewish Voice) (Yiddish), Kovno 27.9.1928
Der Yiddisher Cooperator (Yiddish), Kovno # 3-1928
HaMelitz, St.Petersburg (Hebrew), 4.1.1881; 22.2.1881; 20.4.1901
Birzieciu Zodis (The word of the Birzher) (Lithuanian), Birzh 30.10.1990
Shakhar-Gertner, Sheina: The Trees Stood Still: Holocaust Survivors Publishing Co., Framingham, Mass., 1984
Naujienos Chicago (Lithuanian), 11.6.1949

Appendix 1
List of 41 Vabolnik Jewish donors for the victims of the great Persian famine as published in *Hamagid* # 17, 1972
(from JewishGen>Databases>Lithuania>*HaMagid* by Jeffrey Maynard)

Surname	Given Names	Comments
ATLES	Moshe Dov	
ATLES	Zev	
BARA"M	Eliezer	
BARA"M	Yosef	
BEILESH	Avraham Yechiel	
BEKER	Abba	
BEKER	Aharon Zev	
BITON	Moshe	
BLOCH	Yehoshua Yitzchok	
FEINBERG	Meir Dov	
FRIDMAN	Zelig	
GEFEN	Dovid Bentzion	
GORDON	Mendil	
GORDON	Tzvi	
HACOHEN	Pinchas	
HER	Meir	
KADISHEWITZ	Leib	from Viesintos (Wishinte)
KANTOR	Yoel Lipman	
KANTZIPOWITZ	Shlomo	
KAPLEN	Yosef	
KUSNIR	Eli	
KUTNIR	Moshe	
LEWIN	Yakov	
LEWIN	Yisroel Leib	
LEWIT	Bentzion	

LURIA	Aharon	
NITZIN	Betzalel	
ROM	Tzvi Hirsh	
RUBIN	Leib	
SANDLER	Nachum	
SHLAPKOWITZ	Eli Yechezkel	
SHLAWIN	Binyamin	
SHU"B	Avraham	
TZESISKE	Mordechai Bentzion	
WALK	Eliezer Lipman	from (Primose)
YAFE	Mendil	
YUZUNT	Mendil	
	Eli ben Tz	
	Meshulam Moshe	
	Pinchas ben Sh	
	Pinchas Zelig ben A	

Vaiguva (Vaigeve)

Vaiguva (Vaigeve in Yiddish) lies in the northwestern part of Lithuania, in the Zamut (Zemaitija) region, about 55 km. to the southwest of the district administrative center Shavl (Siauliai). The Vaiguva River flows nearby. An estate has existed there since 1557 and a village was established in 1598.

Until 1795 Vaiguva was included in the Polish-Lithuanian Kingdom. According to the third division of Poland in the same year by the three superpowers of those times, Russia, Prussia and Austria, Lithuania was divided between Russia and Prussia. As most of the other towns of Lithuania, Vaiguva became part of the Russian Empire, first under the auspices of the Vilna province (*Gubernia*) and from 1843 under the Kovno Gubernia in the Siauliai district. At that time Vaiguva became a county administrative center. It held this status also during the period of independent Lithuania.

Jews probably first settled in Vaigeve in the nineteenth century. Until World War I and in the first years after the war the Jews comprised a third of the total population, but later their numbers dropped to such an extent that just before World War II only ten Jewish families remained in the town.

According to the all-Russian census of 1897, 530 residents lived in Vaigeve, 193 of them being Jewish (36%).

Before World War I Vaigeve Jews made their living in the trades and crafts, mainly in tailoring. The tailors would work in nearby villages during the week and return home for *Shabbath*.

In times of famine the Jewish and Christian residents left the town and looked for food elsewhere. The wealthiest man in the town, Barukh Faivelzon, who ran the estate and the hotel that belonged to a Polish nobleman, set up long tables with food near his home and every passer-by, Jew or Christian, could eat his fill before going on his way. Barukh's wife delivered provisions to every passer-by for his journey, that included a piece of bread, a herring and 10 Kopeikas. When the hunger worsened a help committee headed by Dr. Rilf, the rabbi of Memel, was established in town that would send every week money to Vaigeve.

A first aid station was set up in the house of Barukh Faivelzon. The doctor from Uzhvent, P. Girbudas worked there. During Nazi rule he tried to help the Jews imprisoned in the *Beth Midrash*.

At the end of the nineteenth century the children of the *Heder* established the *Kinyan Torah* society, whose goal was to buy books for the *Beth Midrash*. With the help of the Kopeikas they collected enough holy books to fill a cupboard in the *Beth Midrash*. The climax of this project was the purchase of a *Talmud* that was carried into the *Beth Midrash* with great ceremony.

The rabbis who officiated in Vaugeve during the years were:
Hayim-Hirsh Shulevitz
Yeshayahu Mamush
Efraim-Dov Berezinsky, from 1902 in Vaigeve
Mosheh Luria, the last rabbi of the community, murdered by Lithuanians in 1941.
For some time the town also had a Hazan, a Shohet and a Melamed.

During the period of Independent Lithuania (1918-1940) most Vaigeve Jews were farmers. According to the first census performed by the new Lithuanian government in 1923, 389 residents lived in Vaigeve, 118 of them Jewish (30%).

According to the government survey of 1931 there were two Jewish shops in the town: one sold food products and the other textiles. According to the same survey a wool-combing workshop operated in the town and two flourmills in villages of the county were Jewish-owned. In 1937 there were four Jewish artisans: two tailors, one baker and one butcher.

In 1921 a fire burned down 22 Jewish houses.

A street in Vaigeve after the fire of 1921

In the summer of 1940 Lithuania was annexed to the Soviet Union and became a Soviet Republic. Under new regulations, the factories owned by Jews were nationalized, as were some of the Jewish shops. Some of the former owners were employed in them and the others had to look for another source of income. By this time about ten Jewish families remained.

A few days after the outbreak of war between Germany and the Soviet Union on June 22, 1941, the Germans entered Vaigeve. The Lithuanians immediately took control and began to harass the Jews. An order was issued but not executed, that all the Jews should concentrate in one of the Jewish farms of the vicinity. At the beginning of July the Jews were ordered to leave their houses and concentrate in the *Beth Midrash*. They were not permitted to take anything with them. There they were kept in terrible conditions without food or water. At the end of July 1941 they were transferred to nearby Kelm (Kelme). The seventeen children were separated by force from their mothers and were placed under the supervision of the two Faivelzon sisters. On July 29, 1941 (5th of Av, 5701) all Vaigeve Jews together with the Kelm Jews were murdered at the nearby sand quarries. The children were transferred to Zhager (Zagare) where they were murdered on the day after Yom Kippur 5702 (October 2, 1941).

The mass grave in Kelm

The monument at the massacre site with the inscription in Hebrew and
Lithuanian: "In memory of the scholars and residents of the town of
Kelm and surroundings, who were murdered by the bloody Nazi
scoundrels - damn them - in 5701 (1941). Immortalized by the remnant
of the Broida-Ziv families of Kelm."

Sources:
Yad Vashem archives, Jerusalem, M-1/E-1023/930; M-9/15(6);
M-33/973, 995; Koniukhovsky collection 0-71, files 47, 48
Fridman, Eliezer-Eliyahu, Memoirs 5618-5686, (Hebrew), Tel Aviv 1926
Gotlib; *Ohalei Shem*, page 50
Komunistu Zodis (Word of Communists) (Lithuanian) Kelme, 11.6.1988

Vainutas (Vainute)

Vainutas (*Vainute* in Yiddish) lies in the western part of Lithuania, in the Zamut (*Zemaitija*) region, about 35 km. to the northwest of the district administrative center Tavrig (*Taurage*). The narrow Sisa (*Shisha*) River flows through the town.

The town of Vainute has existed since the sixteenth century. In 1792 it was granted the right of self rule as a town.

A view of Vainute

Until 1795 Vainute was included in the Polish-Lithuanian Kingdom. According to the third division of Poland in the same year by the three superpowers of those times, Russia, Prussia and Austria, Lithuania was divided between Russia and Prussia. As was the case with most of the other towns of Lithuania, Vainute became part of the Russian Empire, first within the province (*Gubernia*) of Vilna and from 1843 in the Kovno *Gubernia* in the Rasein district. During the period of Independent Lithuania (1918-1940) Vainute was a county administrative center in the Taurage district.

After the Memel (*Klaipeda*) district was annexed to Germany in 1939 the border between Germany and Lithuania was drawn five kilometers from Vainute.

Jewish settlement before World War II
Jews are first believed to have settled in Vainute in the middle of the seventeenth century. In 1766 there were 515 Jews. Before World War I about 80 Jewish families lived in Vainute, making their living in agriculture, trade and crafts.

In a list of donors for the great Persian famine in 1871-72 the names of 57 Vainute Jews appear (see **Appendix 1**).

During the period of Independent Lithuania (1918-1940) the Jewish population decreased. The first census conducted by the new Lithuanian government in 1923 counted 1,291 residents in Vainute, 348 of them being Jewish (27%).

Vainute, on the road from the mill to the town
(Courtesy of Naomi Musiker, from the Jewish Board of Deputies archive in Johannesburg, scanned by Barry Mann and Maurice Skikne)

In the 1921 elections for the Local Council nineteen men were elected, two of them Jewish. At that time most of the Jews made their living in agriculture, with a minority in the small trades and crafts. The farmers held large fields, pasture areas and plantations, cultivating them intensively using agricultural machinery. The other Jews also had small plots for auxiliary farms that brought them additional income. Some families were peddlers and other families were supported by relatives living abroad.

According to the government survey of 1931 there were eleven shops and businesses in the town, ten of them (91%) owned by Jews: five textile shops, three businesses with meat and horses, one pharmacy and one mixed goods shop. According to the same survey Vainute Jews owned a wool-combing workshop, a bakery, a sawmill, a flourmill and a power plant.

In 1937 there were fifteen Jewish tradesmen: seven butchers, three tailors, one wool knitter, one shoemaker, one barber and two others.

The Jewish Popular Bank (*Folksbank*) played an important role in the economic life of Vainute's Jews and their economic condition was generally sound.

In 1939 there were twenty-two telephones listed, half of them in Jewish homes and businesses.

In the years before World War II relations between the Jews and the Lithuanians worsened. The open propaganda of the Lithuanian Merchants Association (*Verslas*) to boycott Jewish shops and the Nazi propaganda from across the nearby border had their influence. Every year, before *Pesakh*, Vainute Jews were afraid to go out in the evenings because of risk of blood libel that was raised from time to time. Before *Pesakh* in 1940 a Lithuanian housemaid falsely accused her Jewish employer of slaughtering her son to use his blood to bake his *Matsoth*. Other peasants believed the libel and created a pogrom against the Jews. In the middle of the night they smashed the windows of all the Jewish houses, injured some Jews and looting homes.

A wedding in 1938: the bride is L. Leibovitz
(Courtesy of Naomi Musiker, from the Jewish Board of Deputies archive in Johannesburg, scanned by Barry Mann and Maurice Skikne)

The Jewish children received their elementary education at a *Heder* and at the Hebrew *Tarbuth* school. After graduating, most of the youngsters either worked with their parents or began to learn a trade. Only a few continued to study at the Hebrew gymnasium in Tavrig and in the Telz *yeshivah*. The community maintained a library with Yiddish and Hebrew books.

Zionism was embraced by the Vainute Jews at the end of the nineteenth century. Regular fundraising was conducted for settlement of *Eretz-Yisrael*.

The names of twenty-one Vainute Jews appear in lists of donors, as published in the Hebrew newspaper *HaMelitz* in 1898 and 1900 (see **Appendix 2**). The fund raiser was Yisrael Yavetz. Subsequent fund raisers included Shalom-Yits'hak Levitov (1903), Yisrael Yavetz, Yosef Aizikovitz, Yehudah-Avraham Asherovitz and Leib Sheinberg (1909) and Tsevi Rabinovitz (1914).

In 1901 *Agudath Benei Zion* (The Sons of Zion Society) was active in Vainute; that group and others collected donations for the settlement of *Eretz-Yisrael*. In that year many Vainute Jews signed up to buy shares in the bank of the Zionist movement *Otzar Hityashvuth HaYehudim* (Jewish Colonical Trust [in *Eretz-Yisrael*]).

In the years of Independent Lithuania, Vainute Jews took part in the voting for Zionist congresses as shown:

Cong No.	Year	Tot Shek	Total Votes	Labor Party		Rev	Gen Zion		Gros	Miz
				Z"S	Z"Z		A	B		
18	1933	---	86	16		---	1	---	56	13
19	1935	---	144	14		---	---	2	84	44

Key: Cong No. = Congress Number, Tot Shek = Total Shekalim, Rev = Revisionists, Gen Zion = General Zionists, Gros = Grosmanists, Miz = Mizrahi

The Jewish youth belonged to Zionist youth organizations. Sport activities were run by the local Maccabi branch with its 50 members. A few young people joined the underground Communist party.

Religious life concentrated around the *Beth Midrash*. Among the rabbis who officiated in town were:
    Benyamin Lifshitz (?-1871)
    Benyamin Farber
    Tsevi Ze'ev Shor (?-1929)
    Ezra Altshuler (1858-1938), officiated in Vainute for 35 years, in 1936 he emigrated to *Eretz-Yisrael*, and died in 1938 in a road accident in Kefar Saba; he published several books on Judaism.
    Yosef-Ya'akov Shor, born in Vainute and was appointed as Rabbi in 1936; the last Rabbi of this community, murdered by Lithuanians in1941.

The welfare societies *Gemiluth Hesed* and *Bikur Holim* had branches in the town.

Ya'akov Hodes (1886-1961), who was born in Vainute, emigrated with his family to England as a young boy, and began to write articles in the press (The Manchester Guardian and The Jewish World) from the age of seventeen. From 1945 he lived in *Eretz-Yisrael* where he edited publications for the Jewish Agency. He died in Jerusalem.

During World War II and after

In June 1940 Lithuania was annexed by the Soviet Union and became a Soviet Republic. Under new laws, the majority of Jewish factories and shops were nationalized and commissars were appointed to manage them. All Zionist parties and youth organizations were disbanded and Hebrew educational institutions were closed. Supply of goods decreased and, as a result, prices soared. The middle class, mostly Jewish, was hit hard, and the standard of living gradually dropped. In 1940 about 55 Jewish families lived in the town.

The German army entered Vainute on the first day of the war between Germany and the Soviet Union, June 22, 1941. On that morning a number of Jews harnessed their horses to their carts and fled to the nearby villages to seek shelter with peasant acquaintances. Others tried to escape to Russia but only a few Soviet activists managed to reach there. During that first week all the fugitives returned home because the peasants threw them off their farms. Coming home they found their Lithuanian neighbors had invaded their houses and taken over their property. Some of the Jews settled in the *Beth Midrash* and others at the houses of relatives or acquaintances. The Germans and Lithuanians confiscated their horses and cattle.

The Lithuanian police took control of the town and ordered the Jews to hand over their radios, money, valuables and guns. The order was accompanied with the threat that anyone who did not comply would be shot, together with his entire family. Nonetheless many hid their valuables in the ground. Others gave their valuables to the local priest for safekeeping until after the war.

On June 24, 1941 an order was issued that all males aged twelve years and older to register with the police. For the next four weeks the men were taken for different work projects, such as burying dead horses, repairing roads and culverts, cleaning the streets and serving the Germans and Lithuanians. At noon they were permitted to go home for lunch and afterward they returned to work. The Lithuanian police sometimes entered Jewish homes and demanded that the Jews 'present' them with various items.

One day, in about the third week of the war, when the Jews reported for work, the Lithuanian police led them to the church square. They had brought in the elderly Rabbi Yosef Shor and the *Shamash* Yosef Shtern. The S"S men who were present forced the *shamash* to cut off half of the rabbi's beard. The rabbi was then tied to a horse on which a S"S man sat and rode around the square. The rabbi was forced to run behind the horse while being whipped, and the Lithuanians at the square enjoyed the 'show.'

After this torture the rabbi became very ill. Five other men detained on different pretexts were shot in different places in the vicinity.

One day in July the men were brought from the yard of the police station to the *Beth Midrash*. There they were forced to remove the *Aron Kodesh*, the Torah scrolls and the holy books from the *Beth Midrash* and to stack them all in a pile at the yard. The men were forced to fetch their holy books, *Tefilin* and *Talitoth* and throw them all on the pile. The Lithuanians brought in the ailing rabbi and ordered him to ignite the pile, over which the Germans had poured petrol. The rabbi vehemently refused and begged to be shot. Finally the Jewish tailor who lived near the *Beth Midrash* ignited the pile while the Lithuanians applauded as it all burned.

On July 19, 1941 all the men were brought to the *Beth Midrash*. They were forced to empty their pockets and were then marched through the town in the direction of Naishtot Tavrig (*Zemaiciu Naumiestis*). Three kilometers from the town they were halted in a field. Shortly afterwards an S"S man from Heydekrug arrived, who made a selection from among the men. Of the 120 men in the field 90 were loaded on a towing truck and were taken toward Naishtot. At the ravines of Siaudvyciai, three kilometers east of Vainute, they were murdered and buried. The remaining 30, young strong men, were transferred, with much abuse, to the Heydekrug camp. Jews from other towns, including Kaltinenai and Laukuva were also imprisoned there.

In August another selection was made and 50 to 60 men, mainly the elderly and ill, were separated from the others. They were told they were to be taken home, but on the way they were murdered. In October and November 1941 further selections were made and those chosen were told as before that they would be going home, but, as it was later discovered, they were murdered and buried at the ravines of Siaudvyciai.

At the end of July 1943 the men from the Heydekrug camp were transferred to Auschwitz. There about 100 were annihilated, including ten men from Vainute. After about two months the surviving men were transported to the Warsaw ghetto in order to vacate the ruins. Many died in a typhus epidemic, including the men from Vainute. In summer of 1944 the remaining men were transported to the Dachau concentration camp.

Only three Vainute men survived to be freed by the American army at the end of the war.

The mass grave and the monument at the ravines of Siaudvyciai

The women and children who remained in the town after the men were removed were expelled from their homes and crammed into a few houses around the *Beth Midrash*. Some women were forced to work on farms and the others at different cleaning tasks. The S"S men from Heydekrug and the local police would come into town, drag girls outside and rape them.

At the end of September 1941 the authorities announced that the women and the children would be taken to the place where their men were working. About 125 women and children were brought to the Gerainiai Forest, about four kilometers from Vainute, where they were all murdered and buried.

After the war monuments were erected on the mass graves.

Sources:
Yad Vashem archives, Jerusalem, TR-10/568; 0-3/2580; Koniukhovsky collection 0-71, files 4, 16-19
YIVO, New York, Collection of Lithuanian Jewish Communities, file 1568
Kamzon Y.D., *Yahaduth Lita*, page 61
Gotlib, *Ohalei Shem*, page 50
HaMelitz, St. Petersburg, 18.6.1901

Survivors of Vainute at the mass grave

Appendix 1
List of 57 Vainute donors for the victims of the Persian famine as published in HaMagid, #28, 1872
(From JewishGen>Databases>Lithuania>*HaMagid* by Jeffrey Maynard)

Surname	Given Name	Comments
AVREMES	Shmuel	
BARA"M	Yechezkel	
BASHES	Chaim	
BERILS	Yisroel	
BR"D	Mordechai	
CHATZES	Itzik	
CHAYAT	Leib	
DEGITZER	Dovid	
DOVIDS	Eli	
DOVIDS	Moshe	

Surname	Given Name	Comments
EIZIKS	Shaul	
GAWRER	Fisil Tzvi	
HAWES	Mordechai	father of Zev Avraham
HAWES	Zev Avraham ben Mordechai	
KA"TZ	Eitze Micha	
KA"TZ	Tuvia	
KRETZMER	Dovid	
LEWENZOHN	Yitzchok Meir	
LIPA	Avraham	
LIPSHITZ	Binyamin	Rabbi Gaon
MAGID	Shaul	
MINDES	Tzvi	
MOSHES	Avraham	
REINES	Tzvi	
ROZING	Shraga	
SEGAL	Menachem	
SHAPIRO	Yehiyahu Dov	
SHU"B	Moshe Leib	
SHU"B	Yuda Meir	
SHWEKSNER	Tzvi	
SILTZISKER	Pinchas	
SILTZISKER	Yakov	
TOIBES	Shmuel	
TOIRAG	Rachel	woman
YAKES	Eitze	
YAKOBZOHN	Shimon Shaul ben Yitzchok Meir	
YAKOBZOHN	Tzvi Ari	father of Yitzhak Meir
YAKOBZOHN	Yitzchok Meir ben Tzvi Ari	
ZIGEITZER	Meir	

Surname	Given Name	Comments
ZWINGER	Leizer	
	Aharon ben Kofman	
	Daniel ben G	
	Ete	widow
	Kofman father of Aharon	
	Lv Leizer	
	Micha	
	Nachum Mordechai	
	Reuven	
	Shlomo Yakov ben Y	boy
	Shmuel ben Shalom	
	Todros Leib	
	Tzvi ben Shlomo Yakov	boy
	Yakov Abba	
	Yakov Leizer ben Z	
	Yisroel Bentzion	
	Yisroel Leib ben R Chana	
	Yosef Leib	

Appendix 2
List of Vainute donors for the Settlement of *Eretz-Yisrael* as published in HaMelitz
(From JewishGen>Databases>Lithuania>*HaMagid* by Jeffrey Maynard)

Surname	Given Name	Comments	Source	Year
ABRAMOWITZ	Yehuda Leib		#121	1900
ABRAMOWITZ	Yehuda Leib		#56	1899
GROSMAN	Zechariah		#121	1900
GROSMAN	Zechariah		#56	1899
KLEIN	Yitzchok		#121	1900
KLEIN	Yitzchok		#56	1899
LEWINZOHN	Yitzchok Meir		#56	1899
LEWINZON	Yitzchok Meir		#121	1900
LEWITAN	Shlomo Yitzchok		#140	1900
MARKOWITZ	Yitzchok		#56	1899
MELAZRENAN	Betzalel		#56	1899
MILOZDENAN	Betzalel		#121	1900
RABINOWITZ	Dov Tzvi		#121	1900
RABINOWITZ	Tzvi Dov		#56	1899
ROZIN	Tzvi Zelig		#121	1900
ROZIN	Tzvi Zelig		#56	1899
YABETZ	Yisroel		#121	1900
YAVETZ	Eliahu ben Yisroel	born 1887	#122	1900
YAVETZ	Yisroel		#56	1899
YAVETZ	Yisroel father of Eliahu b-i-l of Nochum Rozing of Taurage		#122	1900
	Yehuda Leib ben Shachna		#121	1900

Veliuona (Velon)

Veliuona (Velon inYiddish) is located in central Lithuania on the right shore of the Neman (Nemunas) river, about 50 km. northwest of Kovno (Kaunas). It was built in the valley and on the hills adjacent to the river.

At the end of the thirteenth and the beginning of the fourteenth centuries a fortress carrying the same name was built in the area. The fortress successfully resisted the recurrent attacks of the Crusader order. After the defeat of the Crusaders in the Zalgiris (Gruenwald) battle in 1410, the Velon fortress lost its strategic importance and the settlement grew into an urban settlement of fishermen and trades people. In 1500 permission was granted to Velon to have its own emblem, to maintain a market and three fairs annually. In 1772 Bernardine monks settled in that area.

Until 1795 Velon was included in the Polish-Lithuanian Kingdom. According to the third division of Poland in the same year by the three superpowers of those times, Russia, Prussia and Austria, Lithuania was divided between Russia and Prussia. Like most of Lithuania, Velon became a part of the Russian Empire, first in the Vilna province (*Gubernia*) and from 1843 in the Kovno *Gubernia* as a county administrative center. It also kept this status during the years of independent Lithuania (1918-1940).

General view of Velon

It seems that the first Jews settled in Velon at the beginning of the fifteenth century, as maintained by elderly people who referred to the tombstones at the old local cemetery. It was also said that the first tombstone in the cemetery was of a girl named Vikhne, a daughter of a couple of beggars; she died while passing through the town. In Velon there was a custom to mention the girl's name during the prayer of *Hazkarath Neshamoth* (Memorial Service of the Dead).

In 1766, there were 166 Jewish tax payers in Velon. According to the all-Russian census of 1897, 820 residents inhabited the town, of whom 573 (about 100 families) were Jewish (aboutr 70%). During that time the Jews made up the majority of the town's population; consequently, many were hurt during the numerous grim events that occurred in the town. One such incident was the Polish rebellion and retribution activities instigated by the Russian army, in particular by the Cossacks.

Many tales were told about the hero of the town, Izik the horse-man, who specialized in long trips to St. Petersburg and back. He was such a strong man that even during his recruitment to army service for Czar Nicolai the First, the recruiters could not catch him to send him to the army.

Religious and public life concentrated mostly around the two *Batei Midrash,* one in the lower part of the town and the second in the upper part where the house of the rabbi and the *yeshivah* were also located. At the end of the nineteenth century approximately thirty students studied in the *yeshivah.* In the years 1870-1874 the head of the *yeshivah* was the local rabbi Ya'akov Yosef (Ya'akov Harif), a student of the famous Rabbi Yisrael Salanter. Among other subjects, he taught the *Musar* doctrine (Ethics). Later he moved to New York where he became the head of a *yeshivah.*

Rabbi Shemuel-Menahem HaLevi Katz

Among the rabbis who served in Velon were:

Ya'akov Braines, in Velon from 1850, who was born in the town and made his living trading in the surrounding villages;

Mosheh-Betsalel Luria (1835-1914) in Velon 1860-1869, who published many books on the Talmud;

Hayim Ratsker, 1869-1870;

Shemuel Neviazhsky, 1874-1876;

Ya'akov Zak, 1876-1913;

Shemuel-Menahem HaLevi Katz (1887-1954), in Velon 1913-1915; in 1940 he emigrated to Eretz Yisrael, and served as rabbi in Tel Aviv, was a member of the Main Rabbinate, died in Tel Aviv.

The list of contributors for the benefit of the victims of the great Persian famine in 1871-72, includes names of 25 Velon Jews (see **Appendix 1**).

At the beginning of World War I, in summer 1915, the Russian rule ordered Velon Jews exiled to the remote regions of Russia. They were given two hours to leave their homes, under heavy threats that those who refused would be hanged.

After the war and the establishment of the independent Lithuania in 1918, a number of the exiled Velon Jews returned home. In 1921, there were 258 Jews living in the town, and the first census performed by the new government in 1923 counted 470 residents, 335 (71%) being Jews.

Following the Law of Autonomies for Minorities issued by the new Lithuanian government, the Minister for Jewish Affairs, Dr. Menakhem (Max) Soloveitshik ordered elections to community committees, *Va'adei Kehilah,* to be held in the summer of 1919. In Velon a community committee of four members was elected which functioned for several years, supported by the ministry for Jewish Affairs in Kovno.

In these and subsequent years many Jews, both single and with families, moved away to the larger towns in Lithuania or emigrated overseas.

The residents who remained in town made their living, as before the war, in small trade and crafts, and raft transport on the Neman River. Relatives from abroad supported many of their families in Velon. Almost every family maintained a small auxiliary farm next to their home.

According to the 1931 government survey Velon had three textile shops, two tool and iron product shops, two heating materials shops, two shoe factories, one sewing machine (Singer) shop, one pharmacy, one bakery, one restaurant, one wool-combing workshop and one leather-processing factory, all owned by Jews.

In 1937 twenty-four Jewish trades people could be counted in Velon: eight tailors, four shoemakers, four butchers, two bakers, two milliners, one oven builder, one carpenter, one blacksmith and one barber.

In 1929 the *Beth Midrash* burned down and also the economic situation of the Jews began to deteriorate. The transfer of the market from the lower part of the town where the Jewish people traded to the mostly Christian upper part damaged the Jewish economy. Jews also suffered from the open propaganda run by the Lithuanian Merchants' Association (*Verslas*) who spread the message not to buy in Jewish shops.

In 1939 there were twenty telephone subscribers in Velon, six of them Jewish.

Jewish children studied at the Yiddish school, and Yiddish culture was prevalent in town. The Yiddishist (*Folkist*) daily newspaper *Folksblat* had twenty subscribers in Velon, while the Zionist daily *Di Yiddishe Shtime* had only two. Nevertheless, there was a Zionist camp in Velon and its members participated in the purchase of Shekalim and voted for Zionist congresses as presented in table below:

Cong No.	Year	Total Shek	Total Votes	Labor Z"S	Party Z"Z	Rev	Gen Zion A	B	Gros	Miz
15	1927	15	6	5	1	---	--	---	---	---
18	1933	---	20	19		---	--	---	1	---
19	1935	---	79	39		---	8	32	---	---
21	1939	31	26	22		---			N.B.2	1

Key: **Cong No. = Congress Number, Tot Shek = Total Shekalim, Rev = Revisionists, Gen Zion = General Zionists, Gros = Grosmanists, Miz = Mizrahi, NB = National Block**

The last rabbi of Velon was Tsevi-Leib Fersky, who was murdered in the Holocaust.

In June 1940, Lithuania was annexed to the Soviet Union and became a Soviet Republic. Following new rules, light industry enterprises owned by Jews were nationalized. A number of Jewish shops were nationalized and commissars were appointed to manage them. The supply of goods decreased and, as a result, prices soared. The middle class, mostly Jewish, bore most of the brunt and the standard of living dropped gradually. All the Zionist parties were disbanded. The secretary of the local communist party was a Jew, P. J. Rodansky. Some Jews were very active in the MOPR (Red Help) organization. During the elections to the Soviet institutions some of them participated in a Yiddish show staged for the local audience. Jews still comprised the majority in the volunteer Fire Brigade. At that time forty Jewish families still lived in town.

The day following the German invasion of Lithuania, Lithuanian nationalists took control of Velon and enthusiastically imposed orders against Jews that were issued by the German and Lithuanian authorities in Kovno. They also began to abuse their Jewish neighbors by forcing hard labor on them, such as carrying stones from place to place with no purpose, pushing Jews into the river fully clothed, and so on. There were no Germans in town yet, but the armed Lithuanians did what they pleased. Lawlessness ruled against Jews. The leaders who guided the murderers included Bronius Zilinskas, Jurgis Antanaitis and Stasys Bartusius.

In July 1941 all Jewish men were forced to gather at the *Beth Midrash* where they were kept without food and water for several days. They were then taken out, forced to stand in line with spades and led to the Augusta estate. But instead of being forced to work once again, they were led to the grove beside the estate where pits were already prepared. There, firing squads ordered Jews to throw away the spades and undress, and then they were shot.

On September 4, 1941 (12th of Elul, 5701) the two surviving men, 81 women and 86 children were taken out of their homes and led to a forest near the Gystus River, 2 km. west of Velon. There they were murdered and buried. After the war the corpses of the victims were exhumed out of the pits and buried again in the mass graves of Vilki (Vilkija) in Pakarkles Forest about 2 km. from Vilki. Details of the murders resurfaced during the trial of the murderers conducted in Soviet Lithuania in 1953 and 1959.

The mass grave and the monument at the Pakarkles forest near Vilki

In the early 1990s, a stone monument was erected at the Old Jewish cemetery with the inscription in Lithuanian and Yiddish: "The Old Jewish Cemetery. May the memory of the deceased live forever."

Sources:
YIVO, New York, Collection of Lithuanian Jewish Communities, files 206-209, 1514
Gotlib, *Ohalei Shem*, page 59
Fridman Eliezer-Eliyahu, Memoirs (Hebrew), 1858-1926, Tel Aviv, 1926
Levin, Dov; *Velon* (Hebrew), *Pinkas Hakehilot-Lita*, Yad Vashem, 1996
HaMelitz, St. Petersburg (Hebrew) # 43-4.11.1879
Folksblat, Kovno, (Yiddish) 21.7.1930; 15.6.1935; 13.8.1935; 15.11.1940; 19.11.1940;
Kovner Tog (Yiddish), 3.7.1926
Masines Zudyned Lietuvoje (Mass Murder in Lithuania) (Lithuanian), Vol. 2, pages 300-306

Appendix 1
List of 25 Velon Jewish donors for the victims of the great Persian famine of 1871-72 as published in *Hamagid* #16, 1872
(From JewishGen>Databases>Lithuania>*HaMagid* by Jeffrey Maynard)

Surname	Given Name
BURLANT	Tzvi Leib
LAFER	Dov
MUROWSKI	Moshe Yitzchok
MUROWSKI	Yona
RADONER	Zev
SANDLER	Boruch
SANDLER	Chaim
SHACHNES	Yitzchok ben Moshe
TRANSPOLSKI	Zev ben Dov
ZALMENSH	Yitzchok ben Moshe
	Avraham ben Sh
	Dov ben Yehuda
	Eli ben Aharon
	Eli Gershon ben M Y

Surname	Given Name
	Ephraim ben Hillel
	Pinchas ben Sh
	Shabasai ben Yakov
	Shabasai ben Yisroel
	Shachna ben Tz
	Shalom ben Yakov
	Shlomo Yosef
	Tzvi ben Yakov
	Yitzchok Boruch
	Yosef Menachem
	Yosef Osher

Viduklė

Vidukle can be found in the northwestern part of Lithuania, in the Zamut (*Zemaitija*) region, stretching along the main Kaunas-Klaipeda road, about 14 km. to the northwest of the Raseiniai district administrative center. The Vidukle railway station is three kilometers away from the town.

Vidukle was first mentioned in historical documents dating back to the fifteenth century where it was referred to as a settlement belonging to the Catholic bishops of Zemaitija.

Before 1795 Vidukle was included in the Polish-Lithuanian Kingdom. According to the third division of Poland the same year by the three superpowers of those times Russia, Prussia and Austria, Lithuania was divided between Russia and Prussia. As most of Lithuania, Vidukle became a part of the Russian empire, first in the Vilna province (*Gubernia*) and from 1843 in the Kovno *Gubernia* as a county administrative center. It preserved its status during the period of independent Lithuania as well. (1918-1940).

The Jewish settlement till World War II
Most likely Jews began to settle in Vidukle in the middle of the seventeenth century. In 1662 four Jews lived in town. The number increased following King August the Third's declaration on May 21, 1742 that Jews will be granted some privileges. Jews made their living in shop keeping, crafts and agriculture, mainly on leased terrains. In 1879 a new *Beth Midrash* replaced the ruins of the old one. As indicated in the Hebrew newspaper *HaMelitz* dating back to the years 1899 and 1901, the list of contributors for the settlement of Eretz Yisrael included the names of 61 Vidukle Jews (see **Appendix 1**). The fundraiser was Ze'ev Telem.

During World War I, the Russian military set May 5, 1915 as the date for the exile of Vidukle Jews to inner Russia, but the Germans occupied the town a week before, consequently permitting the Vidukle Jews to stay.

After the war, in 1918, an independent Lithuanian state was established. Vidukle Jews participated in the October 1922 elections to the first Lithuanian *Seimas* (Parliament). The Zionist list received 86 votes, *Akhduth* (*Agudath Yisrael*) received 13 votes and the Democrats received 10 votes. According to the first government census of 1923, the total population of Vidukle was 694 people, 221 among them were identified as Jewish (32%).
During that period Vidukle Jews continued to deal in the small trades, crafts and agriculture. According to the government survey of 1931, four shops were operating in town, two of them were Jewish, a textile shop and a

pharmacy. According to the same survey, Jews also owned a sawmill, a flourmill, a wool-combing shop and a leather factory.

In 1937, fifteen Jewish tradesmen worked in Vidukle: three tailors, two bakers, two glaziers, two butchers, one oven builder and five others.

Among the seven Vidukle telephone subscribers in 1939, only one was Jewish.

Jewish children acquired their elementary education at the Hebrew *Tarbuth* School, and some of the boys attended the *Heder.* Some graduates continued their studies at the Kelm or Telz *yeshivoth.* The community maintained a library filled with Hebrew and Yiddish books.

Many of the Vidukle Jews belonged to the Zionist camp and were supporters of almost all Zionist parties, as one can see in the distribution of votes for the Zionist congresses in the table below:

Cong No.	Year	Shek	Total Voter	Labor Party		Rev.	Gen. Zion		Gro	Miz
				Z"S	Z'Z					
14	1925	20	----	----	----	--	----	----	----	----
15	1927	11	10	---	10	---	---	----	----	---
16	1929	7	---	---	---	---	---	----	----	---
18	1933	---	9	6		---	3	----	----	---
19	1935	---	63	10		---	3	23	----	27

Key: Cong No. = Congress Number, Tot Shek = Total Shkalim, Rev. = Revisionists, Gen Zion = General Zionists, Gros = Grosmanists, Miz =Mizrakhi,

A few young people from Vidukle joined the *Akhvah* (Fraternity) group from Kovno that emigrated to *Eretz Yisrael* in 1920 and joined the founders of the Kibbutz Sarid.

Religious life centered around the great *Beth Midrash.* Among the rabbis who served Vidukle were:

Yehezkel Rabinovitz

Yedidyah Gorbinsky

Yehoshua HaCohen Kaplan (1873-1941); he published several books on religious issues and was the last rabbi of Vidukle, murdered together with his community in 1941.

Among the charitable associations of Vidukle one could find the *Bikur Holim* and *Gemiluth Hesed.*

Among the well known personalities born in Vidukle were Yisrael Kaplan (1902 - died in the 1990s in Tel Aviv), the son of a rabbi, historian, teacher and writer, he survived the Kovno ghetto, the Riga and Dachau concentration camps and arrived in Israel in 1949 where he published many articles and books in Yiddish.

Meir HaCohen Kaplan, he was the rabbi's second son and became a member of the rabbinical court in Tel Aviv.

During World War II
With the annexation of Lithuania to the Soviet Union and the change of its status to a Soviet republic in the summer of 1940, nationalization of factories and larger shops owned mostly by Jews, followed. All Zionist parties and youth organizations were disbanded, and Hebrew educational institutions were closed.

In the morning of June 22, 1941, when war between Germany and the Soviet Union began, Jews from Tavrig (*Taurage*) reached Vidukle by carts and cars and told people that war broke out and that their town was burning. The next morning Vidukle Jews loaded their belongings on carts and went to the neighboring villages to look for shelter at their Lithuanian friends. On that day, Monday afternoon the Germans entered Vidukle, and Jews returned home. Only one Vidukle Jew who worked in Rasein managed to escape to Russia.

The German soldiers occupied the region concentrating at the Vidukle railway station while Lithuanian activists took over governance of the town. They immediately began to mistreat Jews, bread was rationed, and although baked by Jewish bakers, it was given to Jews only if there was some bread left over; Jews were forced into labor, were mistreated and beaten; two Germans would come by cart from the near town of Nemoksht and would together with local Lithuanians enter Jewish homes, evict the residents and loot the property; every Jews was forced to sow on a yellow *Maged David* on his outer garments. About fifteen Jewish men and women, suspected being Communists were detained and transferred to jail in Rasein. The women were released later, but the men were never seen again.

One day an order was issued for all men fourteen years old and older to come to the building of the local council. The old people were sent back to their homes, but others were taken to the railway station under heavy guard and locked in the house of the Fridman family and in the barns in the yard. Men from Nemoksht were also brought to this site. These men were forced to carry heavy loads on their backs from on place to another and then run back from the start again. They were also forced to perform so-called "gymnastics" which was another kind of torture.

On July 24, 1941 (29th of Tamuz, 5701) old men were taken out of the *Beth Midrash* where they were locked and led to the railway station. Among them was the elderly Rabbi Yehoshua HaCohen Kaplan who had difficulty walking at the requested speed and the guards pushed him. Frail old men from Nemoksht were also brought to this place. All were taken to a nearby pool, where they were ordered to undress and dip in. While in the pool their clothes were taken away, and naked, in groups of ten they were led to the prepared pit and shot. Every group was eyewitness to the murder of the previous one.

Women and children remaining in town were ordered to leave their homes and gather in the *Beth Midrash* and in the four houses nearby. For some time the young women would work different jobs, such as washing the floors in the police station and at the local councilor's home. On August 21, the women began to sense that something bad was going to happen and some of them escaped the homes of Lithuanian peasants. A few managed to get to the Shavl ghetto.

On Friday, August 22, 1941 (29th of Av 5701) armed Lithuanians led all the women and children out of the *Beth Midrash* and on to the Jewish cemetery, where they shot them and buried them in a mass grave. According to the testimony of Lithuanian women who lived near the site, the women were forced to undress naked, and the children were thrown in the pit still alive.

According to the Soviet-Lithuanian sources, near the railway station of Vidukle, about 100 meters right of the road, a mass grave was found with approximately 200 male corpses. Another mass grave was found near the Jewish cemetery with about 100 corpses of women and children.

At the beginning of the 1990s, monuments were built on the murder sites. At about the same time, a stone monument was built on the site of the Jewish cemetery with an inscription in Yiddish and Lithuanian: "The old Jewish cemetery. Sacred is the memory of the deceased."

The mass grave with the monument near the railway station of Vidukle

The monument next to the railway station with the inscription in Yiddish and Lithuanian: "In this place in July 1941 the Hitlerist murderers and their local helpers murdered about 200 Jewish men."
In the Lithuanian language an inscription is added: " Sacred be the memory of the innocent victims."

The mass grave and the monument near the Jewish cemetery with the inscription in Yiddish and Lithuanian: "In August 1941 in this place the Hitlerist murderers and their local helpers murdered about 100 Jewish women and children".
In Lithuanian it is added: "Sacred be the memory of the innocent victims".

Sources:
Yad Vashem archives, Jerusalem, M-1/E-1655/1939; M-33/971; 0-3/2582
Koniukhovsky collection 0-71, files 42, 52, 53
Gotlib, Ohalei Shem, page 57
Di Yiddishe Shtime, Kovno, 25.4.1938
Fun Letsten Hurban (Yiddish) Munchen, # 10, December 1948
Naujienos, Chicago, 11.6.1949

Appendix 1
The lists of the Vidukle donors for the settlement of Eretz Yisrael as published in HaMelitz
(From JewishGen>Databases>Lithuania>HaMelitz-by Jeffrey Maynard)

Surname	Given Name	Comments	Source	Year
ABELSOHN	Shmuel		HaMelitz #27	1901
ABELSON	Mordechai Hillel		#56	1899
ABELSON	Shmuel		#56	1899
ARELOWITZ	Moshe Zev		#56	1899
AVRAMOWITZ	Aba		#27	1901
BEKER	Yakov Yitzchok		#27	1901
BERELOWITZ	Pinchos		#27	1901
BERLOWITZ	Meir		#56	1899
BLUM	Pinchos		#27	1901
BROIDA	Kalman		#56	1899
BROIDA	Kalman		#27	1901
EITZIKOWITZ	Avraham		#56	1899
EITZIKOWITZ	Avraham		#27	1901
EZRIELOWITZ	Moshe Zev		#27	1901
FEIWELOWITZ	Shmuel Yitzchok		#56	1899
FEIWELOWITZ	Shmuel Yitzchok		#27	1901
FIRMANSKI	Yosef		#27	1901
FISH	Moshe		#56	1899
FLOIM	Tzvi Moshe		#27	1901
FLOIM	Yakov		#56	1899

Surname	Given Name	Comments	Source	Year
FLOIM	Zundl		#27	1901
GRINBERG	Nechemiah		#27	1901
GRINBERG	Zelig		#56	1899
HIRSKOWITZ	Eli Shraga		#56	1899
KAMBER	Yisroel		#56	1899
KAPLAN	Eliezer Ari		#56	1899
KROM	Meir		#27	1901
KROS	Avraham Aharon		#56	1899
LEIZEROWITZ	Moshe		#27	1901
MAGELNITZKI	Pinchos		#56	1899
MALINOWSKI	Avraham		#27	1901
MEIEROWITZ	Yechiel		#27	1901
MICHELOWITZ	Zusman		#56	1899
MICHELOWITZ	Zusman		#27	1901
MILNER	Tzvi		#56	1899
PEREMANIK	Mendil		#56	1899
PEREWOZNIK	Mendel		#27	1901
PORMANSKI	Yosef		#56	1899
ROZAEITZKE	Avraham Mordechai		#56	1899
ROZEITZKI	Avraham Mordechai		#27	1901
ROZEITZKI	Shaul		#27	1901
ROZENTZWEIG	Meir		#56	1899
ROZENTZWEIG	Meir		#56	1899
ROZENTZWEIG	Meir		#27	1901
ROZENTZWEIG	Shraga Zalman		#56	1899

Surname	Given Name	Comments	Source	Year
ROZENTZWEIG	Yakov		#27	1901
ROZENTZWEIG	Yekil		#56	1899
SENDEROWITZ	Avraham Mordechai		#27	1901
SHABASEWITZ	Tzvi		#56	1899
SHABASHEWITZ	Eliezer Yisroel		#27	1901
SHABASHEWITZ	Shraga		#27	1901
SHABASOWITZ	A Y		#56	1899
SHABASOWITZ	Binyomin		#56	1899
SHLOMOWITZ	A Yeshiyahu		#27	1901
SHLOMOWITZ	Yeshiyahu		#27	1901
SMIATZKI	Reuven		#27	1901
SUPOZNIK	Eliahu		#27	1901
TELEM	Zev		#56	1899
TELES	Zev ben Moshe		#27	1901
ZINGER	Yisroel Yitzchok		#56	1899

Viekšniai (Vekshne)

Vieksniai (Vekshne in Yiddish) can be found in the northwestern part of Lithuania, in the Zamut (Zemaitija) region, on the shores of the Venta River, about 15 km. southeast of the district administrative center of Mazheik (Mazeikiai). A village and an estate with the name Vieksniai were mentioned in historical sources dating back to the sixteenth century. Over the years the town developed into an important north Lithuanian trade center known for its pottery products. In 1772 the town was granted the Magdeburg rights of self-rule.

Until 1795 Vekshne was included in the Polish-Lithuanian Kingdom. According to the third division of Poland in the same year by the three superpowers of those times, Russia, Prussia and Austria, Lithuania was divided between Russia and Prussia. As most of Lithuania, Vekshne became part of the Russian Empire, first in the Vilna province (*Gubernia*) and from 1843 in the Kovno *Gubernia*.

Vekshne underwent significant development during Russian rule (1795-1915). The construction of the Libau (Liepaja)-Romni railway in 1872 contributed to its growth. At that time about 60 shops were in operation, the first pharmacy in the Zamut region opened and weekly market days and annual fairs were held. On May 15, 1886 a fire broke out in the area, and most of the houses burned down.

For many years Vekshne was a county administrative center, retaining this status during independent Lithuania (1918-1940) and during World War II.

Jewish settlement before World War I
According to the tombstones at the local Jewish cemetery the first Jews settled in Vekshne in the middle of the seventeenth century. From that time most of the Jewish people made their living in trade, crafts and light industry. A few dealt in agriculture. The economic situation was generally fair for the majority. Grain and timber merchants were known to be affluent. In 1847, there were 1,120 Jewish residents in Vekshne. The big fire of 1886 destroyed about 100 Jewish homes, mostly those of the wealthy. An aid committee headed by the local rabbi Shalofer raised 600 rubles, donated by those whose property could be salvaged. The committee also made an appeal in the Hebrew newspaper *HaMelitz* targeting former Vekshne residents in Lithuania and abroad as well as neighboring communities. About 200 rubles were contributed by the Dubeln community (in Latvia) and several hundred rubles were donated by the Riga Jewish community. Jews of the nearby Zhager community responded immediately as did Jews from Hazenput in Latvia (Kurland). However, since these donations were still not sufficient another heartfelt appeal was published in *HaMelitz*, signed by seven

distinguished men of the town: Josef Gordon, Aba Heler, Leib Goldmagen, Mosheh Shub, Leib Nathanzon, Avraham-Ber Epl and Mordehai Garbel.

Thanks to outside support and the efforts of the victims themselves, the town recovered economically. However, young people continued to emigrate to South Africa, America and *Eretz-Yisrael*, to be followed later by their families. At least fifteen headstones of Vekshne Jews can be found at the old cemetery in Jerusalem.

During these years the religious, social and public life of Vekshne Jews concentrated around the *Shulhoif*, which housed the local *yeshivah* and two prayer houses (one for winter and one for summer).

A partial list of rabbis who served during this period in Vekshne, is given in **Appendix 1.**

The list of contributors for the benefit of the victims of the great famine in Persia in 1871-1872 published in the Hebrew newspaper *HaMagid* contains the names of 118 Vekshne Jews (see **Appendix 2**).

Most of the Jewish children were educated at *Heder*-type institutions affiliated with the local *yeshivah*. A few students, mostly girls, acquired general education with private teachers while others studied in local non-Jewish schools or in Libau in Kurland.

Vekshne Jews supported the *Hibath Zion* movement. The list of contributors to the Settlement of *Eretz-Yisrael* for the years 1895, 1897, 1898 and 1903 contains the names of 58 Vekshne Jews (see **Appendix 3**). The list for 1914 contains 80 names. The fundraisers were Mosheh-Zalman Heler and Rabbi Barukh Levenberg.

According to the all-Russian census of 1897, there were 2,951 residents in Vekshne, 1,646 of them Jewish (56%).

In the summer of 1915, one year after the outbreak of World War I, Vekshne Jews were exiled deep into Russia by an order of the Russian military, due to so-called suspicion of collaboration with the German army.

During Independent Lithuania (1918-1940)
With the establishment of independent Lithuania only a small number of the exiled Jews returned home. Among the expatriates was the rabbi of Vekshne, Shelomoh Fainzilbcr. Upon their return, they found that most of the homes were burnt down or in ruins due to wartime military activities.

Following the Law of Autonomies for Minorities issued by the new Lithuanian government, the Minister for Jewish Affairs, Dr. Menachem (Max) Soloveitshik, ordered elections to community committees, *Va'adei Kehilah,* to be held in the summer of 1919. In Vekshne in 1921 a community committee of seven members was elected, which operated until April 1925.

An important part of its budget was raised through compulsory tax collected from the Jewish population. Objectors were confronted with various measures against them according to the law. The committee also appealed for help from former residents living abroad. The minutes of the meetings of the committee covering four years of its activity are preserved in the archives of YIVO in New York.

In 1921 there were about 300 Jewish residents in Vekshne.

Due to demolition of farms in the surrounding areas and border disputes with Latvia, the economic situation deteriorated considerably. Consequently, more young people began leaving town. Only in the mid-1920s was an improvement felt, which continued through the decade. Many of the Jews made their living in retail trade, but large timber merchants such as brothers Shimon and Mihael Vax flourished, as did grain merchants, the brothers Betsalel and Leibl Berzhansky, brothers Meir and Josef Shain, Tsirl Erdman, Alter Yudes, Aizik Shishi, Ya'akov Gibor, Zelig Laf and others.

Vekshne Jews again engaged in the development of light industry. Some merchants were known all over Lithuania, including Yisrael Kalvarisky who owned leather processing shops, Aryeh Yenka, Zelig Shuster and Honeh Raif, and Josef Leshem who owned a wool-spinning factory. Yeshayahu, Mihal and David Gindon owned pottery factories. The flourmill and the power plant of Vekshne town were also owned by Jews.

The Jewish Popular Bank (*Folksbank*) fulfilled an important function in the economic life of Vekshne Jews. In 1920 it had 40 members and in 1927 the number reached 170. The United Credit Association for Jewish Agrarians in Lithuania had a branch in Vekshne. In 1939 there were 37 telephone subscribers, 20 of them Jewish.

The welfare societies of Vekshne were *Linath Hatsedek* and *Gemiluth Hesed,* with a financial capacity enabling them to make loans of up to 500 litas. On occasion fundraising activities were initiated for different charity goals such as for *Maoth Hitim* (for *Pesakh*) or *Ma'ahal Kasher* (Kosher food for the Jewish soldiers in the Lithuanian army). Zlata and Hayah Berzhansky, Paya Vigoder, Tsirl Erdman and other women excelled in various women's societies. The participants of the local volunteer fire brigade, headed by Berl Yashchik, were mostly Jewish.

According to government survey of 1931, there were 53 shops in town; 45 of them belonged to Jews (85%).

The business distribution of these shops is presented in the table below:

Type of business	Total	Owned by Jews
Grocery	8	6
Grain and flax	4	4
Butcher shop and cattle trade	3	3
Restaurant and tavern	7	4
Food products, eggs	7	7
Beverages	2	1
Textile products and furs	7	6
Leather and shoes	3	3
Haberdashery and house utensils	3	3
Medicine and cosmetics	1	0
Radios, bicycles, sewing machines	1	1
Tools and iron products	2	2
Heating materials and cattle food	1	1
Machines, transportation	1	1
Other	3	3

In the same survey twenty light industry enterprises are listed, thirteen of them owned by Jews (65%).

Type of Factory	Total	Jewish owned
Headstones, glass, bricks	1	1
Textile: wool, flax, knitting	4	3
Sawmills and furniture	1	0
Flour mills, bakeries, beverages, confectionery	4	3
Dresses, footwear	4	2
Leather industry: production, cobbling	2	2
Others: barbers, photographers, jewelers	4	2

In 1937 fourteen skilled Jewish workers resided in Vekshne - two tinsmiths, two butchers, two needle trade persons, one oven builder, one glazier, one tailor, one milliner, one shoemaker, one barber, one corset maker and one seamstress.

At the beginning of the 1920s two schools opened in Vekshne, a religious-orthodox school of the *Yavneh* chain and one of the secular-Zionist *Tarbuth* chain. During their early years, they competed for students. The local rabbi Fainzilber, one of the leaders of the Association of Lithuanian Rabbis, was involved in discussion on this issue. The *yeshivah* that opened before World War I was by then closed for of lack of students, but regular lessons on the Bible and *Gemarah* were maintained by the *Tifereth Yisrael* society, headed by Rabbi Paramut until his emigration to *Eretz-Yisrael* in 1923. Secular cultural activities were organized by the Jewish library, which had about 1,200 books in the Yiddish and Hebrew languages. There was also a drama circle, some youth organizations and a few political groups.

The political leanings of Vekshne Zionists can be seen in the distribution of their votes for the Zionist congresses:

Cong No.	Year	Total Shek	Total Votes	Labor Party		Rev	Gen Zion		Gros	Miz
				Z"S	Z"Z		A	B		
15	1927	30	26	13	---	2	---	---	---	11
16	1929	20	---	---	---	---	---	---	---	---
17	1931	38	38	2	15	7	11	---	---	3
18	1933	---	72	37		17	12	---	1	5
19	1935	---	182	65		---	2	40	37	38

Key: **Cong No. = Congress Number, Tot Shek = Total Shekalim, Rev = Revisionists, Gen Zion = General Zionists, Gros = Grosmanists, Miz = Mizrahi, NB = National Block**

The Vekshne *Maccabi* branch boasted 100 members at its heyday.

Among the personages born in Vekshne and well-known in the Jewish world were the Zionist leader Avraham Idelson; the Zionist activist Yehudah-Leib Apel; Miriam Shakh, the secretary of Dr. Herzl; her brother, the writer Fabius Shakh; the writer Yisrael Efroikin; the journalist Aharon-Yits'hak Grodzensky; the writer Meir-Joel Vigoder; and Yits'hak Shapiro (1895-1941), the chairman and one of the founders of the Association of Jewish Fighters for the Independence of Lithuania and deputy mayor of Yanishok, who was hanged by the Nazis.

The last rabbi of the Vekshne community was Kalman Magid, one of the heads of the *Mizrahi* party in Lithuania. He was murdered by the Lithuanian collaborators in the summer of 1941.

Rabbi Kalman Magid

Rabbi Shelomoh Fainzilber

During World War II and afterwards

In June 1940, Lithuania was annexed to the Soviet Union and became a Soviet Republic. Following new rules, light industry enterprises owned by Jews were nationalized. A number of Jewish shops were also nationalized and commissars were appointed to manage them. The supply of goods decreased and as a result, prices soared. The middle class, mostly Jewish, bore the brunt and the standard of living dropped gradually. All the Zionist parties and youth organizations were disbanded and the Hebrew school was closed. Some people of the leftist camp integrated into the local government institutions.

With the invasion by the German army into Lithuania on June 22, 1941, many Vekshne Jews tried to escape to the Soviet Union, but only a few succeeded. The others were murdered on the way or returned home. Armed Lithuanian nationalists, headed by the local school headmaster Kostas Milchis, immediately took control. They welcomed the representatives of the German army who entered Vekshne, and were willing and ready to collaborate with them.

Their main activity was to arrest the pro-Soviet activists and murder the Jews. The collaborators' first victim was David Levin.

In the beginning of July the Jewish men were forced into the winter *Beth Midrash*, whence they were taken out every morning for hard labor. Women and children were allowed to bring food to the detainees.

On July 7, 1941 the men were released to their homes and told to prepare for transfer to Lublin in Poland, but almost immediately all Jews were ordered to present themselves in the market square. Doctor Hayim Lipman was ordered to point out Jews who were Communists. The doctor said that there were no Jewish Communists in Vekshne. Consequently, the beards of Rabbi Magid and other Jews were cut off.

Women and children were imprisoned in the *Beth Midrash,* while men were herded into the *Shulhoif* (the yard of the synagogue). All the Jews, including the rabbi, were forced to dance and perform gymnastic exercises. Other Jews were forced to wash horses while tied to their tails. Rabbi Mihael Blokh was made to tip a bucket of water over the head of Rabbi Magid. After all this abuse in front of a cheering Lithuanian crowd, the Jews were all imprisoned in the grain storehouses of Shimon Vax.

They were kept there for four weeks, during which time they were starved and tortured by Lithuanian guards, resulting in some deaths.

On August 4, 1941 (11th of Av 5701) guarded by armed Lithuanians, the Jews were transferred to the Mazheik (Mazeikiai) district administrative center. There, they were herded to the Jewish cemetery together with other Jews from Mazheik and the neighboring towns Siad (Seda), Akmyan (Akmene), Veger (Vegeriai), Tirkshle (Tirksliai), Zhidik (Zidikai) and Klikol (Klykuoliai). Lithuanian guards forced some of the men to dig pits, and after the work was completed all were shot the next day and buried in the prepared pits. Only one Jew, Hone Raif, managed to escape from the murder site to the Shavl ghetto. In 1943 he ran away from the ghetto to Telz and went into hiding with Lithuanian peasants. One of the peasants reported him but the next day soldiers from the Red Army arrived and liberated him. Other Jews who managed to escape to the Soviet Union or to the Kovno ghetto at the beginning of the war, survived as well. Among them were Dr. Pesia Kisin (nee Blumberg) and Bluma Levin (nee Vigoder).

The mass grave and the monument near the Jewish cemetery in Mazheik

The monument with the inscription in Yiddish and Lithuanian: "At this site Hitler's murderers and their local helpers executed about 4000 Jews and people of other nationalities"

At the beginning of the 1990s, in the place where old Jewish cemetery once stood, a monument was erected carrying an inscription in Yiddish, Hebrew and Lithuanian: "The Old Cemetery. Let Their Memory live Forever."

Sources:
Yad Vashem archives, Jerusalem, M-1/E-1670/1555, testimony of Elhanan (Hone) Raif; 1637/1771; M-1/Q-1407/181; Konioukhovsky collection, 0-71, file 0-37; testimony of Dr. Pesia Kisin-Blumberg
YIVO, New York, Collection of Lithuanian Jewish Communities, files 1568, 370-386
Gotlib, *Ohalei Shem* (Hebrew), page 67
Vigoder Meir, Book of Memory, Dublin 1931
Levin Yits'hak; *Eile Ezkora* (I will remember these) (Hebrew), Vol.6, pages 208-209
Shakh Miriam; *Asher Itam Hithalakhti* (Those with whom I would walk), (Hebrew), Tel-Aviv 1951, pages 5-21
Levin Dov; *Vekshne* (Hebrew), *Pinkas HaKehiloth Lita*, Yad Vashem, Jerusalem 1996
Yiddisher Lebn (Jewish Life), Telz, # 20, 20.4.1923
Yiddishe Kooperatsie, Kovno, 3.10.1929
Dos Vort (Yiddish), Kovno, 26.12 1934
Di Yiddishe Shtime (Yiddish), Kovno, 18.1.1922; 17.8.1922; 23.12.1934; 2.8.1937
HaMelitz (Hebrew) St.Petersburg, 4.6.1886; 20.8.1886; 8.12.1904
Morgen Journal (Yiddish), New York, 13.10.1946
Masines Zudynes Lietuvoje (Mass Murder In Lithuania) (Lithuanian), Vol. 2, pages 181-182

Appendix 1
Partial list of rabbis and yeshivah heads who officiated in Vekshne
Shabtai Yofe-till 1840;
Yekutiel Zalman-till 1848;
Mosheh Shapiro;
Josef Shalofer;
Eliyahu-Barukh Komai (1840-1917), in Vekshne 1881-1888;
Aba-Ya'akov Borohov, until 1900;
Aryeh-Leib Lipkin (1840-1902), in Vekshne 1901-1902
Yekutiel-Zalman Levitas;
Ben-Zion-Ze'ev Karnitz, until 1913;
Barukh Levenberg (1875-1920), in Vekshne 1898-1914
Shelomoh Fainzilber (1871-1941), in Vekshne 1919-1924, murdered in summer 1941 in Keidan
Kalman Magid (1874-1941), the last rabbi of Vekshne, was murdered in summer 1941 together with his community in Mazheik

Appendix 2
List of 118 Vekshne Jewish donors for the victims of the great famine in Persia in 1872 as published in HaMagid # 20, 1872
(From JewishGen>Databases>Lithuania>HaMagid by Jeffrey Maynard)

Surname	Given Name	Comments
AIDELZOHN	Dovid	
ARANSHTAM	Aran	
BLOCH	Leib	
BLODIN	Yakov	
BRON	Sh B	
CHOWEDANSKI	Hershil	
COHEN	Hirsh	
EIZIKZON	Sh	
FRIDMAN	Dovid	
GARBIL	Ch	brother of D
GARBIL	D	brother of Ch
GARBIL	Yakov	
GLANT	Yechezkel	

Surname	Given Name	Comments
GOLDBERG	Yisroel	
GORDON	Sh	f-i-l of N Rabinowitz
HENICH	Dov Zev	
HERZMARK	M	
IZRELSHTAM	Chaim	bridegroom
IZRELZOHN	Ch	
KA"TZ	Avraham Yehoshua	
KAHANA	Leib	
KATZ	Asher	
KATZ	Mordechai Yitzchok	
KIMEL	Bendit	
KIMEL	Herz	
KIMEL	Uri	
KLAMPESH	Moshe	
KLEIN	E	
KRIS	Moshe Shalom	
KUMIN	Chaim Leizer	
LAPIDOS	Ephraim Chaluna	
LEKUZIN	Yona	
LEWINSHTEIN	Levi	
LEWINSHTEIN	Liberman	
LIPSHITZ	Moshe Zalman	
NAHTENZOHN	Feivel	brother of Leib Bentzion
NAHTENZOHN	Leib Bentzion	brother of Feivel
NATKIN	Y	Harav
PEKER	Y	
PIL	M	
RABINOWITZ	N	s-i-l of Sh Gordon
RABINOWITZ	Shaul	

Surname	Given Name	Comments
RAWI	Sender	
SEGAL	Avraham Yitzchok	
SEGAL	Feivush	
SEGAL	Sh	
SHEFETZ	Yisroel	
SHEMESH	Uri	DBHCh"N
SHEMESH	Yehoshua	DBHM"D
SHETZ	Shalom	
SHIF	B ben Y	
SHIF	Y	father of B
SHMIT	Binyomin	
SHMIT	D	
SHMIT	E	
SHU"B	Elchanan	
SHU"B	Sh	
SHULMAN	Dov	Rabbi morenu
SHULMAN	Yakov	
TINE	Sh	
TRACHTENBERG	N	
WAKS	Leib	
WAKS	Yitzchok	
WOLPERT	Mrs. N	widow
YAFE	Leib son of Rabbi Shimon	son of the Rabbi Gaon
YECHEZKEL	Gershon ben M	
ZAK	Boruch	
ZAKSH	Uri	
ZILBERT	D	
	A ben Z	

Surname	Given Name	Comments
	Aharon ben Ch	
	Avraham ben B	
	Avraham ben Y	
	Avraham Dov	
	Avraham Moshe	
	Avraham Pinchas	
	Benny Yechezkel	
	Binyamin ben Y	
	Ch ben Y	
	Chaikel Leib	
	Chaim Zev	
	Chaya	widow
	Dovid ben N	
	Elimelech	
	Feivush Ber	
	Gershon ben Y	
	Hirsh ben A B (brother of Leib)	
	Lamech ben Sh	bridegroom
	Leib ben A B	brother of Hirsh
	Leib ben M	
	Leib Moshe ben Y	
	Leib Zarzin	
	Levi ben Sh	
	M	Sha"tz here
	M ben Ch	
	M ben M	
	M ben Reuven	
	M ben Y	
	M ben Y	

Surname	Given Name	Comments
	Meir ben N	
	Sh ben L	
	Sh ben L	
	Sh Y	
	Shmuel ben Tzvi	
	Tzvi ben B	
	Yakov ben M	
	Yakov Moshe	
	Yehiahu ben Ch	
	Yisroel ben Sh	
	Yitzchok ben Asher	
	Yitzchok ben R	
	Yitzchok Zev	
	Yosef	
	Yosef Eli	
	Z ben A	
	Z ben Chaim	
	Zalata Yocheved	widow
	Zelda	widow

Appendix 3

List of 58 Vekshne Jewish donors for the settlement of Eretz Yisrael as published in HaMelitz
(From JewishGen>Databases>Lithuania>HaMelitz by Jeffrey Maynard)

Surname	Given Name	Comments	Source	Year
	Aharon Reuven	wed 1902/3	#30	1903
BLOCH	Gitel wife of Benzion Nachum Tankel from Zager	wed in Zager 1897	#9	1898
COHEN	tzvi		#156	1898
ERMANN	Avraham husband of Tzvia		#156	1898
ERMANN	Tzvia wife of Avraham		#156	1898
FRIDMAN	Feige sister or s-i-l of L Y Pil wife of Philip Fridman	in Pretoria, Transvaal	#57	1897
FRIDMAN	Fridman husband of Feige	in Pretoria, Transvaal	#57	1897
FRIDMAN	son of Philip and Feige born 1896/7	in Pretoria, Transvaal	#57	1897
HELLER	Aba husband of Beile father of Moshe Zalman		#241	1897
HELLER	Beile wife of Abba		#241	1897
HELLER	Dvora bas Aba sister of M Z		#241	1897
HELLER	Eliahu Hirsh ben Aba brother of M Z		#241	1897
HELLER	Isser brother of Moshe Zalman		#142	1897
HELLER	Libe bas Aba sister of M Z		#241	1897
HELLER	Moshe Zalman		#57	1897

Surname	Given Name	Comments	Source	Year
HELLER	Moshe Zalman		# 188	1898
HELLER	Moshe Zalman		#68	1898
HELLER	Moshe Zalman ben Aba fianceof Feige Yoselowitz	engaged	#241	1897
HELLER	Moshe Zalman brother of Isser		#142	1897
HELLER	Sarah Hene bas Aba sister of M Z		#241	1897
HELLER	Zalman		#9	1898
IZRAELSHTAM	Naphtali		#30	1903
KAPLAN	Henriette wife of Filip Yafe	wed 4 Nisan	#123	1897
KIMMEL	Bendet father of Zenni		#161	1895
KIMMEL	Bendet father of Zenni		#161	1895
KOLMAN	Meir		#156	1898
KOPELOWITZ	Betzalel		# 188	1898
KOPELOWITZ	Feiga		# 188	1898
KOPELOWITZ	Reitze bas Zelig wife of Leib Shub	wed 1898 in Mozeik	# 188	1898
KURSHAN	Tzvi husband of Mina Tzalelsohn of Zager	wed 10 Elul	#195	1900
LEWIN	Moshe Yitzchok		#9	1898
LEWIN	Yosef Moshe		#9	1898
MICHALOWITZ	Yechiel Michel f-i-l of Rabbi Dov Ber Borochow from Gorzd		#57	1897
MILLER	Moshe Tzvi husband of Rachel Waks	wed 1897/8	#9	1898
MILLER	Moshe Tzvi husband	wed 1897	#9	1898

Surname	Given Name	Comments	Source	Year
	of Rochel Waks			
NAFTALIN	Mendil		#68	1898
PEKER	Reuven		#156	1898
PEKER	Reuven		#9	1898
PIL	Ester		#241	1897
PIL	Leib Yitzchok brother or b-i-l of Feige Fridman		#57	1897
REITZ	Brocha		# 188	1898
ROLNIK	hena		#156	1898
SHISHI	Reuven father of Yehoshua Leib		#156	1898
SHISHI	Yehoshua Leib ben Reuven	deceased TRNZ	#156	1898
SHUB	Leib		#156	1898
SHUB	Yakov Moshe		#156	1898
TANKEL	Benzion Nachum husband of Gitel Bloch	wed in Zager 1897	#9	1898
TODEROWITZ	Yitzchok		#156	1898
WAKS	Michel		#9	1898
WAKS	Rachel bride of Moshe Tzvi Miller	wed 1897/8	#9	1898
WAKS	Shimon		#9	1898
WAKS	Yitzchok		#9	1898
WOLPERT	Leib brother of Yosef		#123	1897
WOLPERT	Yosef brother of Leib		#123	1897
YAFE	Filip husband of Henriette Kaplan	wed 4 Nisan	#123	1897
YOSELOWITZ	Feige fiancée of Moshe Zalman Heller	engaged	#241	1897

Ylakiai (Yelok)

Ylakiai (Yelok in Yiddish) lies in the Zamut (Zemaitija) region in northwestern Lithuania, 30 km. west of the district administrative center of Mazheik (Mazeikiai) and 13 km. from the Latvian border. A settlement bearing this name was part of a property of the aristocratic family of Sapiega, and was first mentioned in a historical document dating from the eighteenth century. Yelok developed particularly in the nineteenth century and was known for its great markets and fairs. During World War I some houses were destroyed, but after the war the town was rebuilt and during independent Lithuania it became a county administrative centre.

Yelok Jews had established a settled community by the beginning of the nineteenth century. Public life centered around the *Beth Midrash*. Yelok was one of the first communities to open a branch of *Agudath Yisrael*. Thirty Yelok Jews were named in two lists of donors to the *Agudah* Fund for the years 1913 and 1914. There were also donors to funds for the settlement of *Eretz-Yisrael*. Two lists of donors published in the Hebrew newspaper *HaMelitz* mention nineteen names of Yelok Jews (see **Appendix 1**). The fundraisers were K. J. Ziman and Yehudah Blumental.

Until World War I Jews made their living in trade, small scale agriculture and peddling. Two large flourmills were Jewish-owned. Important commercial activities took place on the weekly market days (Wednesdays) and during the five yearly fairs.

During these years the Jews comprised more than half of the population. According to the 1897 Russian census, 1,367 people lived in Yelok, 775 of them being Jews (57%). Before World War I, in 1913, 150 Jewish families with about 800 persons resided in Yelok.

After the war and with the establishment of independent Lithuania in 1918, Yelok was rebuilt. The first census performed by the new government in 1923 showed 999 residents in Yelok, 409 being Jews (41%).

Following the Law of Autonomies for Minorities issued by the new Lithuanian government, the Minister for Jewish Affairs, Dr. Menachem (Max) Soloveitshik, ordered elections to Community Committees, *Va'adei Kehilah,* to be held in the summer of 1919. In Yelok a community committee of eleven members was elected which functioned for several years and was supported by the Ministry for Jewish Affairs in Kovno. The first meeting of the committee took place on October 30, 1920 when J. Bernshtein was elected chairman, K. Yamin deputy chairman and A. Katz treasurer. It was also decided to revive the *Ezra* (Aid) society.

During this period Yelok Jews made their living in trade and crafts. According to the government survey of 1931 there were twenty shops in town, seventeen of them Jewish-owned (85%), as shown:

Type of the business	Total	Owned by Jews
Grocery stores	3	2
Grain and flax	1	1
Butcher's shops and cattle trade	2	1
Restaurants and taverns	2	1
Food products	3	3
Textile products and furs	4	4
Leather and shoes	1	1
Haberdashery and house utensils	1	1
Medicine and cosmetics	1	1
Bicycles and electrical equipment	1	1
Other	1	1

Seven Jewish craftsmen worked here in 1937: two tailors, two butchers, one shoemaker, one knitter and one needle worker. The Jewish Popular Bank (*Folksbank*) played an important role in the local economy; in 1927, 93 members were registered there. In 1939 Yelok had eleven telephone subscribers, four of them Jewish.

A Jewish House in Yelok, 1938

Many Yelok Jews emigrated to America, South Africa and *Eretz-Yisrael*. Those who remained continued to maintain the Hebrew *Yavneh* School, where about 40 pupils studied, the *Talmud Torah*, the *Gemiluth Hesed* fund and the library. Thus Zionist activities continued and even grew stronger. During this period the Zionist youth organization *HaShomer HaTsair* and a branch of the sport organization *Maccabi* were active locally. Most Zionist parties had members, as we can see from the votes for the Zionist congresses in the table below:

Cong No.	Year	Total Shek	Total Votes	Labor Party		Rev	Gen Zion		Gros	Miz
				Z"S	Z"Z		A	B		
15	1927	20	17	10	---	---	5	---	---	2
16	1929	51	22	11	3	---	6	---	---	2
17	1931	22	15	3	4	---	6	---	---	2
18	1933	---	25	22		---	2	---	---	1
19	1935	---	77	62		---	---	2	---	13

Key: Cong No. = Congress Number, Total Shek = Total Shekalim, Rev = Revisionists, Gen Zion = General Zionists, Gros = Grosmanists, Miz = Mizrahi

Among the rabbis who officiated in Yelok were Yehoshua Leibovitz; Shemuel-Ya'akov Rabinovitz, who was Yelok's rabbi for most of his life until his death in 1930, and who published many books on religious issues; Meir-Mordehai Zilberman; Nakhman Hirshovitz. The last rabbi was Meir Pakalnishky who was murdered in the summer of 1941.

In the summer of 1940 Lithuania was annexed to the Soviet Union and became a Soviet Republic. As elsewhere, local factories, Jewish shops and Jewish flourmills were nationalized, all Zionist parties and youth organizations were disbanded and the Hebrew school was closed.

On June 22, 1941 the German army invaded Lithuania. A few days later Lithuanian nationalists took over in Yelok and began to abuse the Jews. One Lithuanian, restaurant owner, Mikas Glaubartas, cut the beards of elderly Jews with a knife, injuring them badly. In July and August a band of armed Lithuanians, headed by the chairman of the local council, Kazis Venckus, led groups of Jews to the Jewish cemetery to the southwest of the town, and shot them. Thus all Yelok Jews were murdered and buried in a large mass grave. According to a Soviet-Lithuanian source, the number of victims during Nazi rule amounted to 475 men, women and children.

The mass grave with the entrance gate

The monument with an inscription in Lithuanian, Yiddish and Hebrew: "On this site Hitler's murderers and their local helpers murdered 446 Jews, 25 Zamuts and 4 Karaims in 1941."

The entrance gate

Sources:
Yad Vashem archives, Jerusalem, Z-4/2548, 13/15/131, 55/1701, 55/1788
YIVO, New York, Collection of Lithuanian Jewish Communities, files 510-516
Gotlib; *Ohalei Shem*, page 94
Mirsky; Torah Institutions in Europe (Hebrew), page 186
Levin, Dov; *Yelok, Pinkas HaKehiloth-Lita* (Hebrew) Yad Vashem 1996
HaMelitz, St.Petersburg, 26.6.1883; 23.4.1893
Di Yiddishe Shtime, Kovno, 31.10.1935
Dos Yiddisher Lebn (Jewish Life) (Yiddish). Telz, 5.5.1938
Masines Zudynes Lietuvoje (Mass Murder In Lithuania), Vol. 2. page 399
Neuzmirsime (We will not forget) (Lithuanian), Vilnius, 1950

Appendix 1
List of 19 Yelok donors for the settlement of Eretz Yisrael as published in *Hamelitz*
(From JewishGen>Databases>Lithuania>Hamelitz-by Jeffrey Maynard)

Surname	Given Name	Comments	Source	Year
BALKIND	Yakov brother of Chaim Bentzion in Chwedana		#229	1899
BLUMENTHAL	Yehuda		#7	1903
BORIN	Beinish father of Chaya		#7	1903
BORIN	Chaya bas Beinish wife of Sh D Shif	wed 1902	#7	1903
BORIN	Yakov		#7	1903
COHEN	L		#7	1903
COHEN	Yakov		#7	1903
DORIN	Leah	widow	#7	1903
DORIN	Naphtali		#7	1903

Surname	Given Name	Comments	Source	Year
EDELMAN	Alte		#7	1903
FRIEDBERG	husband of widow Miriam Nurok from Shavel	doctor, wed 15 Sivan	# 120	1893
GLIKMAN	L		#7	1903
SHATZ	Yakov		#7	1903
SHIF	M		#7	1903
SHIF	Sh D husband of Chaya Borin	wed 1902	#7	1903
SHITZ	Mordechai		#7	1903
SHITZ	Tzirel		#7	1903
SHLEZ	Yakov		#7	1903
ZIMAN	K Y		#7	1903

Zapyškis (Sapizishok)

Zapyskis (Sapizishok in Yiddish) is situated on the left bank of the Neman (*Nemunas*) River, about fourteen kilometers west of Kovno. The town is first mentioned in historical documents from the end of the sixteenth century.

Until 1795 Sapizishok was included in the Polish-Lithuanian Kingdom. According to the third division of Poland the same year by the three superpowers of those times, Russia, Prussia and Austria, Lithuania was divided between Russia and Prussia. The part of Lithuania on the left bank of the Neman River and including Zapyskis was handed over to Prussia. During the period of Prussian rule (1795-1807) decreased commerce with Kovno, which at that time was under Russian control, caused the economic decline of the town. A statistical document of that time describes Sapizishok as a poor village with 150 residents.

From 1807 to 1815 Sapizishok was under the auspices of the Great Dukedom of Warsaw and was considered a county center in the Bialystok District. In 1813, after the defeat of Napoleon, all of Lithuania was annexed to Russia, and Sapizishok was included in the Augustowa province (*Gubernia*). In 1866 it became part of the Suwalk *Gubernia*.

Russian rule brought a revival of trade and occasional fairs were organized in Sapizishok. In 1825 Sapizishok acquired the Magdeburg rights to call itself a town. The flood of 1864 and later World War I caused significant damage to Sapizishok. During the period of Independent Lithuania (1918-1940) Sapizishok was a county administrative center.

Jews probably began to settle in Sapizishok at the beginning of the nineteenth century. It is known that Sapizishok Jews took part in the 1831 rebellion against the Czar. Jews made their living in timber trade and transporting logs along the Neman River. They were village folk, and like their neighbors they would react to injustice with fists. At the same time they had warm Jewish hearts and open minds towards charity issues. The welfare societies *Gemiluth Hesed* and *Linath HaTsedek* were very active, and the town had many educated people, among them many subscribers to Hebrew newspapers.

A Hebrew school opened in 1910 and continued to offer education through the times of Independent Lithuania. Students of different ages studied in one room and with one teacher.

Following the passage of the Law of Autonomies for Minorities issued by the new Lithuanian government in 1918, the Minister for Jewish Affairs, Dr. Menachem (Max) Soloveitshik, ordered elections to community committees *(Va'adei Kehilah)* to be held in the summer of 1919. In 1919 a *Va'ad* (community committee) with five members was elected in Sapizishok: two from the *Tseirei Zion* list, two unaffiliated and one from the General Zionists. The committee was active in all fields of Jewish life until the end of 1925. Of 97 people with voting rights, only 75 voted.

According to the first government census in 1923, the population of the town reached 589, of whom 293 were Jews (50%).

During that period Sapizishok Jews made their living in the small trades, timber and crafts. Jewish people owned the flourmill and the sawmill.

In 1937 fifteen Jewish tradesmen worked in the town: seven butchers, three shoemakers, two glaziers, one baker, one tinsmith and one photographer. In 1939 there were twenty telephone subscribers; only two were Jewish.

Among Sapizishok Jews a Zionist atmosphere prevailed and there were supporters of almost all of the Zionist parties. The Zionists purchased *Shekalim* and voted for the Zionist Congresses, as seen in the table below:

Cong No.	Year	Tot Shek	Total Votes	Labor Party		Rev	Gen Zion		Gros	Miz
				Z"S	Z"Z		A	B		
16	1929	18	---	---	---	---	---	---	---	---
18	1933	---	17	16		---	---	---	--	1
19	1935	---	105	56		---	1	2	40	6

Key: Cong No. = Congress Number, Tot Shek = Total Shekalim, Rev = Revisionists, Gen Zion = General Zionists, Gros = Grosmanists, Miz = Mizrahi

Sport activities were run by the local Maccabi Branch with 26 members in the 1920s.

Religious life centered on the local synagogue. The rabbis who served in Sapizishok during those years were:
   Yisrael Avigdor
   Hayim Ze'ev Kriger (?-1903)
   Aharon-Shelomoh Zalmanovitz
   Meir Verzhbolovsky (1881-1941), published many books on religious issues, was murdered in the Shoah.
   Yohanan Zarkhi (Zupovitz) (1874-1946), was active in the Mizrahi party and in the National Funds, emigrated to *Eretz-Yisrael* in 1934 and became a rabbi in Tiberias. He was well liked by farmers in the agricultural settlements in the Jordan valley, and died in Tiberias.
   Yits'hak Grin (1880-1941), the last Rabbi of Sapizishok, murdered in the Shoah.

Rabbi Meir Verzhbolovsky   **Rabbi Yohanan Zarkhi**

Among the personages born in this town were Dr. Mosheh Kriger, director of the Hospital in Zefat and deputy chairman of the Medical Association in Israel, and the well-known artist Yehezkel Shtraikhman (died in 1993 in Tel Aviv).

In the summer of 1940 Lithuania was annexed to the Soviet Union and became a Soviet Republic. Following new regulations, many Jewish businesses were nationalized. All Zionist parties and youth organizations were disbanded, the Hebrew school was closed and a Yiddish school was opened instead. Supply of goods decreased, and as a result, prices soared. The middle class, mostly Jewish, bore the brunt, and the standard of living dropped gradually.

Several days after the German invasion of the Soviet Union on June 22, 1941, the German army entered Sapizishok. The Lithuanian nationalists, who took control, began to victimize and rob the Jews.

On August 7, 1941, Jews were forced out of their homes and their property looted while they were detained in a ghetto. In the middle of August Lithuanian police took forty young men from the ghetto to a place next to the Jewish cemetery, where they were murdered and buried. On September 4, 1941 (12th of Elul, 5701) the remaining men, women and children were led to the bank of the Neman River, near the neighboring villages of Dievogaila and Kluoniskiai where they were murdered and buried in a mass grave. According to German sources 47 men, 118 women and 13 children were murdered at that location.

The monument near the mass grave: the inscription in Hebrew and
Lithuanian states, "In this place in 1941 the Hitlerist murderers and
their local helpers murdered approximately 282 Jews, children, women
and men."

The mass grave near the village of Dievogaila

Sources:
YIVO, New York, Collection of Lithuanian Jewish Communities,
files 670-672
Di Yiddishe Shtime, Kovno, 1.10.1919
Teviskes Zinios, Kaunas, 6.4.1991

Žarėnai (Zharan)

Zarenai (Zharan in Yiddish) is located in the northwestern part of Lithuania, in the Zamut (Zemaitija) region, about eighteen kilometers from the district administrative center Telz (Telsiai). Zharan is mentioned in historical documents beginning in the fourteenth century. In the fifteenth century Zharan was a district center. In 1665 King Jan Kazimir granted it the privilege to hold weekly markets and three yearly fairs.

Until World War I a Polish squire family owned the estate and the town. They did not lease their lands, but built houses and rented them to the Jews of the town. During the period of Independent Lithuania (1918-1940) Zharan was a county administrative center.

In 1918 the independent Lithuanian state was established. Following the Law of Autonomies for Minorities issued by the new Lithuanian government, the Minister for Jewish Affairs, Dr. Menachem (Max) Soloveitshik, ordered elections to community committees *(Va'adei Kehilah)* to be held in the summer of 1919. In Zharan a *Va'ad (*community committee) of five members was elected. The committee was active in all fields of Jewish life until the end of 1925.

According to the first government census in 1923, the population of the town was 385; among them were 174 Jews (45%). Many of them emigrated to South Africa and their number continued to decrease until before World War II there were fewer than one hundred Jews remaining. Most of the young people left the town and those who remained found they had little to do.

After World War I more than half of the Zharan Jews acquired their homes from the Polish family together with plots of lands of three to fifteen hectares. According to the agrarian reform undertaken by the government, the lands of the estate were divided among the peasants who cultivated them. The Jews who had farmed rented lands from the estate for many years, did not receive any land. The Jewish landowners had them cultivated by Lithuanian peasants and took half of the yield. The Jews owned small shops and butcher shops but most of them were poor. Only one Jewish family a few kilometers from the town cultivated their own farm.

According to the government survey of 1931 Jewish businesses included three Jewish-owned textile shops and a wool combing shop, and four flourmills in nearby villages. In 1937 there were six Jewish artisans in the town: two tailors, two butchers, one baker and one shoemaker.

There was a *Beth Midrash,* a rabbi and a shokhet in Zharan. In the 1920s the rabbi was Ya'akov-Mosheh Abelov.

Sixteen Zharan Zionists took part in the elections for the nineteenth Zionist Congress in 1935. They voted as follows: thirteen gave their votes for the

Mizrahi party, two voted for the General Zionists B and one voted for the Labor party. Many homes had a *Keren Kayemeth LeYisrael* Blue Box.

One young Zharan girl emigrated to *Eretz-Yisrael* as a *Halutsah* (pioneer).

With the annexation of Lithuania to the Soviet Union and becoming a Soviet republic in summer of 1940, the lives of Zharan Jews didn't change much. There was no nationalization of Jewish shops because the Jews were so poor. In 1940 about 95 Jewish families lived in the town.

With the outbreak of war between Germany and the Soviet Union on June 22, 1941, a great part of Zharan was burnt down. The Jews did not try to escape but remained in the town. After the Lithuanian police took control, their first victim was the rabbi, Ya'akov-Mosheh Abelov. He was a young man who had arrived in Zharan from Minsk (Belarus). Lithuanian police grabbed him off the street and began to beat him. After the rabbi collapsed a policeman shot and killed him with a pistol. Another young Jew was killed because before the war he refused to sell liquor on credit to the police. A short time later 28 Jewish youth from Zharan and nearby settlements were murdered near the estate and buried there. In the middle of July 1941 some Zharan Jews were transferred to the Rainiai camp where a number of other men were still being held. All these men were badly beaten and later murdered between July 15 and 17, 1941.

Other men, and the women and children from the town were taken to a place near the (Vishoven) Viesvenai estate about 9 km. to the southeast of Telz. There, Jews from the following towns were concentrated: Alsiad (Alsedziai), Riteve (Rituva), Vorne (Varniai), Luknik (Luoke), Loikeve (Laukuva), Zharan (Zarenai) and Naveran (Navarenai). Their fate was the same as that of the Jews of Telz and the surrounding area.

One of the mass graves in Viesvenai

The mass grave near the estate of Zharan

Only seven Zharan Jews survived; six women and one man. Four of these emigrated to Israel after the war and the other three remained in Lithuania.

Sources:
Yad Vashem Archives, Jerusalem, M-9/15(6); 0-57 the Yekhiel Dambe
Testimony; Koniukhovsky collection 0-71, files 57, 117
Dos Vort, Kovno, 17.12.1934
Naujienos, Chicago, 11.6.1949

Židikai (Zhidik)

Zidikai (Zhidik in Yiddish) is in the northwest part of Lithuania in the Zamut (Zemaitija) region, about 20 km. west of the district administrative center of Mazheik (Mazeikiai). Most of its houses were built on a hill. The Zidikai village and an estate granted by the king to the noble Hudkevitz are listed in legal documents dating back to the sixteenth century. In the middle of the nineteenth century Zhidik became a county administrative center.

Until 1795 Zhidik was part of the Polish-Lithuanian Kingdom. According to the third division of Poland in the same year by the three superpowers of those times, Russia, Prussia and Austria, Lithuania was divided between Russia and Prussia. As most of Lithuania, Zhidik became a part of the Russian Empire, first in the Vilna province (*Gubernia*) and from 1843 in the Kovno *Gubernia*.

According to the all Russian census of 1897, there were 1,243 residents in town, 914 being Jews (73%). That year the town had three leather-processing shops and twenty stores and conducted regular market days and fairs.

After World War I the population of Zhidik dropped considerably. According to the first government census of 1923, there were 893 residents in town, 799 being Jewish (89%). They lived in 119 small wooden houses and 55 others lived on the nearby estate. During the period of independent Lithuania (1918-1940) Zhidik was a county administrative center.

Jewish settlement till after World War I
The first Jews are believed to have arrived in Zhidik at the end of the seventeenth century. In the ensuing years their numbers increased, and they made their living in the small trades. A few were peddlers who traded in the nearby Kurland villages.

In 1780 a wooden synagogue was built in town, and was known as the "cold synagogue" as it was not heated in winter. Later, a *Beth Midrash* was built where mostly less-educated people prayed. One of the oldest institutions was the *Hevrah Kadisha* where a record (*Pinkas*) was kept of all its activities. A sample of this *Pinkas* is preserved at the YIVO archives in New York.

Rabbis who served in Zhidik before World War I included Tsevi-Hirsh; Dov Dimand; Shelomoh-Mosheh Levenberg who worked in Zhidik for 38 years until his death at the age of 75 in 1896; Hayim Nathanzon (1838-1904), who served in Zhidik for seven years; and Avraham-Ze'ev HaLevi Heler (1886-1941), who was murdered in Mariampol in the summer of 1941.

Because of its geographic remoteness from larger towns and centers of education, the Zhidik community was very traditional, and every innovative idea evoked strong opposition. At the end of the nineteenth century a boy and a girl were punished because they walked alone in the nearby forest. They were tied up and led through the streets of the town while being spanked by the public.

A dispute erupted following the decision of the synagogue *Gabai* to replace the prayer stands (*shtenders*) with more comfortable benches for praying. It took years to defeat the conservatism but the decision was implemented after rabbis from the nearby communities of Yelok (Ylakiai), Siad (Seda) and Pikeln (Pikeliai) intervened.

Prayer Stands (*Shtenders*)

In 1888 Zhidik faced intense controversy following the initiative of the local rabbi Shelomoh-Mosheh Levenberg to bring a permanent doctor to the town. In order to finance his salary of six rubles per week, the majority decided to impose a tax on the sale of yeast. But the yeast sellers and their supporters strongly opposed this decision. Their arguments sometimes ended in loud discussions and even fights during *Shabbath* prayers; at times the intervention of the local police was needed. At the end of 1890 Rabbi Heler was detained when someone informed authorities that his two sons had left town to evade military service. Only after personal assurances from a few community noblemen, was the old rabbi was released and the informers left Zhidik.

The list of contributors for the victims of the great Persian famine of 1871-72, as published in the Hebrew newspaper *HaMagid* included the names of 43 Zhidik Jews (see **Appendix 1**).

Before World War I the *Agudath Yisrael* party was very active. The list contains the names of paying 78 members. The economic situation of Zhidik deteriorated in these years to such an extent that the estate owners had to donate flour and firewood to the needy people. Emigration to America and South Africa increased and almost every week a family departed to a new country.

During World War I, in the summer of 1915, the remaining Zhidik Jews were exiled to remote parts of Russia.

During independent Lithuania (1918-1940)
With the establishment of the independent Lithuanian state in 1918, some of the exiled Jews returned to Zhidik. The delineation of the border with Latvia severed ties with villages in Kurland in Latvia worsening an already bad economic situation. This in turn caused Jewish families to move from Zhidik to the larger towns in Lithuania. Only a few dozen Jewish families remained. Some worked in agriculture while others made their living in the six leather processing shops and in the flour mill, all of which belonged to Jews.

According to the government survey of 1931, seventeen stores operated in Zhidik at that time, thirteen of them (86%) belonging to Jews: eight textile shops, two food stores, two tools and iron stores, one haberdashery shop, one engaged in grain trade and one butcher shop.

According to the same survey Jews owned the power station, the flour mill, the wool combing shop, the millinery shop for men's hats and four leather processing factories.

Below is an exerpt from the original survey listing two Jewish leather factories of Zhidik.

·MAŽEIKIŲ APSKR.
Bubas Leiba, Židikiai.
Fliorensas Dovydas, Židikiai.
Grinblatas Šaja, Ylakiai.

In 1937 there were thirteen skilled Jewish workers: six tailors, four butchers, a baker, a shoemaker and one other tradesperson.

The Jewish Popular Bank (*Folksbank*) had a considerable impact on the economy in Zhidik. In 1927 the bank had 96 registered members and in 1929 the membership dropped to 87.

During those years Rabbi Yits'hak Begon served in Zhidik. The last rabbi of the community was Eliyahu Lutsky who was murdered in the Holocaust.

The *Beth Midrash* in Zhidik

The conservative nature of the community had an impact on the education of the town's children. For a long time boys studied at the *Heder*-type institution, but when, at the beginning of the 1920s, a Hebrew school of the *Tarbuth* chain was formed, it brought about intense objections. More controversy was caused by the fact that the school was to be housed in the "cold" synagogue which was neglected and no longer used for prayer. In the end the school was opened, but the number of students decreased from year to year.

Among the famous personages born in Zhidik were rabbis Barukh Levenberg and Gershon Gutman; also David Levin, the activist for orthodox education and one of the leaders of *Agudath Yisrael*; and the writer Tsevi-Hirsh Shlez.

The reduction in numbers of Jews in Zhidik did not interrupt the activities of community institutions or their social and political groups. One can see the distribution of power among different Zionist parties according to the votes for the Zionist congresses at the table below:

Cong No.	Year	Total Shek	Total Votes	Labor Party		Rev	Gen Zion		Gros	Miz
				Z"S	Z"Z		A	B		
15	1927	20	19	18	---	---	1	---	---	---
16	1929	49	27	24	---	2	1	---	---	---
17	1931	---	17	16	---	---	1	---	---	---
18	1933	---	24	23		---	1	---	---	---
19	1935	---	66	50		---	---	---	---	16
21	1939	22	21	16		---	---		N.B.5	---

Key: **Cong No. = Congress Number, Total Shek = Total Shekalim, Rev = Revisionists, Gen Zion = General Zionists, Gros = Grosmanists, Miz =Mizrahi, NB = National Block**

During World War II and afterwards

In June 1940, Lithuania was annexed to the Soviet Union and became a Soviet Republic. Following new regulations, light industry enterprises owned by Jews were nationalized. A number of Jewish shops were nationalized and commissars were appointed to manage them. The supply of goods decreased and as a result, prices soared. The middle class, mostly Jewish, bore the brunt and the standard of living dropped gradually. All the Zionist parties were disbanded and the Hebrew school was closed.

In that year approximately 40 Jewish families (150 people) lived in Zhidik. Upon the invasion of the German army into Lithuania on June 22, 1941 many Zhidik Jews tried to escape to the Soviet Union, but only a few succeeded. Most of them perished on the roads, while a few reached Kovno and ended up in the Kovno ghetto.

When the Germans entered Zhidik on June 25, 1941, the town was already controlled by local Lithuanian nationalists. They began to loot Jewish property and Jews were injured and killed, among them the storeowner J. N. Neiman. A Lithuanian competitor seized the opportunity to eliminate him. He forced Neiman to dig a pit, then grabbed the shovel and beat him to the ground with it. He then buried Neiman alive in the pit.

Several days after the Germans entered the town, an order was issued for the Jews to gather in the *Beth Midrash*. They were kept there for a week without food and water, in inhumane and unsanitary conditions. Meanwhile their Lithuanian neighbors looted their homes. After a week the Jews were taken away to Lastik, a few kilometers from the town. Many risked their lives trying to buy food at the neighboring Lithuanian farms in exchange for money or belongings.

After a week the men and women were separated. The men were transferred to Mazheik and locked in barns near the Jewish cemetery where Mazheik Jews were already imprisoned. For a short time they were forced to work at the neighboring Lithuanian farms. On August 3, 1941 (10th of Av 5701) they were murdered by Lithuanian executioners next to the Jewish cemetery. Six days later, women and children were murdered at the same place. Only two Jewish girls managed to escape the massacre. They hid for two years in farms before they were handed over to the German police. They were later handed over to Lithuanian auxiliary police and murdered.

The monument at the entrance to the murder site with the inscription in Yiddish and Lithuanian: "At this site Hitler's murderers and their local helpers executed about 4000 Jews and people of other nationalities."

The mass murder site near the Jewish cemetery

Sources:
Yad Vashem archives, Jerusalem, testimony of Mikhael Tsipin M-1/Q-1455-297; testimony of Hone Raif M-1/E-1650-1555.1771/1631
Koniukhovsky Collection 0-71. File 21; testimony of Prof. Meir Bril, New Orleans 0-57
YIVO, New York, Collection of Lithuanian Jewish Communities, files 453-455
Levin, Dov; Zhidik, *Pinkas HaKehiloth-Lita* (Hebrew), Yad Vashem, Jerusalem 1996
Yakobi Y. Survivors from Lithuania Tell, Davar - Tel Aviv,18.9.1945
Di Yiddishe Shtime (Yiddish), Kovno, 22.6.1931
HaMelitz, St. Petersburg (Hebrew), 23.12.1890; 14.1.1891; 5.2.1891
Naujienos, Chicago (Lithuanian), 11.6.1949

Appendix 1
List of 43 Zhidik Jewish donors for the victims of the great Persian famine as published in HaMagid 1872

(From JewishGen>Databases>Lithuania>*HaMagid*-by Jeffrey Maynard)

Surname	Given Name	Comments
BROIDA	Natel	
CHIN	Dovid	
GOLDBERG	Hoshea	
HEIMAN	Boruch	
KOHN	Binyomin	
KOHN	Tzvi	
LEIBOWITZ	Zundil	
MANZANSKE	Yakov Eliezer	
MAZUR	Tzvi	
MIZATON	Yakov	
PAS	Reuven	
PAS	Yosef	
PERL	Dovid	
RUBIN	Dov Ber	
SHPINDMAN	Shimon	
TUCH	Eliahu	
TUCH	Gershon	father of Tzvi
TUCH	Tzvi ben Gershon	
TUCH	Yakov	
YAFE	Leib Sheftil	
ZAK	Avraham	
ZAKS	Eli	
ZEINGER	Moshe	
	Asher Chaim	

Surname	Given Name	Comments
	Avraham Mordechai	
	Avraham Moshe	
	Chaim Yudik	
	Dovid Chaim	
	Eliezer Dovid	
	Feiwil Menachem	
	Hoshea Meir	
	Meir Yehuda	
	Moshe Shlomo	Rabbi ABD
	Shalom ben Yisroel Shlomo	
	Tzvi Dovid	
	Tzvi Ephraim	
	Yakov Zev	
	Yisroel Shlomo	father of Shlom
	Yitzchok Ephraim	
	Yitzchok Shlomo	
	Yoel Meir	
	Zelig Yitzchok	
	Zev Kalman	

www.ingramcontent.com/pod-product-compliance
Lightning Source LLC
Chambersburg PA
CBHW050227270326
41914CB00003BA/600